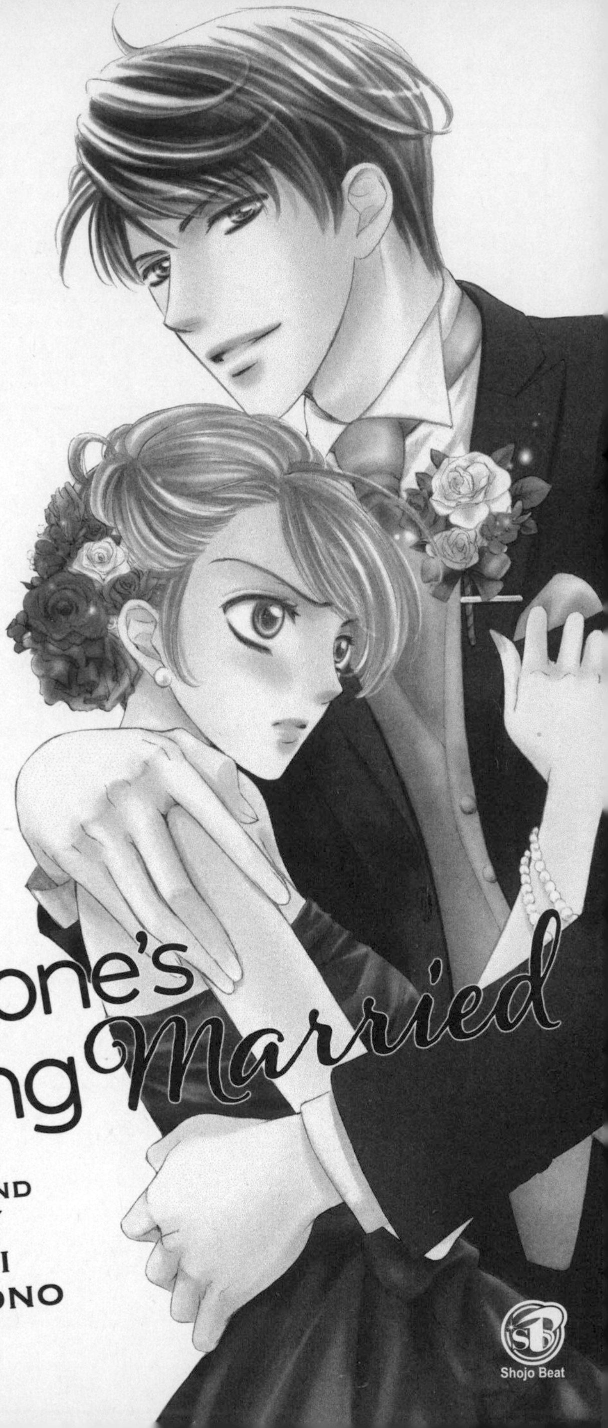

3

Everyone's Getting Married

STORY AND ART BY

IZUMI MIYAZONO

Shojo Beat

CHARACTERS

THE MAN WHO DOESN'T WANT TO GET MARRIED

Ryu Nanami

The handsome, up-and-coming newscaster at PTV. He's returned from the New York office.

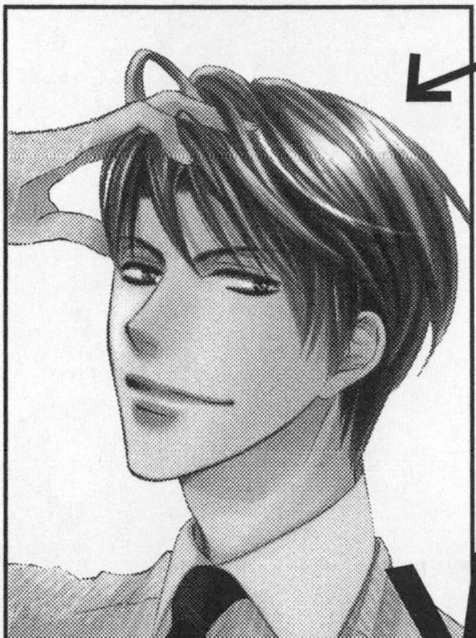
I'd rather die than get married.

VS

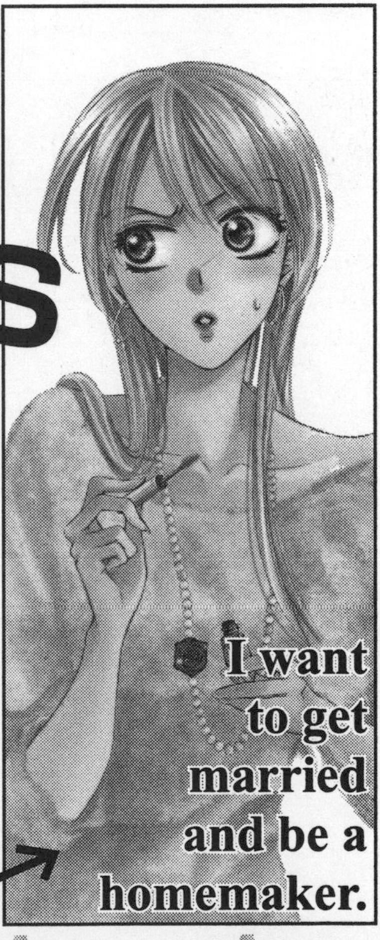
I want to get married and be a homemaker.

Asuka Takanashi

She takes pride in her career at a major bank, but feels strongly about getting married.

THE WOMAN WHO WANTS TO GET MARRIED

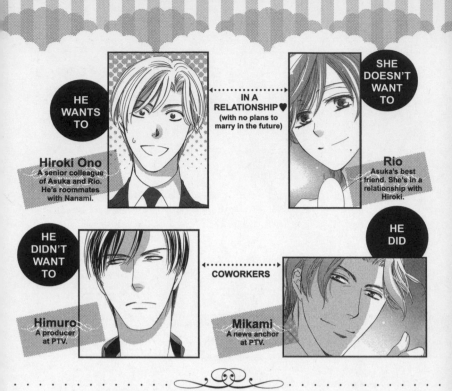

HE WANTS TO
Hiroki Ono
A senior colleague of Asuka and Rio. He's roommates with Nanami.
IN A RELATIONSHIP♥
(with no plans to marry in the future)
SHE DOESN'T WANT TO
Rio
Asuka's best friend. She's in a relationship with Hiroki.
HE DIDN'T WANT TO
Himuro
A producer at PTV.
COWORKERS
HE DID
Mikami
A news anchor at PTV.

STORY THUS FAR

Asuka hits rock bottom after her boyfriend—who she'd been sure would propose to her soon—suddenly dumps her. But at a friend's wedding she meets Ryu Nanami, a handsome TV newscaster. His kindness touches her heart, and she soon falls for him even though Ryu has no interest in getting married. They both know they want different things, but they've fallen in love and decide to give dating a try. However, due to their busy schedules, the two barely have a chance to see each other...

Ryu is selected to host a big music festival that he had a bad experience hosting in the past. Shaking off his previous failure, he proves himself by excelling.

Ryu and Asuka argue over a scheduling conflict, but their love for each other is unwavering. The couple consummates their love, but who is this woman from Ryu's past who has appeared?!

Contents

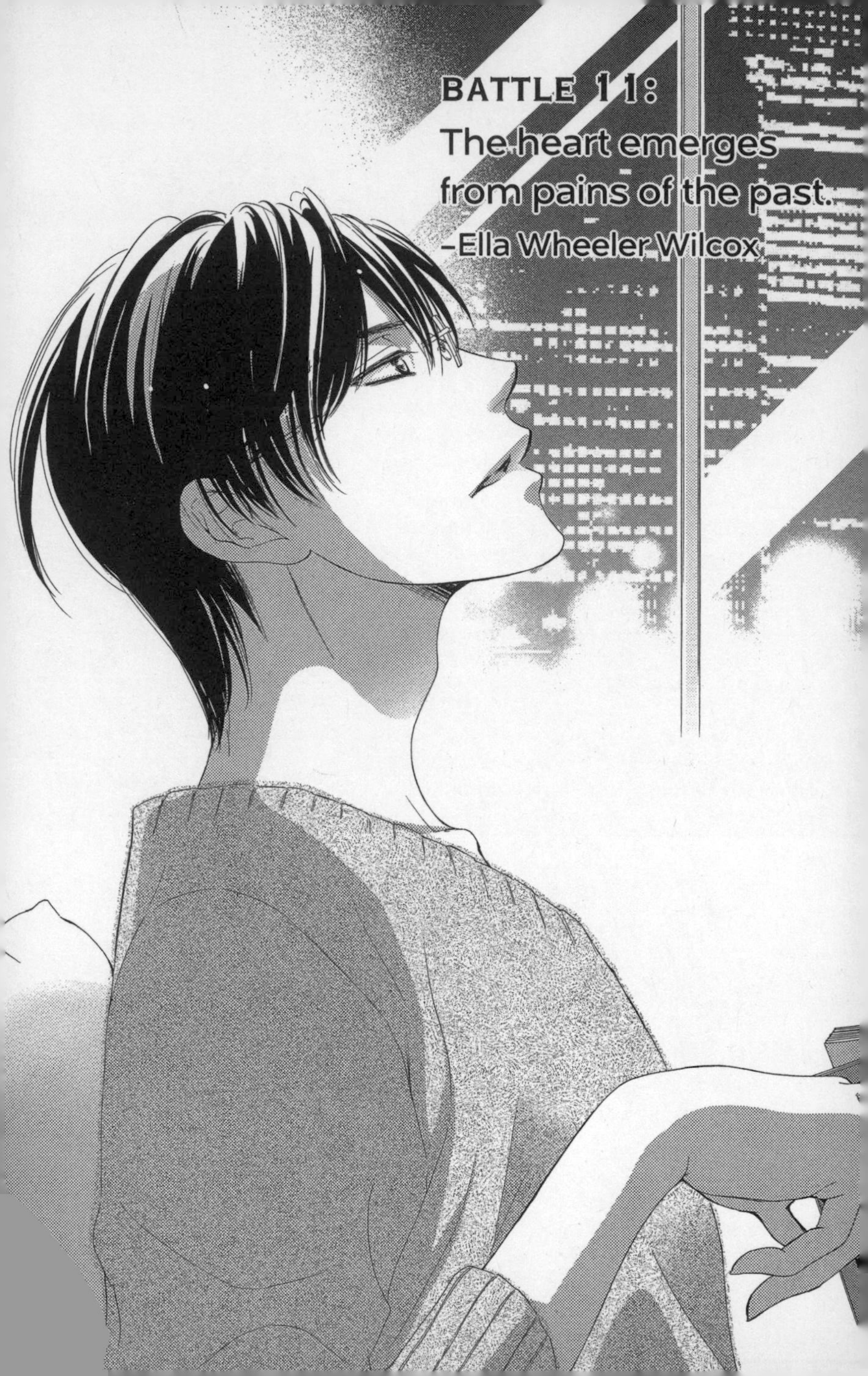
BATTLE 11:
The heart emerges from pains of the past.
–Ella Wheeler Wilcox

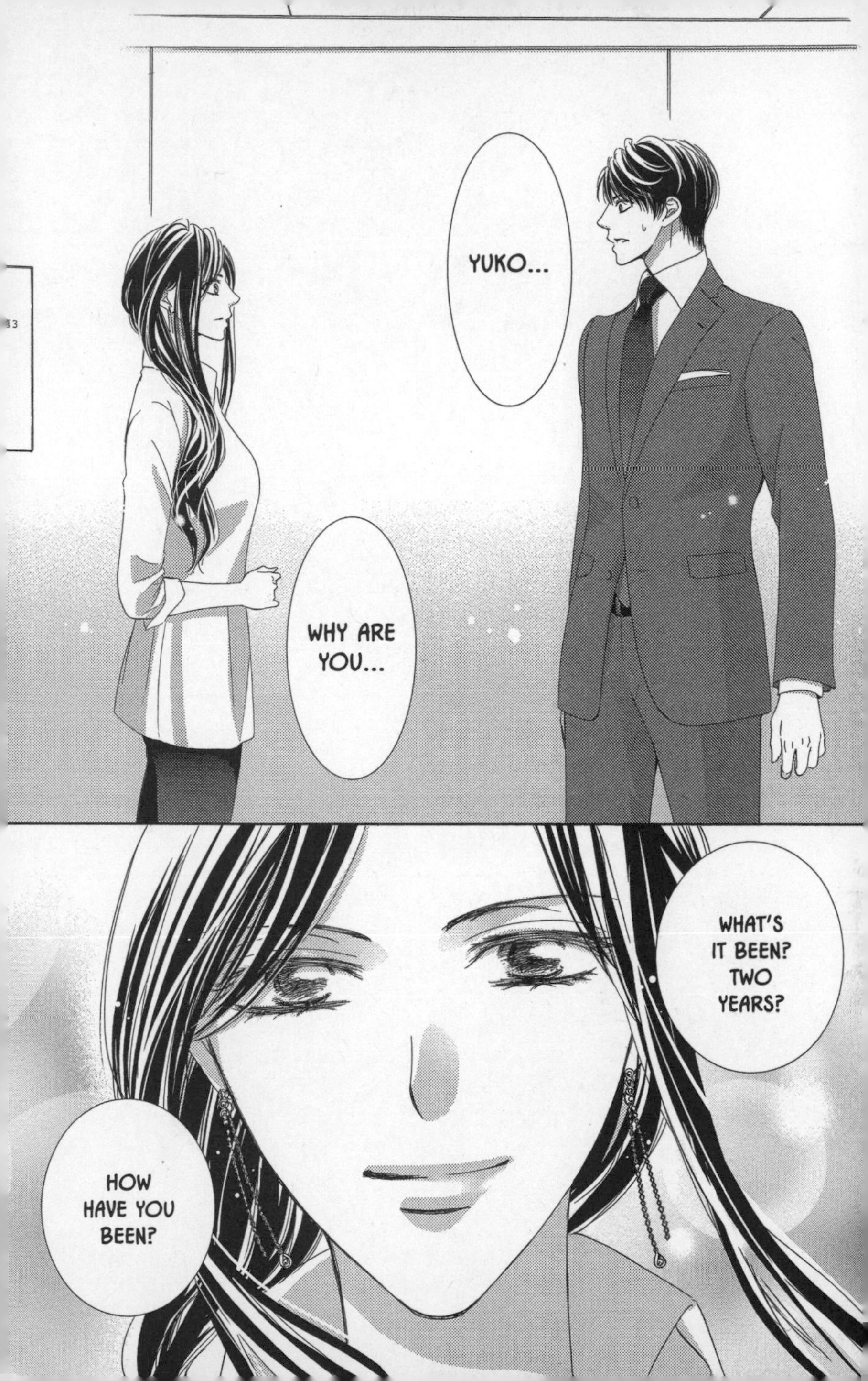
YUKO...
WHY ARE YOU...
WHAT'S IT BEEN? TWO YEARS?
HOW HAVE YOU BEEN?

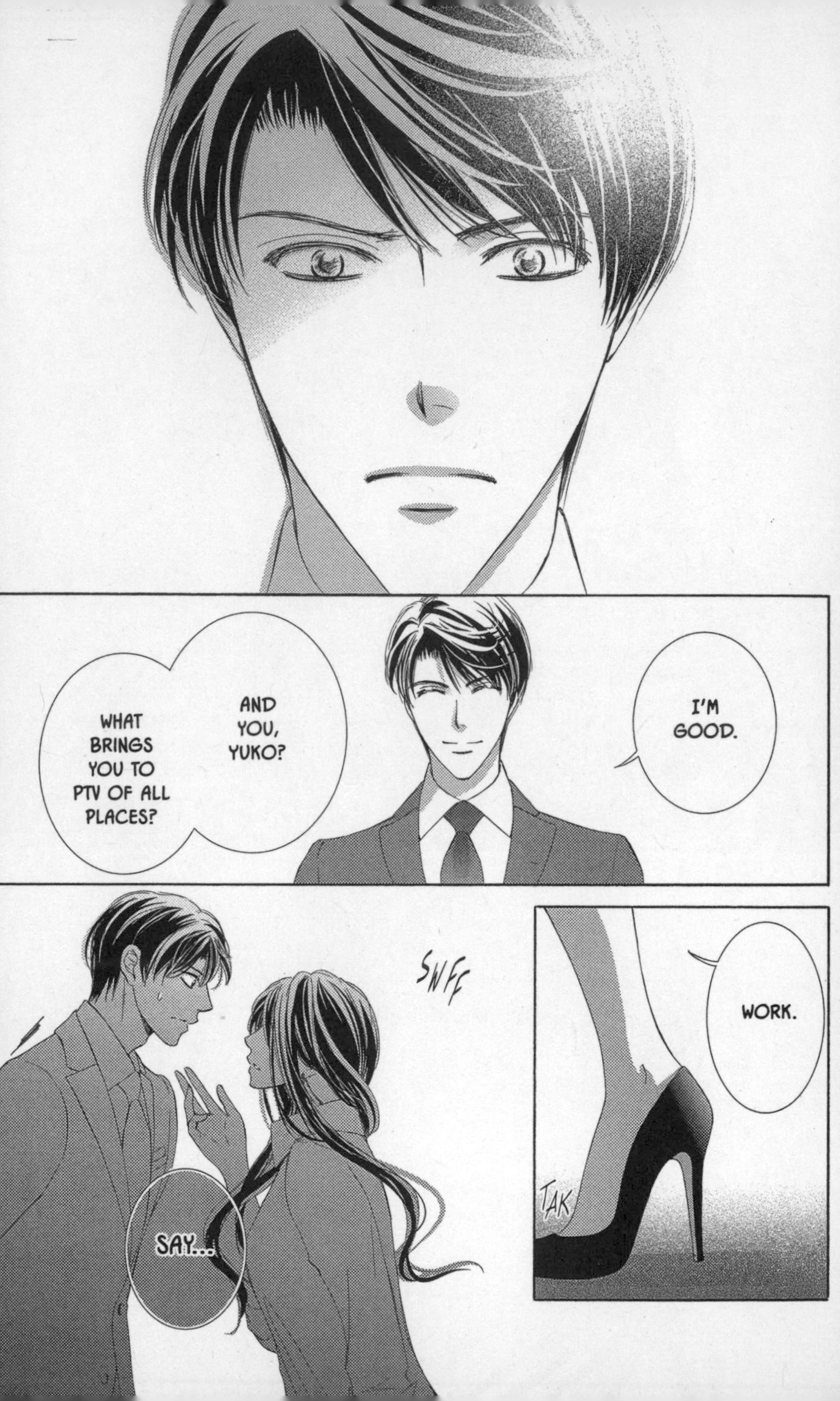
I'M GOOD.
AND YOU, YUKO?
WHAT BRINGS YOU TO PTV OF ALL PLACES?
WORK.
TAK
SNFF
SAY...

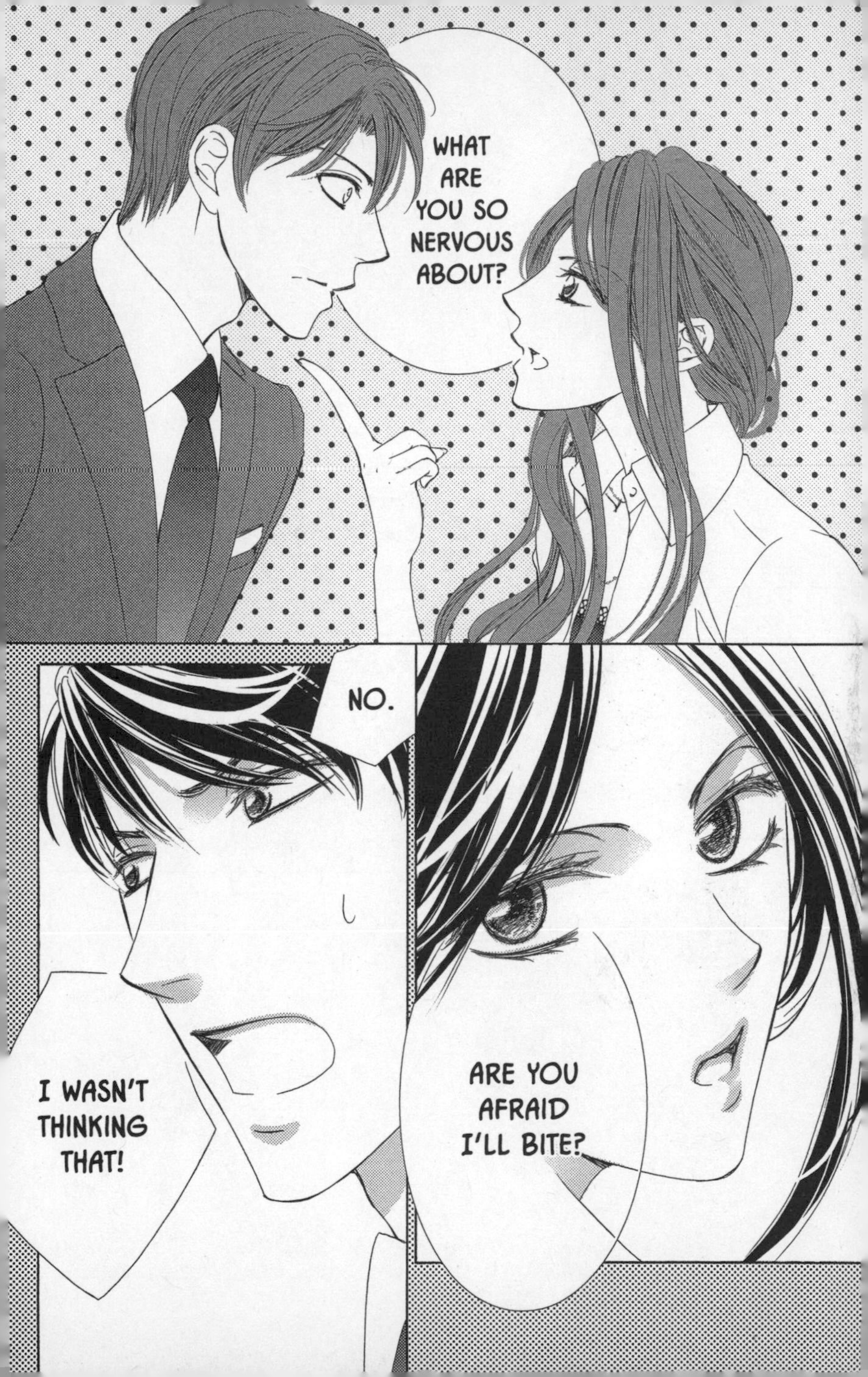
WHAT ARE YOU SO NERVOUS ABOUT?
ARE YOU AFRAID I'LL BITE?
NO.
I WASN'T THINKING THAT!

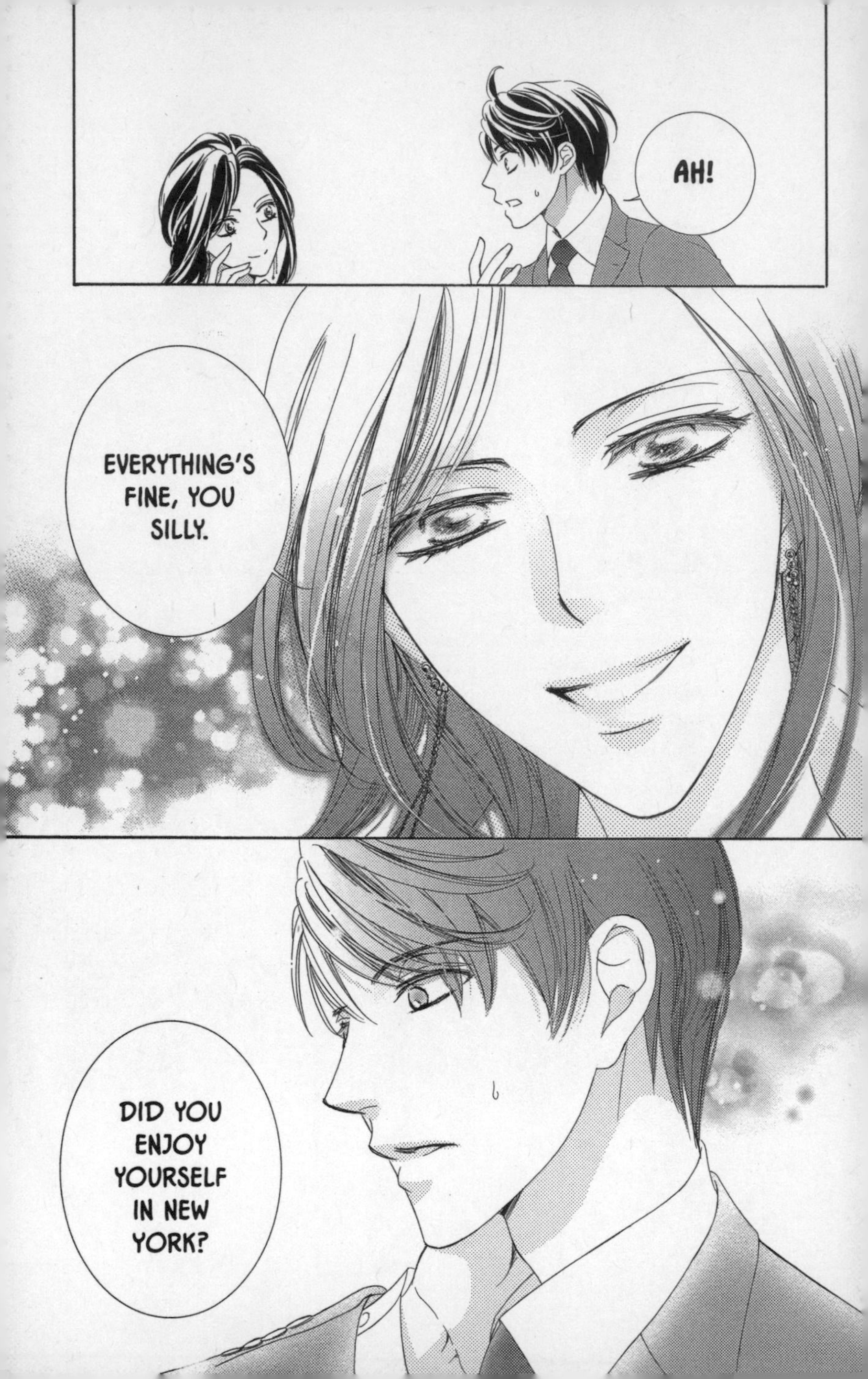
AH!
EVERYTHING'S FINE, YOU SILLY.
DID YOU ENJOY YOURSELF IN NEW YORK?

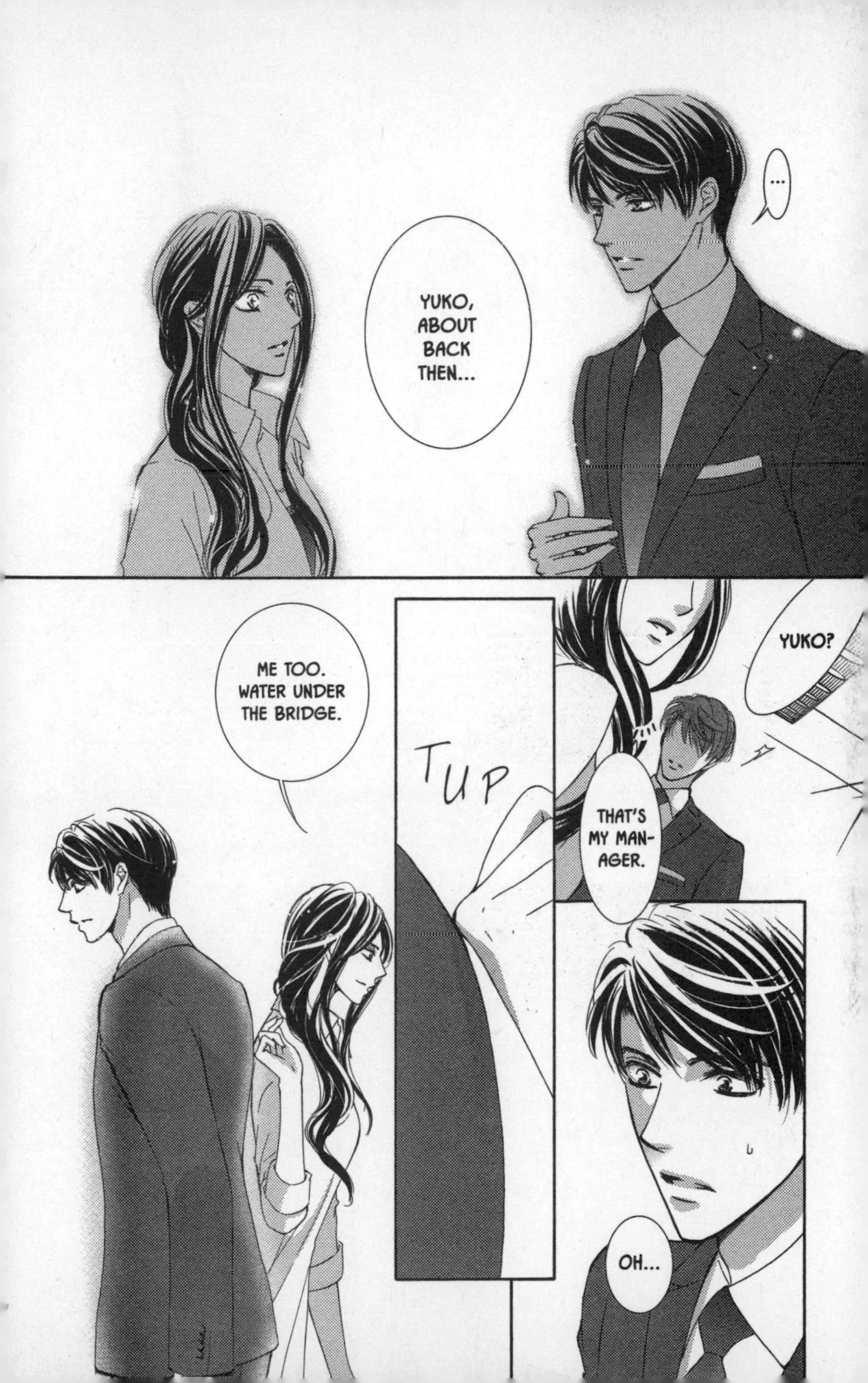
...
YUKO, ABOUT BACK THEN...
YUKO?
THAT'S MY MAN-AGER.
OH...
TUP
ME TOO. WATER UNDER THE BRIDGE.

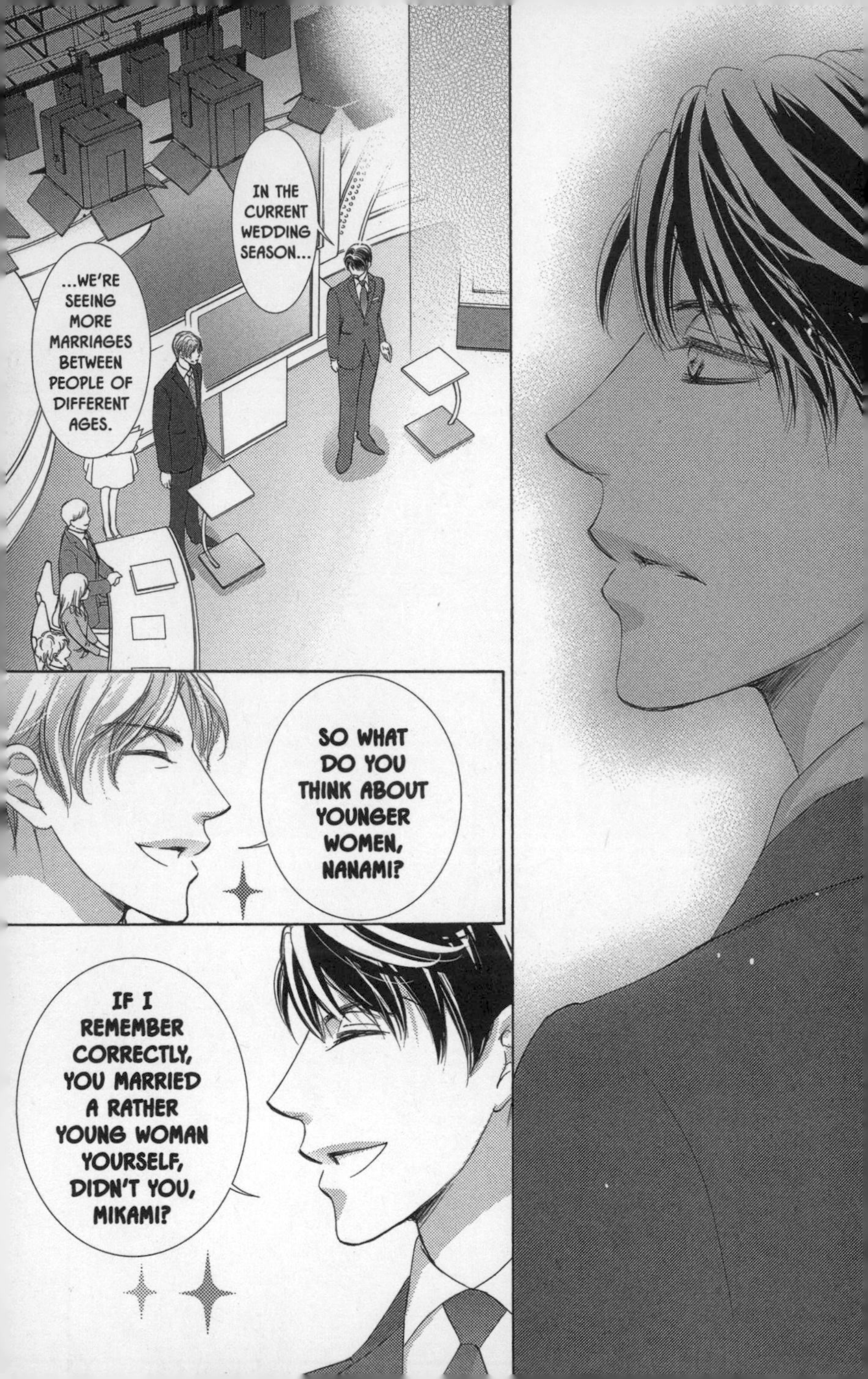
IN THE CURRENT WEDDING SEASON...
...WE'RE SEEING MORE MARRIAGES BETWEEN PEOPLE OF DIFFERENT AGES.
SO WHAT DO YOU THINK ABOUT YOUNGER WOMEN, NANAMI?
IF I REMEMBER CORRECTLY, YOU MARRIED A RATHER YOUNG WOMAN YOURSELF, DIDN'T YOU, MIKAMI?

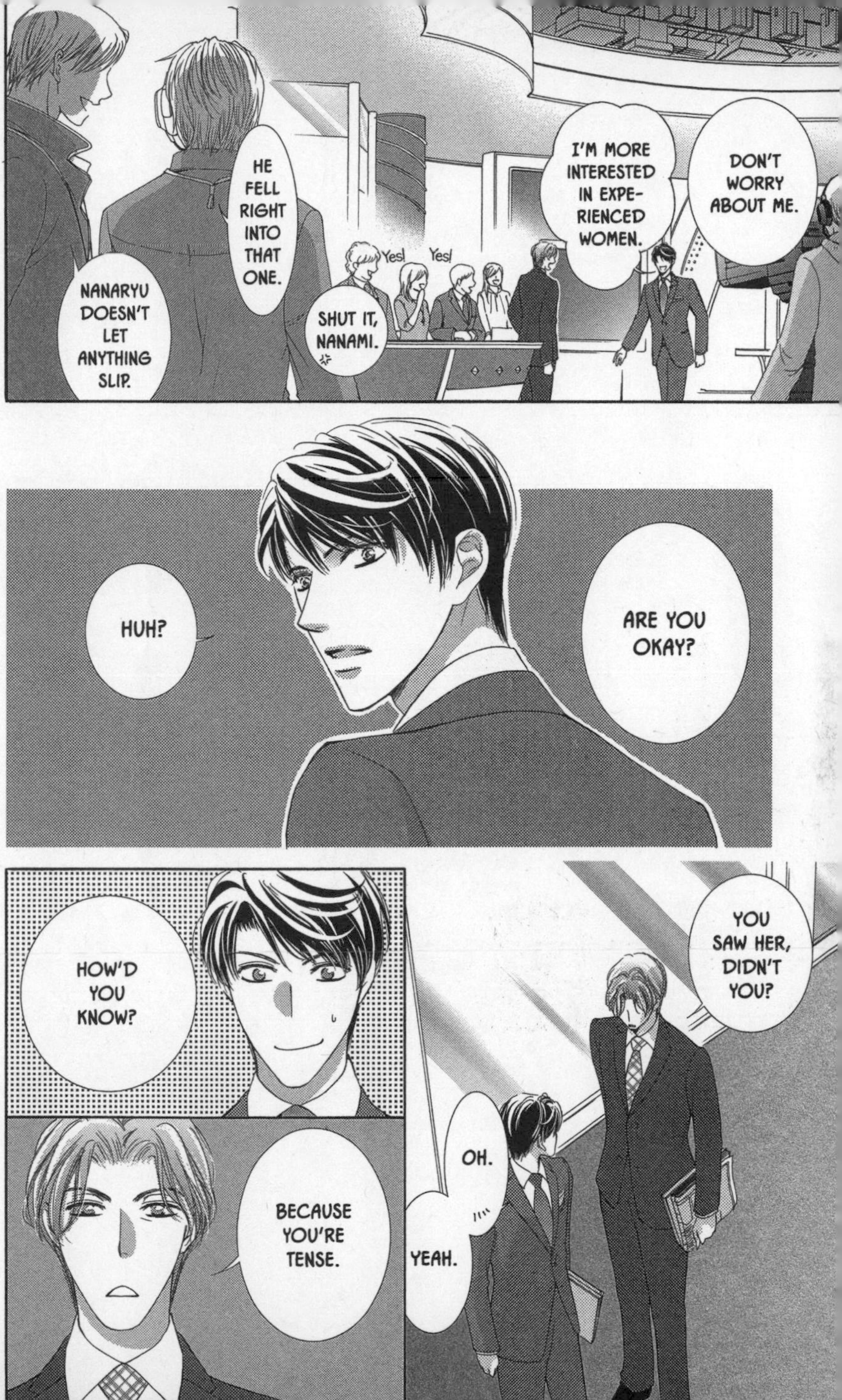
DON'T WORRY ABOUT ME.
I'M MORE INTERESTED IN EXPE-RIENCED WOMEN.
Yes!
Yes!
SHUT IT, NANAMI.
HE FELL RIGHT INTO THAT ONE.
NANARYU DOESN'T LET ANYTHING SLIP.
ARE YOU OKAY?
HUH?
YOU SAW HER, DIDN'T YOU?
OH.
YEAH.
HOW'D YOU KNOW?
BECAUSE YOU'RE TENSE.

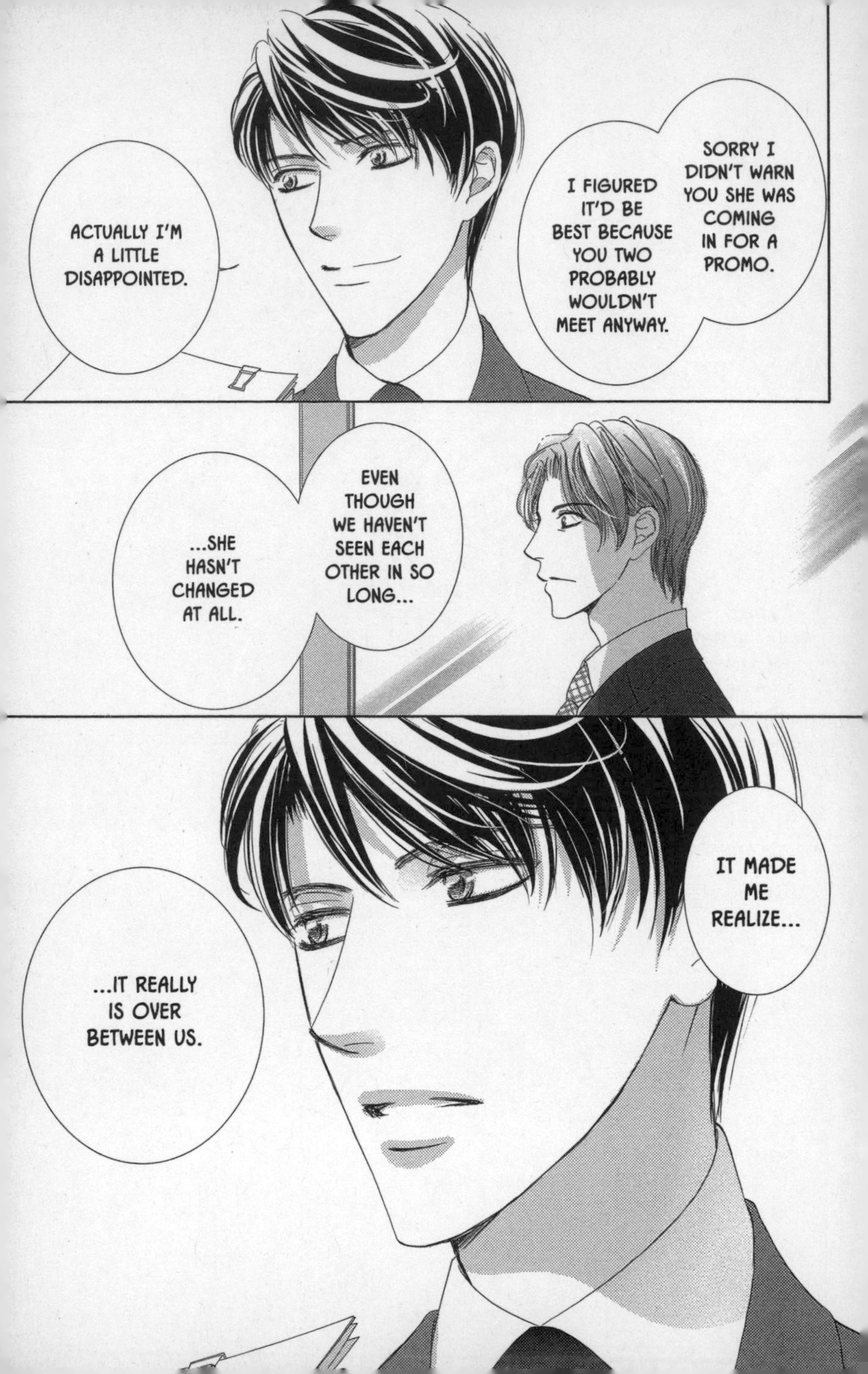
SORRY I DIDN'T WARN YOU SHE WAS COMING IN FOR A PROMO.
I FIGURED IT'D BE BEST BECAUSE YOU TWO PROBABLY WOULDN'T MEET ANYWAY.
ACTUALLY I'M A LITTLE DISAPPOINTED.
EVEN THOUGH WE HAVEN'T SEEN EACH OTHER IN SO LONG...
...SHE HASN'T CHANGED AT ALL.
IT MADE ME REALIZE...
...IT REALLY IS OVER BETWEEN US.

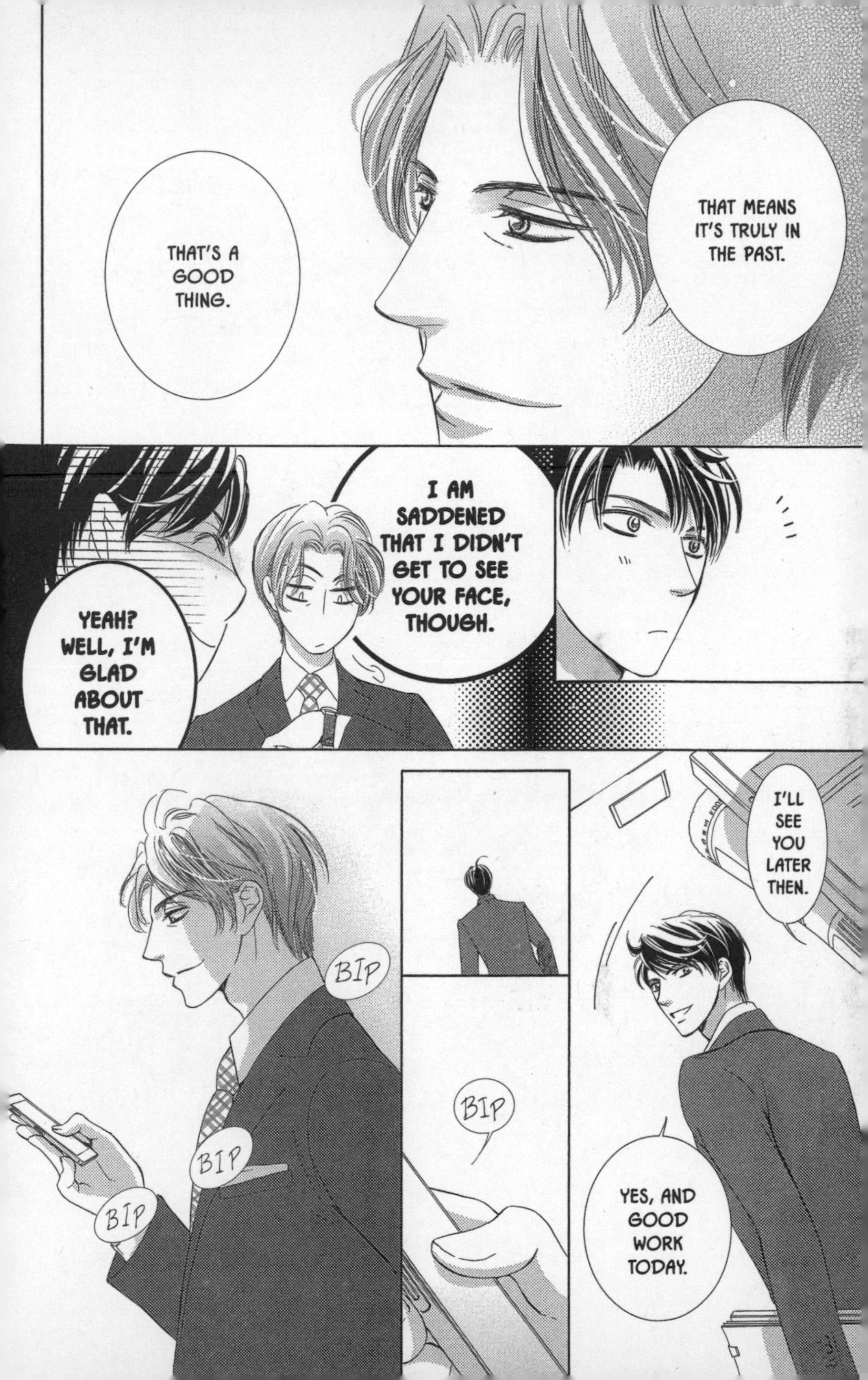
THAT MEANS IT'S TRULY IN THE PAST.
THAT'S A GOOD THING.
I AM SADDENED THAT I DIDN'T GET TO SEE YOUR FACE, THOUGH.
YEAH? WELL, I'M GLAD ABOUT THAT.
I'LL SEE YOU LATER THEN.
YES, AND GOOD WORK TODAY.
BIP
BIP
BIP
BIP

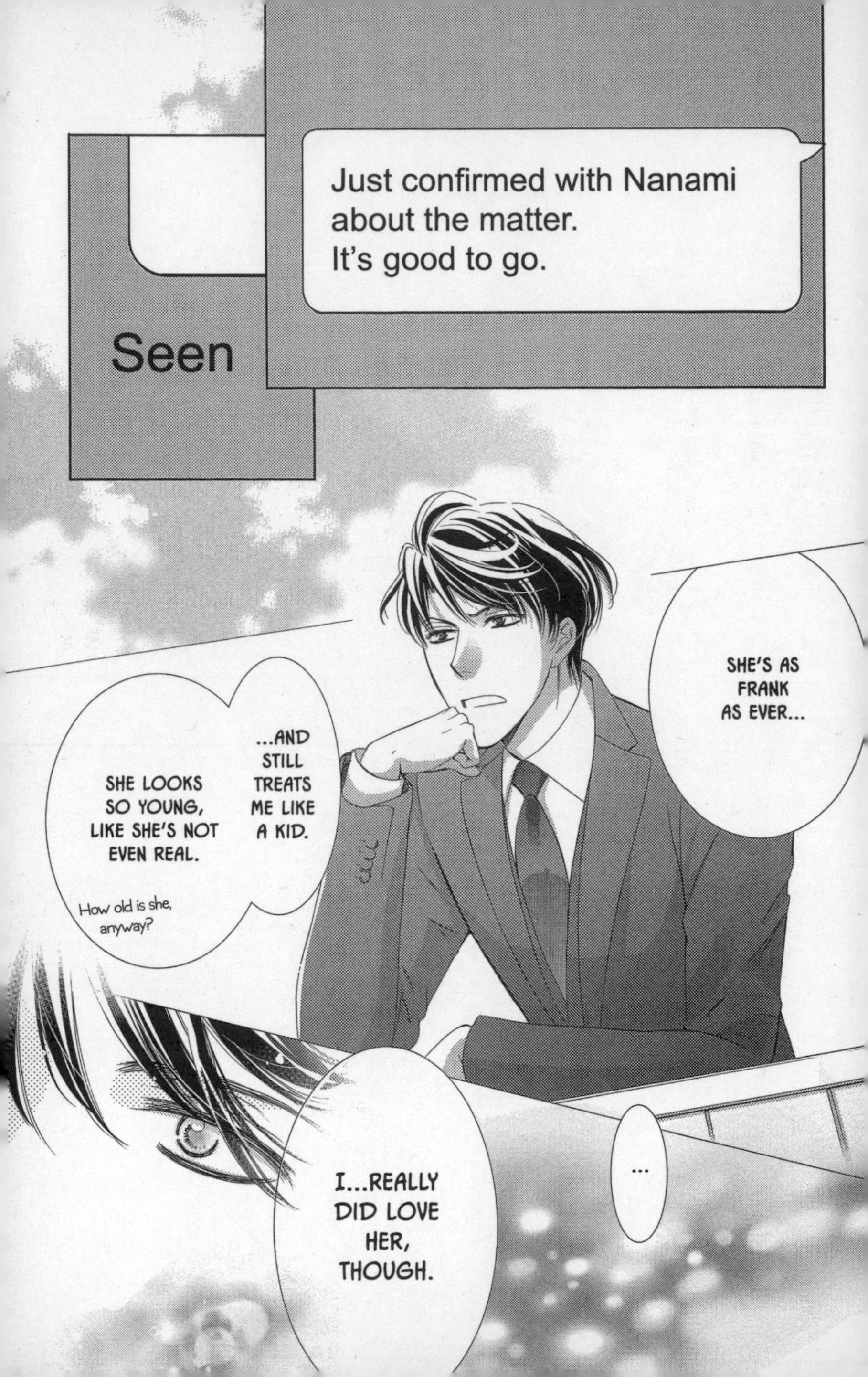
Just confirmed with Nanami about the matter. It's good to go.
Seen
SHE'S AS FRANK AS EVER...
...AND STILL TREATS ME LIKE A KID.
SHE LOOKS SO YOUNG, LIKE SHE'S NOT EVEN REAL.
How old is she, anyway?
...
I...REALLY DID LOVE HER, THOUGH.

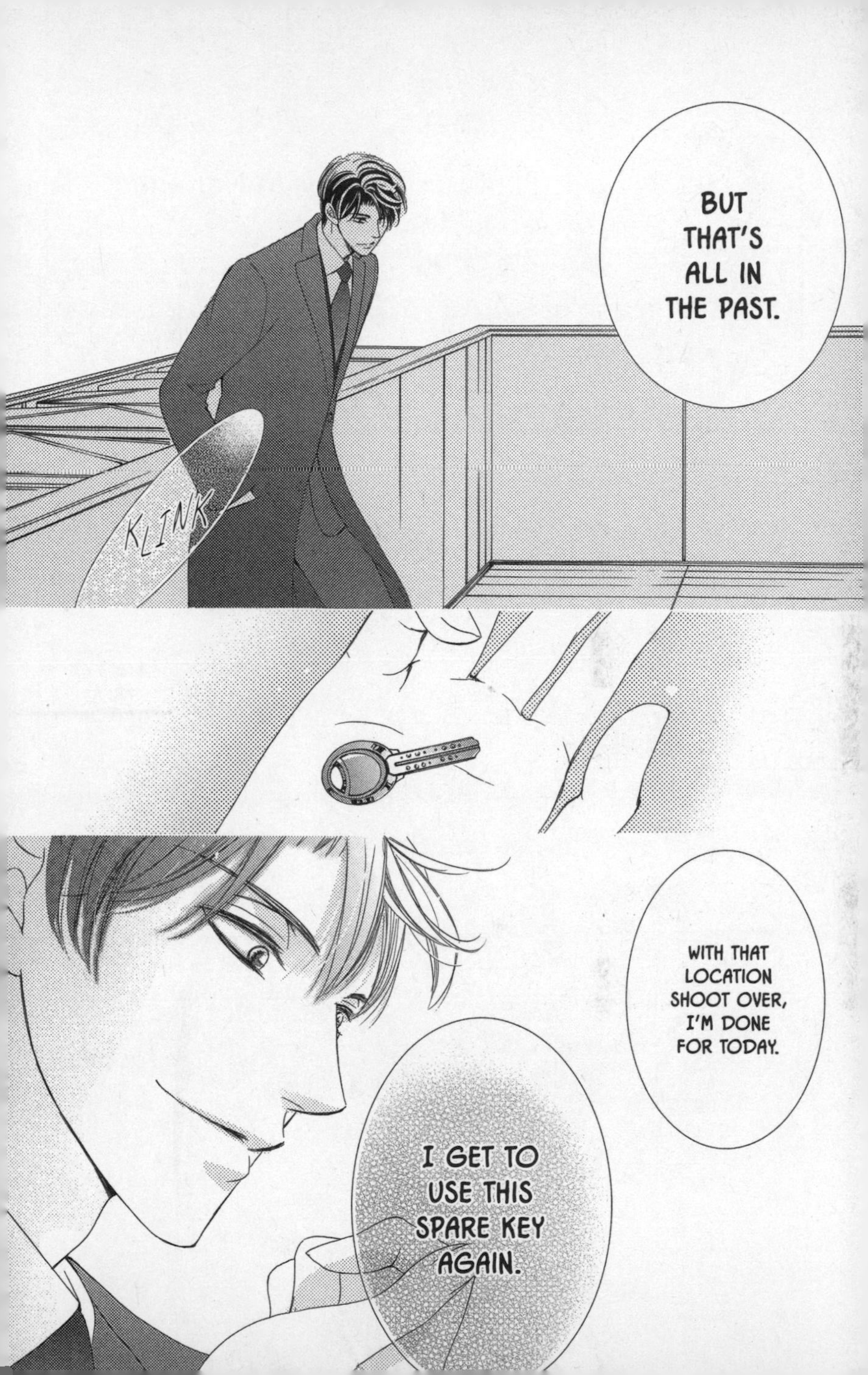
BUT THAT'S ALL IN THE PAST.
KLINK
WITH THAT LOCATION SHOOT OVER, I'M DONE FOR TODAY.
I GET TO USE THIS SPARE KEY AGAIN.

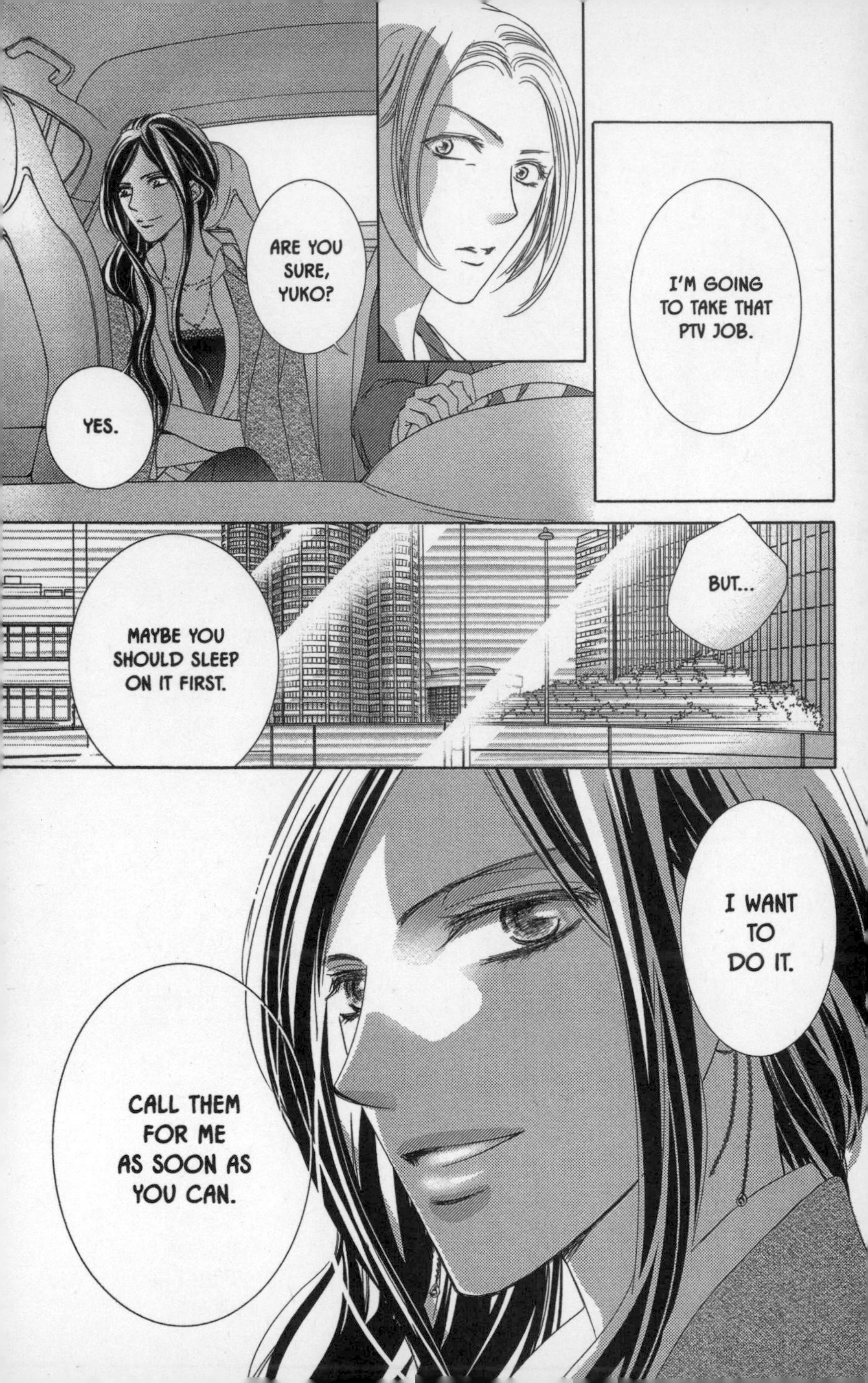
I'M GOING TO TAKE THAT PTV JOB.
ARE YOU SURE, YUKO?
YES.
BUT...
MAYBE YOU SHOULD SLEEP ON IT FIRST.
I WANT TO DO IT.
CALL THEM FOR ME AS SOON AS YOU CAN.

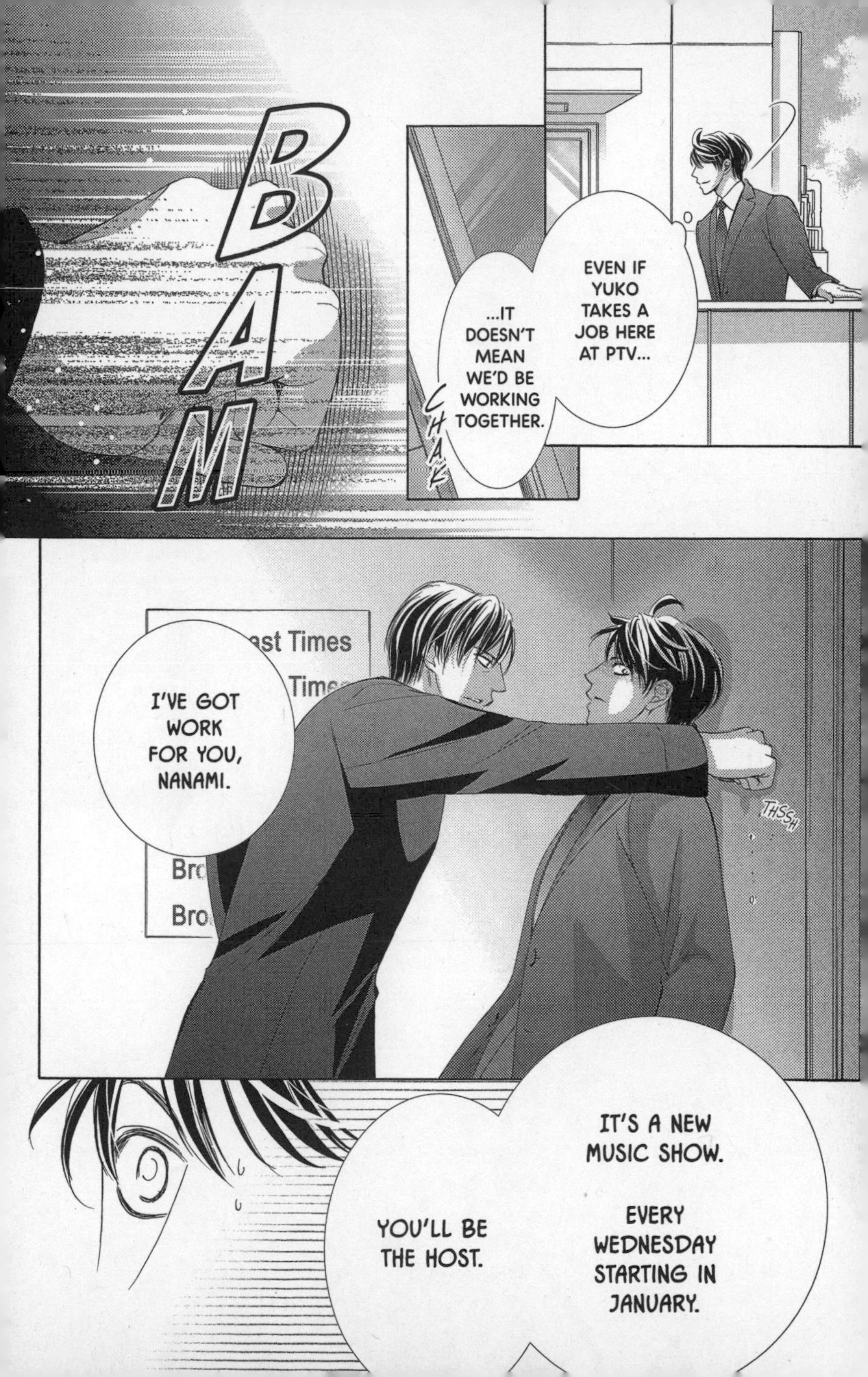

EVEN IF YUKO TAKES A JOB HERE AT PTV...
...IT DOESN'T MEAN WE'D BE WORKING TOGETHER.
CHAK
BAM
THSSH
I'VE GOT WORK FOR YOU, NANAMI.
IT'S A NEW MUSIC SHOW.
EVERY WEDNESDAY STARTING IN JANUARY.
YOU'LL BE THE HOST.

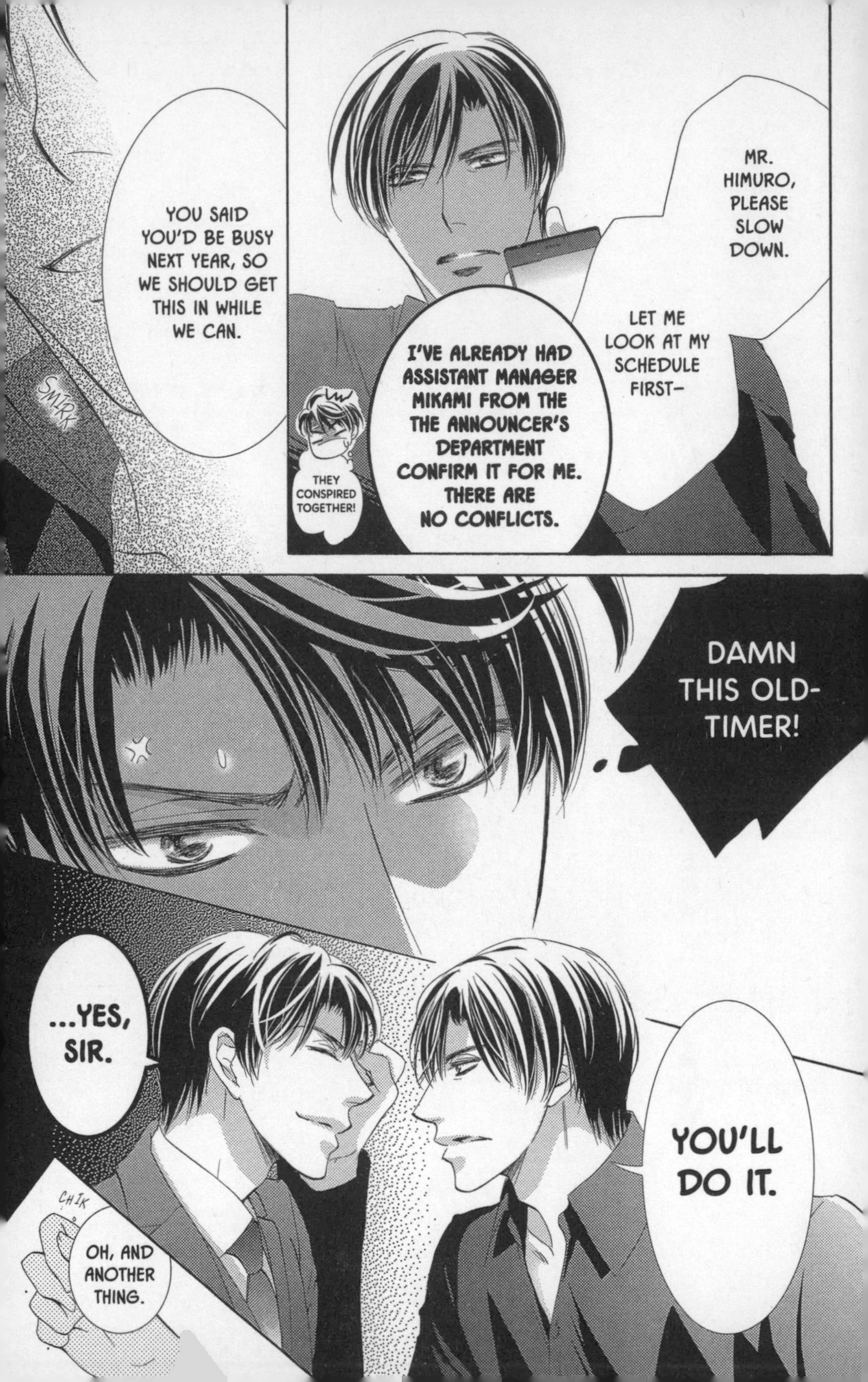
MR. HIMURO, PLEASE SLOW DOWN.
LET ME LOOK AT MY SCHEDULE FIRST—
I'VE ALREADY HAD ASSISTANT MANAGER MIKAMI FROM THE THE ANNOUNCER'S DEPARTMENT CONFIRM IT FOR ME. THERE ARE NO CONFLICTS.
THEY CONSPIRED TOGETHER!
YOU SAID YOU'D BE BUSY NEXT YEAR, SO WE SHOULD GET THIS IN WHILE WE CAN.
SMIRK
DAMN THIS OLD-TIMER!
YOU'LL DO IT.
...YES, SIR.
CHIK
OH, AND ANOTHER THING.

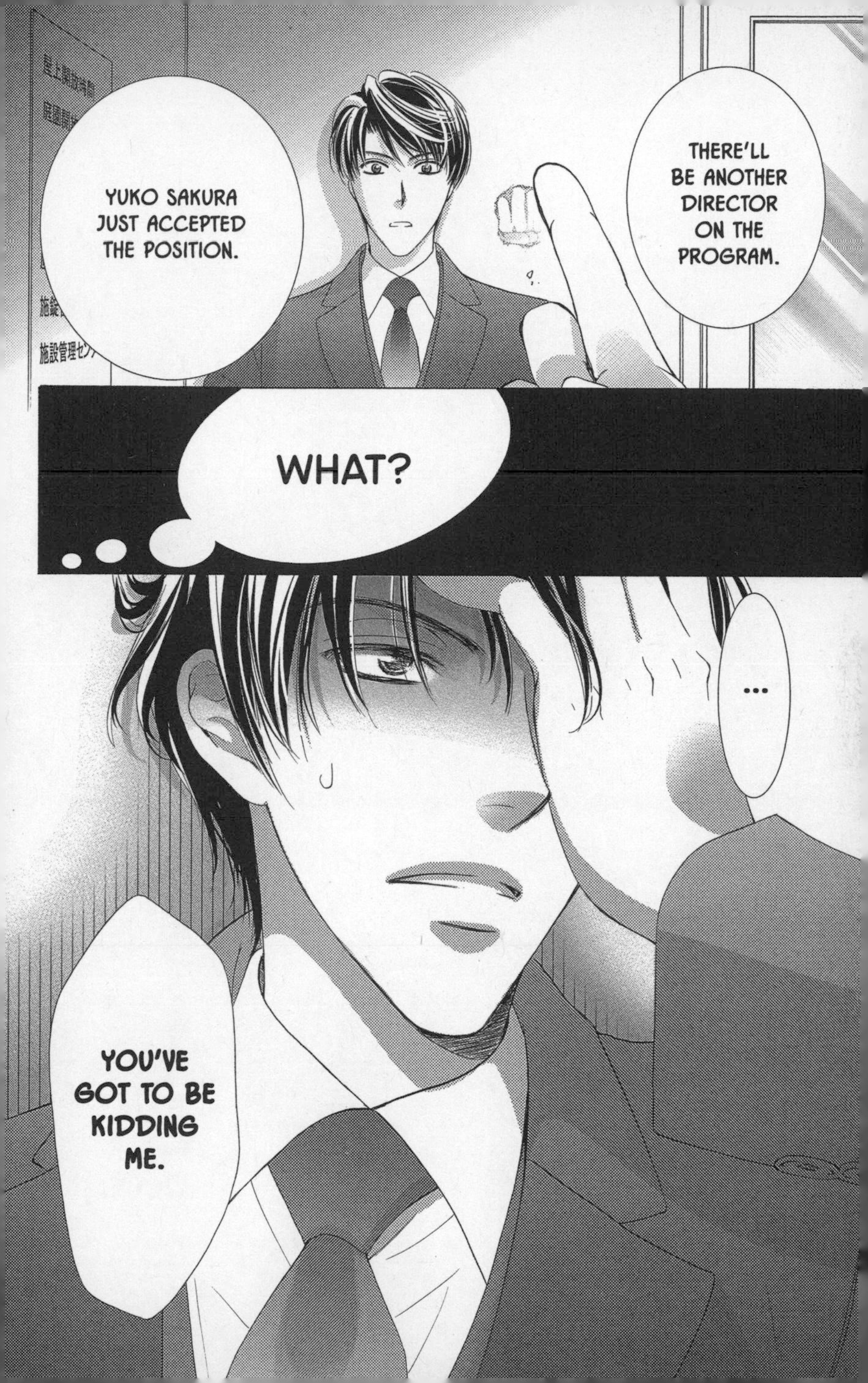
THERE'LL BE ANOTHER DIRECTOR ON THE PROGRAM.
YUKO SAKURA JUST ACCEPTED THE POSITION.
WHAT?
...
YOU'VE GOT TO BE KIDDING ME.

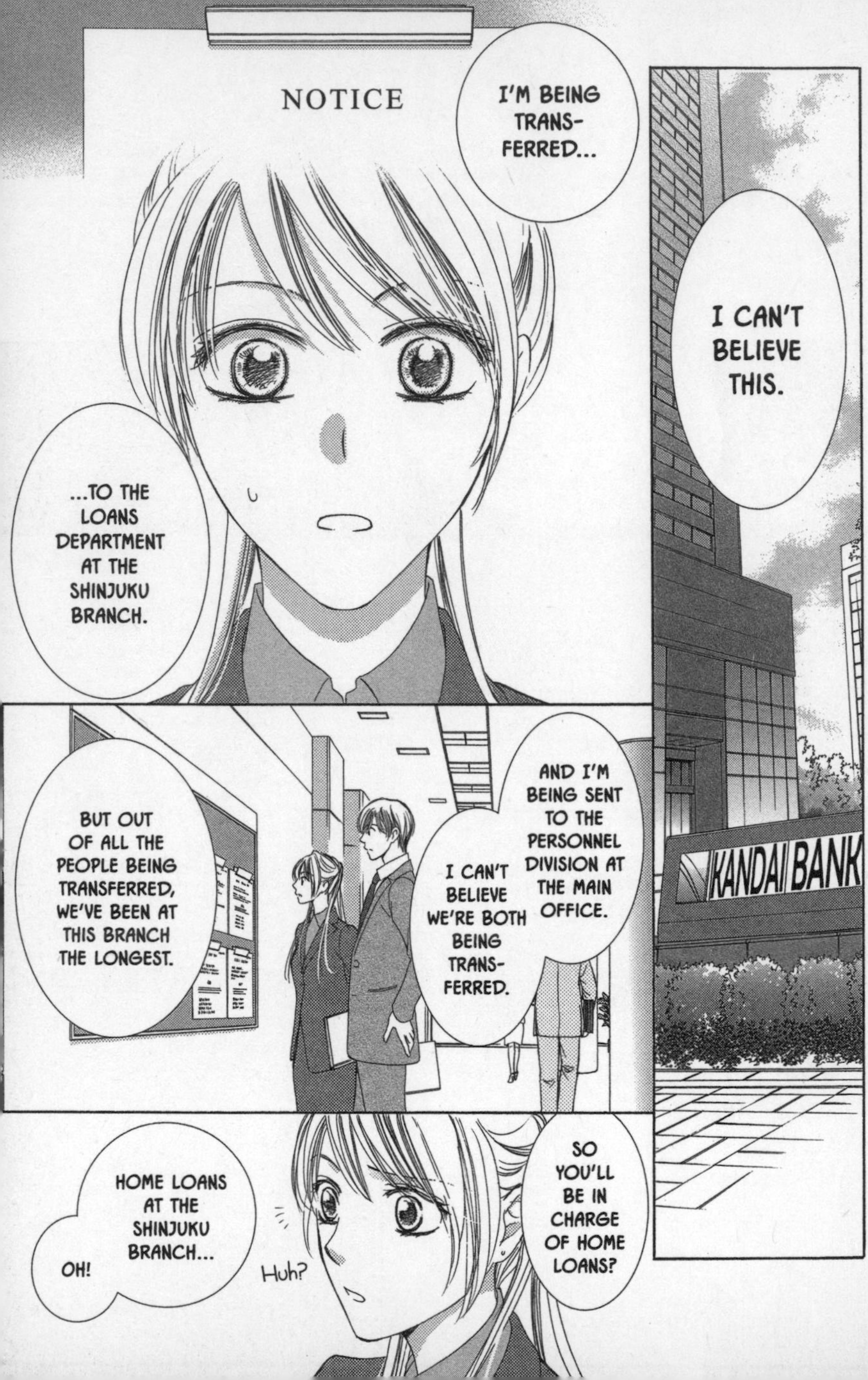
I CAN'T BELIEVE THIS.
NOTICE
I'M BEING TRANS-FERRED...
...TO THE LOANS DEPARTMENT AT THE SHINJUKU BRANCH.
AND I'M BEING SENT TO THE PERSONNEL DIVISION AT THE MAIN OFFICE.
I CAN'T BELIEVE WE'RE BOTH BEING TRANS-FERRED.
BUT OUT OF ALL THE PEOPLE BEING TRANSFERRED, WE'VE BEEN AT THIS BRANCH THE LONGEST.
KANDAI BANK
SO YOU'LL BE IN CHARGE OF HOME LOANS?
Huh?
HOME LOANS AT THE SHINJUKU BRANCH...
OH!

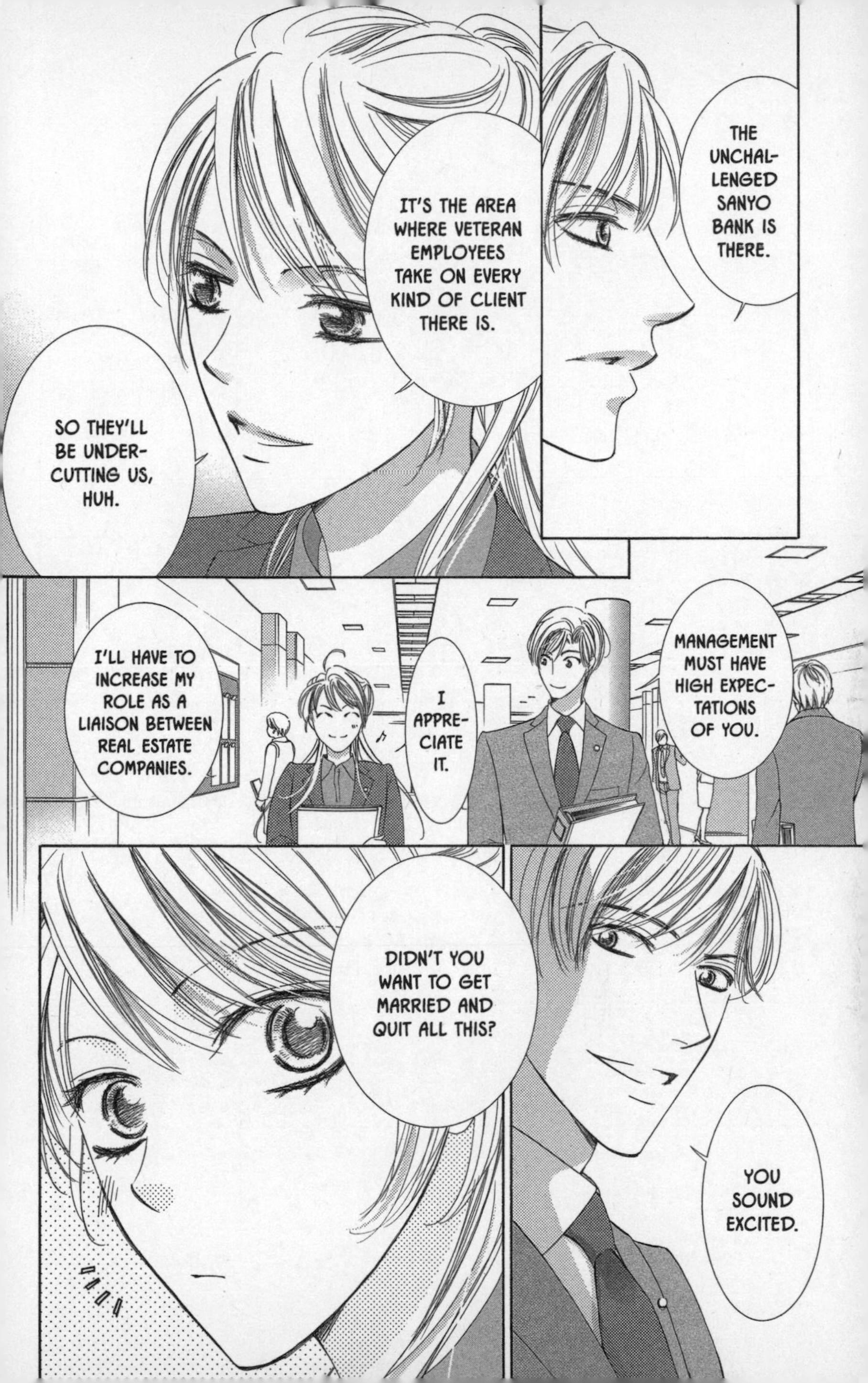
THE UNCHAL-LENGED SANYO BANK IS THERE.
IT'S THE AREA WHERE VETERAN EMPLOYEES TAKE ON EVERY KIND OF CLIENT THERE IS.
SO THEY'LL BE UNDER-CUTTING US, HUH.
MANAGEMENT MUST HAVE HIGH EXPEC-TATIONS OF YOU.
I APPRE-CIATE IT.
I'LL HAVE TO INCREASE MY ROLE AS A LIAISON BETWEEN REAL ESTATE COMPANIES.
YOU SOUND EXCITED.
DIDN'T YOU WANT TO GET MARRIED AND QUIT ALL THIS?

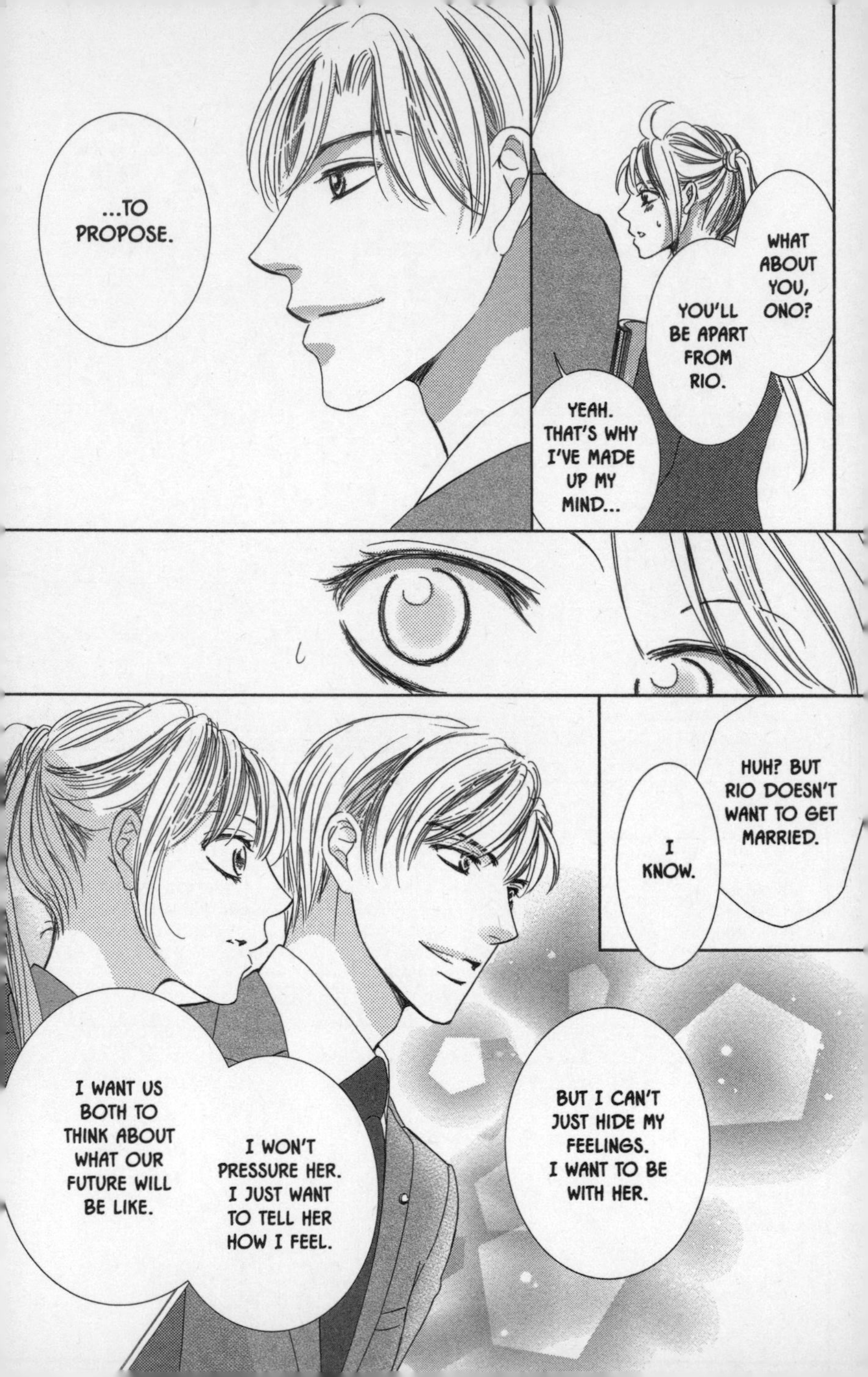
WHAT ABOUT YOU, ONO?
YOU'LL BE APART FROM RIO.
YEAH. THAT'S WHY I'VE MADE UP MY MIND...
...TO PROPOSE.
HUH? BUT RIO DOESN'T WANT TO GET MARRIED.
I KNOW.
BUT I CAN'T JUST HIDE MY FEELINGS. I WANT TO BE WITH HER.
I WON'T PRESSURE HER. I JUST WANT TO TELL HER HOW I FEEL.
I WANT US BOTH TO THINK ABOUT WHAT OUR FUTURE WILL BE LIKE.

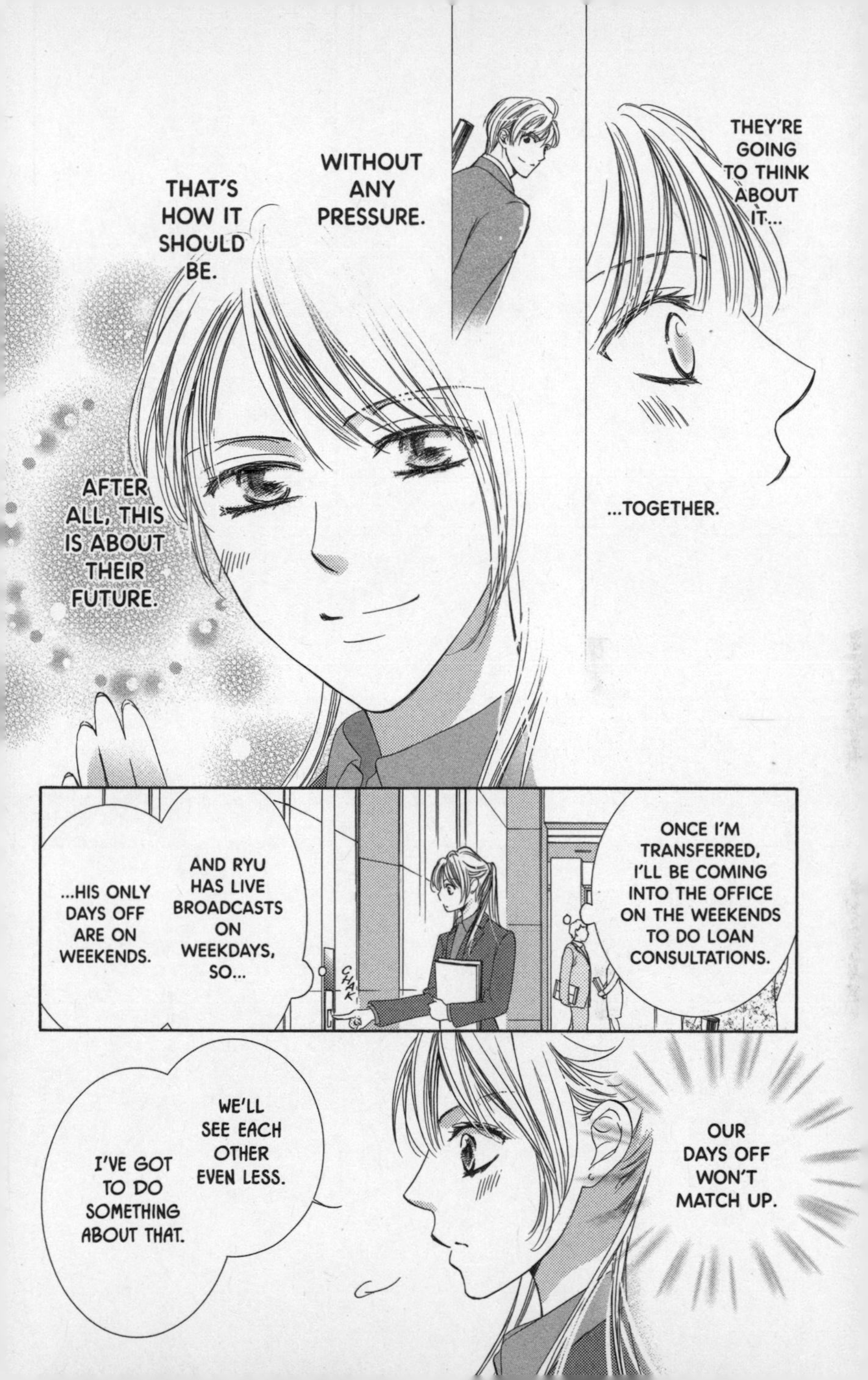
THEY'RE GOING TO THINK ABOUT IT...
...TOGETHER.
WITHOUT ANY PRESSURE.
THAT'S HOW IT SHOULD BE.
AFTER ALL, THIS IS ABOUT THEIR FUTURE.
ONCE I'M TRANSFERRED, I'LL BE COMING INTO THE OFFICE ON THE WEEKENDS TO DO LOAN CONSULTATIONS.
CHAK
AND RYU HAS LIVE BROADCASTS ON WEEKDAYS, SO...
...HIS ONLY DAYS OFF ARE ON WEEKENDS.
OUR DAYS OFF WON'T MATCH UP.
WE'LL SEE EACH OTHER EVEN LESS.
I'VE GOT TO DO SOMETHING ABOUT THAT.

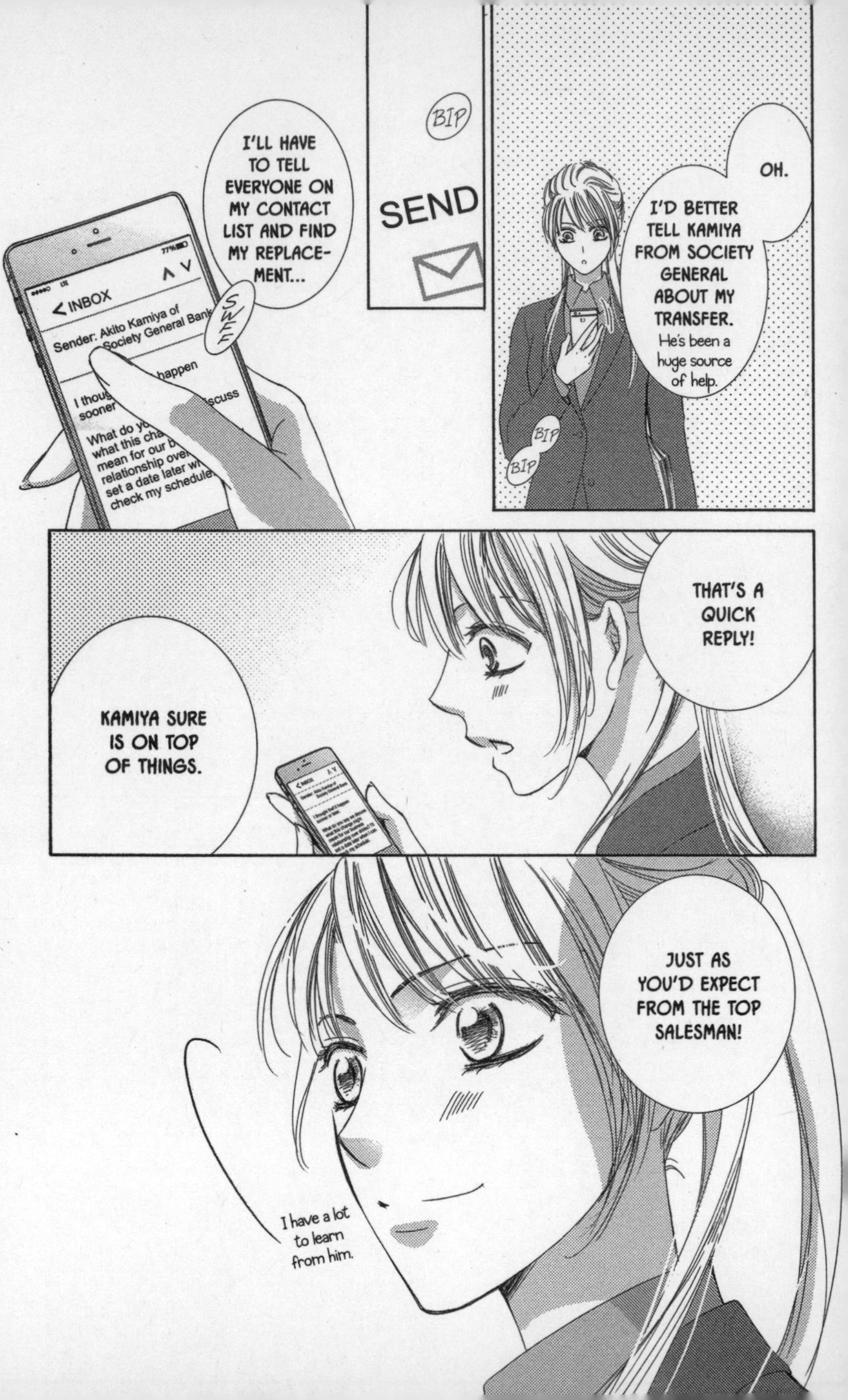
OH.
I'D BETTER TELL KAMIYA FROM SOCIETY GENERAL ABOUT MY TRANSFER. He's been a huge source of help.
BIP
BIP
BIP
SEND
I'LL HAVE TO TELL EVERYONE ON MY CONTACT LIST AND FIND MY REPLACEMENT...
SWFF
INBOX
Sender: Akito Kamiya of Society General Bank
THAT'S A QUICK REPLY!
KAMIYA SURE IS ON TOP OF THINGS.
JUST AS YOU'D EXPECT FROM THE TOP SALESMAN!
I have a lot to learn from him.

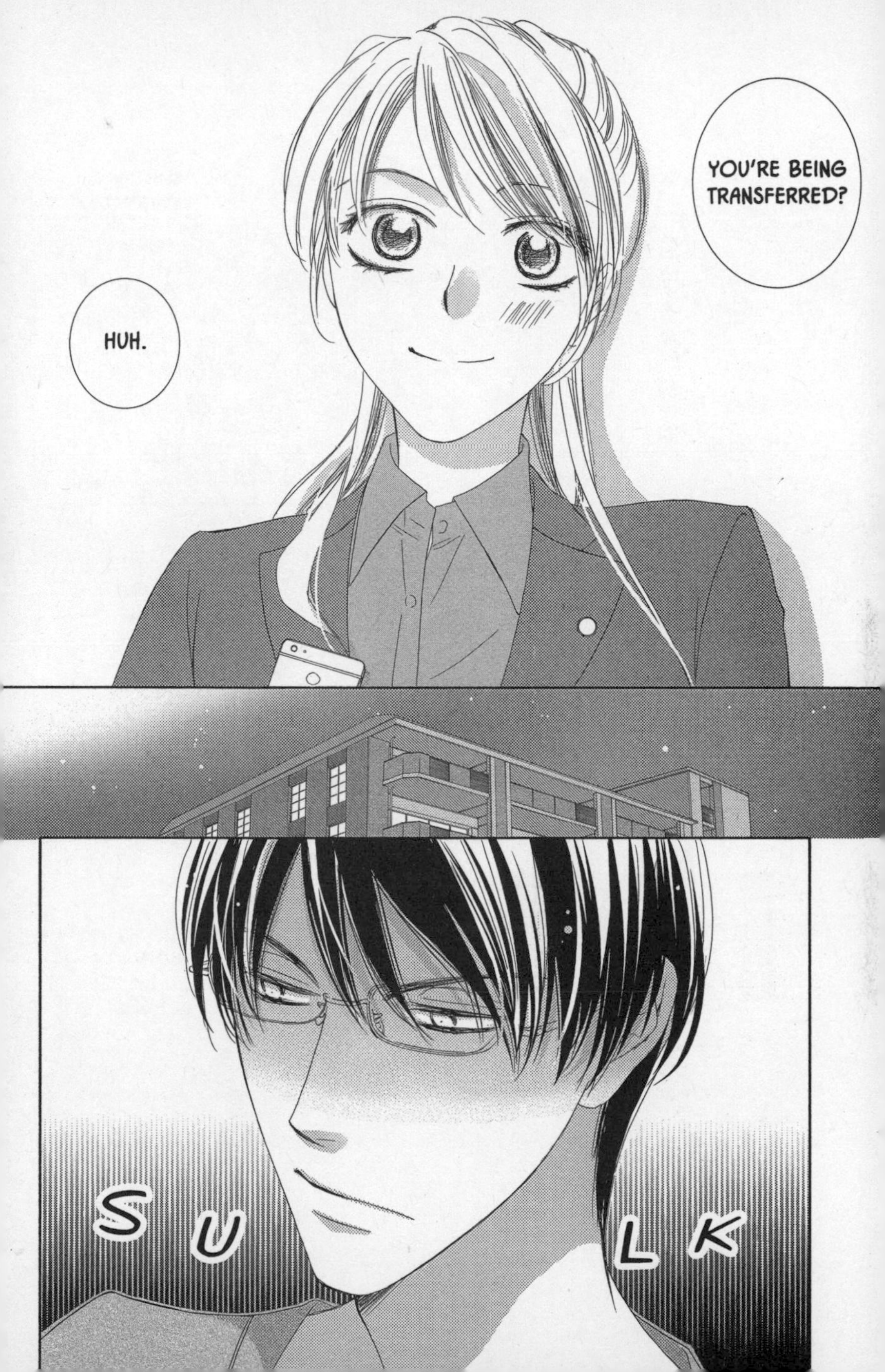
YOU'RE BEING TRANSFERRED?
HUH.
SULK

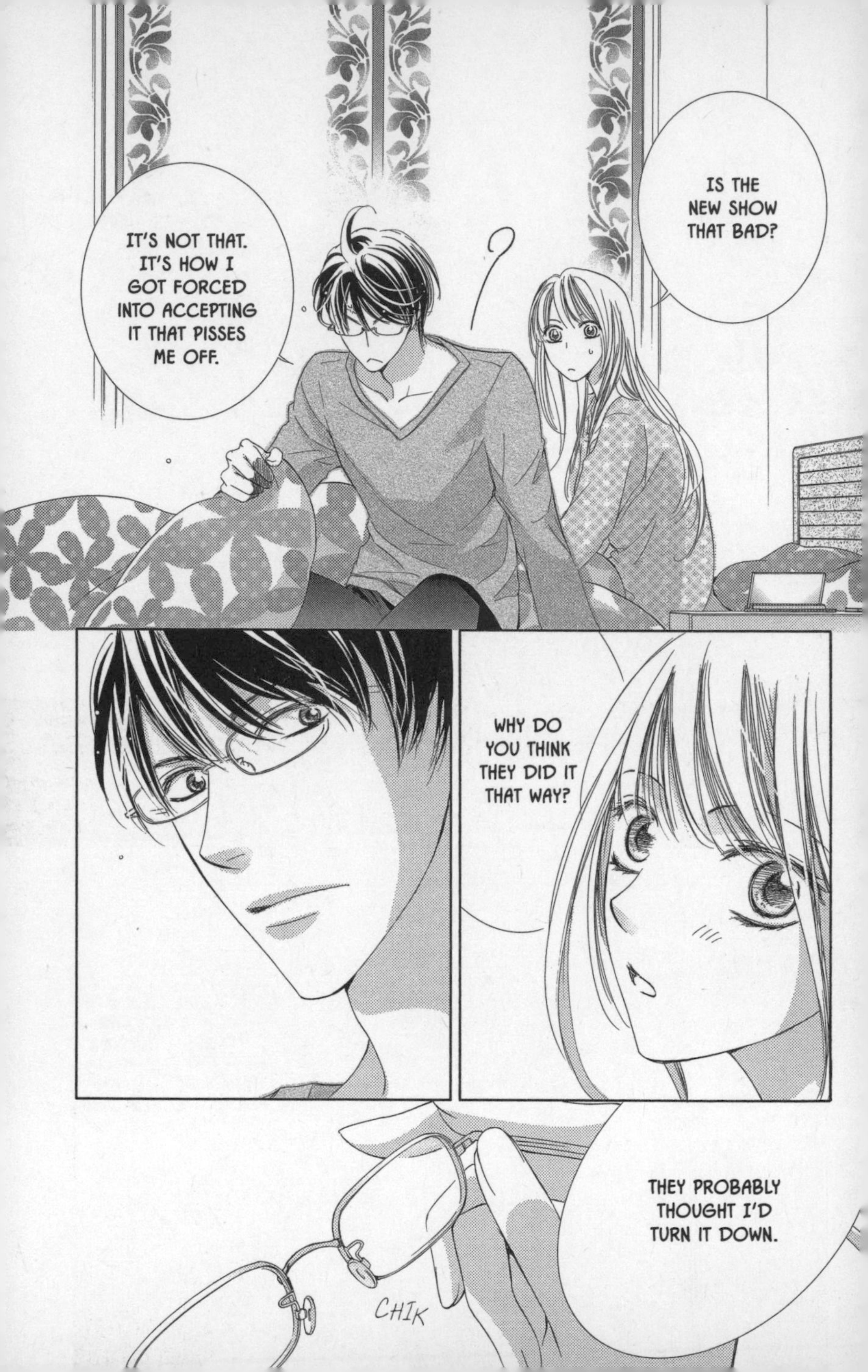
IS THE NEW SHOW THAT BAD?
IT'S NOT THAT. IT'S HOW I GOT FORCED INTO ACCEPTING IT THAT PISSES ME OFF.
WHY DO YOU THINK THEY DID IT THAT WAY?
THEY PROBABLY THOUGHT I'D TURN IT DOWN.
CHIK

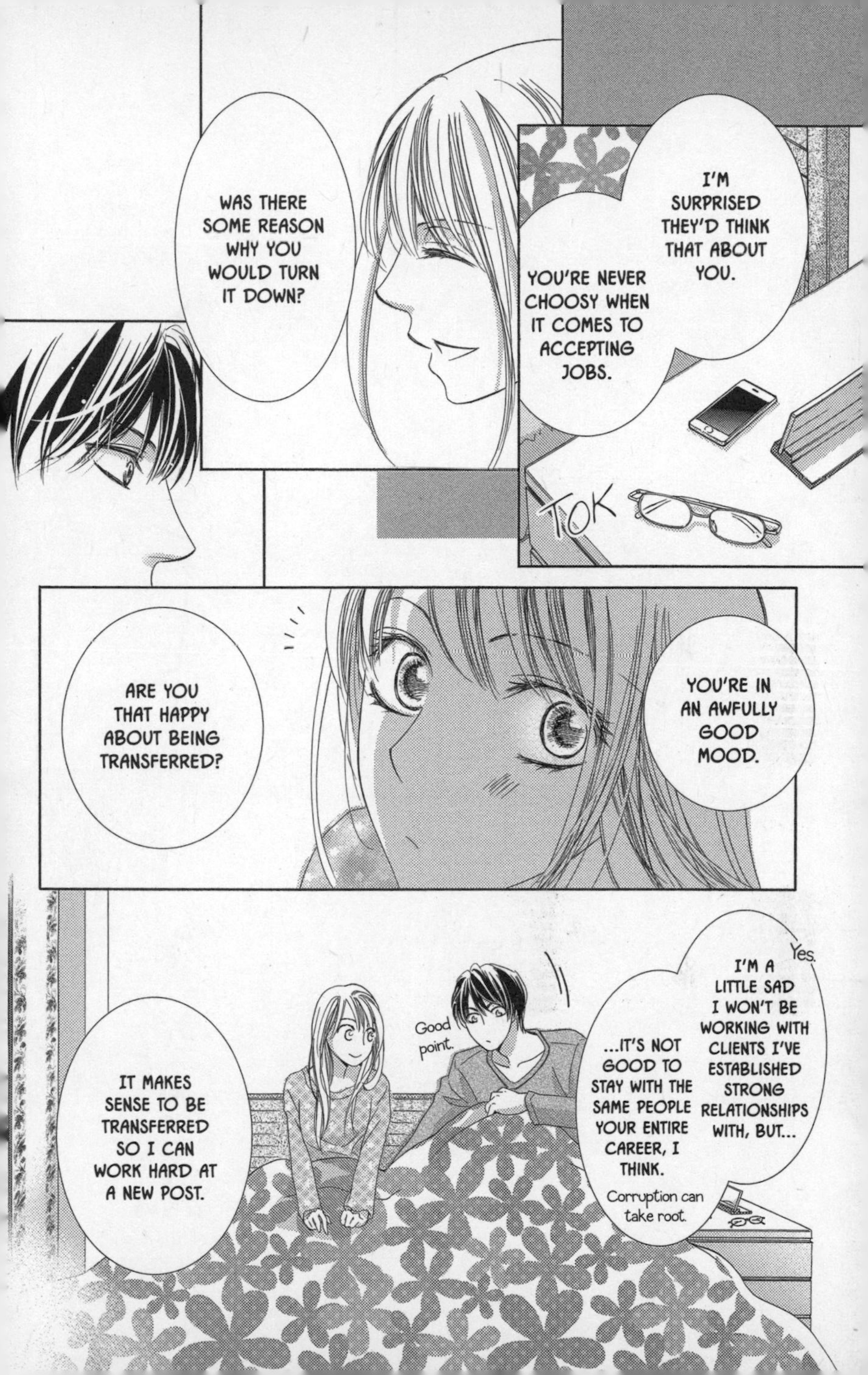
I'M SURPRISED THEY'D THINK THAT ABOUT YOU.
YOU'RE NEVER CHOOSY WHEN IT COMES TO ACCEPTING JOBS.
TOK
WAS THERE SOME REASON WHY YOU WOULD TURN IT DOWN?
YOU'RE IN AN AWFULLY GOOD MOOD.
ARE YOU THAT HAPPY ABOUT BEING TRANSFERRED?
Yes.
I'M A LITTLE SAD I WON'T BE WORKING WITH CLIENTS I'VE ESTABLISHED STRONG RELATIONSHIPS WITH, BUT...
...IT'S NOT GOOD TO STAY WITH THE SAME PEOPLE YOUR ENTIRE CAREER, I THINK.
Corruption can take root.
Good point.
IT MAKES SENSE TO BE TRANSFERRED SO I CAN WORK HARD AT A NEW POST.

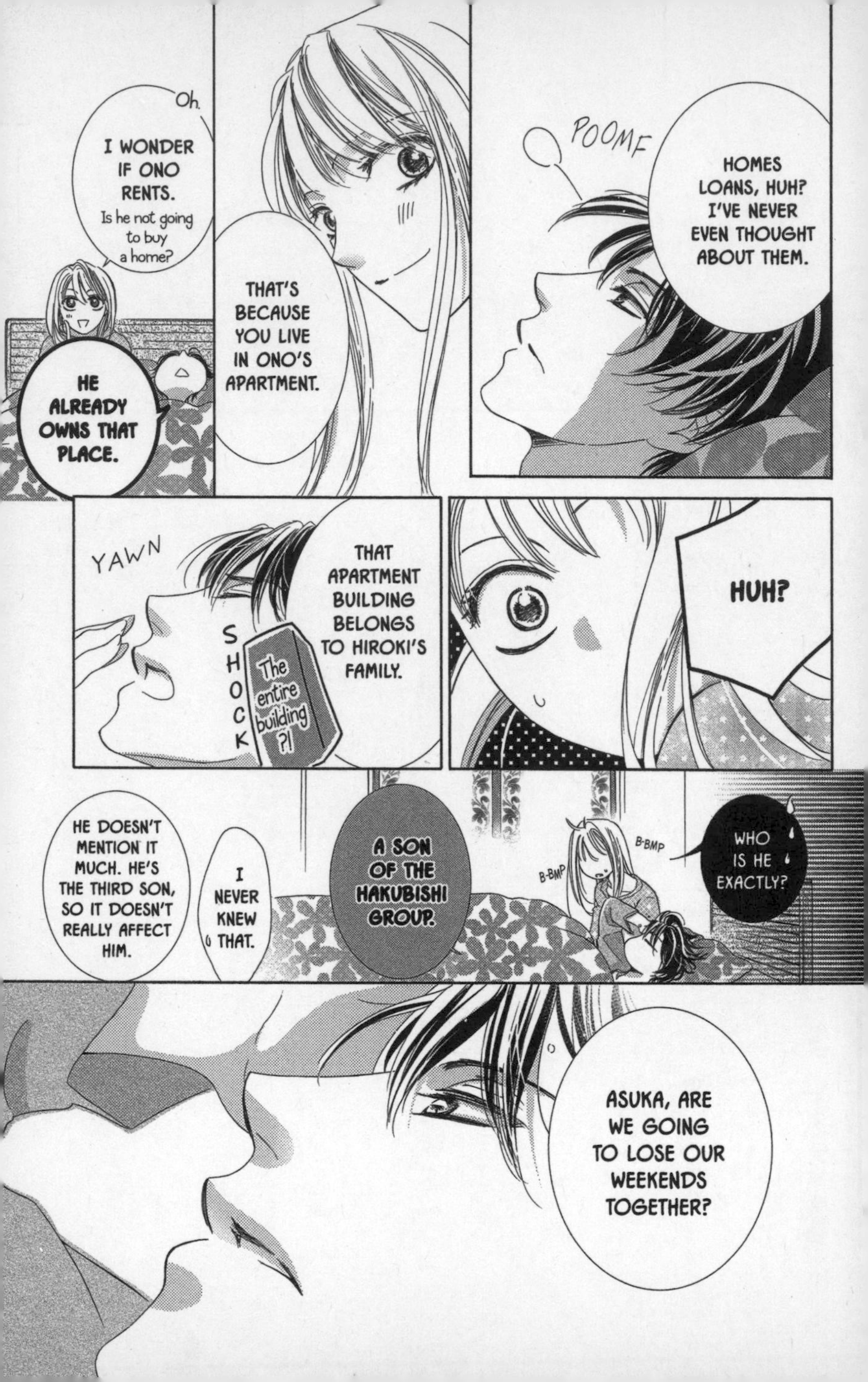
POOMF
HOMES LOANS, HUH? I'VE NEVER EVEN THOUGHT ABOUT THEM.
THAT'S BECAUSE YOU LIVE IN ONO'S APARTMENT.
Oh.
I WONDER IF ONO RENTS.
Is he not going to buy a home?
HE ALREADY OWNS THAT PLACE.
HUH?
YAWN
THAT APARTMENT BUILDING BELONGS TO HIROKI'S FAMILY.
SHOCK
The entire building?!
B-BMP
B-BMP
WHO IS HE EXACTLY?
A SON OF THE HAKUBISHI GROUP.
I NEVER KNEW THAT.
HE DOESN'T MENTION IT MUCH. HE'S THE THIRD SON, SO IT DOESN'T REALLY AFFECT HIM.
ASUKA, ARE WE GOING TO LOSE OUR WEEKENDS TOGETHER?

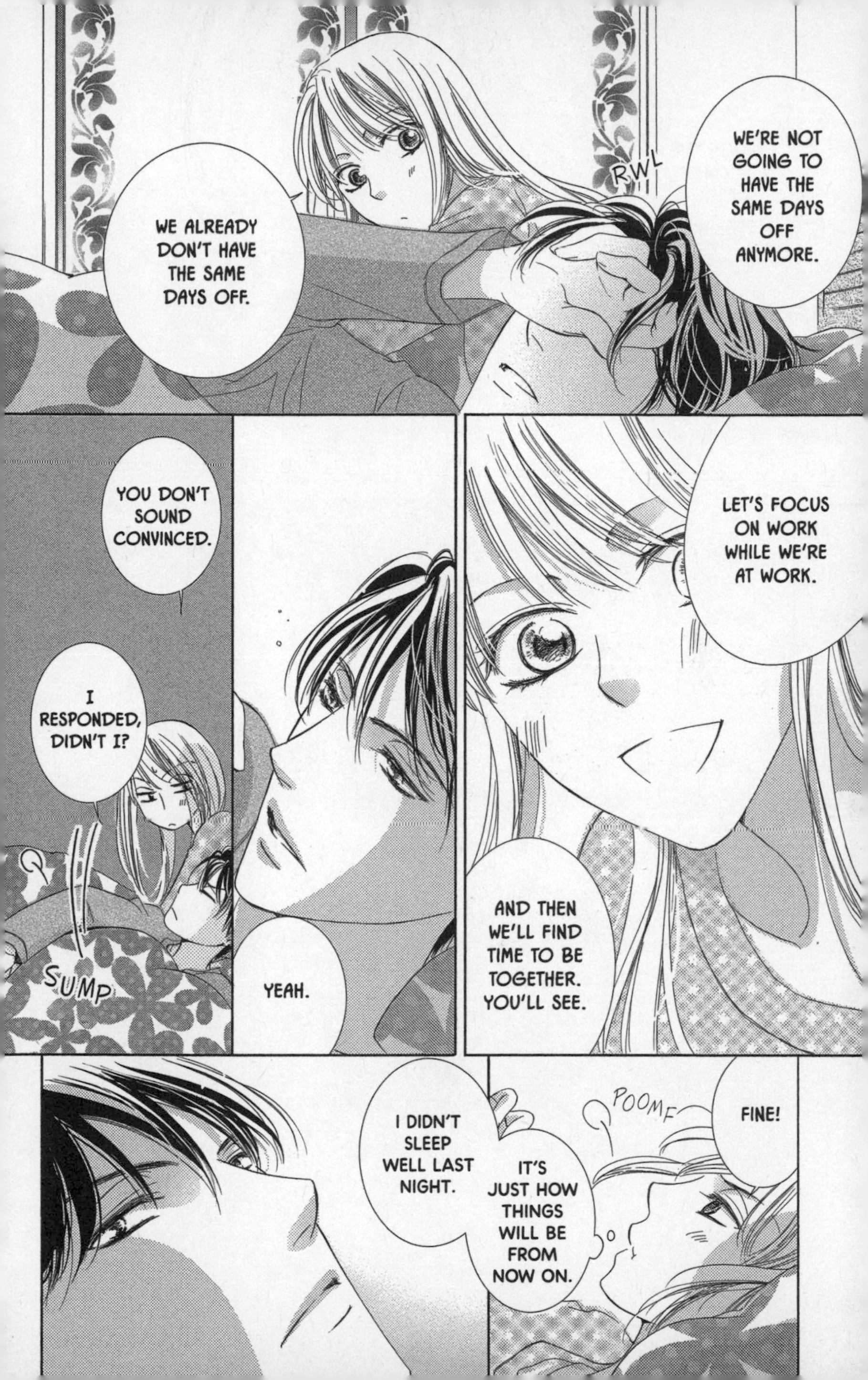
WE'RE NOT GOING TO HAVE THE SAME DAYS OFF ANYMORE.
RWL
WE ALREADY DON'T HAVE THE SAME DAYS OFF.
LET'S FOCUS ON WORK WHILE WE'RE AT WORK.
AND THEN WE'LL FIND TIME TO BE TOGETHER. YOU'LL SEE.
YEAH.
YOU DON'T SOUND CONVINCED.
I RESPONDED, DIDN'T I?
SUMP
FINE!
POOMF
IT'S JUST HOW THINGS WILL BE FROM NOW ON.
I DIDN'T SLEEP WELL LAST NIGHT.

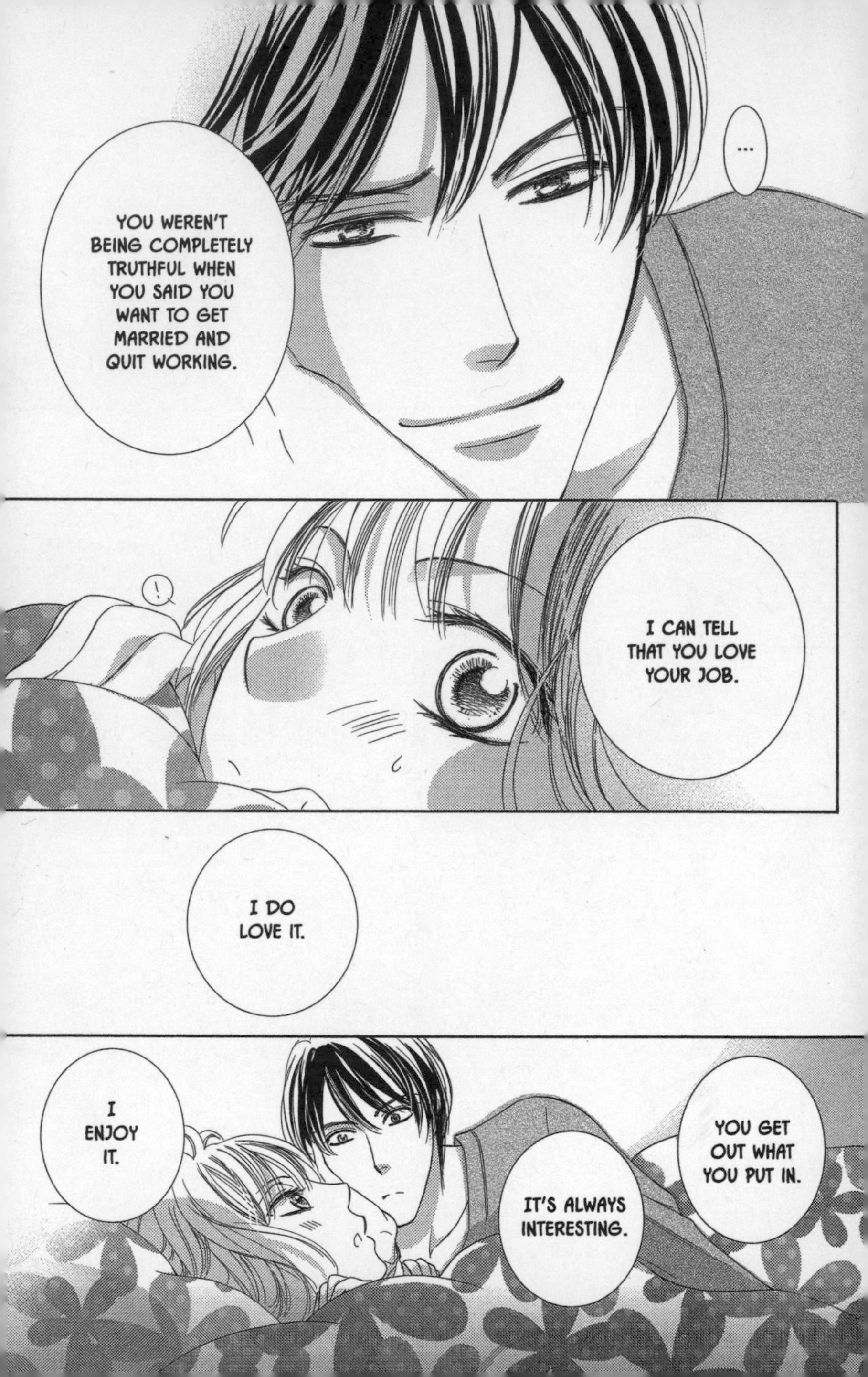
...
YOU WEREN'T BEING COMPLETELY TRUTHFUL WHEN YOU SAID YOU WANT TO GET MARRIED AND QUIT WORKING.
I CAN TELL THAT YOU LOVE YOUR JOB.
!
I DO LOVE IT.
YOU GET OUT WHAT YOU PUT IN.
IT'S ALWAYS INTERESTING.
I ENJOY IT.

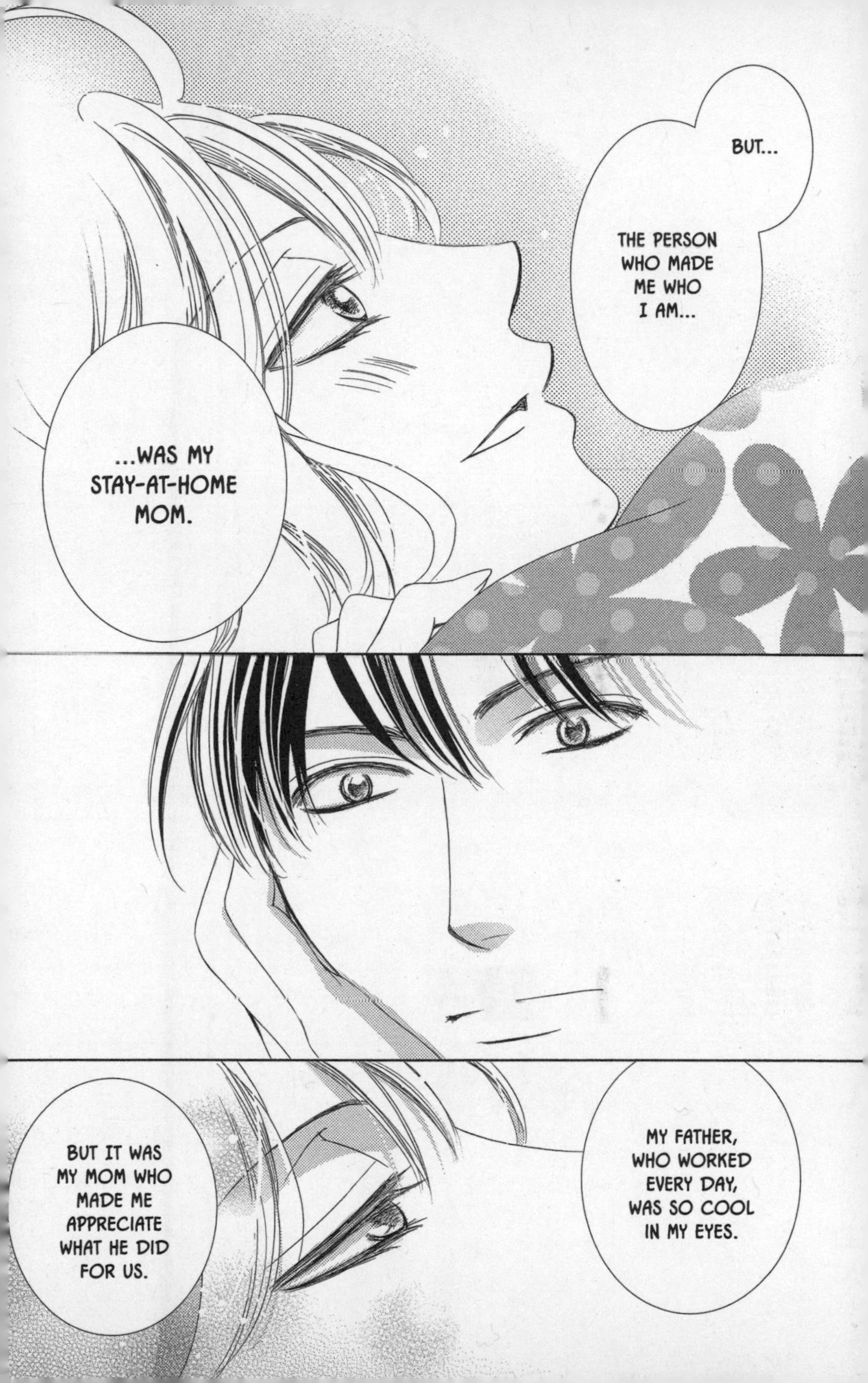
BUT...
THE PERSON WHO MADE ME WHO I AM...
...WAS MY STAY-AT-HOME MOM.
MY FATHER, WHO WORKED EVERY DAY, WAS SO COOL IN MY EYES.
BUT IT WAS MY MOM WHO MADE ME APPRECIATE WHAT HE DID FOR US.

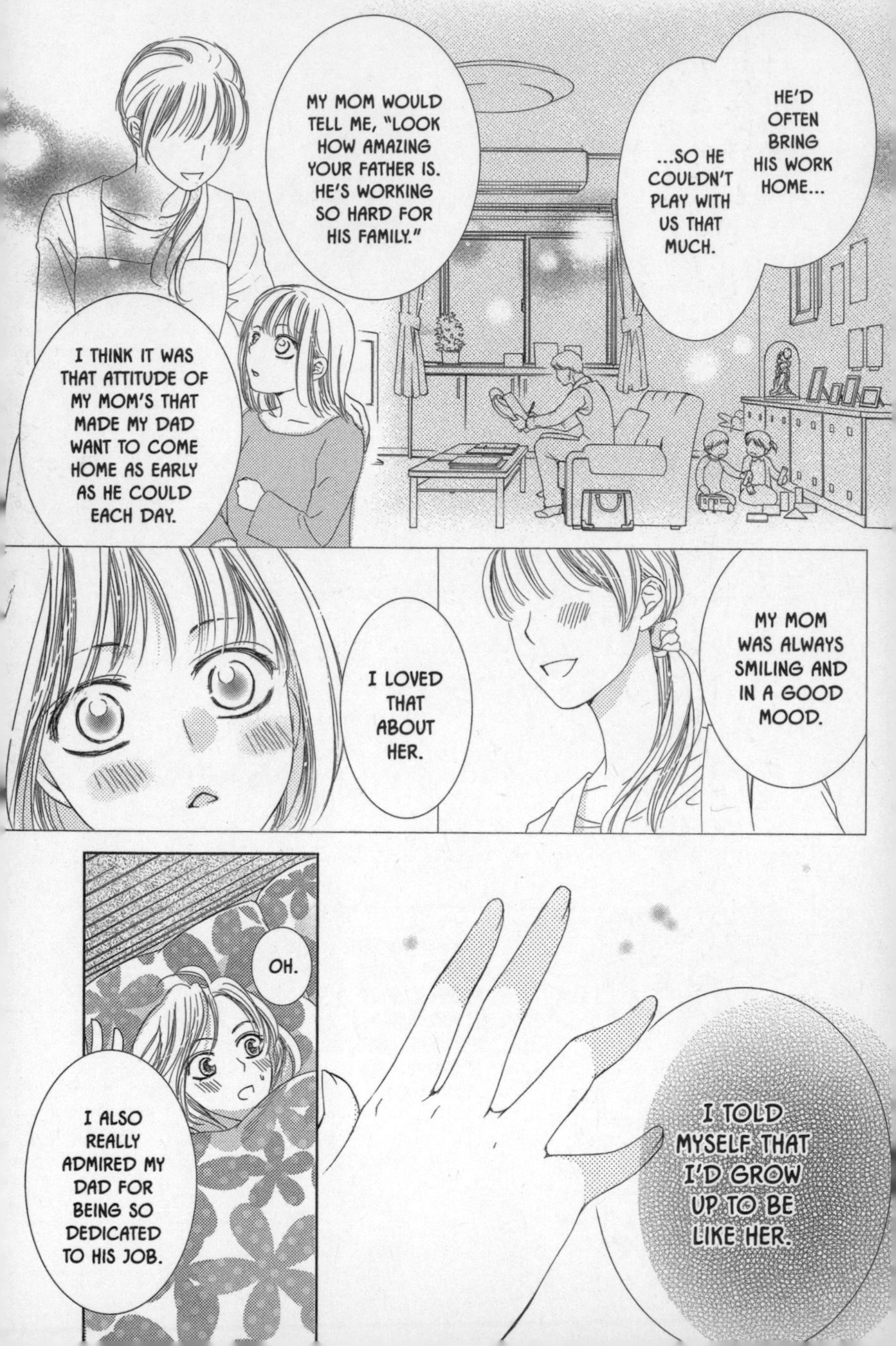
HE'D OFTEN BRING HIS WORK HOME...
...SO HE COULDN'T PLAY WITH US THAT MUCH.
MY MOM WOULD TELL ME, "LOOK HOW AMAZING YOUR FATHER IS. HE'S WORKING SO HARD FOR HIS FAMILY."
I THINK IT WAS THAT ATTITUDE OF MY MOM'S THAT MADE MY DAD WANT TO COME HOME AS EARLY AS HE COULD EACH DAY.
MY MOM WAS ALWAYS SMILING AND IN A GOOD MOOD.
I LOVED THAT ABOUT HER.
I TOLD MYSELF THAT I'D GROW UP TO BE LIKE HER.
OH.
I ALSO REALLY ADMIRED MY DAD FOR BEING SO DEDICATED TO HIS JOB.

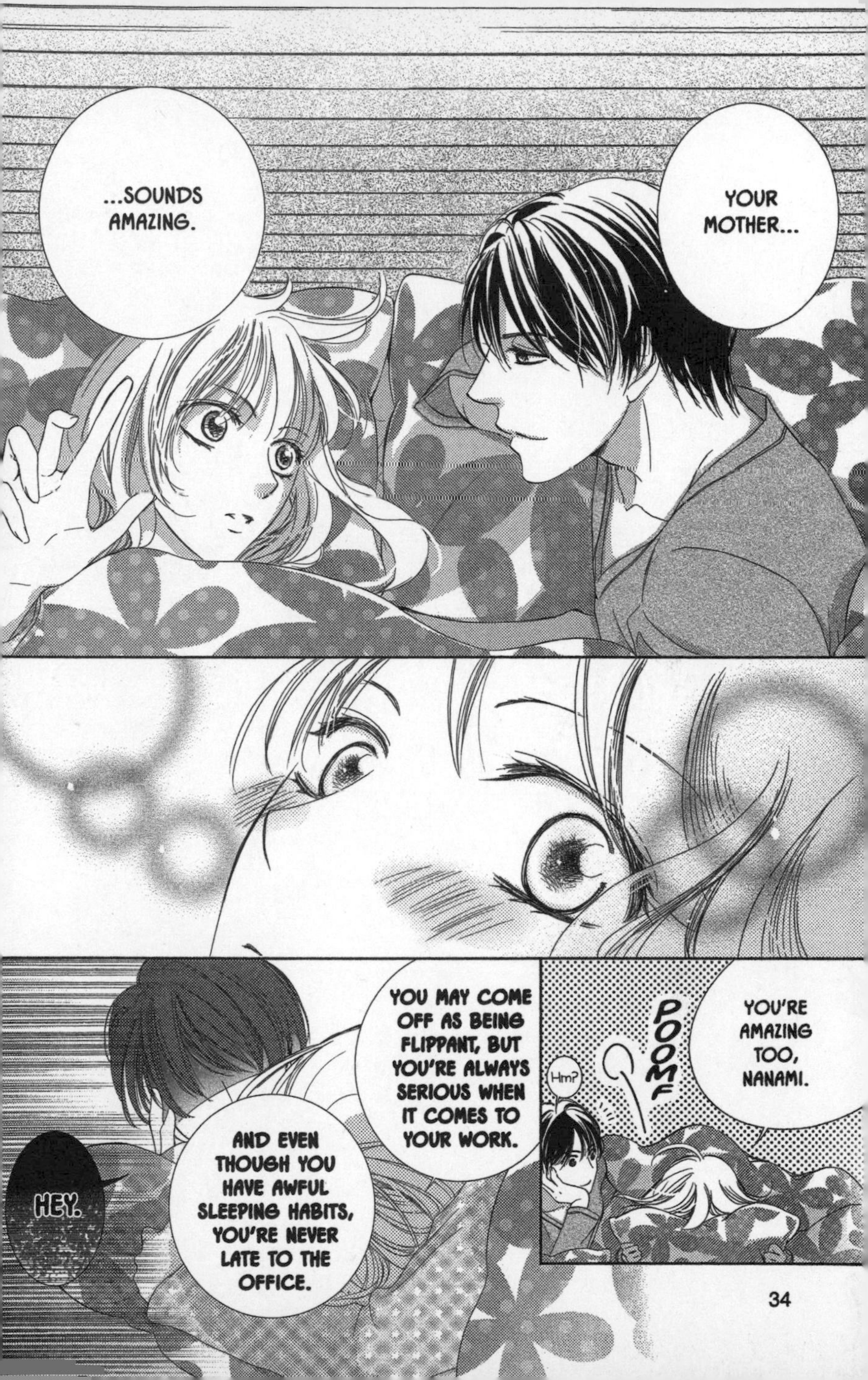
YOUR MOTHER...
...SOUNDS AMAZING.
YOU'RE AMAZING TOO, NANAMI.
POOMF
Hm?
YOU MAY COME OFF AS BEING FLIPPANT, BUT YOU'RE ALWAYS SERIOUS WHEN IT COMES TO YOUR WORK.
AND EVEN THOUGH YOU HAVE AWFUL SLEEPING HABITS, YOU'RE NEVER LATE TO THE OFFICE.
HEY.

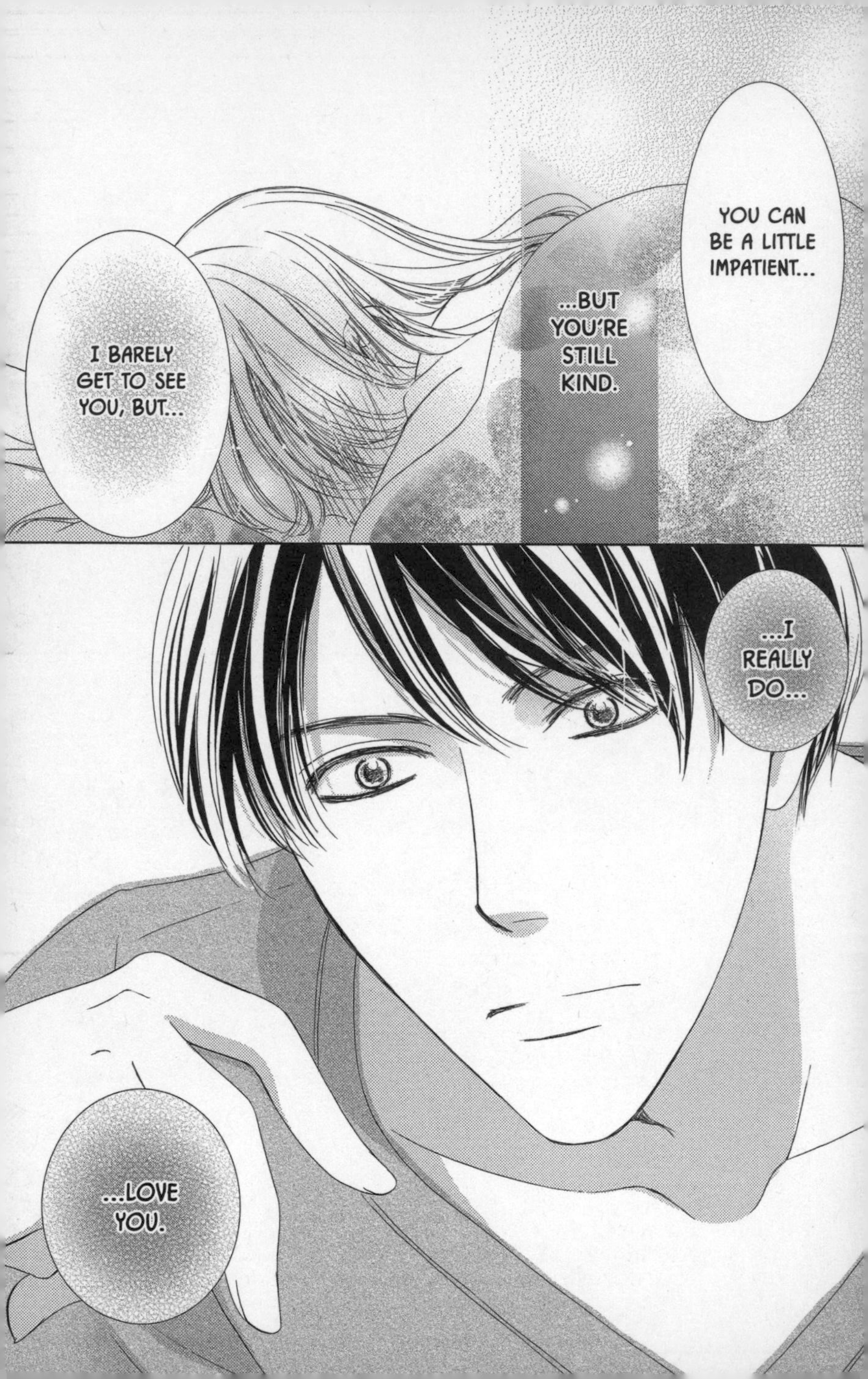
YOU CAN BE A LITTLE IMPATIENT...
...BUT YOU'RE STILL KIND.
I BARELY GET TO SEE YOU, BUT...
...I REALLY DO...
...LOVE YOU.

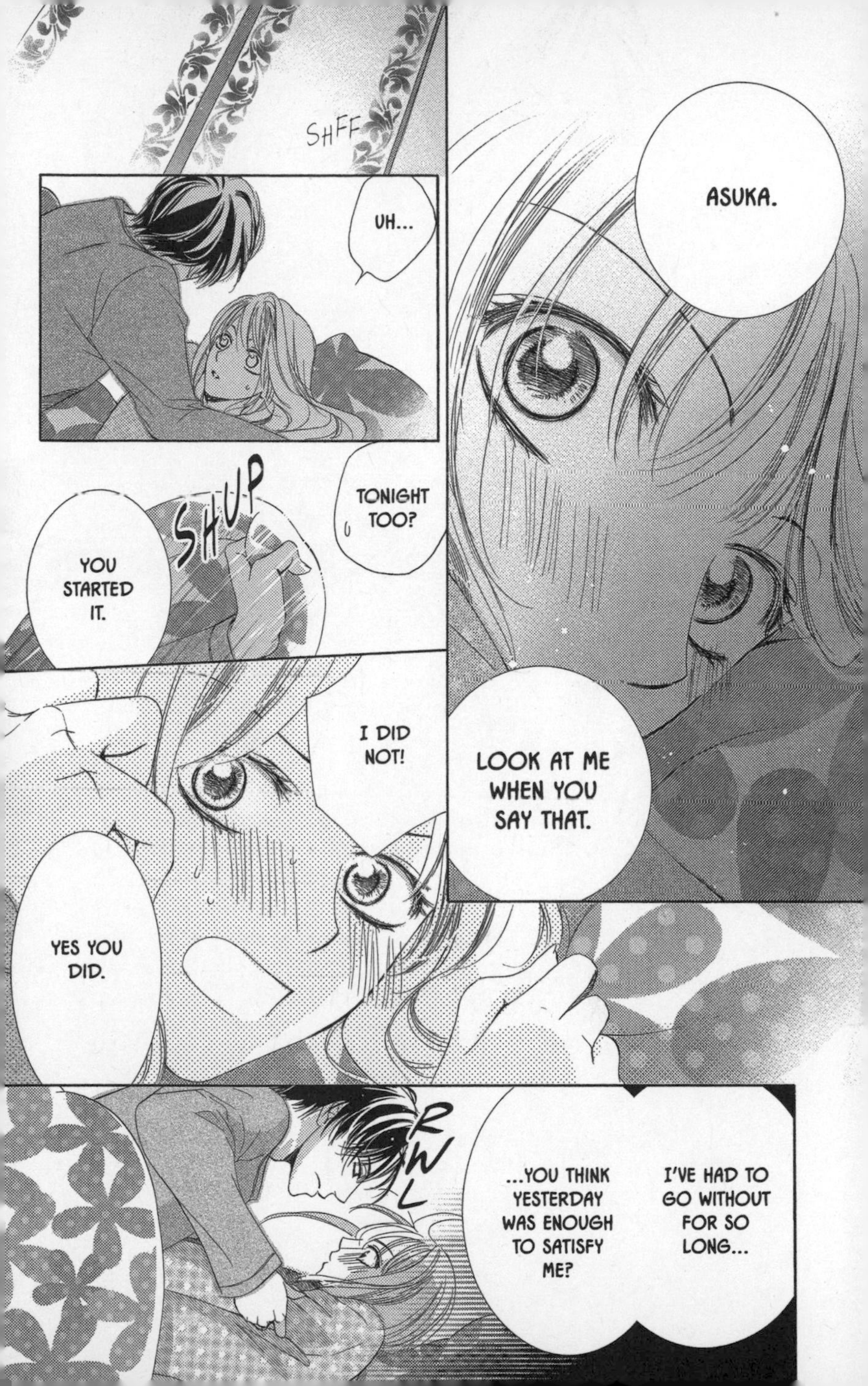
ASUKA.
LOOK AT ME WHEN YOU SAY THAT.
SHFF
UH...
TONIGHT TOO?
SHUP
YOU STARTED IT.
I DID NOT!
YES YOU DID.
I'VE HAD TO GO WITHOUT FOR SO LONG...
...YOU THINK YESTERDAY WAS ENOUGH TO SATISFY ME?
RWL

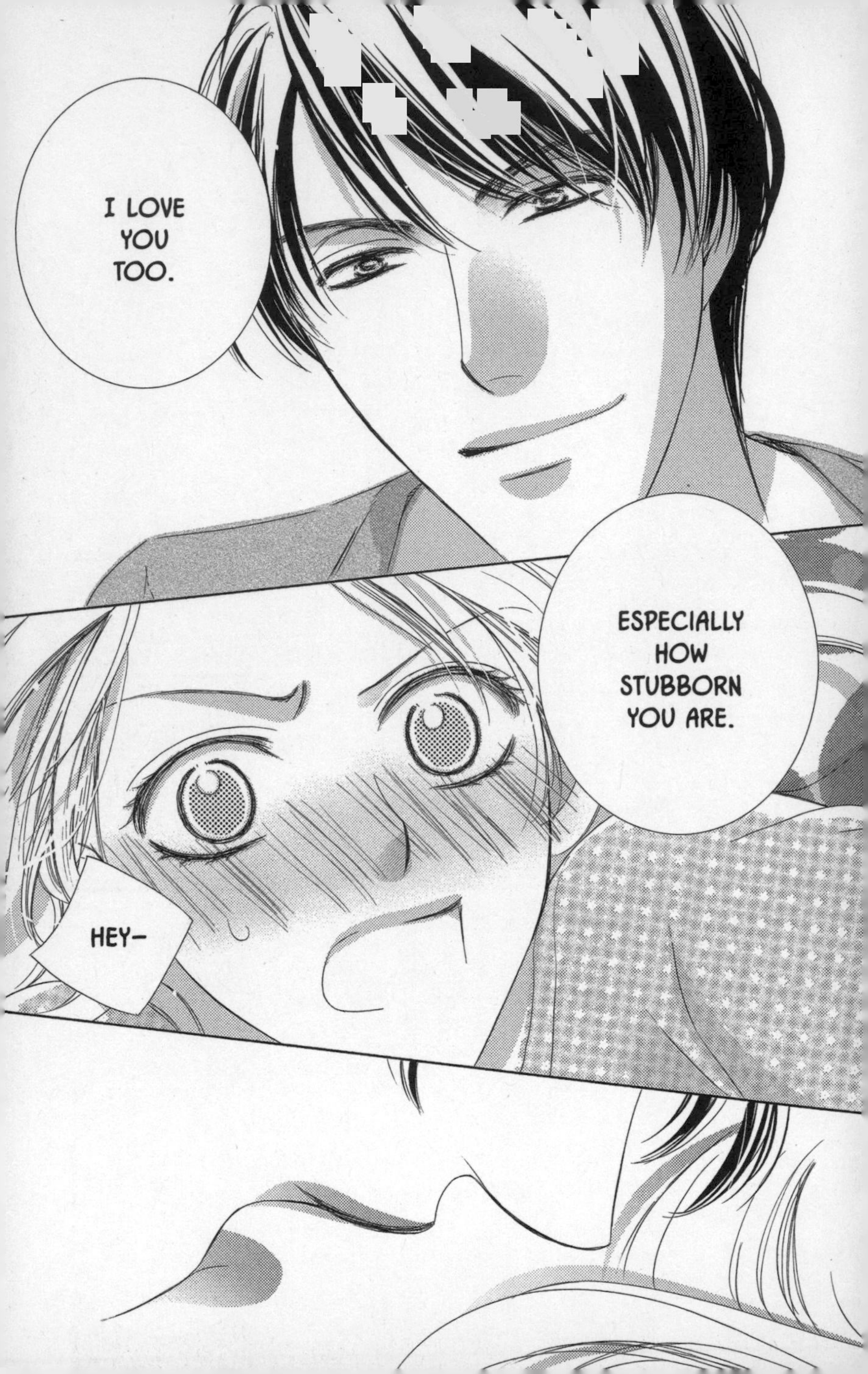
I LOVE YOU TOO.
ESPECIALLY HOW STUBBORN YOU ARE.
HEY–

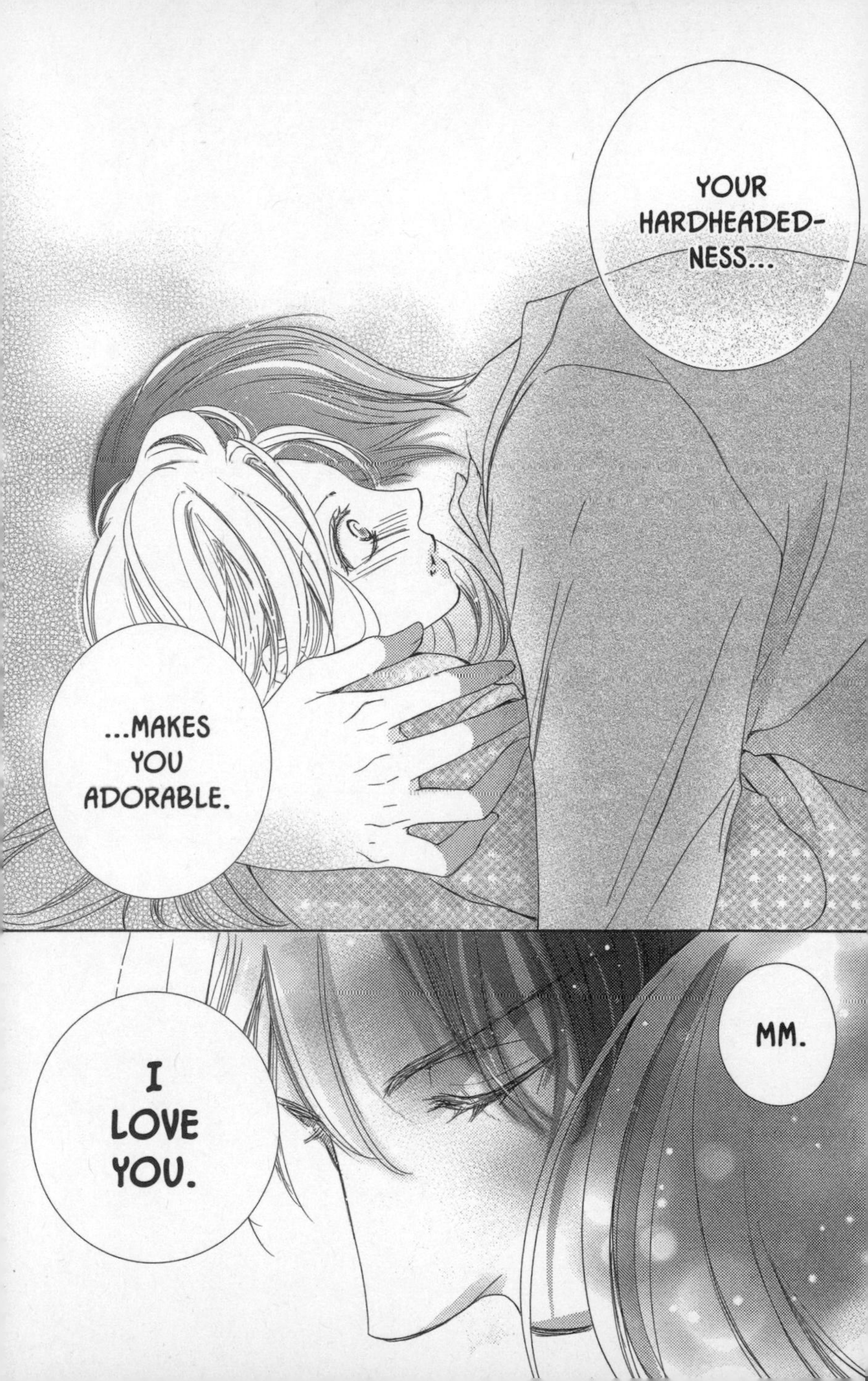
YOUR HARDHEADED-NESS...
...MAKES YOU ADORABLE.
MM.
I LOVE YOU.

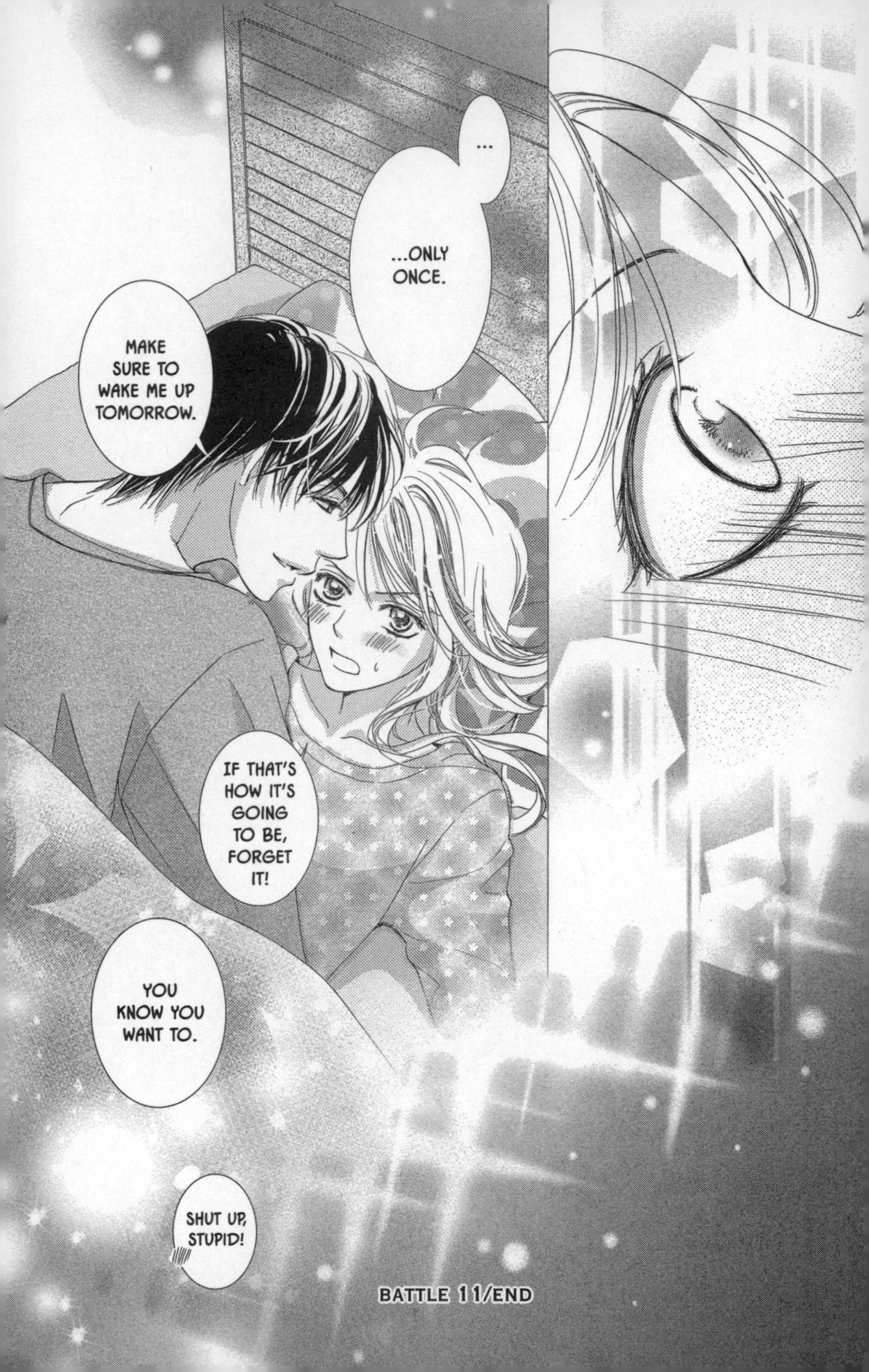
...
...ONLY ONCE.
MAKE SURE TO WAKE ME UP TOMORROW.
IF THAT'S HOW IT'S GOING TO BE, FORGET IT!
YOU KNOW YOU WANT TO.
SHUT UP, STUPID!
BATTLE 11/END

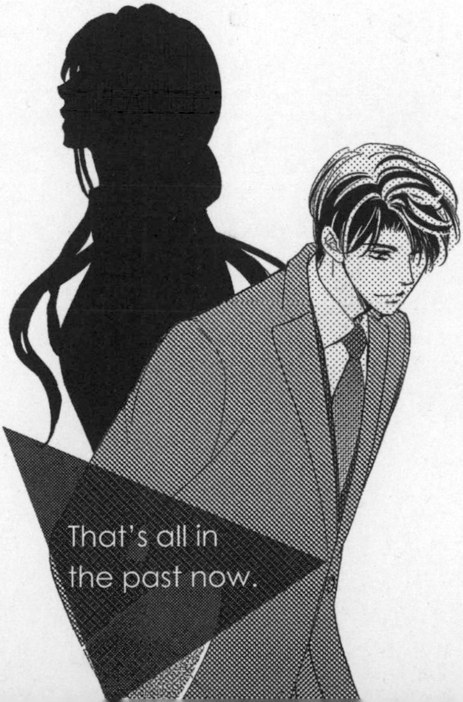
That's all in
the past now.

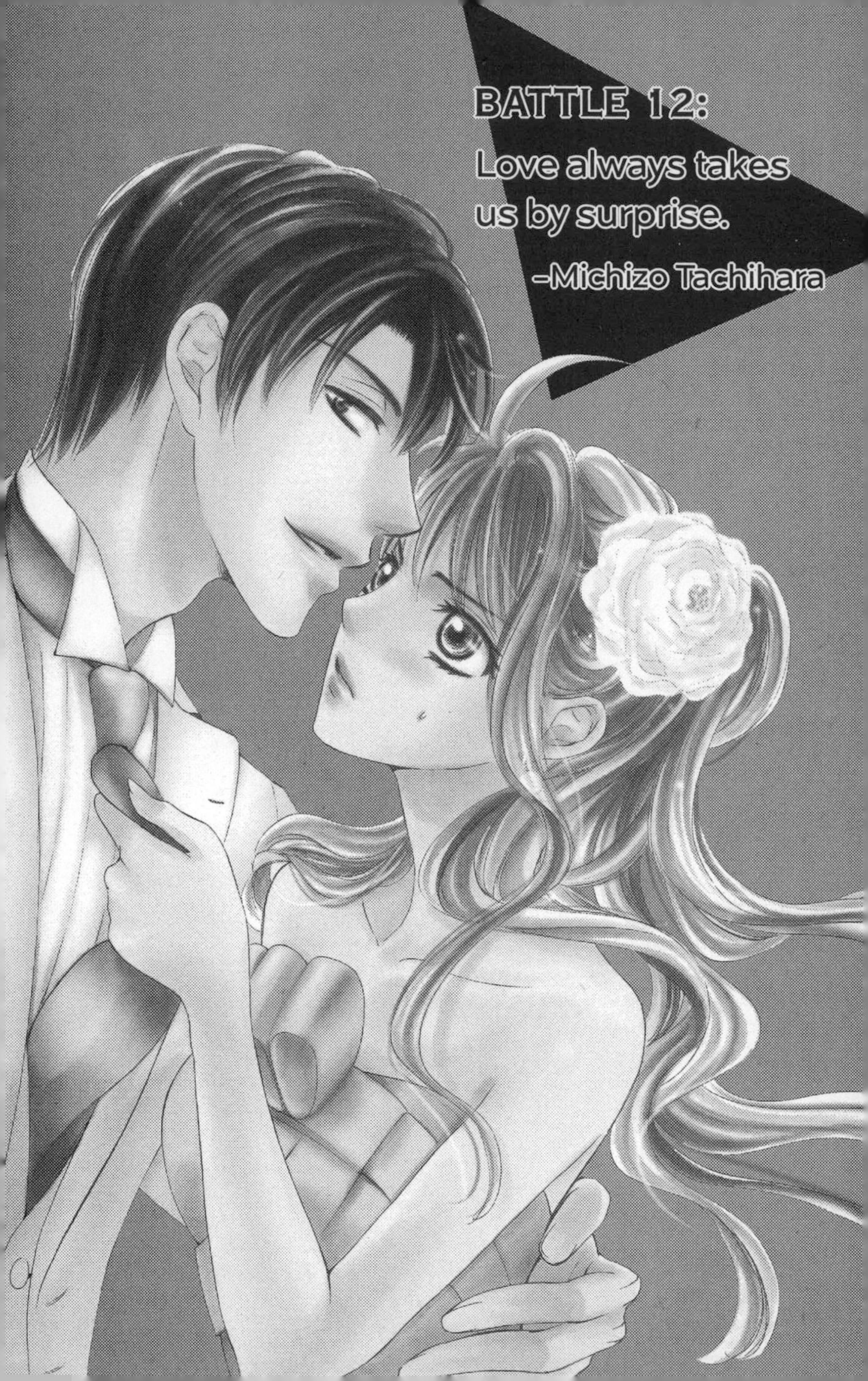
BATTLE 12:
Love always takes us by surprise.
–Michizo Tachihara

Everyone's
Getting
Married

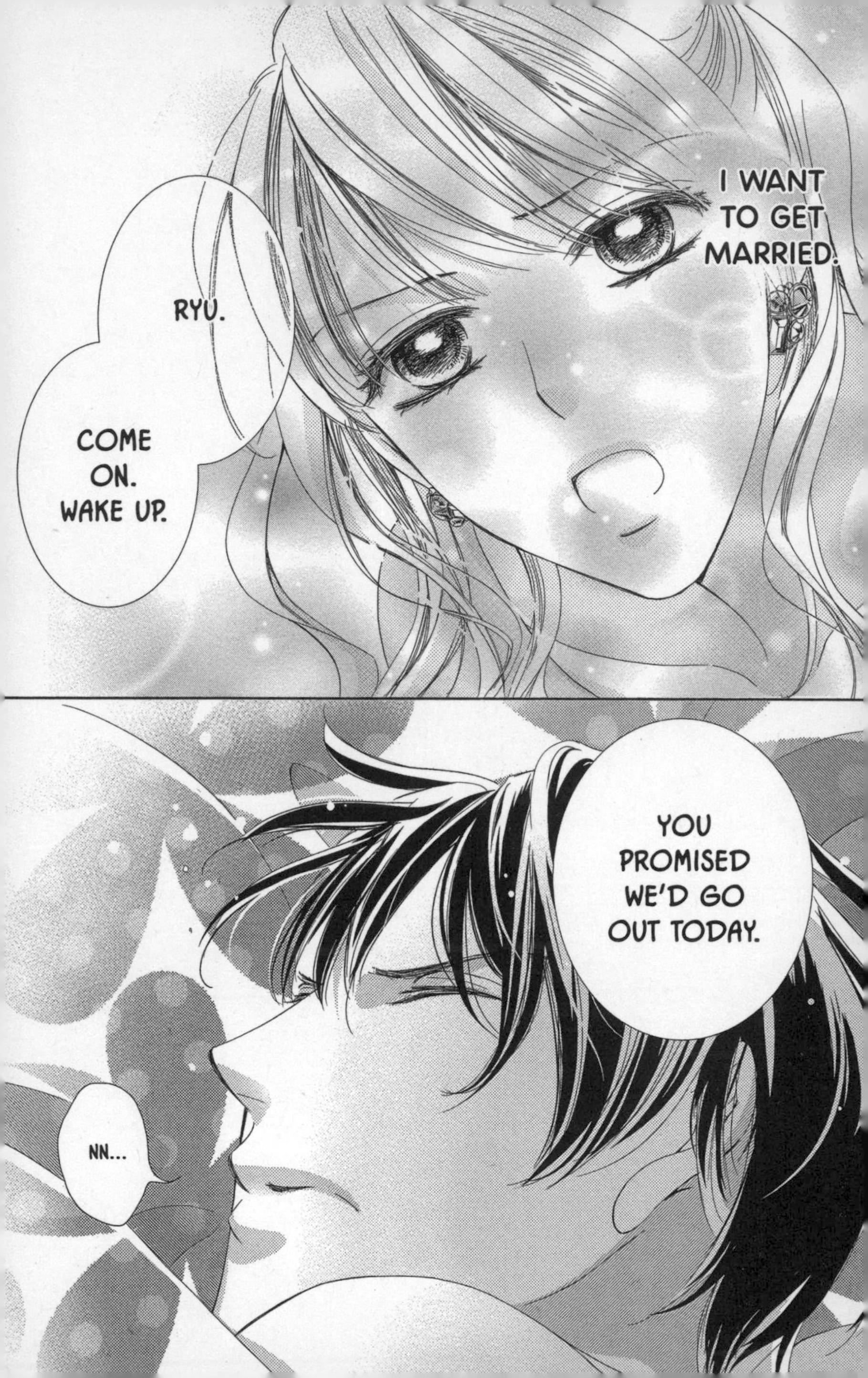
I WANT TO GET MARRIED.
RYU.
COME ON. WAKE UP.
YOU PROMISED WE'D GO OUT TODAY.
NN...

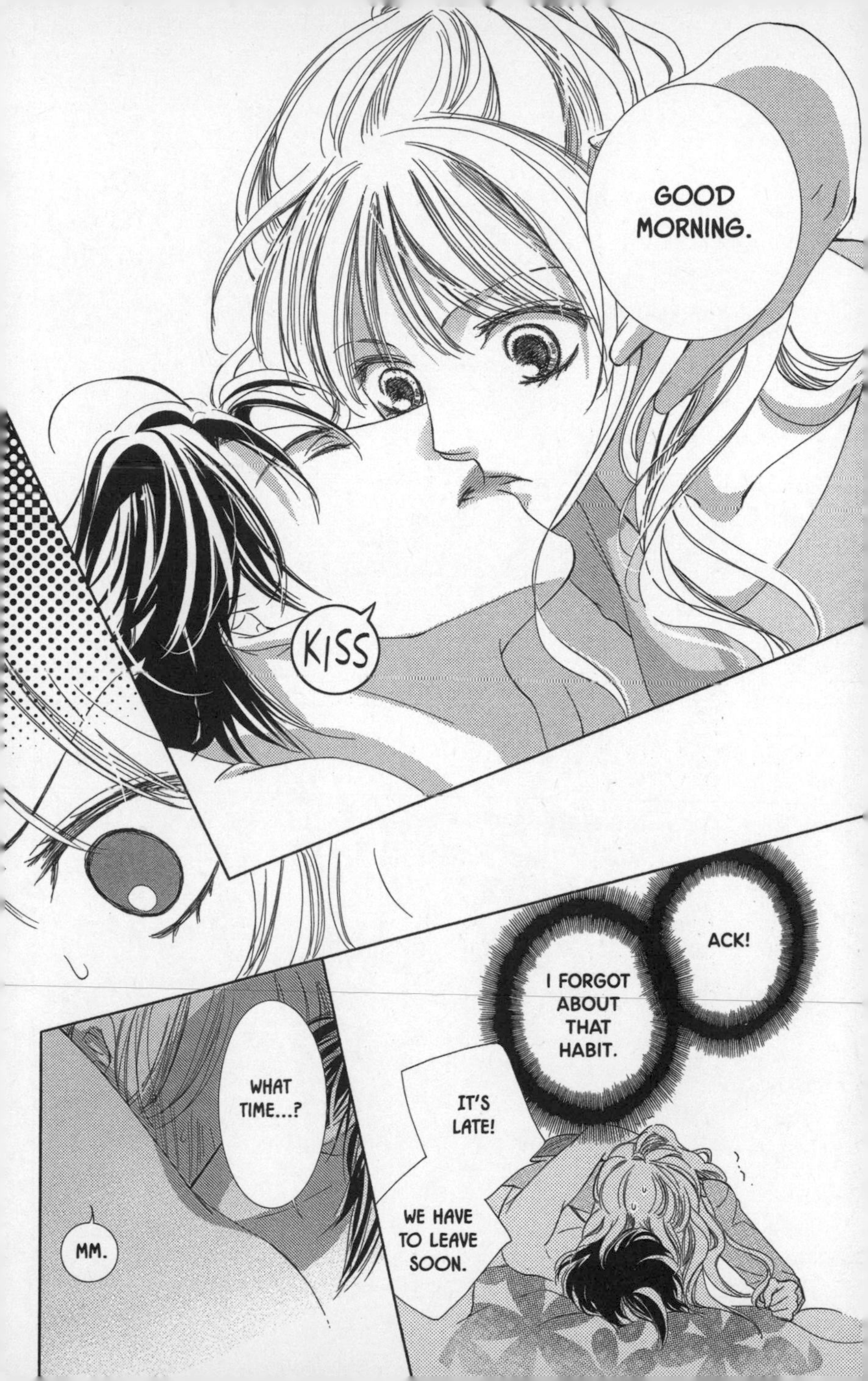
GOOD MORNING.
KISS
ACK!
I FORGOT ABOUT THAT HABIT.
IT'S LATE!
WE HAVE TO LEAVE SOON.
WHAT TIME...?
MM.

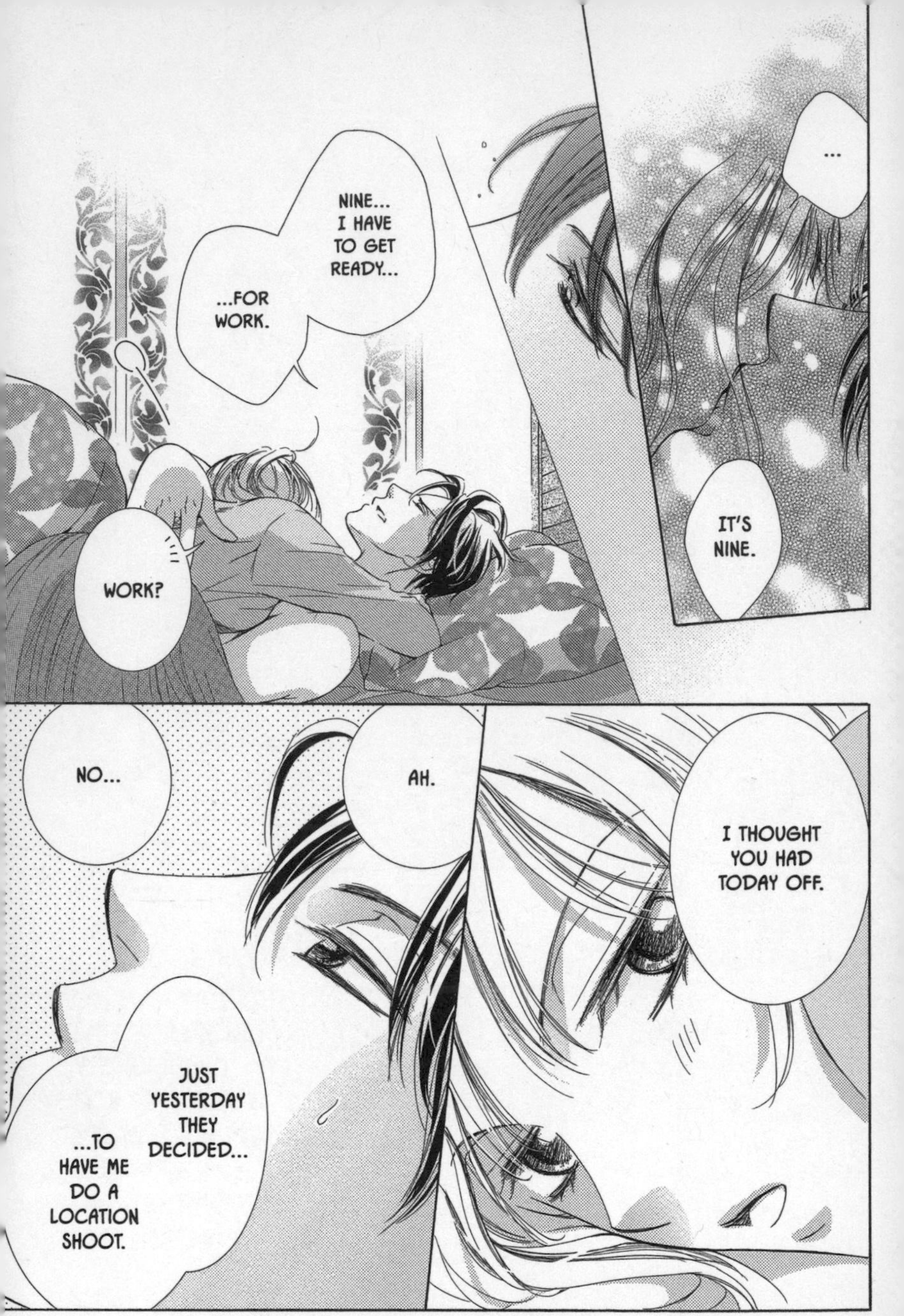
...
IT'S NINE.
NINE... I HAVE TO GET READY...
...FOR WORK.
WORK?
I THOUGHT YOU HAD TODAY OFF.
AH.
NO...
JUST YESTERDAY THEY DECIDED...
...TO HAVE ME DO A LOCATION SHOOT.

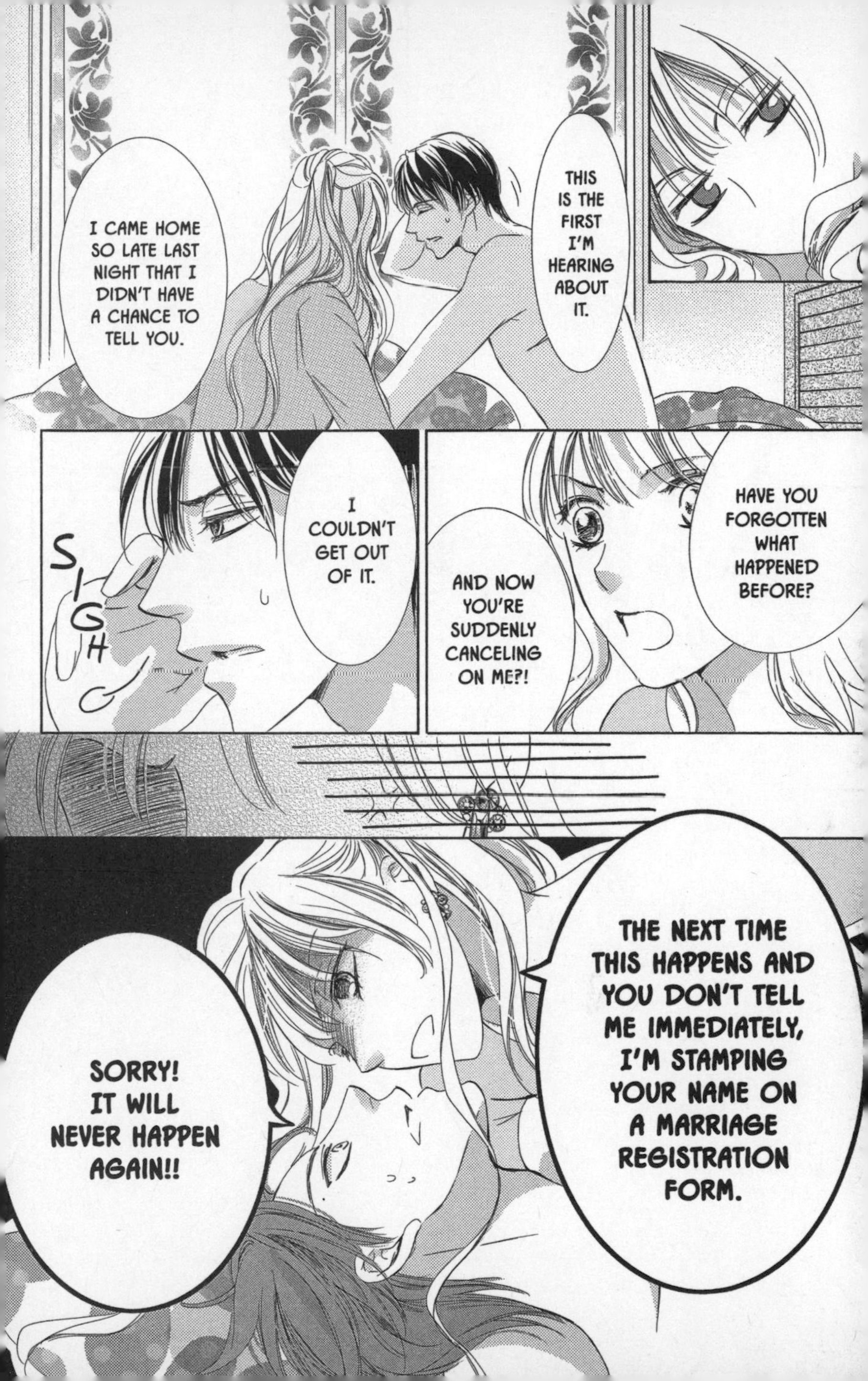
THIS IS THE FIRST I'M HEARING ABOUT IT.
I CAME HOME SO LATE LAST NIGHT THAT I DIDN'T HAVE A CHANCE TO TELL YOU.
HAVE YOU FORGOTTEN WHAT HAPPENED BEFORE?
AND NOW YOU'RE SUDDENLY CANCELING ON ME?!
I COULDN'T GET OUT OF IT.
SIGH
THE NEXT TIME THIS HAPPENS AND YOU DON'T TELL ME IMMEDIATELY, I'M STAMPING YOUR NAME ON A MARRIAGE REGISTRATION FORM.
SORRY! IT WILL NEVER HAPPEN AGAIN!!

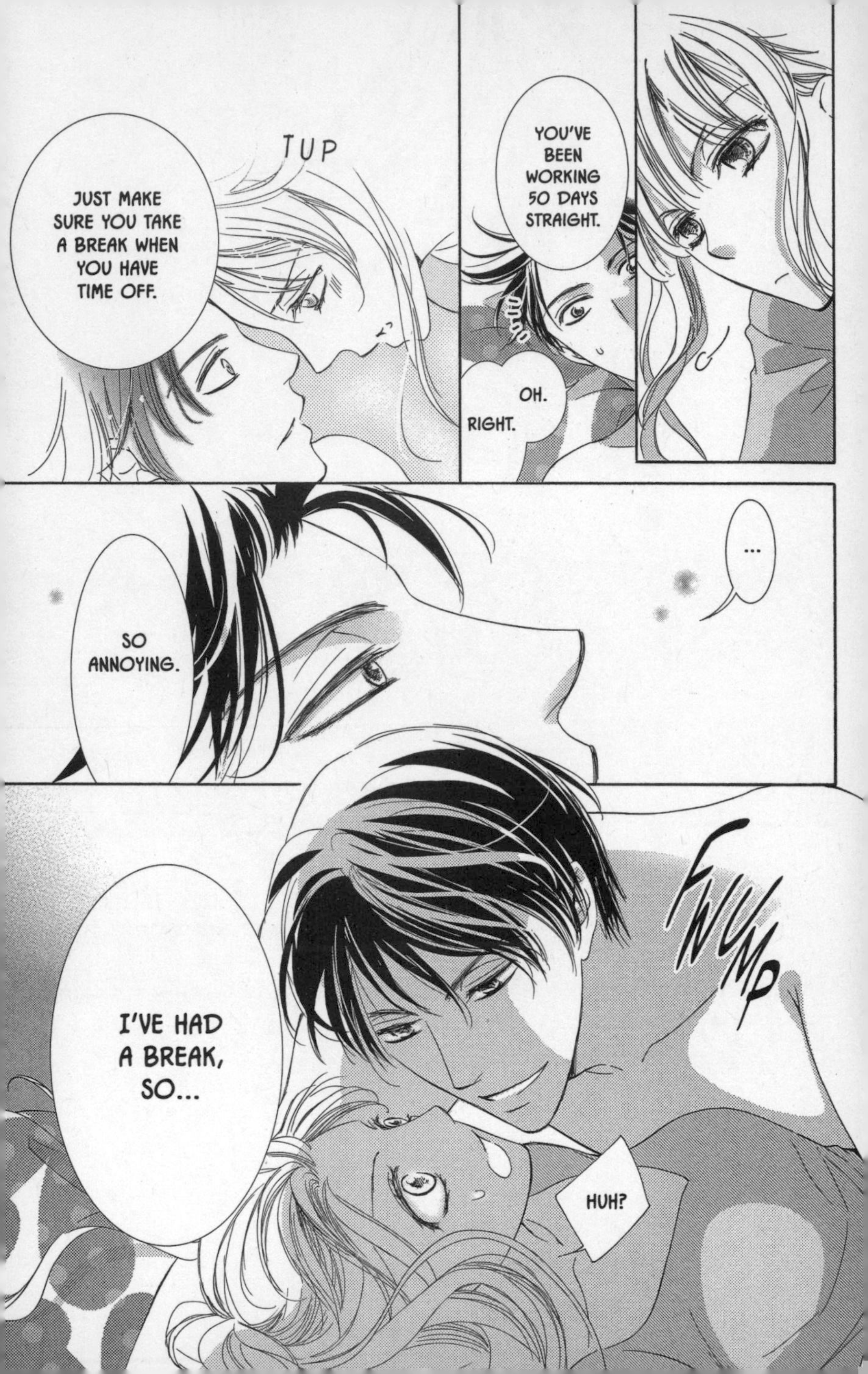
YOU'VE BEEN WORKING 50 DAYS STRAIGHT.
OH.
RIGHT.
TUP
JUST MAKE SURE YOU TAKE A BREAK WHEN YOU HAVE TIME OFF.
...
SO ANNOYING.
FWUMP
I'VE HAD A BREAK, SO...
HUH?

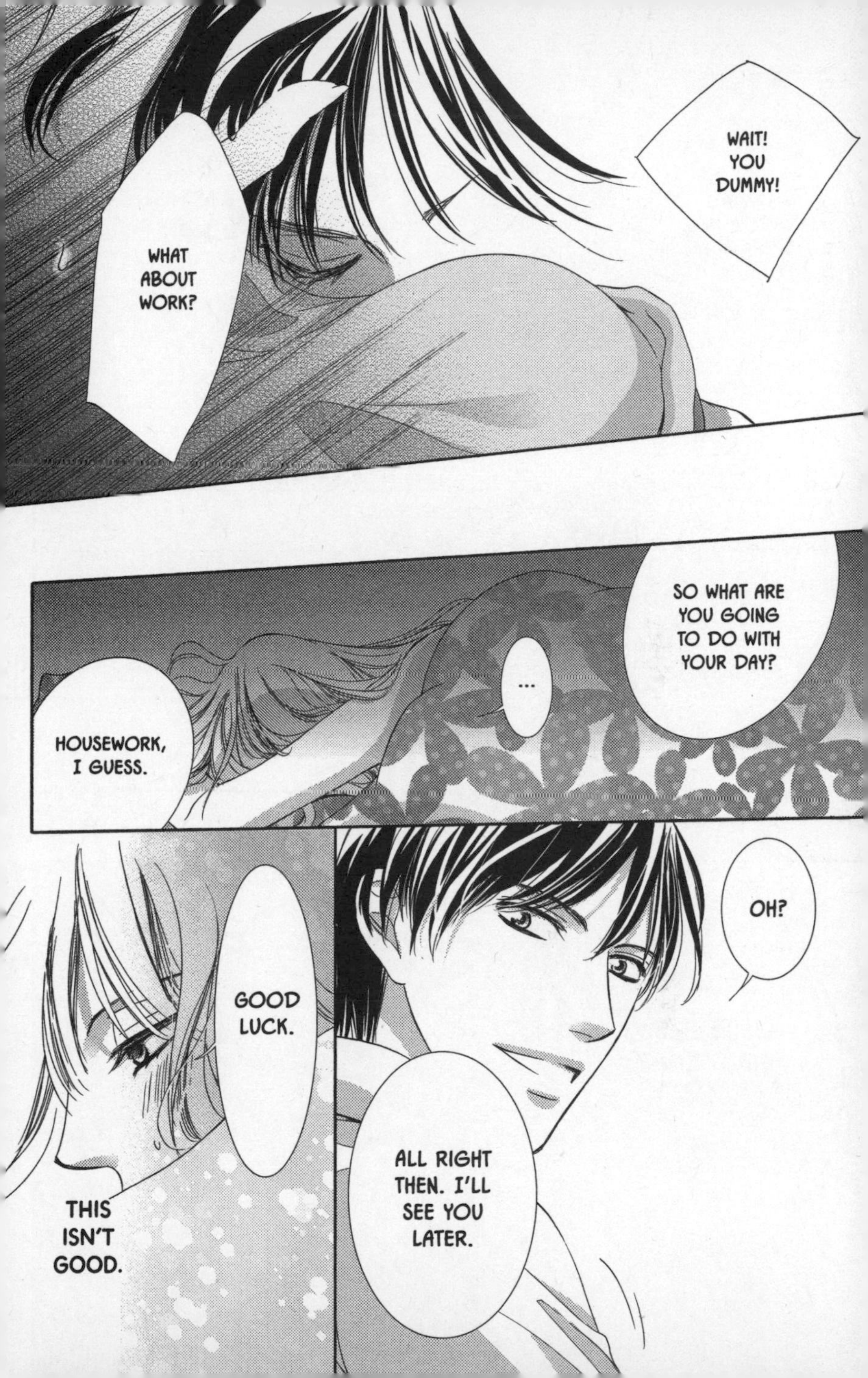
WAIT! YOU DUMMY!
WHAT ABOUT WORK?
SO WHAT ARE YOU GOING TO DO WITH YOUR DAY?
...
HOUSEWORK, I GUESS.
OH?
ALL RIGHT THEN. I'LL SEE YOU LATER.
GOOD LUCK.
THIS ISN'T GOOD.

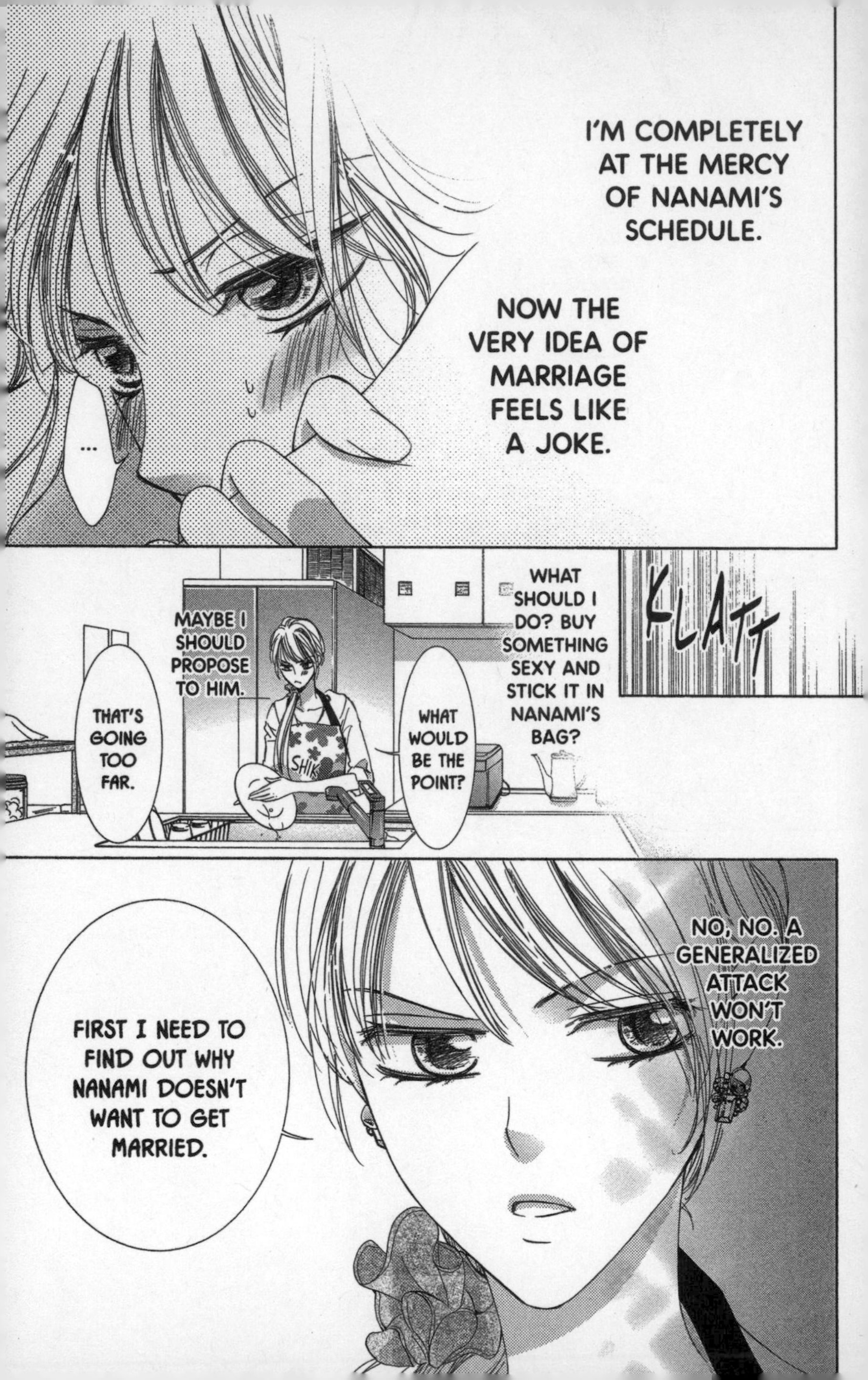
I'M COMPLETELY AT THE MERCY OF NANAMI'S SCHEDULE.
NOW THE VERY IDEA OF MARRIAGE FEELS LIKE A JOKE.
...
KLATT
WHAT SHOULD I DO? BUY SOMETHING SEXY AND STICK IT IN NANAMI'S BAG?
WHAT WOULD BE THE POINT?
MAYBE I SHOULD PROPOSE TO HIM.
THAT'S GOING TOO FAR.
NO, NO. A GENERALIZED ATTACK WON'T WORK.
FIRST I NEED TO FIND OUT WHY NANAMI DOESN'T WANT TO GET MARRIED.

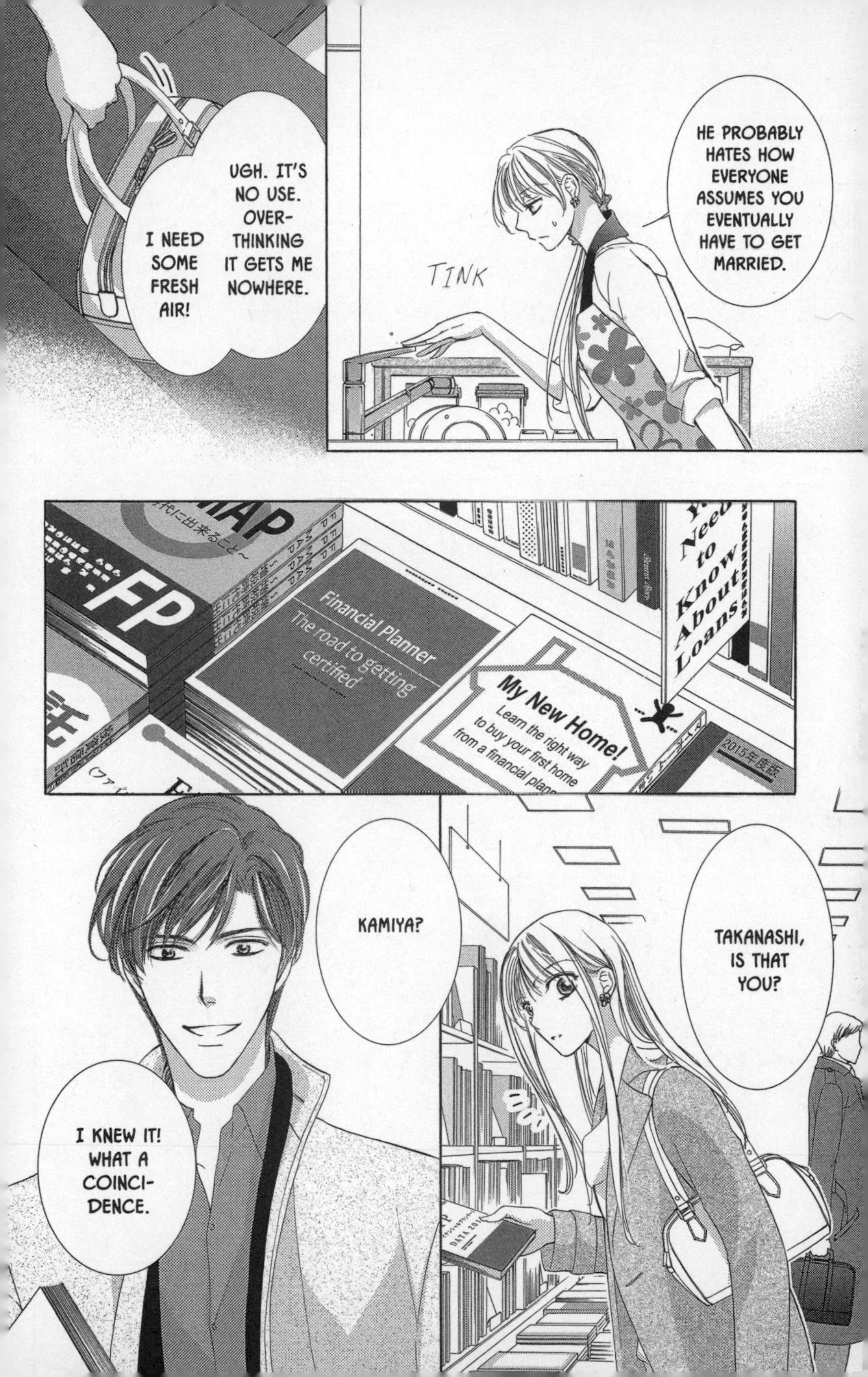
HE PROBABLY HATES HOW EVERYONE ASSUMES YOU EVENTUALLY HAVE TO GET MARRIED.
TINK
UGH. IT'S NO USE. OVER-THINKING IT GETS ME NOWHERE.
I NEED SOME FRESH AIR!
Need to Know About Loans
MAP
FP
Financial Planner
The road to getting certified
My New Home!
Learn the right way to buy your first home
2015年度版
TAKANASHI, IS THAT YOU?
KAMIYA?
I KNEW IT! WHAT A COINCIDENCE.

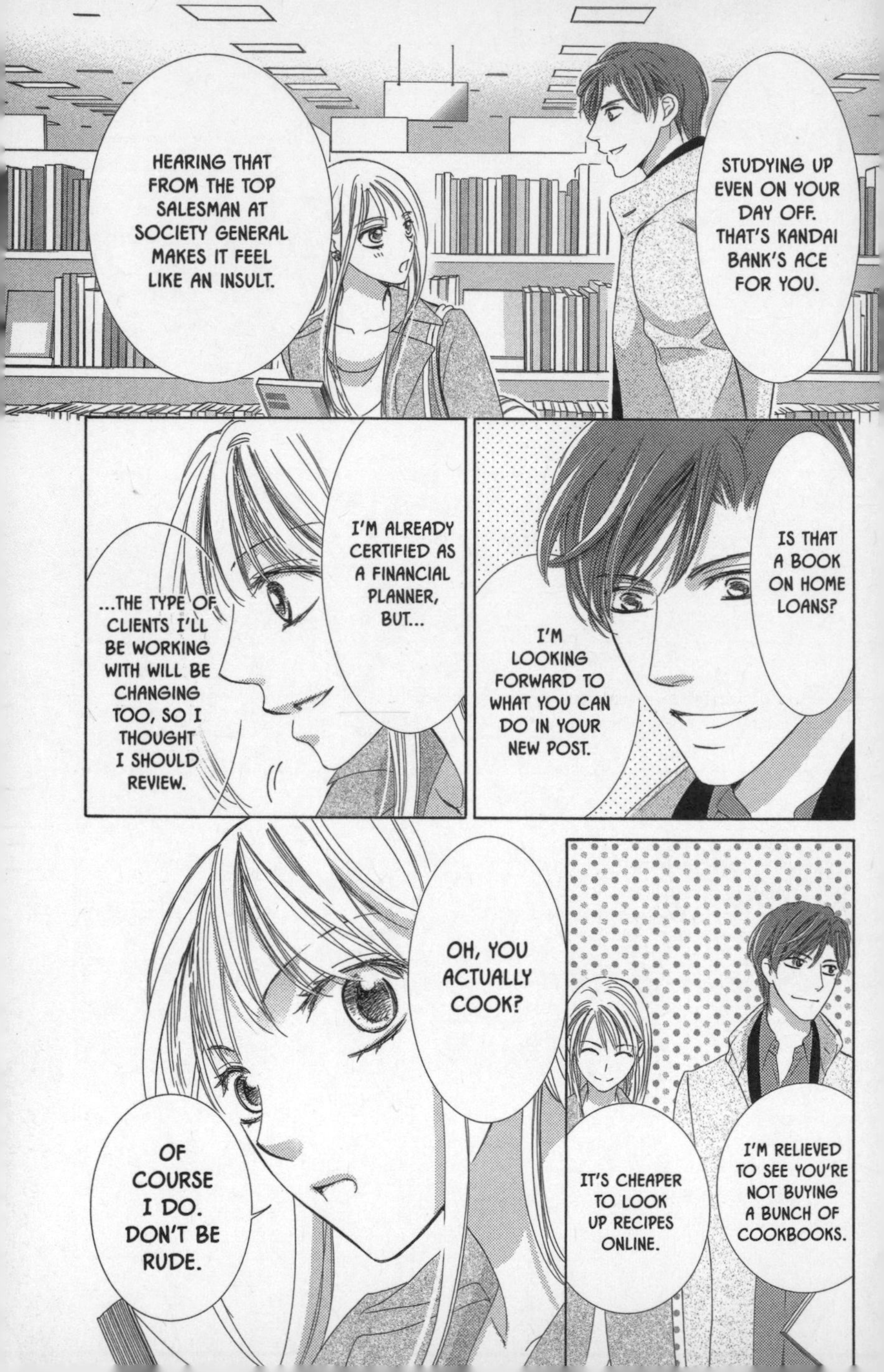
STUDYING UP EVEN ON YOUR DAY OFF. THAT'S KANDAI BANK'S ACE FOR YOU.
HEARING THAT FROM THE TOP SALESMAN AT SOCIETY GENERAL MAKES IT FEEL LIKE AN INSULT.
IS THAT A BOOK ON HOME LOANS?
I'M LOOKING FORWARD TO WHAT YOU CAN DO IN YOUR NEW POST.
I'M ALREADY CERTIFIED AS A FINANCIAL PLANNER, BUT...
...THE TYPE OF CLIENTS I'LL BE WORKING WITH WILL BE CHANGING TOO, SO I THOUGHT I SHOULD REVIEW.
I'M RELIEVED TO SEE YOU'RE NOT BUYING A BUNCH OF COOKBOOKS.
IT'S CHEAPER TO LOOK UP RECIPES ONLINE.
OH, YOU ACTUALLY COOK?
OF COURSE I DO. DON'T BE RUDE.

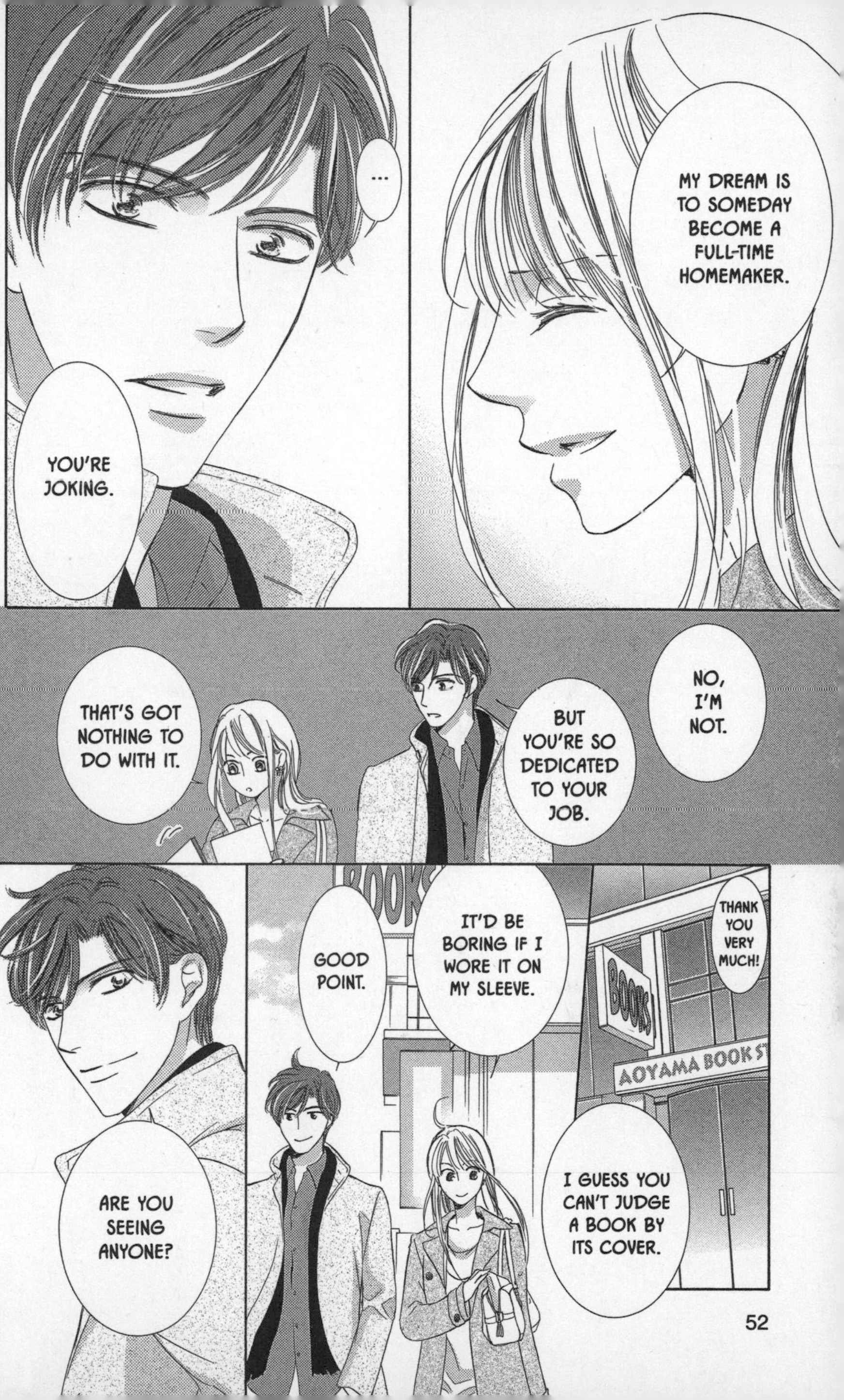
MY DREAM IS TO SOMEDAY BECOME A FULL-TIME HOMEMAKER.
...
YOU'RE JOKING.
NO, I'M NOT.
BUT YOU'RE SO DEDICATED TO YOUR JOB.
THAT'S GOT NOTHING TO DO WITH IT.
BOOKS
THANK YOU VERY MUCH!
I GUESS YOU CAN'T JUDGE A BOOK BY ITS COVER.
IT'D BE BORING IF I WORE IT ON MY SLEEVE.
GOOD POINT.
ARE YOU SEEING ANYONE?

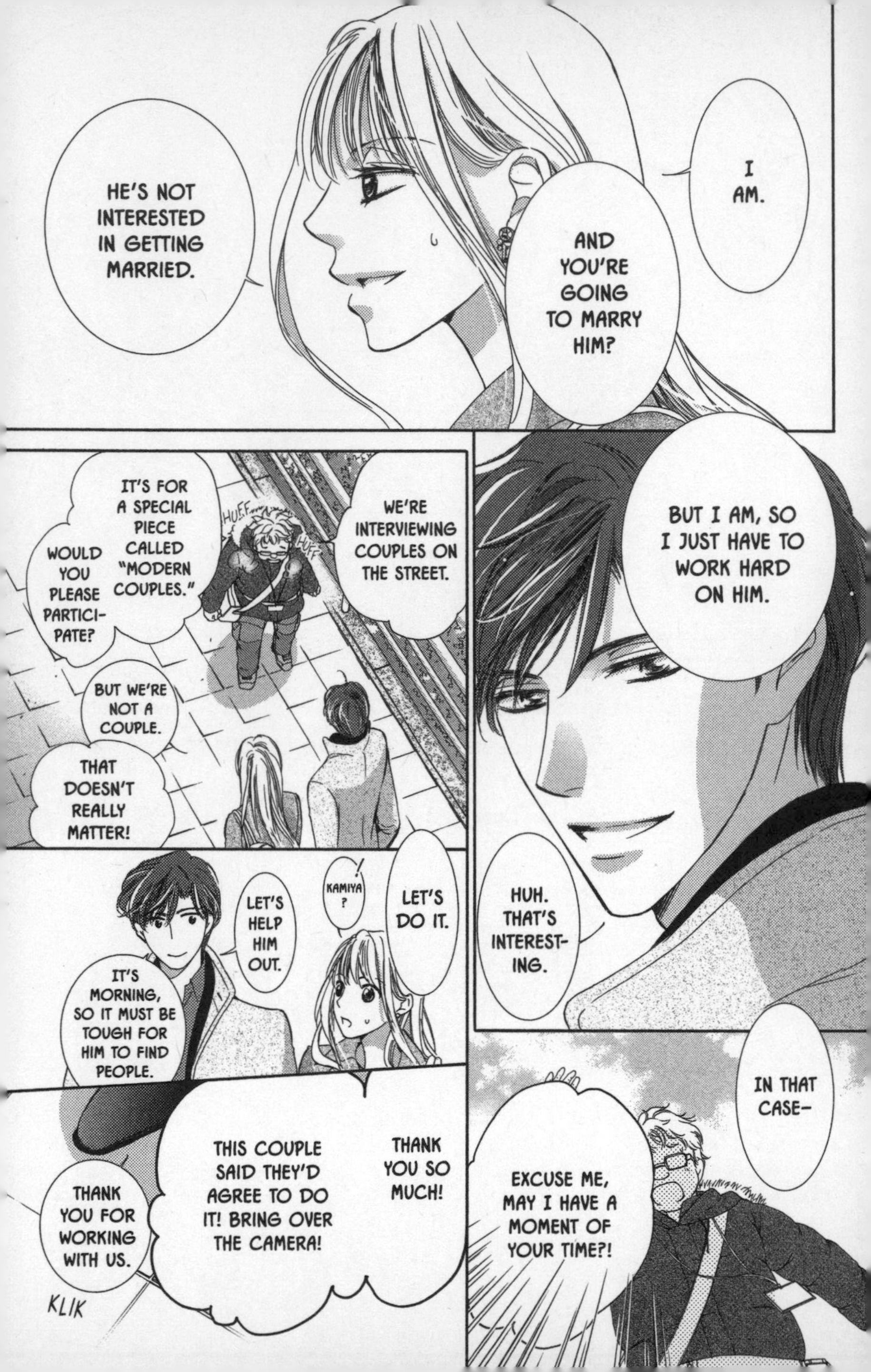
I AM.
AND YOU'RE GOING TO MARRY HIM?
HE'S NOT INTERESTED IN GETTING MARRIED.
BUT I AM, SO I JUST HAVE TO WORK HARD ON HIM.
HUH. THAT'S INTERESTING.
IN THAT CASE–
EXCUSE ME, MAY I HAVE A MOMENT OF YOUR TIME?!
WE'RE INTERVIEWING COUPLES ON THE STREET.
HUFF
HUFF
IT'S FOR A SPECIAL PIECE CALLED "MODERN COUPLES."
WOULD YOU PLEASE PARTICIPATE?
BUT WE'RE NOT A COUPLE.
THAT DOESN'T REALLY MATTER!
LET'S DO IT.
! KAMIYA?
LET'S HELP HIM OUT.
IT'S MORNING, SO IT MUST BE TOUGH FOR HIM TO FIND PEOPLE.
THANK YOU SO MUCH!
THIS COUPLE SAID THEY'D AGREE TO DO IT! BRING OVER THE CAMERA!
THANK YOU FOR WORKING WITH US.
KLIK

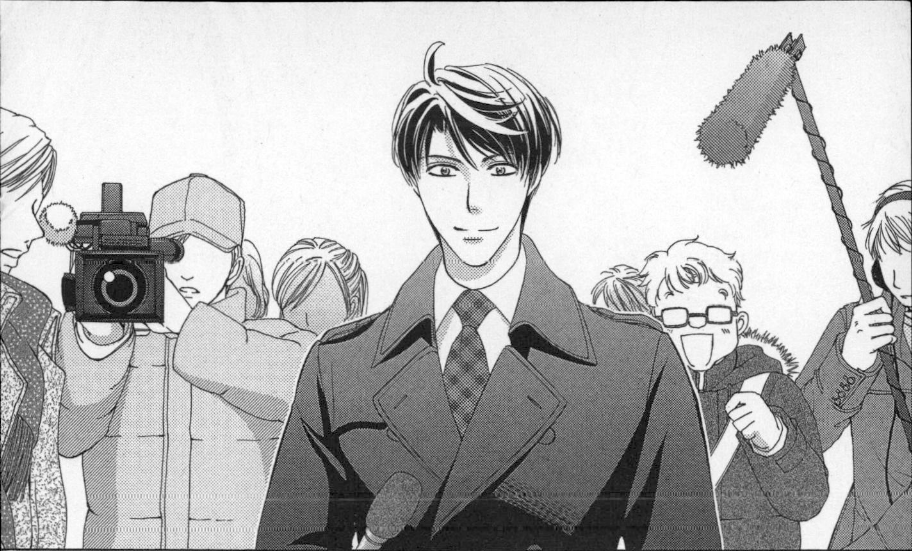

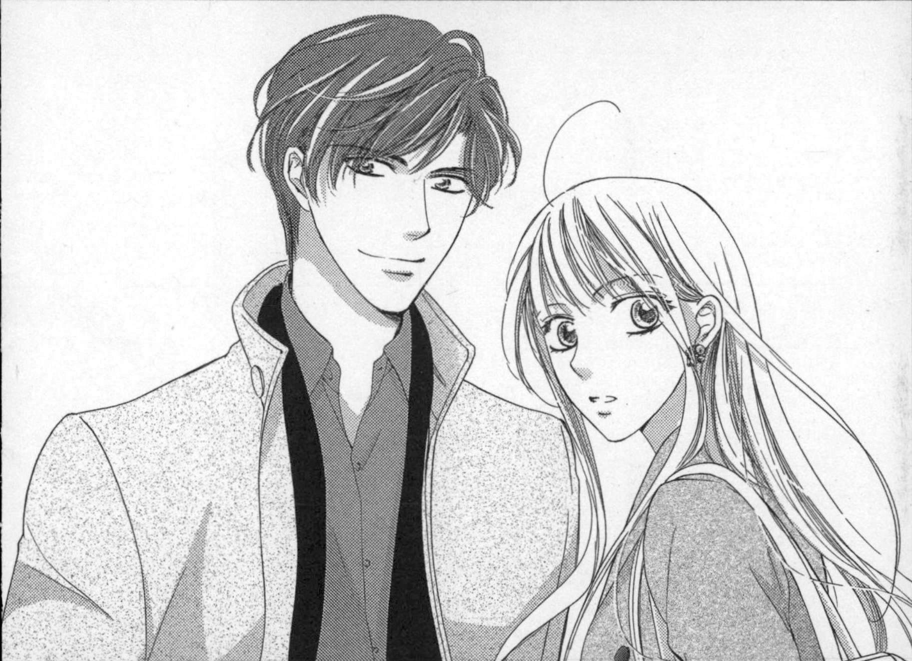

HUH?

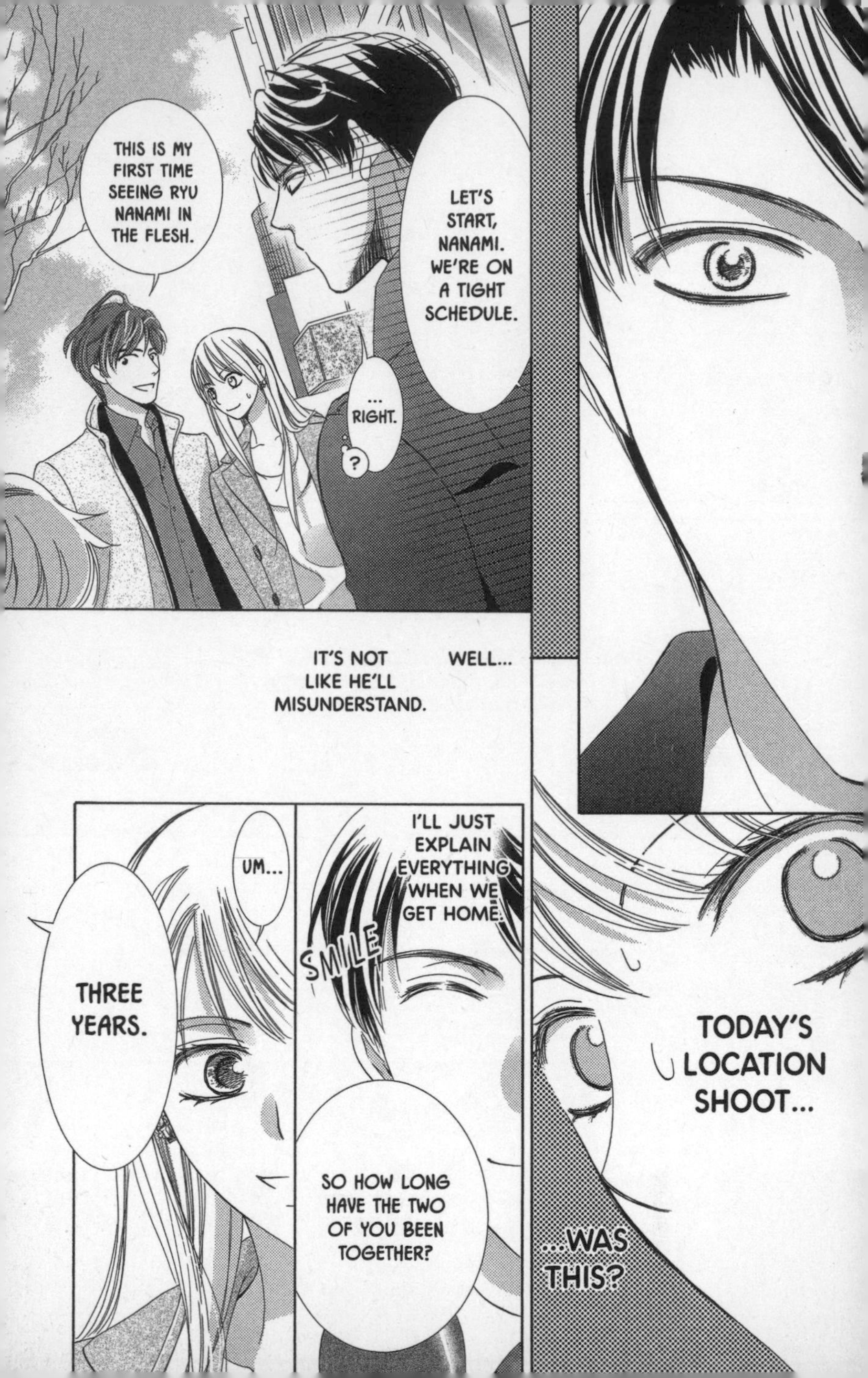

LET'S START, NANAMI. WE'RE ON A TIGHT SCHEDULE.
... RIGHT.
?
THIS IS MY FIRST TIME SEEING RYU NANAMI IN THE FLESH.
WELL...
IT'S NOT LIKE HE'LL MISUNDERSTAND.
TODAY'S LOCATION SHOOT...
...WAS THIS?
I'LL JUST EXPLAIN EVERYTHING WHEN WE GET HOME.
SMILE
SO HOW LONG HAVE THE TWO OF YOU BEEN TOGETHER?
UM...
THREE YEARS.

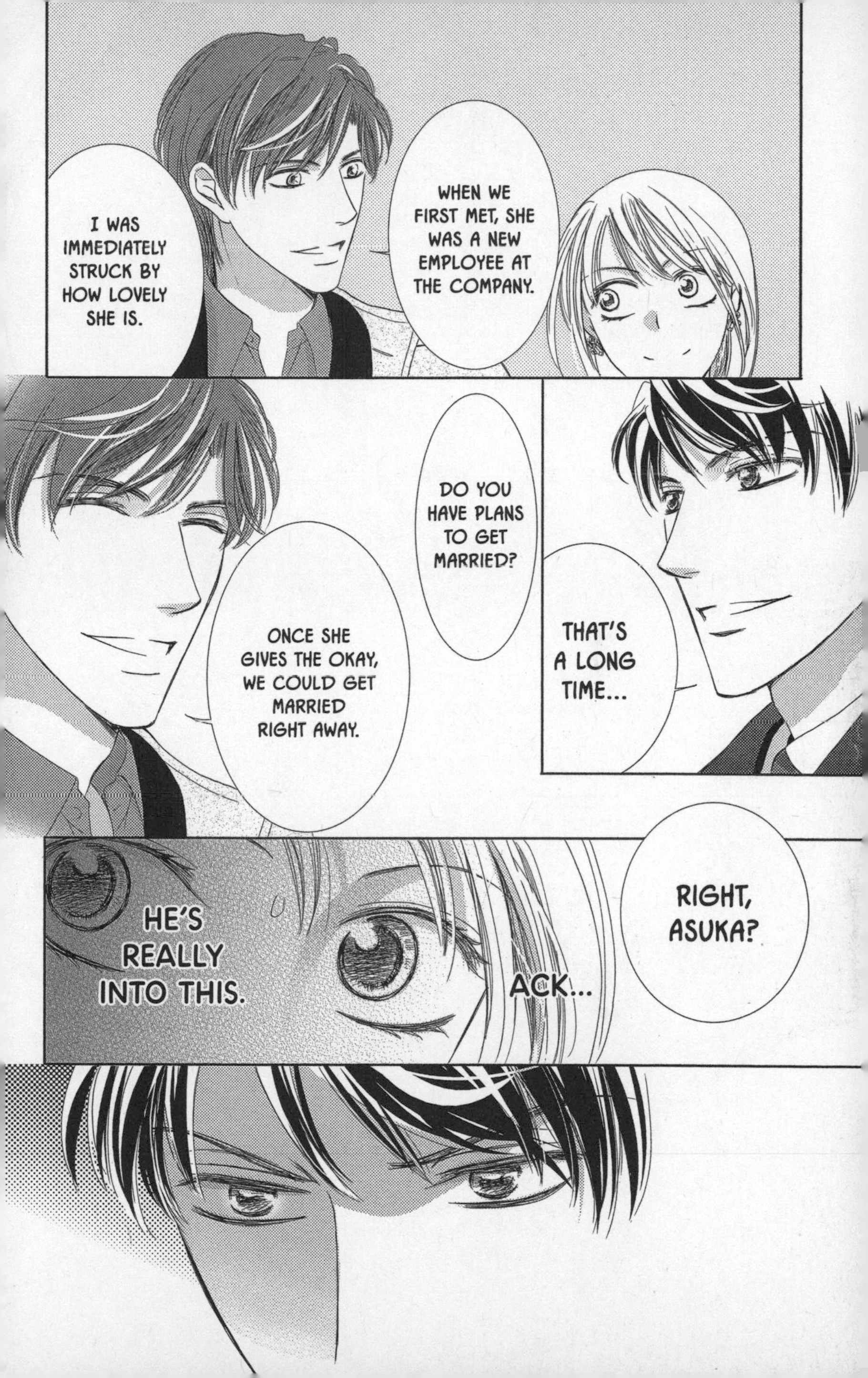
WHEN WE FIRST MET, SHE WAS A NEW EMPLOYEE AT THE COMPANY.
I WAS IMMEDIATELY STRUCK BY HOW LOVELY SHE IS.
THAT'S A LONG TIME...
DO YOU HAVE PLANS TO GET MARRIED?
ONCE SHE GIVES THE OKAY, WE COULD GET MARRIED RIGHT AWAY.
RIGHT, ASUKA?
ACK...
HE'S REALLY INTO THIS.

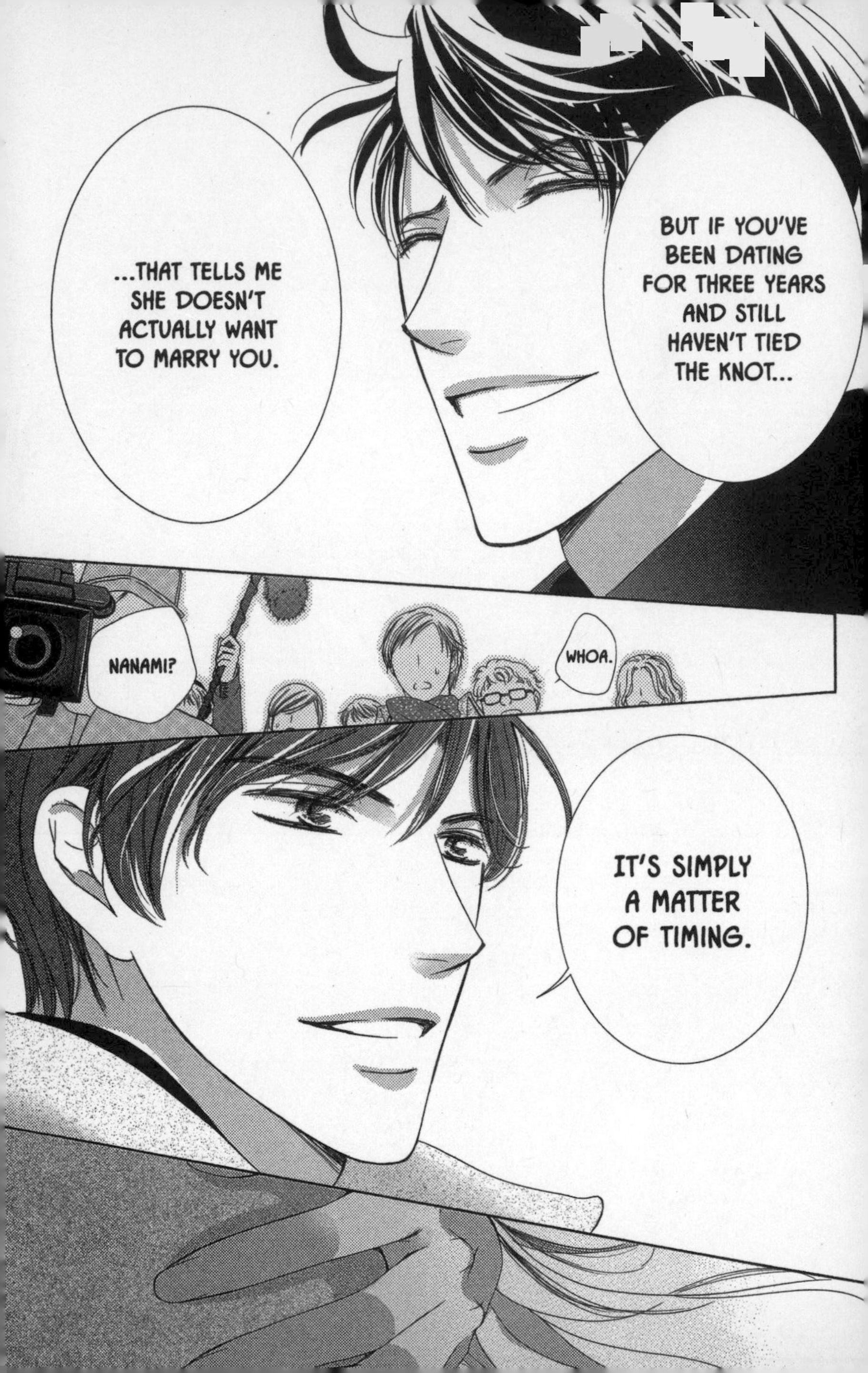
BUT IF YOU'VE BEEN DATING FOR THREE YEARS AND STILL HAVEN'T TIED THE KNOT...
...THAT TELLS ME SHE DOESN'T ACTUALLY WANT TO MARRY YOU.
WHOA.
NANAMI?
IT'S SIMPLY A MATTER OF TIMING.

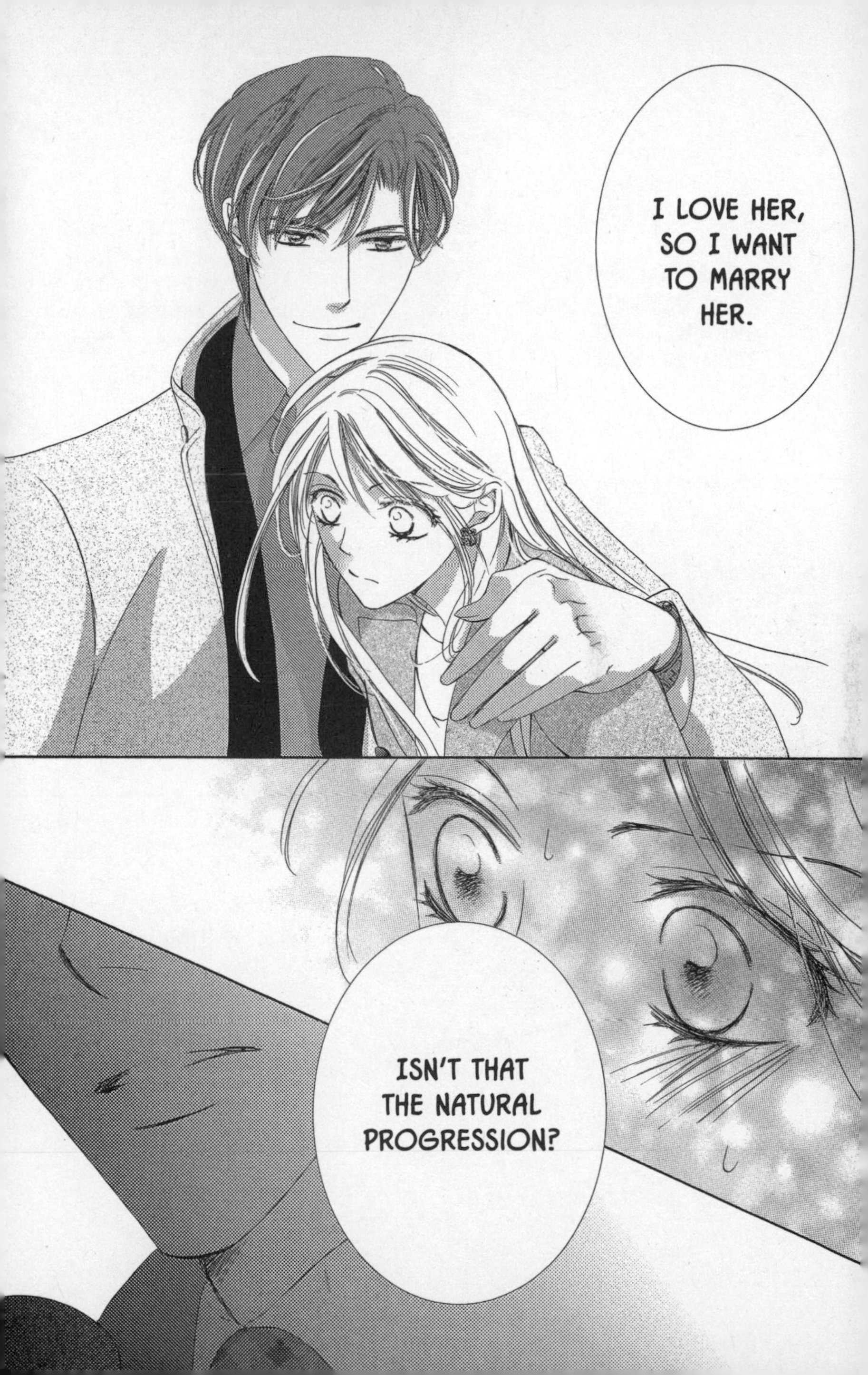
I LOVE HER, SO I WANT TO MARRY HER.
ISN'T THAT THE NATURAL PROGRESSION?

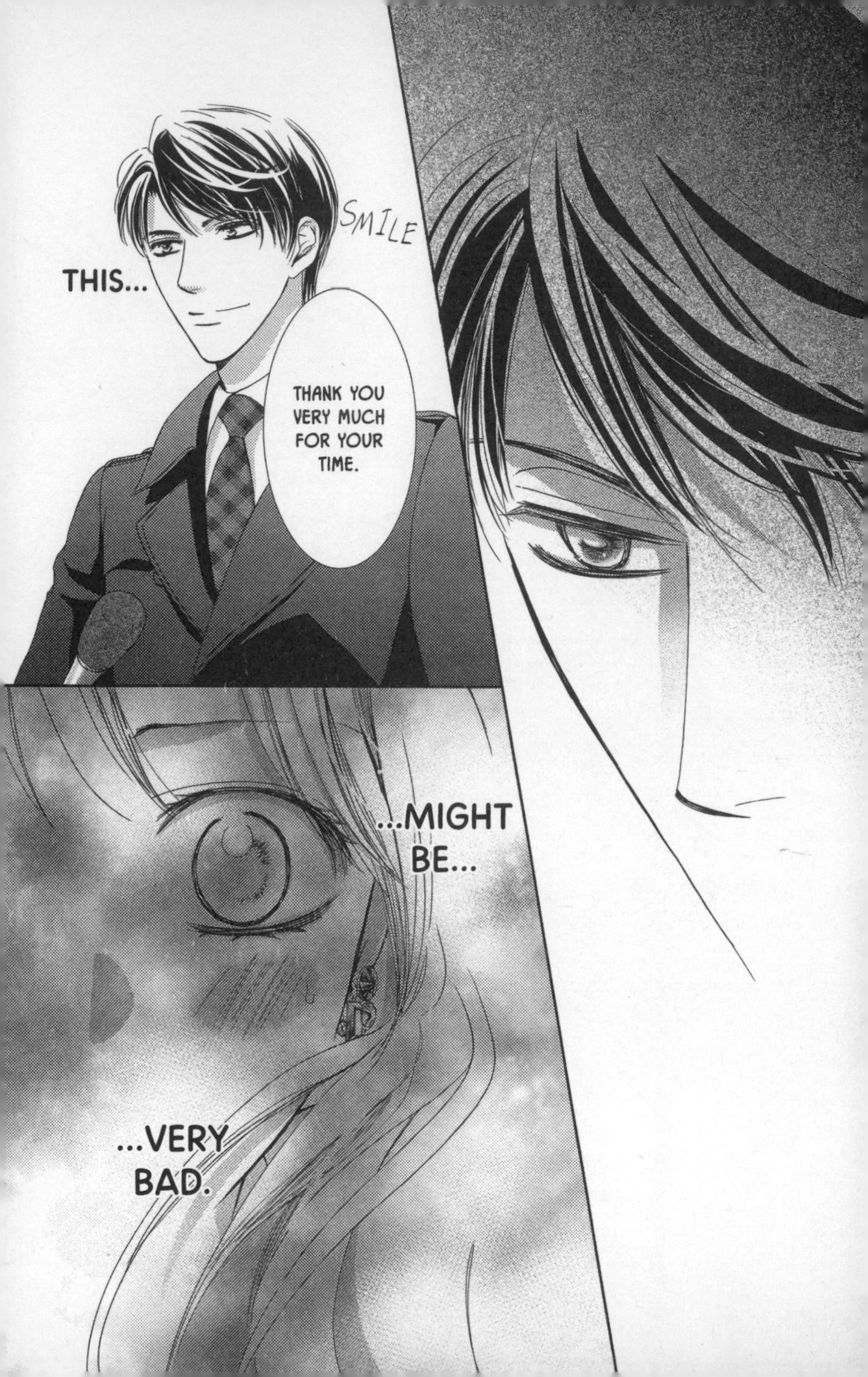
SMILE
THANK YOU VERY MUCH FOR YOUR TIME.
THIS...
...MIGHT BE...
...VERY BAD.

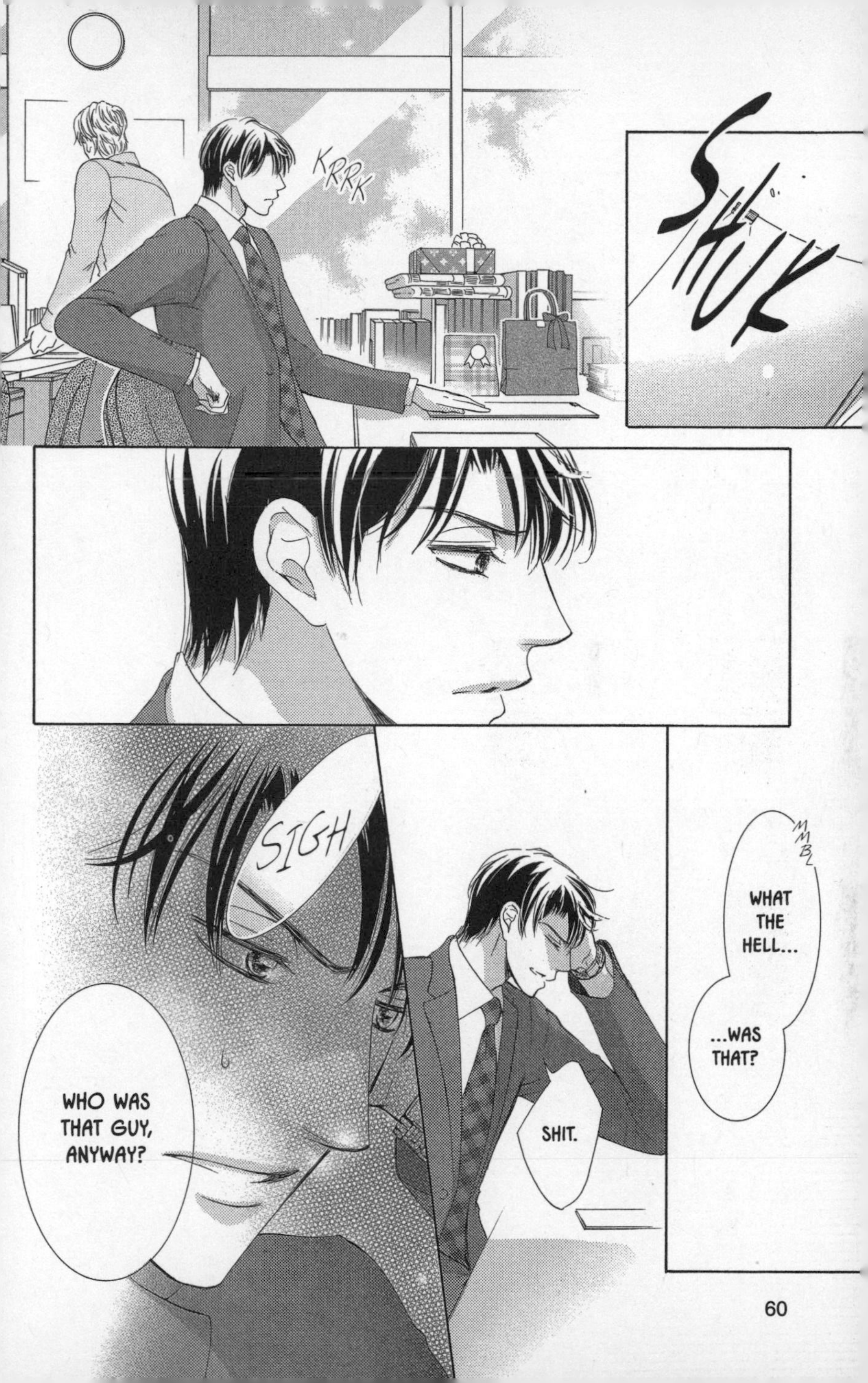
SHUK
KRRK
MMBL
WHAT THE HELL...
...WAS THAT?
SHIT.
SIGH
WHO WAS THAT GUY, ANYWAY?

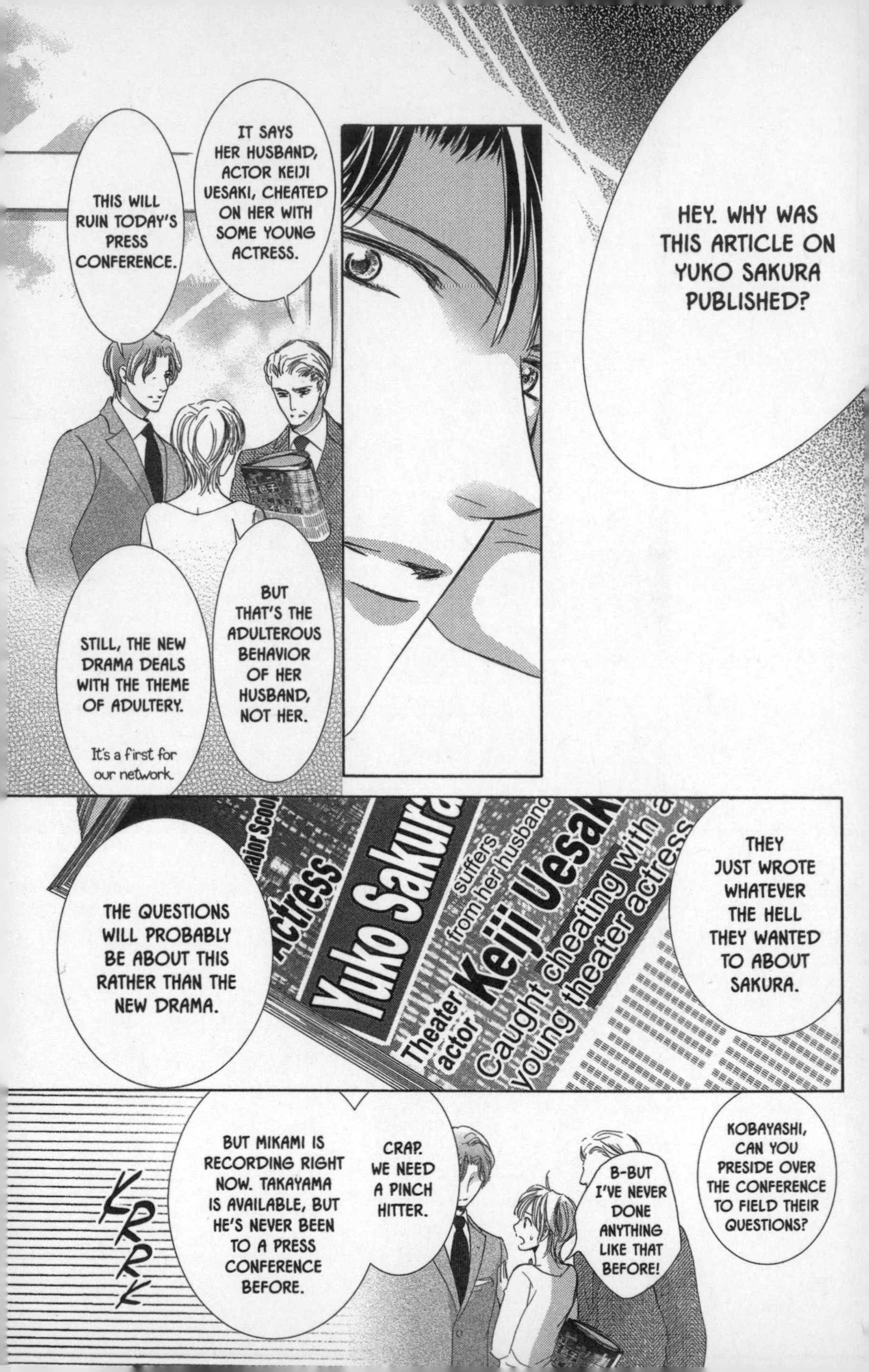
HEY. WHY WAS THIS ARTICLE ON YUKO SAKURA PUBLISHED?
IT SAYS HER HUSBAND, ACTOR KEIJI UESAKI, CHEATED ON HER WITH SOME YOUNG ACTRESS.
THIS WILL RUIN TODAY'S PRESS CONFERENCE.
BUT THAT'S THE ADULTEROUS BEHAVIOR OF HER HUSBAND, NOT HER.
STILL, THE NEW DRAMA DEALS WITH THE THEME OF ADULTERY.
It's a first for our network.
THEY JUST WROTE WHATEVER THE HELL THEY WANTED TO ABOUT SAKURA.
suffers from her husband
Theater actor
Caught cheating with a young theater actress
THE QUESTIONS WILL PROBABLY BE ABOUT THIS RATHER THAN THE NEW DRAMA.
KOBAYASHI, CAN YOU PRESIDE OVER THE CONFERENCE TO FIELD THEIR QUESTIONS?
B-BUT I'VE NEVER DONE ANYTHING LIKE THAT BEFORE!
CRAP. WE NEED A PINCH HITTER.
BUT MIKAMI IS RECORDING RIGHT NOW. TAKAYAMA IS AVAILABLE, BUT HE'S NEVER BEEN TO A PRESS CONFERENCE BEFORE.
KRRK

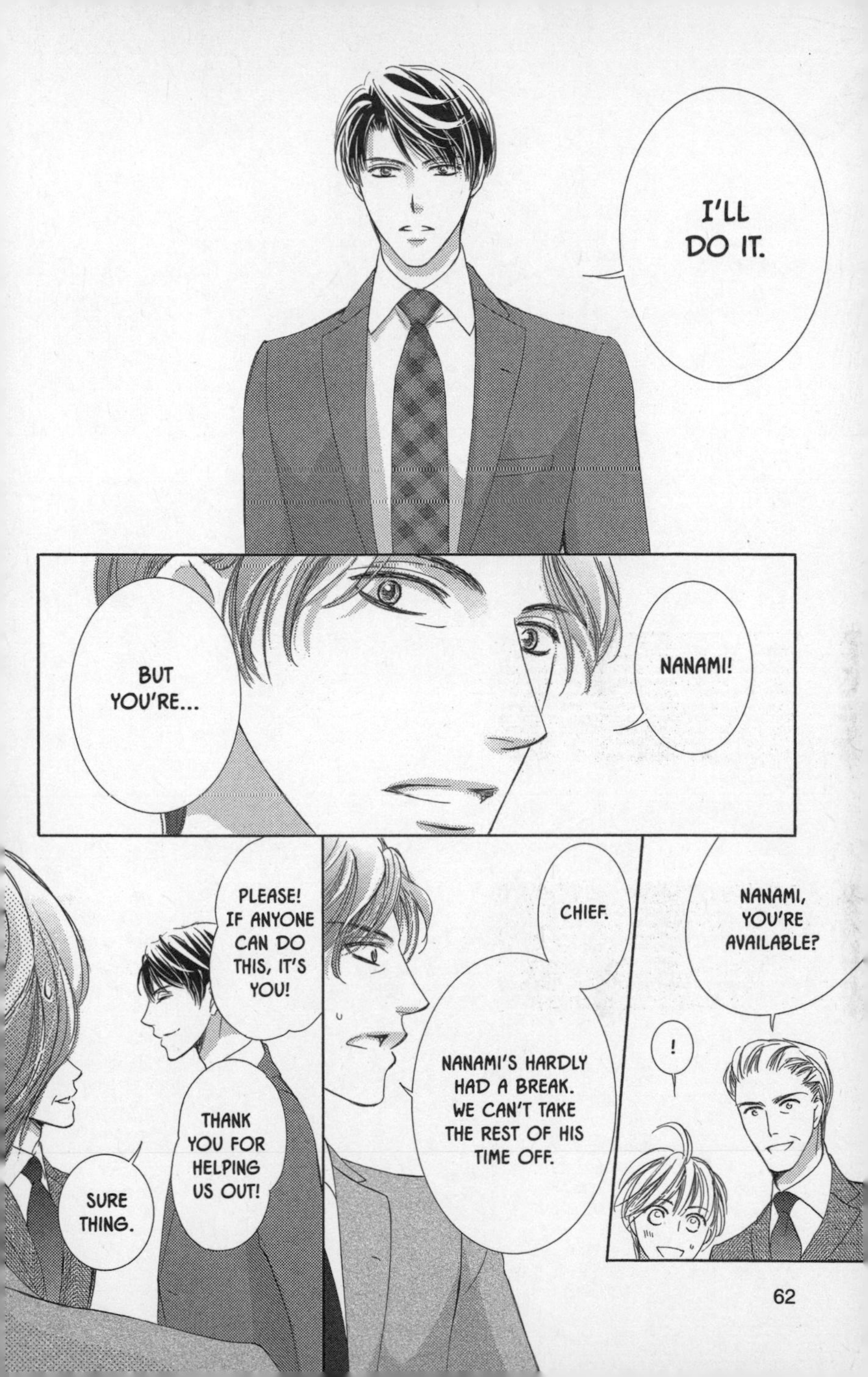
I'LL DO IT.
NANAMI!
BUT YOU'RE...
NANAMI, YOU'RE AVAILABLE?
!
CHIEF.
NANAMI'S HARDLY HAD A BREAK. WE CAN'T TAKE THE REST OF HIS TIME OFF.
PLEASE! IF ANYONE CAN DO THIS, IT'S YOU!
THANK YOU FOR HELPING US OUT!
SURE THING.

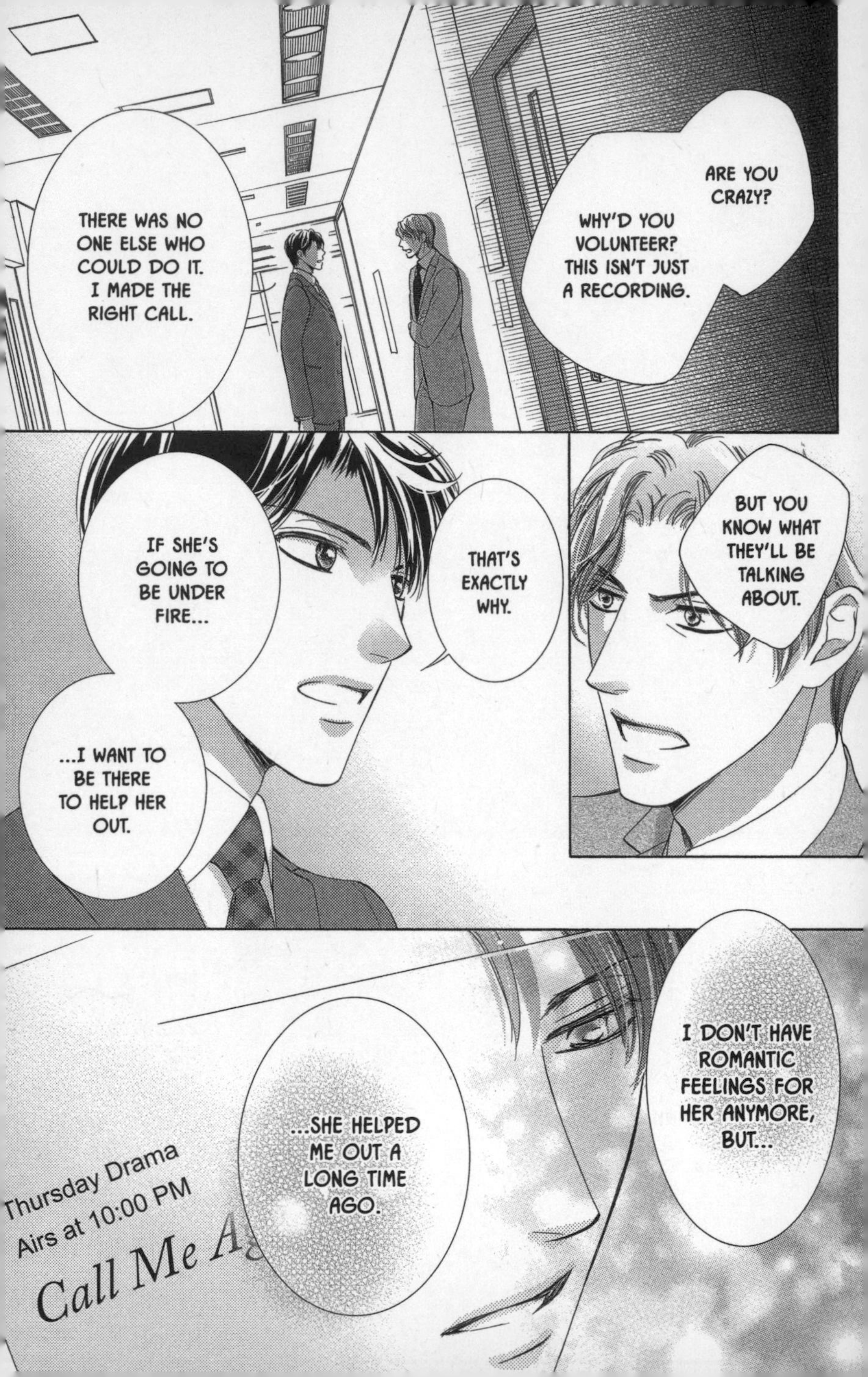
ARE YOU CRAZY?
WHY'D YOU VOLUNTEER? THIS ISN'T JUST A RECORDING.
THERE WAS NO ONE ELSE WHO COULD DO IT. I MADE THE RIGHT CALL.
BUT YOU KNOW WHAT THEY'LL BE TALKING ABOUT.
THAT'S EXACTLY WHY.
IF SHE'S GOING TO BE UNDER FIRE...
...I WANT TO BE THERE TO HELP HER OUT.
I DON'T HAVE ROMANTIC FEELINGS FOR HER ANYMORE, BUT...
...SHE HELPED ME OUT A LONG TIME AGO.
Thursday Drama
Airs at 10:00 PM
Call Me Ag

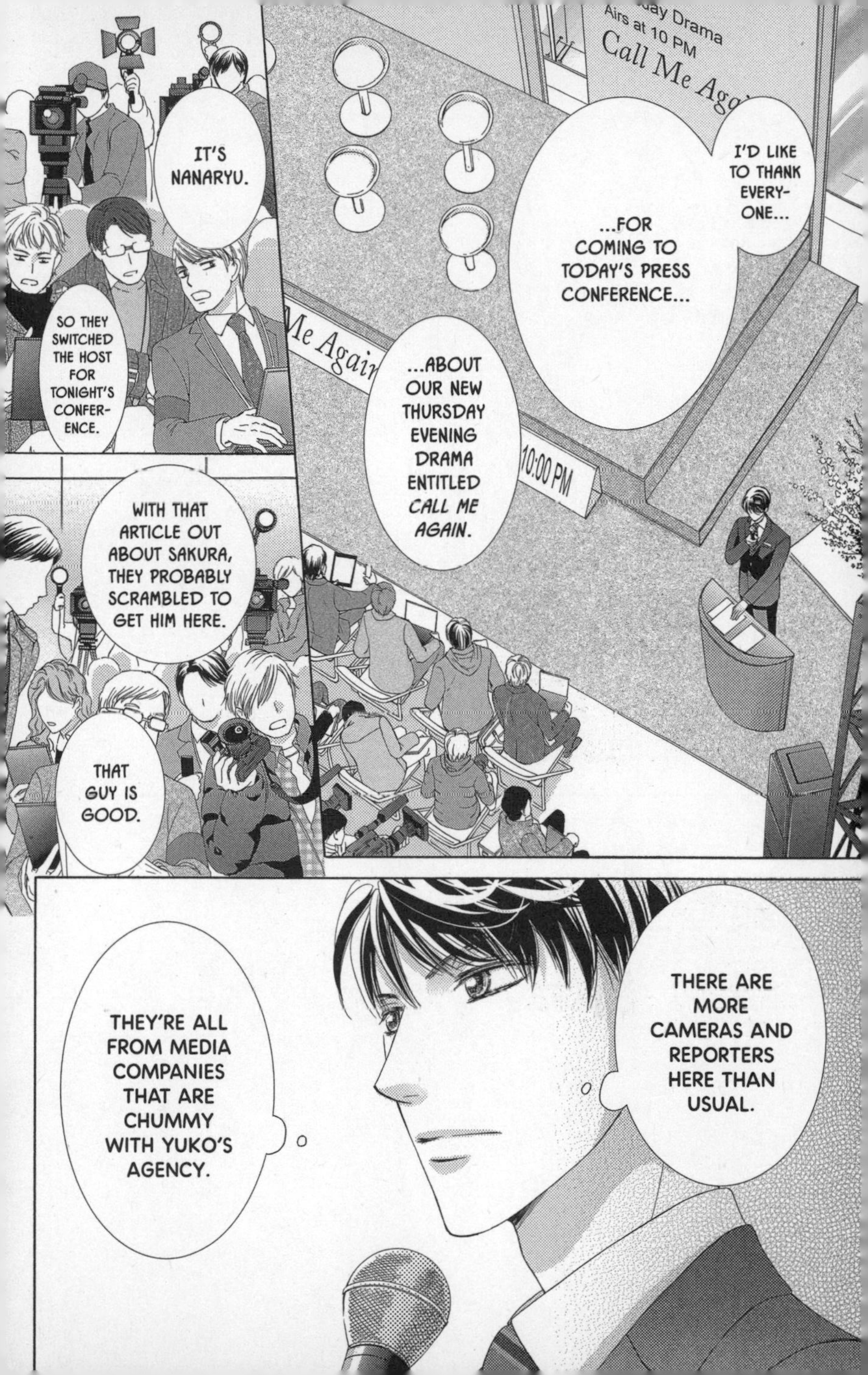
Airs at 10 PM
I'D LIKE TO THANK EVERYONE...
...FOR COMING TO TODAY'S PRESS CONFERENCE...
...ABOUT OUR NEW THURSDAY EVENING DRAMA ENTITLED *CALL ME AGAIN*.
10:00 PM
IT'S NANARYU.
SO THEY SWITCHED THE HOST FOR TONIGHT'S CONFERENCE.
WITH THAT ARTICLE OUT ABOUT SAKURA, THEY PROBABLY SCRAMBLED TO GET HIM HERE.
THAT GUY IS GOOD.
THERE ARE MORE CAMERAS AND REPORTERS HERE THAN USUAL.
THEY'RE ALL FROM MEDIA COMPANIES THAT ARE CHUMMY WITH YUKO'S AGENCY.

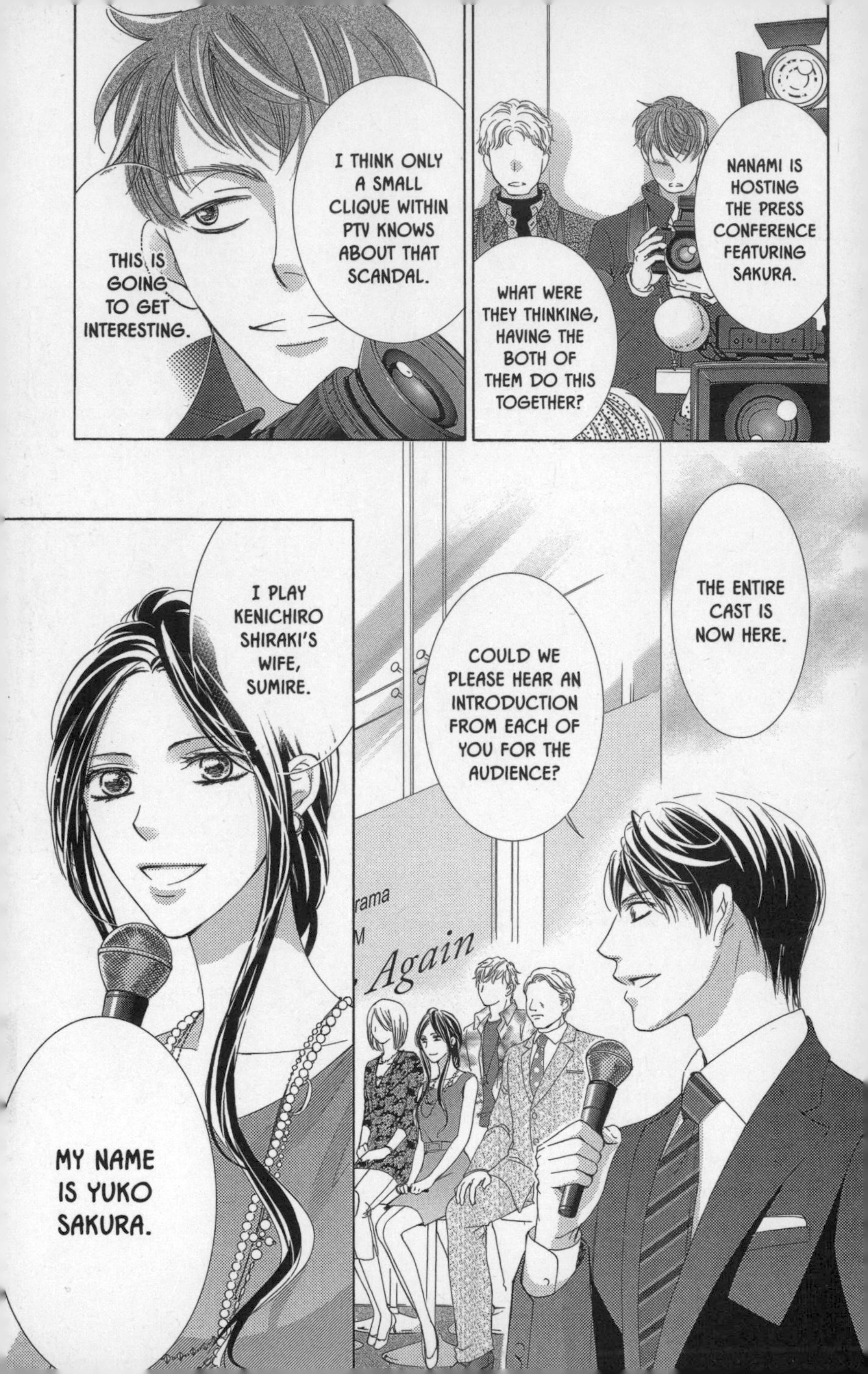
NANAMI IS HOSTING THE PRESS CONFERENCE FEATURING SAKURA.
WHAT WERE THEY THINKING, HAVING THE BOTH OF THEM DO THIS TOGETHER?
I THINK ONLY A SMALL CLIQUE WITHIN PTV KNOWS ABOUT THAT SCANDAL.
THIS IS GOING TO GET INTERESTING.
THE ENTIRE CAST IS NOW HERE.
COULD WE PLEASE HEAR AN INTRODUCTION FROM EACH OF YOU FOR THE AUDIENCE?
Again
I PLAY KENICHIRO SHIRAKI'S WIFE, SUMIRE.
MY NAME IS YUKO SAKURA.

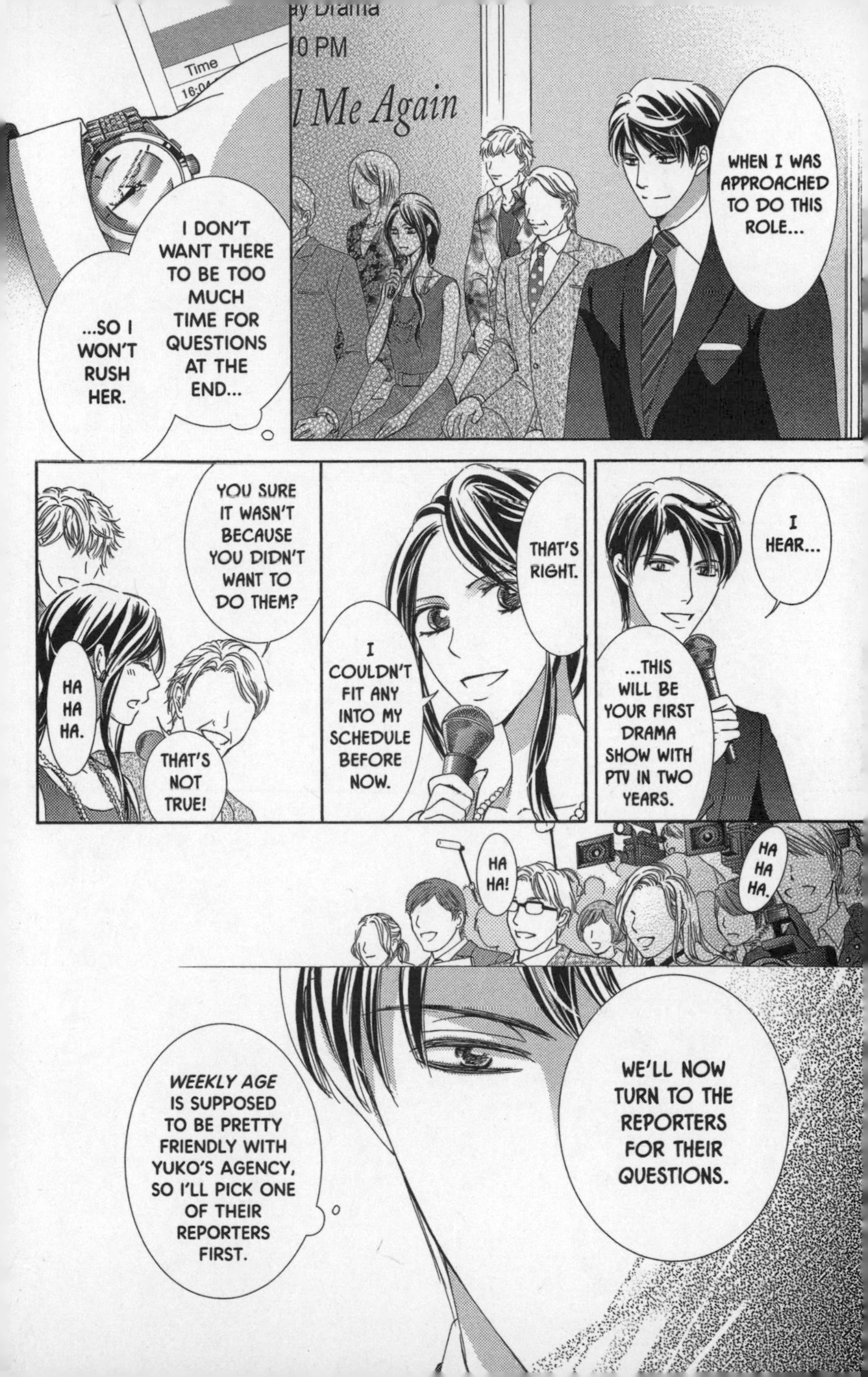
WHEN I WAS APPROACHED TO DO THIS ROLE...
I DON'T WANT THERE TO BE TOO MUCH TIME FOR QUESTIONS AT THE END...
...SO I WON'T RUSH HER.
I HEAR...
...THIS WILL BE YOUR FIRST DRAMA SHOW WITH PTV IN TWO YEARS.
THAT'S RIGHT.
I COULDN'T FIT ANY INTO MY SCHEDULE BEFORE NOW.
YOU SURE IT WASN'T BECAUSE YOU DIDN'T WANT TO DO THEM?
HA HA HA.
THAT'S NOT TRUE!
HA HA HA.
HA HA!
WE'LL NOW TURN TO THE REPORTERS FOR THEIR QUESTIONS.
WEEKLY AGE IS SUPPOSED TO BE PRETTY FRIENDLY WITH YUKO'S AGENCY, SO I'LL PICK ONE OF THEIR REPORTERS FIRST.

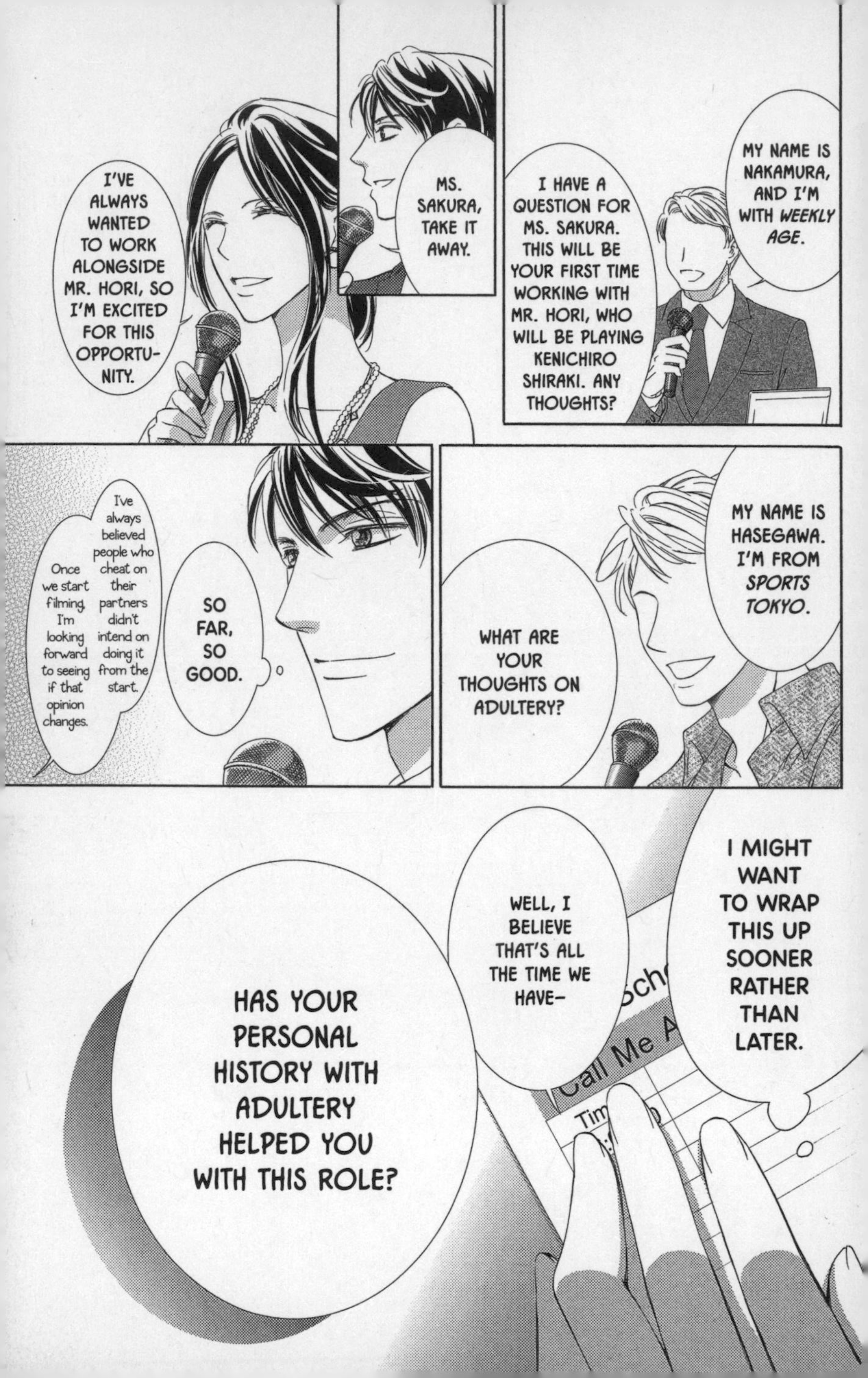
MY NAME IS NAKAMURA, AND I'M WITH *WEEKLY AGE*.
I HAVE A QUESTION FOR MS. SAKURA. THIS WILL BE YOUR FIRST TIME WORKING WITH MR. HORI, WHO WILL BE PLAYING KENICHIRO SHIRAKI. ANY THOUGHTS?
MS. SAKURA, TAKE IT AWAY.
I'VE ALWAYS WANTED TO WORK ALONGSIDE MR. HORI, SO I'M EXCITED FOR THIS OPPORTU-NITY.
MY NAME IS HASEGAWA. I'M FROM *SPORTS TOKYO*.
WHAT ARE YOUR THOUGHTS ON ADULTERY?
SO FAR, SO GOOD.
I've always believed people who cheat on their partners didn't intend on doing it from the start.
Once we start filming, I'm looking forward to seeing if that opinion changes.
I MIGHT WANT TO WRAP THIS UP SOONER RATHER THAN LATER.
WELL, I BELIEVE THAT'S ALL THE TIME WE HAVE–
HAS YOUR PERSONAL HISTORY WITH ADULTERY HELPED YOU WITH THIS ROLE?

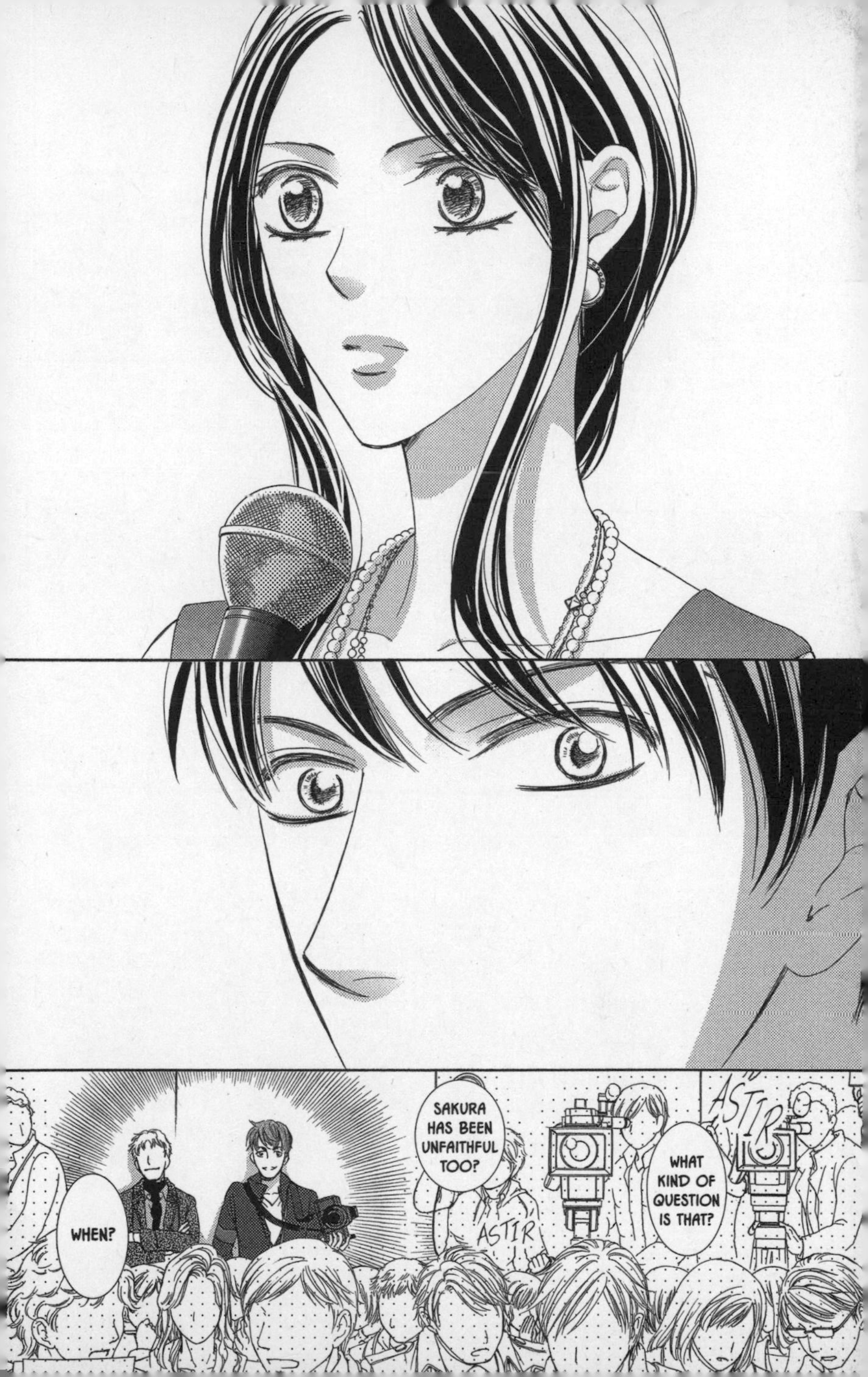
ASTIR
WHAT KIND OF QUESTION IS THAT?
SAKURA HAS BEEN UNFAITHFUL TOO?
ASTIR
WHEN?

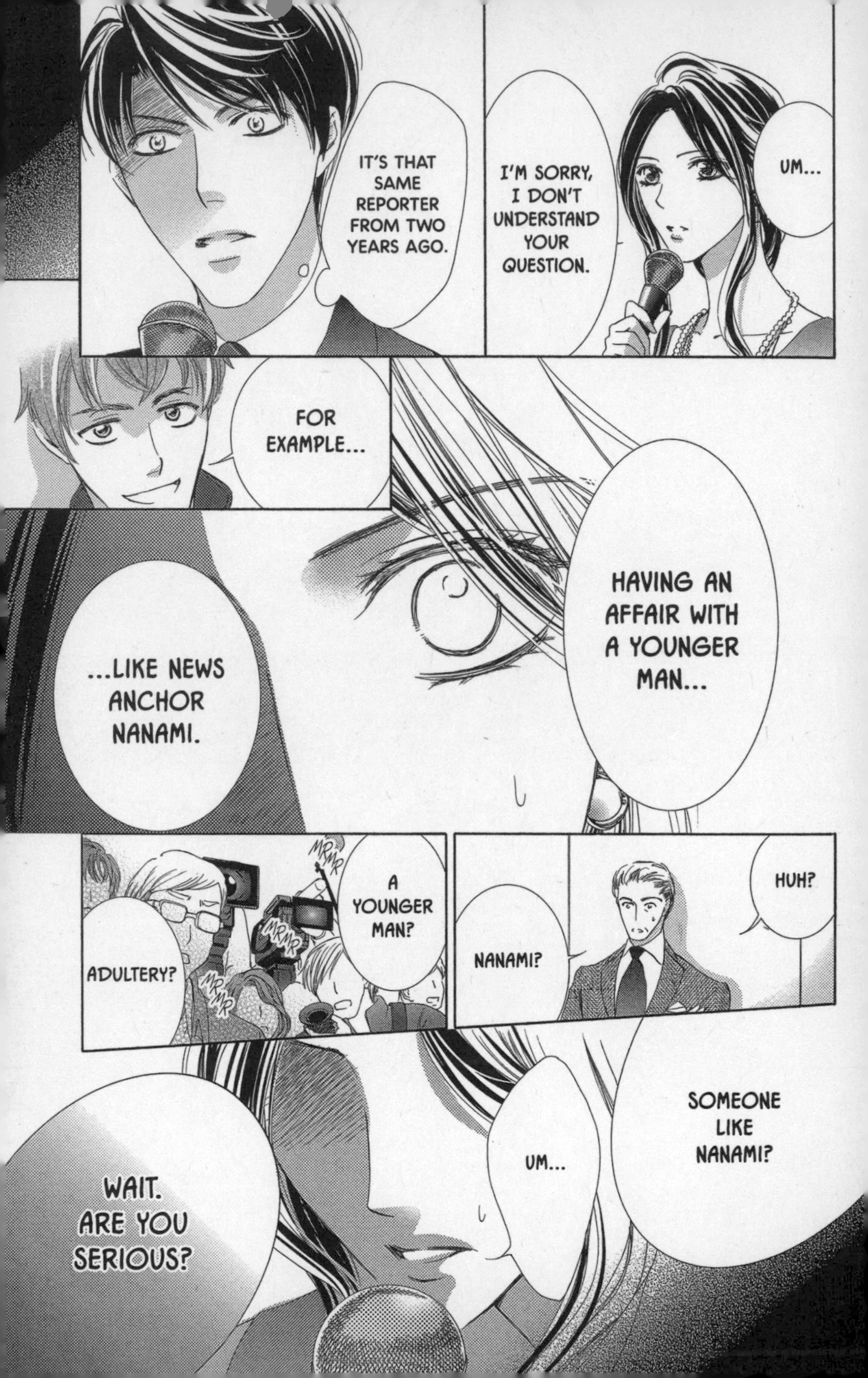
UM...
I'M SORRY, I DON'T UNDERSTAND YOUR QUESTION.
IT'S THAT SAME REPORTER FROM TWO YEARS AGO.
FOR EXAMPLE...
HAVING AN AFFAIR WITH A YOUNGER MAN...
...LIKE NEWS ANCHOR NANAMI.
HUH?
NANAMI?
A YOUNGER MAN?
MRMR
MRMR
MRMR
ADULTERY?
SOMEONE LIKE NANAMI?
UM...
WAIT. ARE YOU SERIOUS?

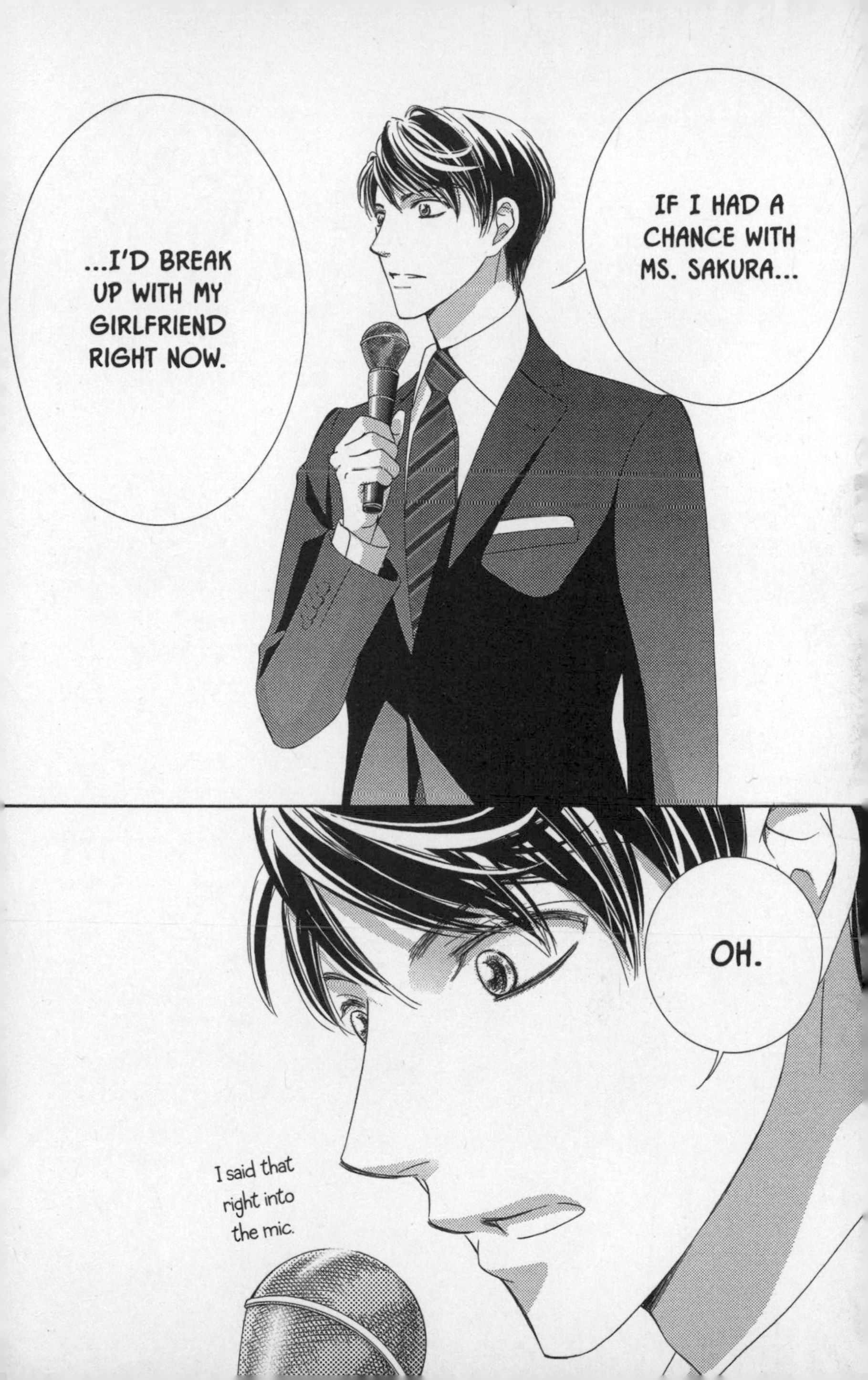
IF I HAD A CHANCE WITH MS. SAKURA...
...I'D BREAK UP WITH MY GIRLFRIEND RIGHT NOW.
OH.
I said that right into the mic.

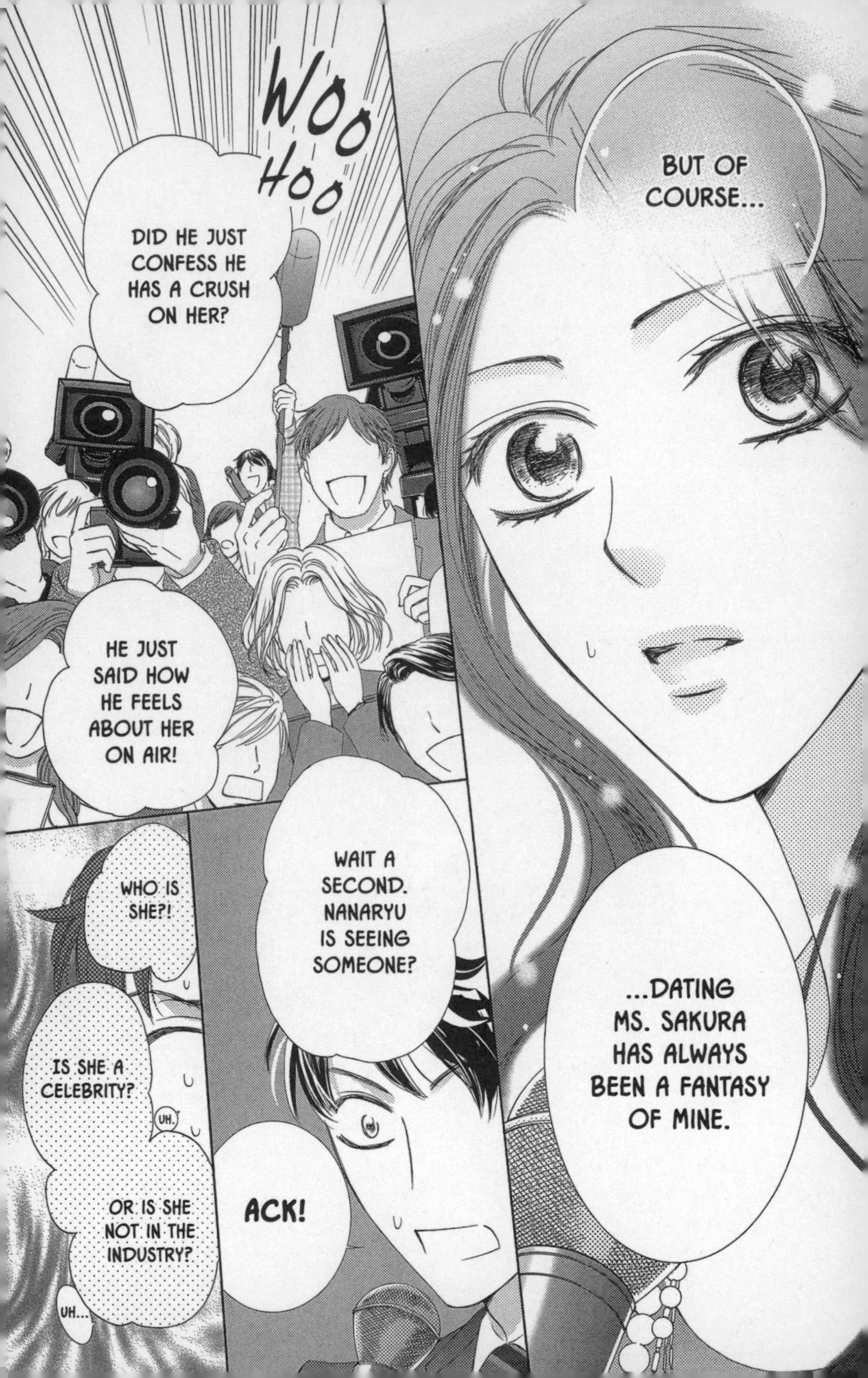
BUT OF COURSE...
...DATING MS. SAKURA HAS ALWAYS BEEN A FANTASY OF MINE.
WOO HOO
DID HE JUST CONFESS HE HAS A CRUSH ON HER?
HE JUST SAID HOW HE FEELS ABOUT HER ON AIR!
WAIT A SECOND. NANARYU IS SEEING SOMEONE?
ACK!
WHO IS SHE?!
IS SHE A CELEBRITY?
UH.
OR IS SHE NOT IN THE INDUSTRY?
UH...

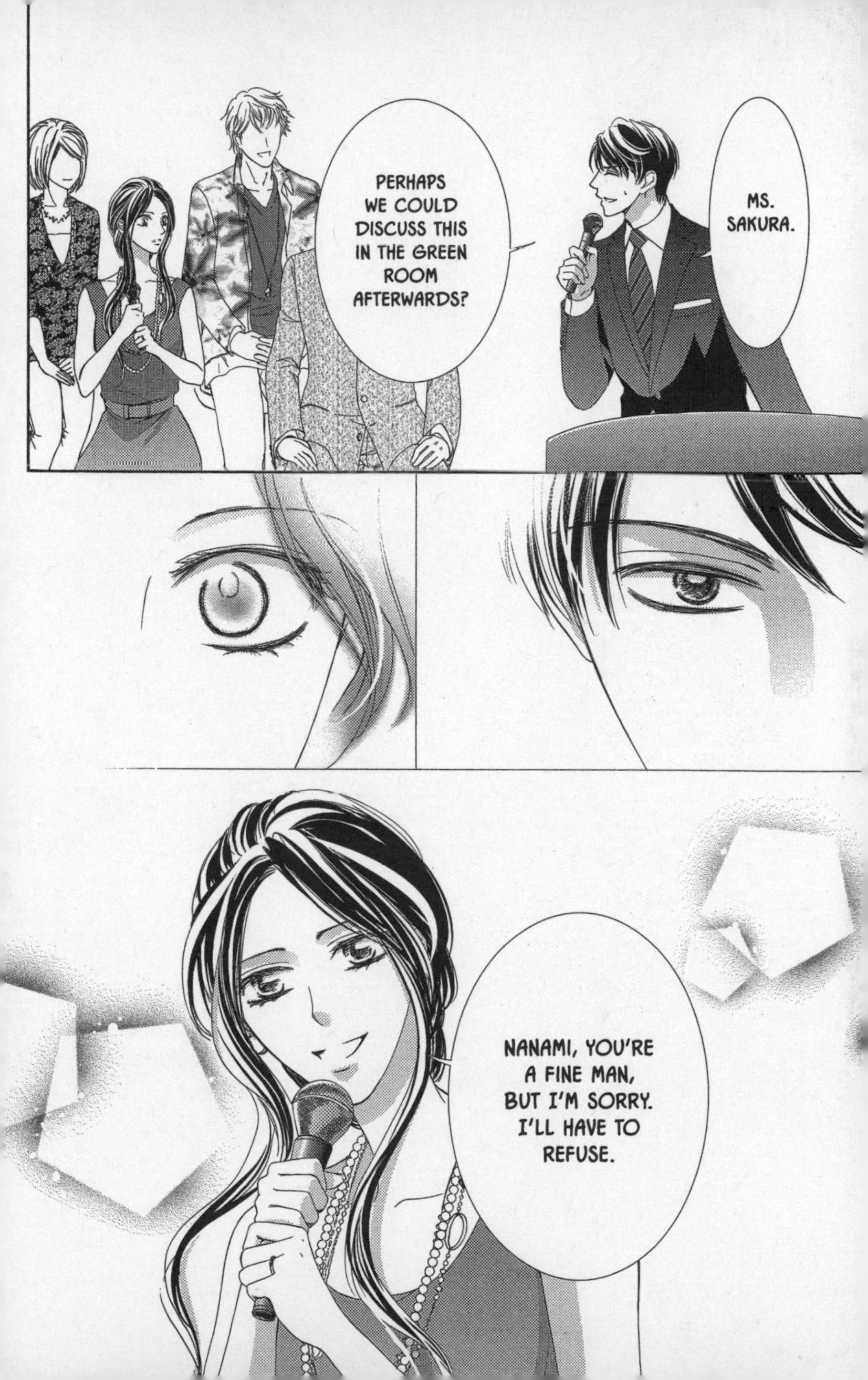
MS. SAKURA.
PERHAPS WE COULD DISCUSS THIS IN THE GREEN ROOM AFTERWARDS?
NANAMI, YOU'RE A FINE MAN, BUT I'M SORRY. I'LL HAVE TO REFUSE.

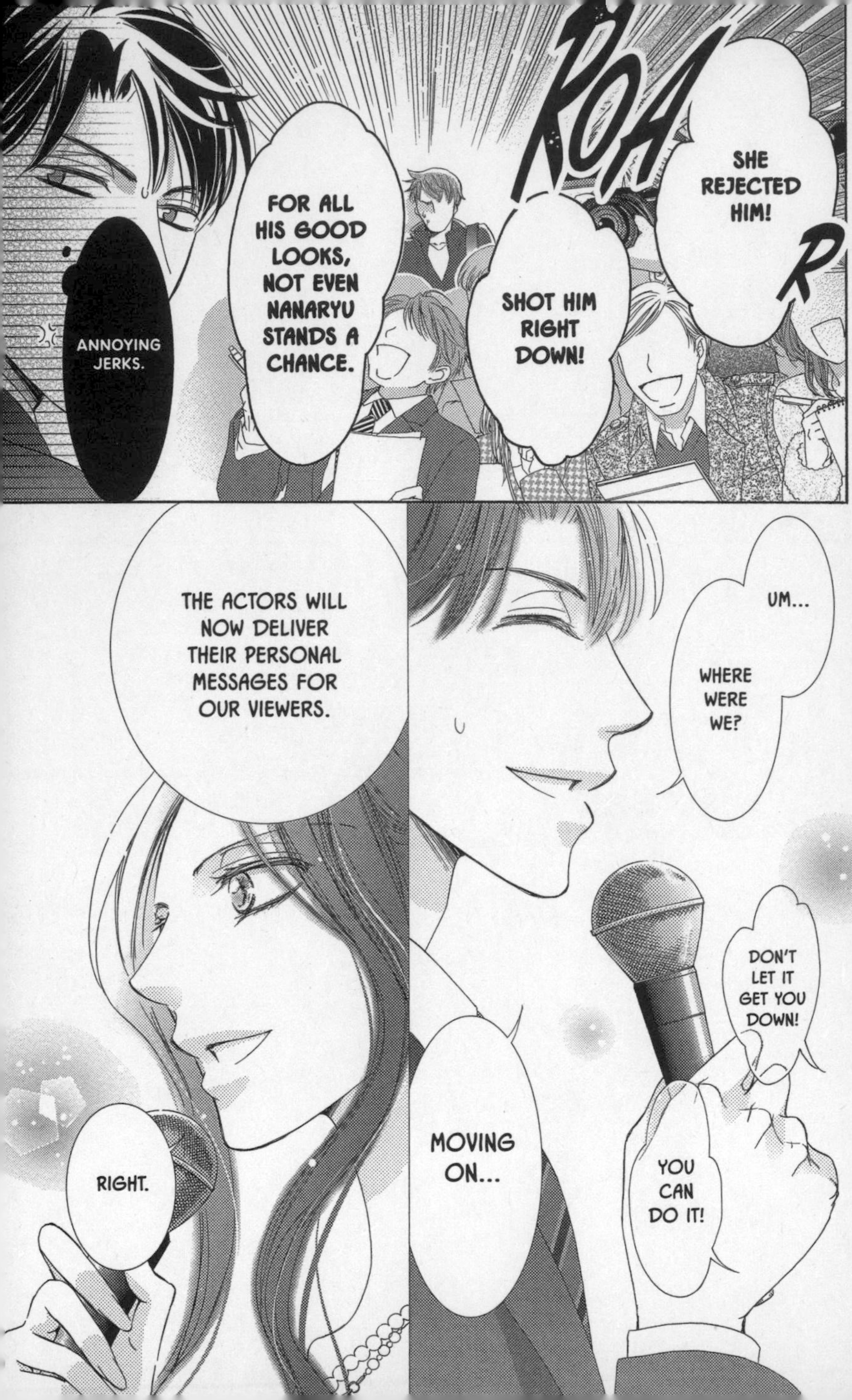
ROAR
SHE REJECTED HIM!
SHOT HIM RIGHT DOWN!
FOR ALL HIS GOOD LOOKS, NOT EVEN NANARYU STANDS A CHANCE.
ANNOYING JERKS.
UM...
WHERE WERE WE?
DON'T LET IT GET YOU DOWN!
YOU CAN DO IT!
MOVING ON...
THE ACTORS WILL NOW DELIVER THEIR PERSONAL MESSAGES FOR OUR VIEWERS.
RIGHT.

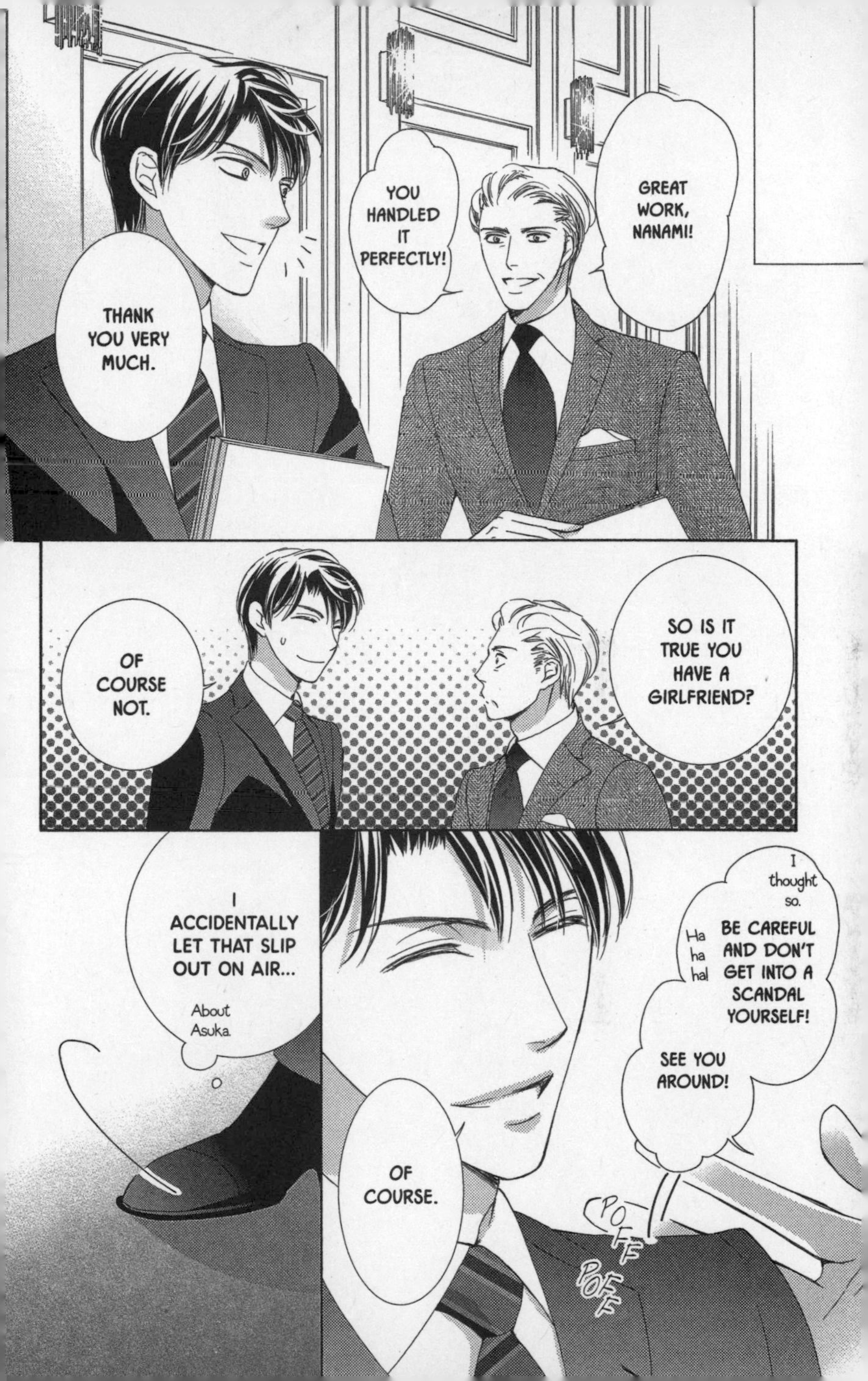
GREAT WORK, NANAMI!
YOU HANDLED IT PERFECTLY!
THANK YOU VERY MUCH.
SO IS IT TRUE YOU HAVE A GIRLFRIEND?
OF COURSE NOT.
I thought so.
Ha ha ha!
BE CAREFUL AND DON'T GET INTO A SCANDAL YOURSELF!
SEE YOU AROUND!
POFF
POFF
OF COURSE.
I ACCIDENTALLY LET THAT SLIP OUT ON AIR...
About Asuka.

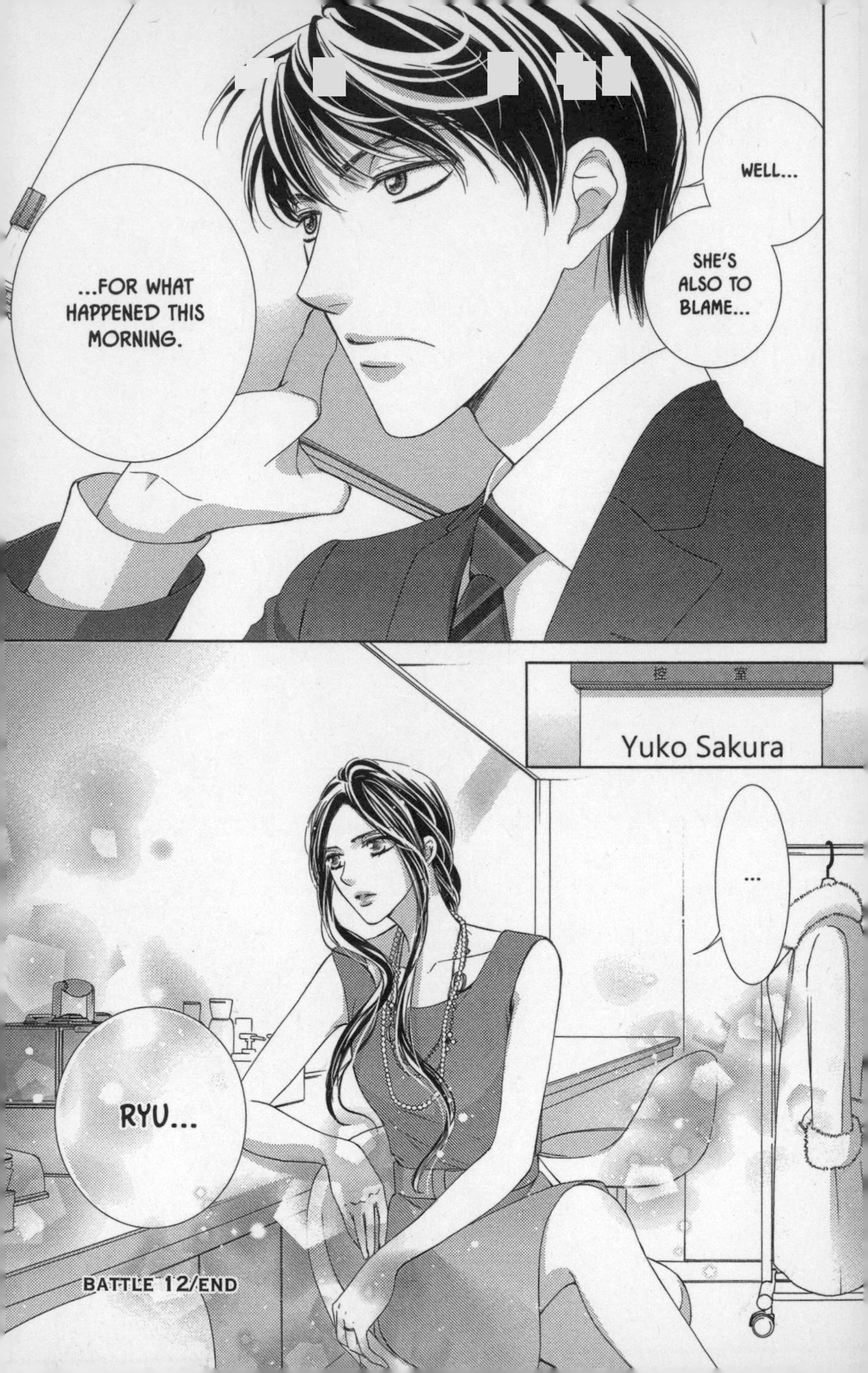
WELL...
SHE'S ALSO TO BLAME...
...FOR WHAT HAPPENED THIS MORNING.
控 室
Yuko Sakura
...
RYU...
BATTLE 12/END

BATTLE 13:

Love is blind, and lovers cannot see the pretty follies that themselves commit.

–William Shakespeare

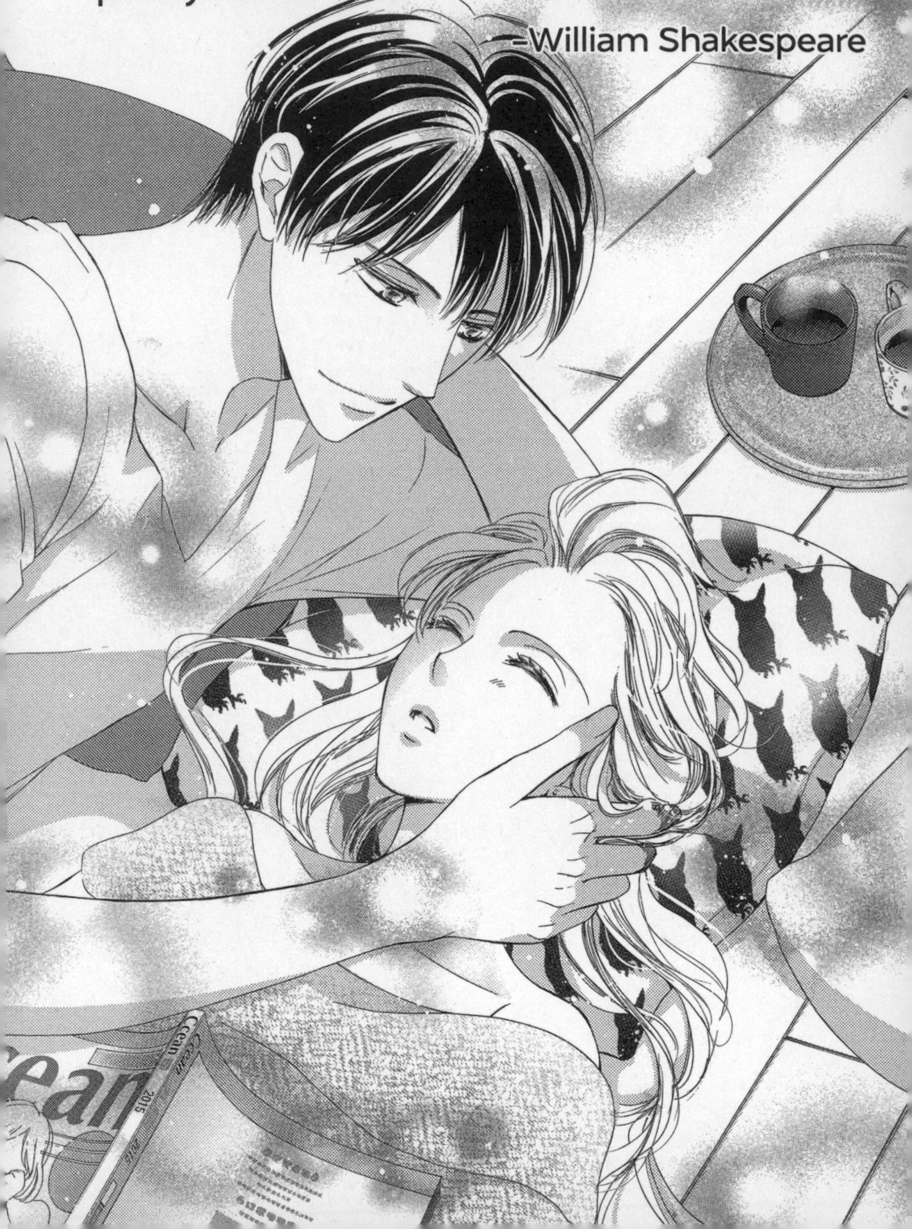
Cean
2015

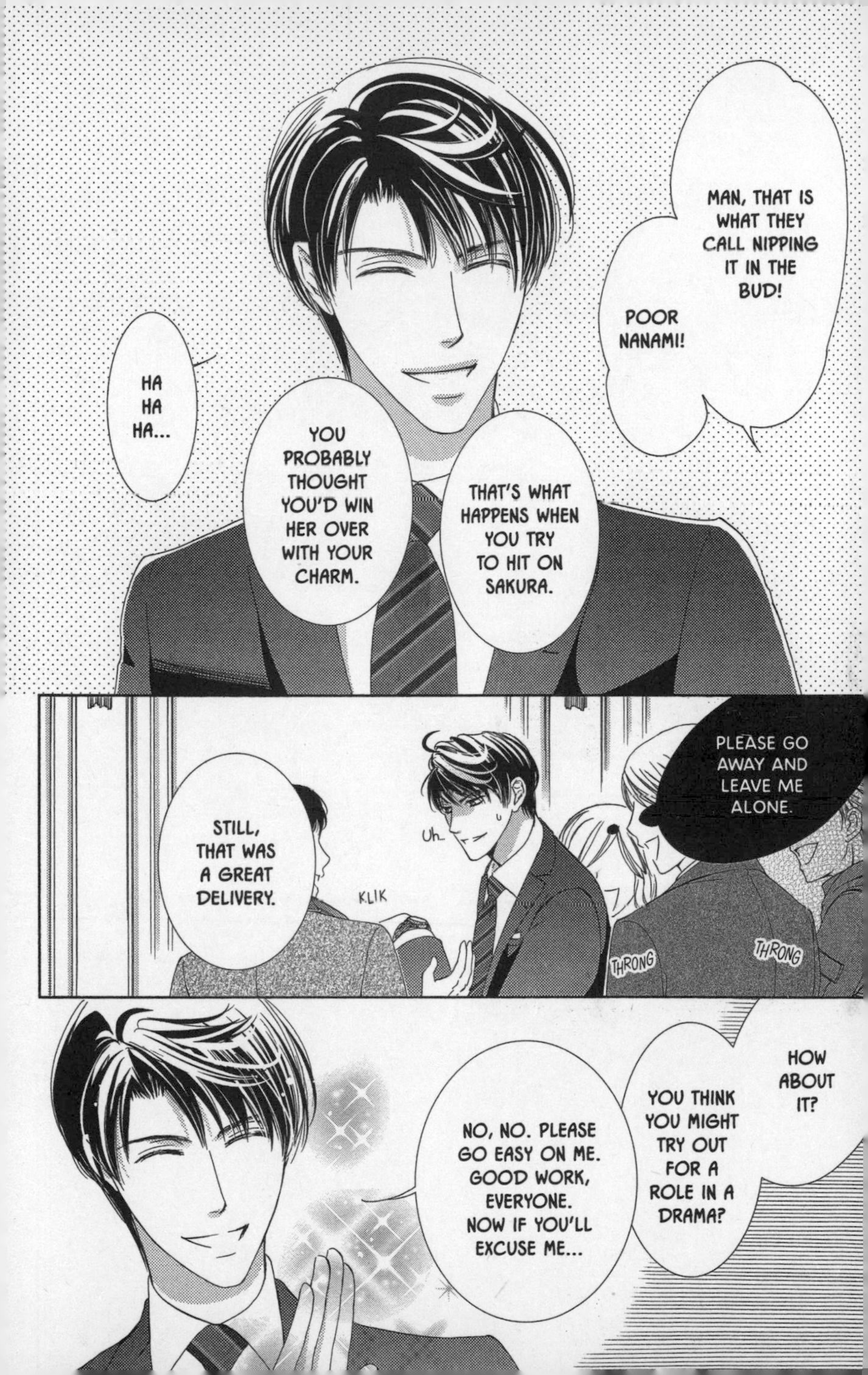
MAN, THAT IS WHAT THEY CALL NIPPING IT IN THE BUD!
POOR NANAMI!
THAT'S WHAT HAPPENS WHEN YOU TRY TO HIT ON SAKURA.
YOU PROBABLY THOUGHT YOU'D WIN HER OVER WITH YOUR CHARM.
HA HA HA...
PLEASE GO AWAY AND LEAVE ME ALONE.
THRONG
THRONG
Uh..
KLIK
STILL, THAT WAS A GREAT DELIVERY.
HOW ABOUT IT?
YOU THINK YOU MIGHT TRY OUT FOR A ROLE IN A DRAMA?
NO, NO. PLEASE GO EASY ON ME. GOOD WORK, EVERYONE. NOW IF YOU'LL EXCUSE ME...

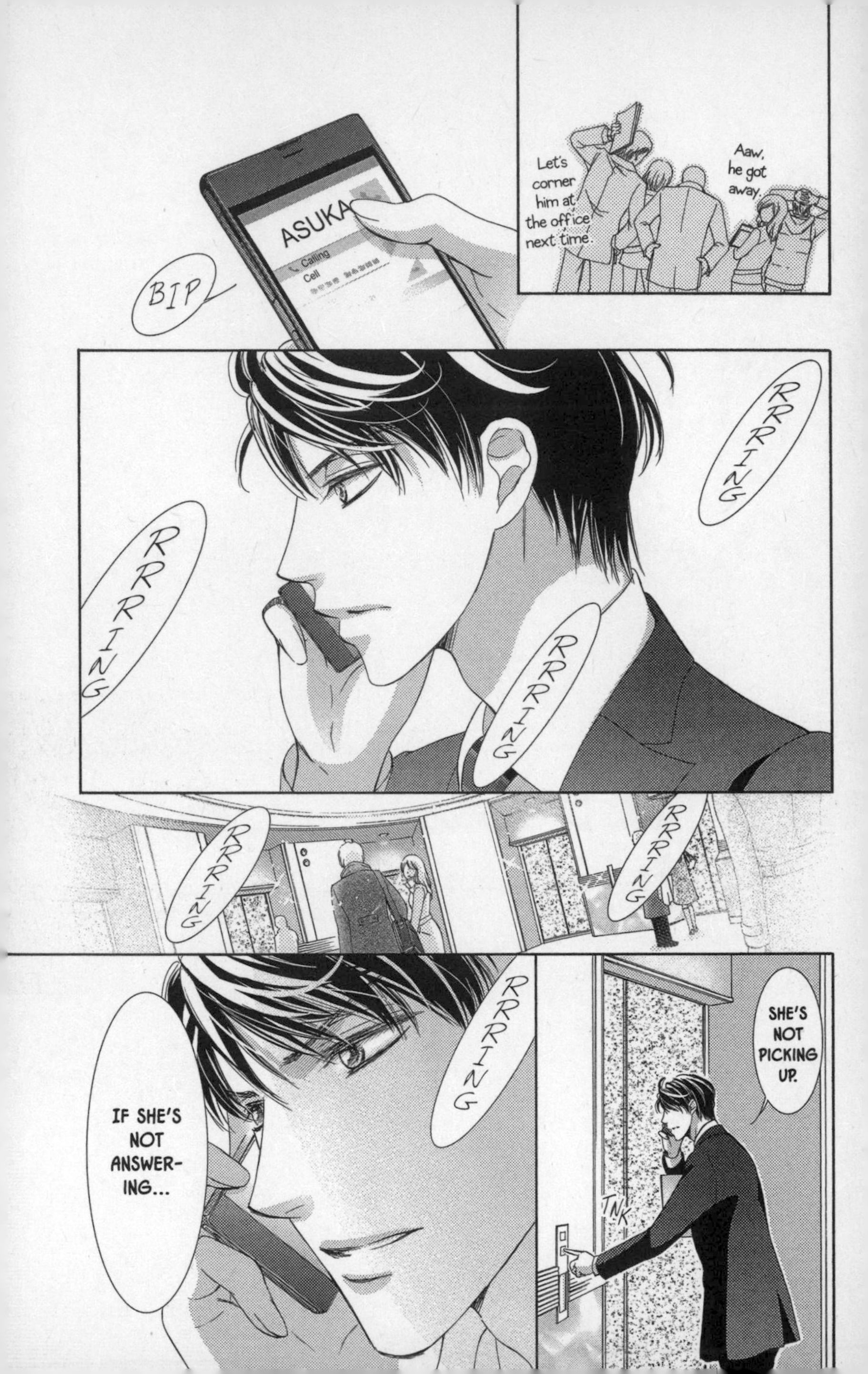
Aaw, he got away.
Let's corner him at the office next time.
ASUKA
Calling
Cell
BIP
RRRING
RRRING
RRRING
RRRING
RRRING
SHE'S NOT PICKING UP.
TNK
RRRING
IF SHE'S NOT ANSWER-ING...

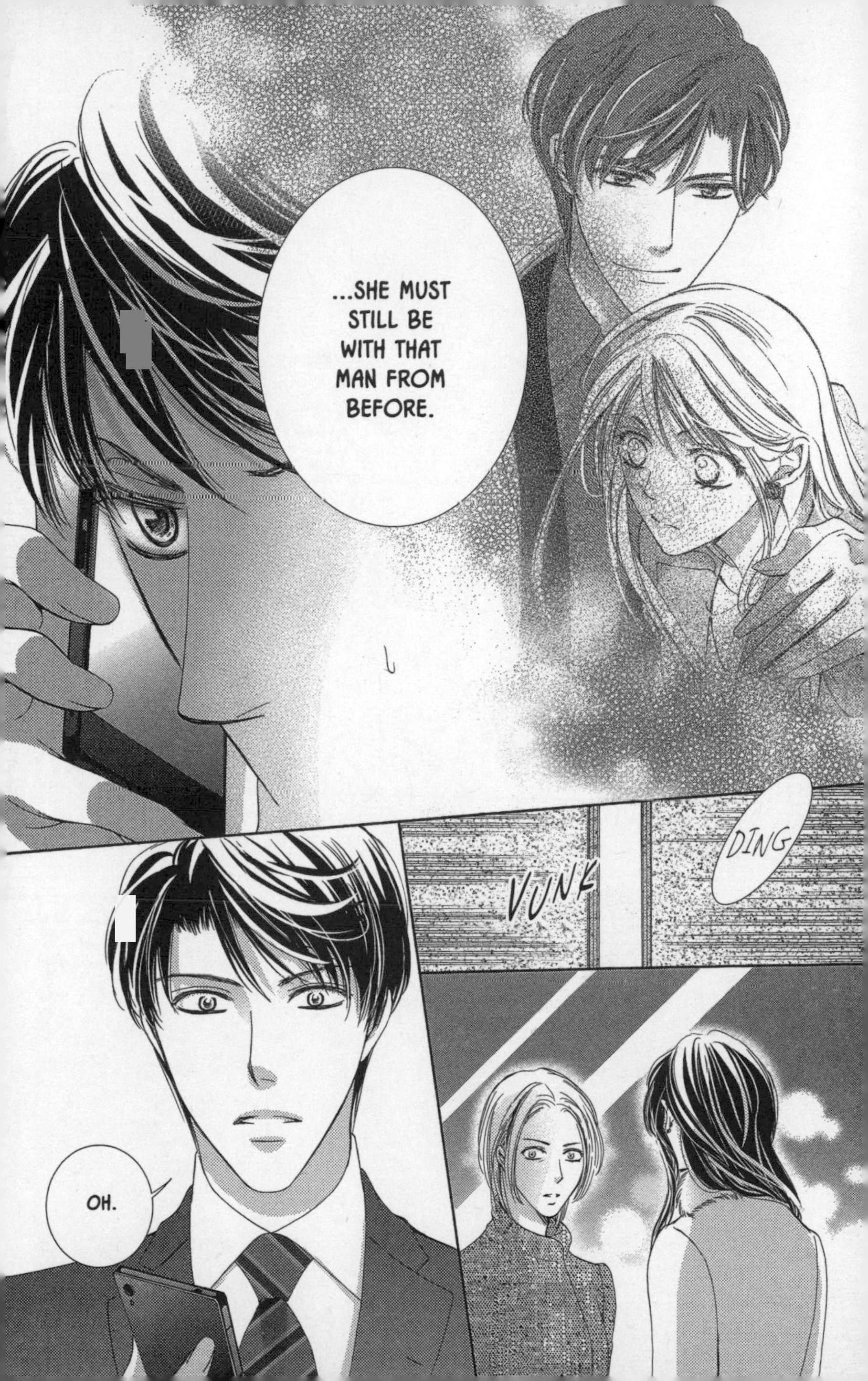
...SHE MUST STILL BE WITH THAT MAN FROM BEFORE.
DING
VUNK
OH.

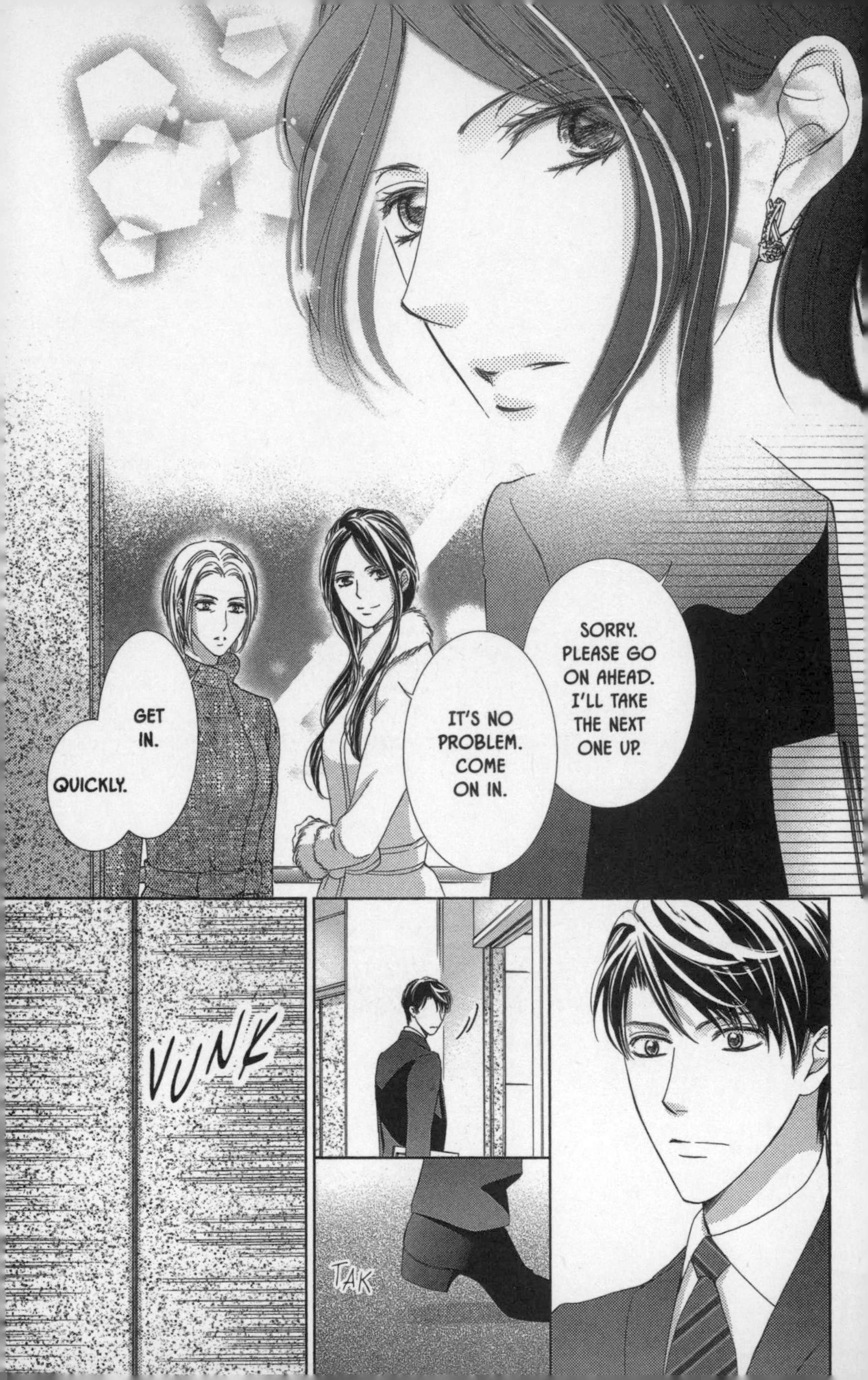
SORRY. PLEASE GO ON AHEAD. I'LL TAKE THE NEXT ONE UP.
IT'S NO PROBLEM. COME ON IN.
GET IN.
QUICKLY.
TAK
VUNK

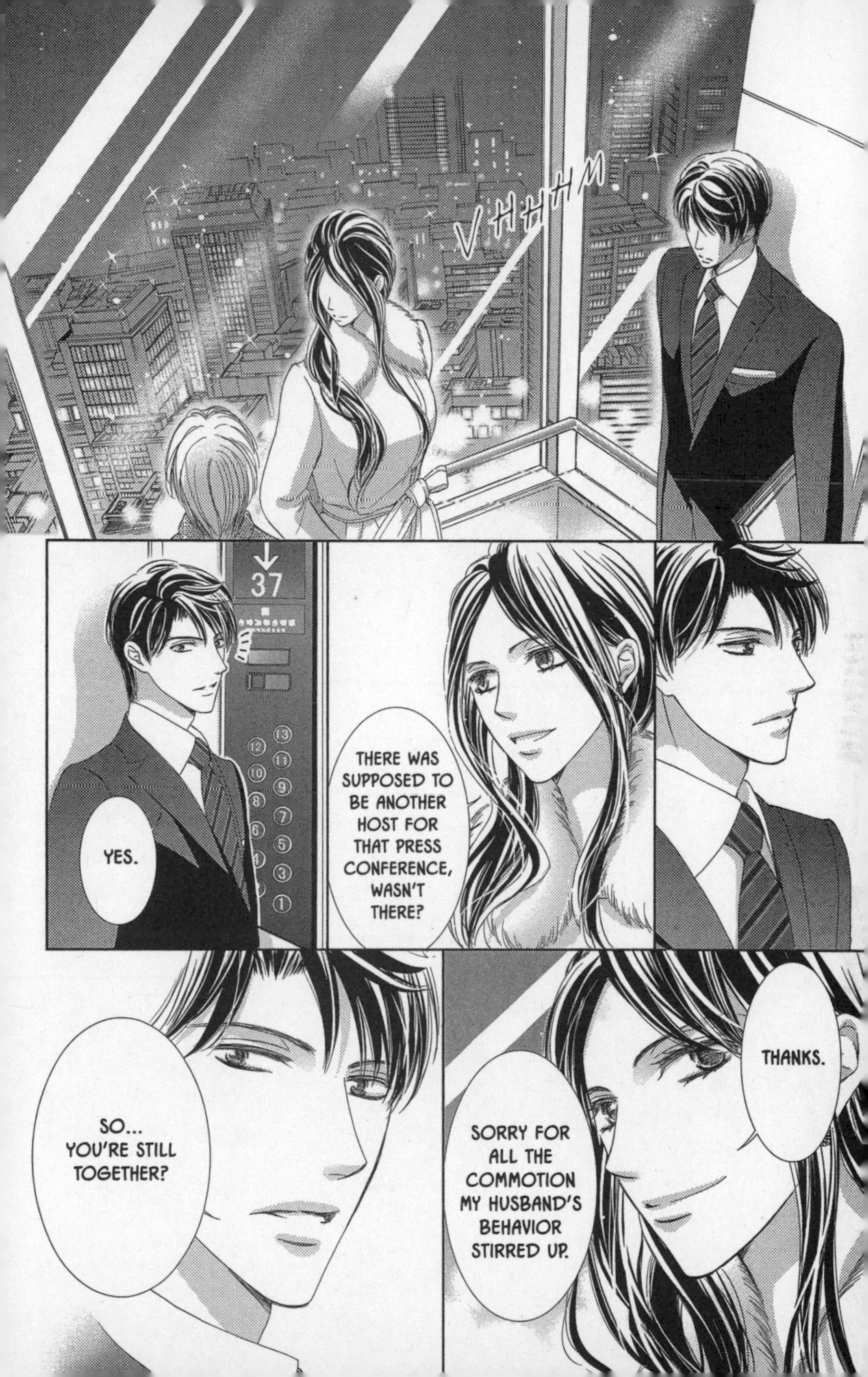
VHHHM
THERE WAS SUPPOSED TO BE ANOTHER HOST FOR THAT PRESS CONFERENCE, WASN'T THERE?
37
YES.
THANKS.
SORRY FOR ALL THE COMMOTION MY HUSBAND'S BEHAVIOR STIRRED UP.
SO... YOU'RE STILL TOGETHER?

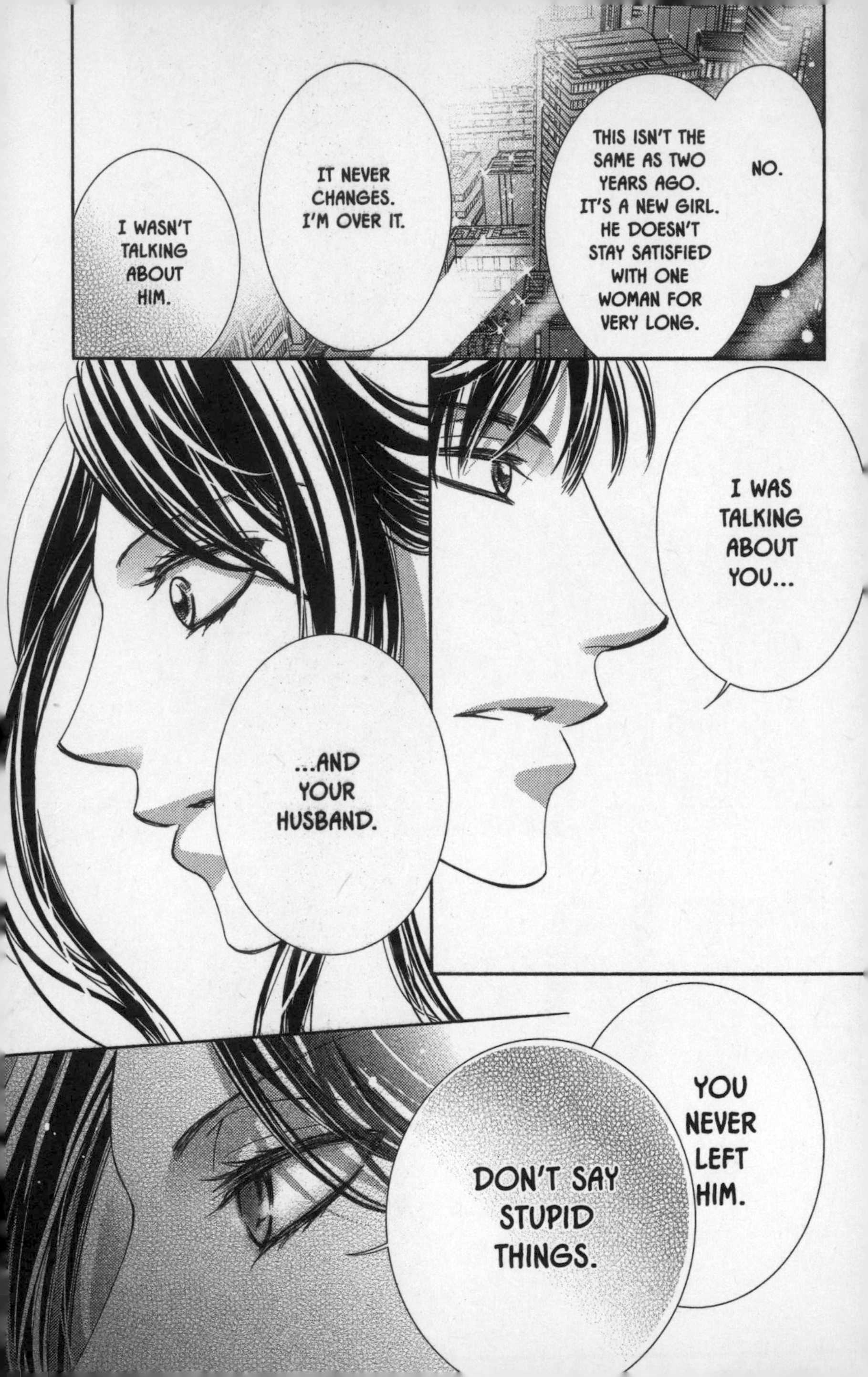
NO.
THIS ISN'T THE SAME AS TWO YEARS AGO. IT'S A NEW GIRL. HE DOESN'T STAY SATISFIED WITH ONE WOMAN FOR VERY LONG.
IT NEVER CHANGES. I'M OVER IT.
I WASN'T TALKING ABOUT HIM.
I WAS TALKING ABOUT YOU...
...AND YOUR HUSBAND.
YOU NEVER LEFT HIM.
DON'T SAY STUPID THINGS.

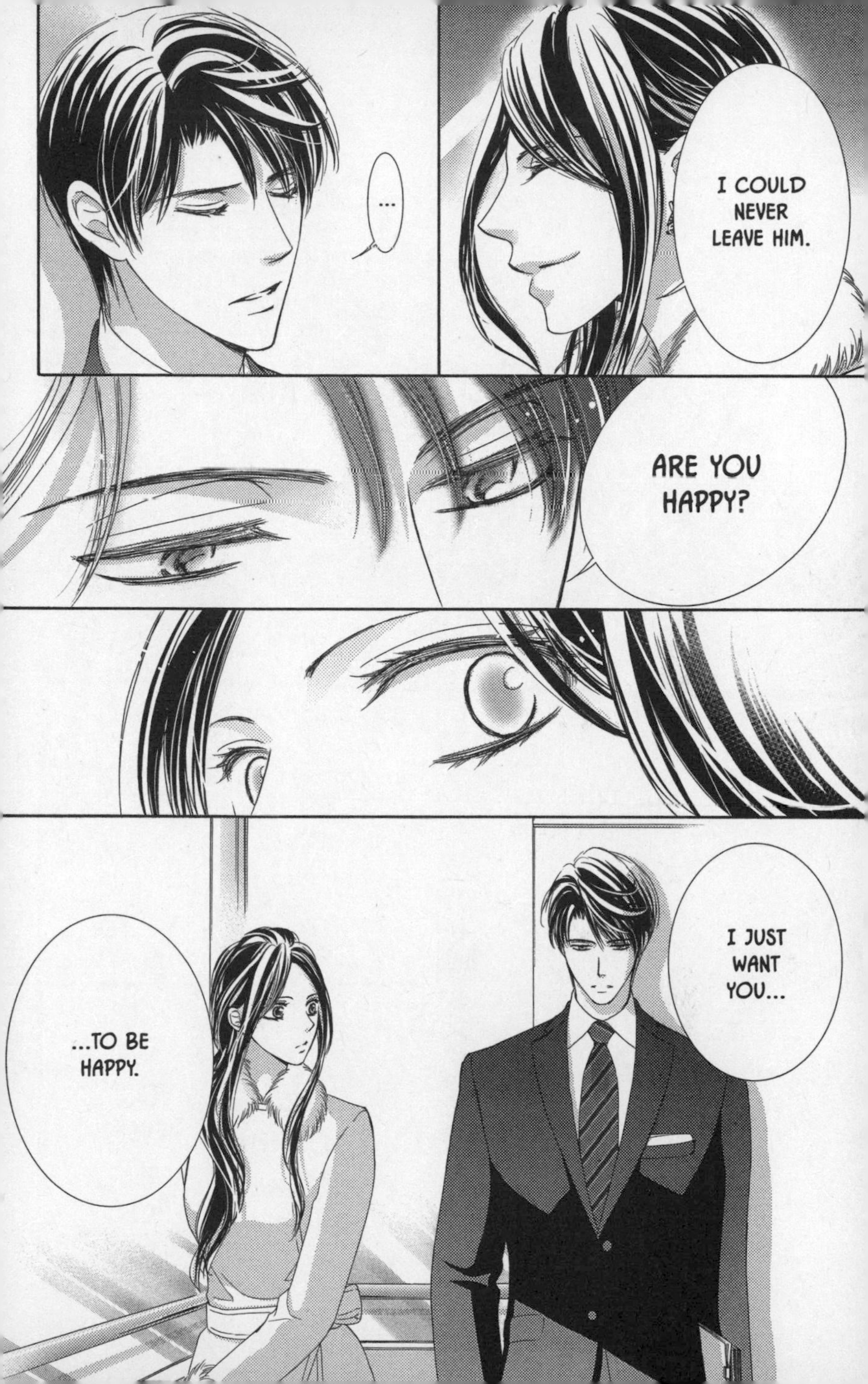
I COULD NEVER LEAVE HIM.
...
ARE YOU HAPPY?
I JUST WANT YOU...
...TO BE HAPPY.

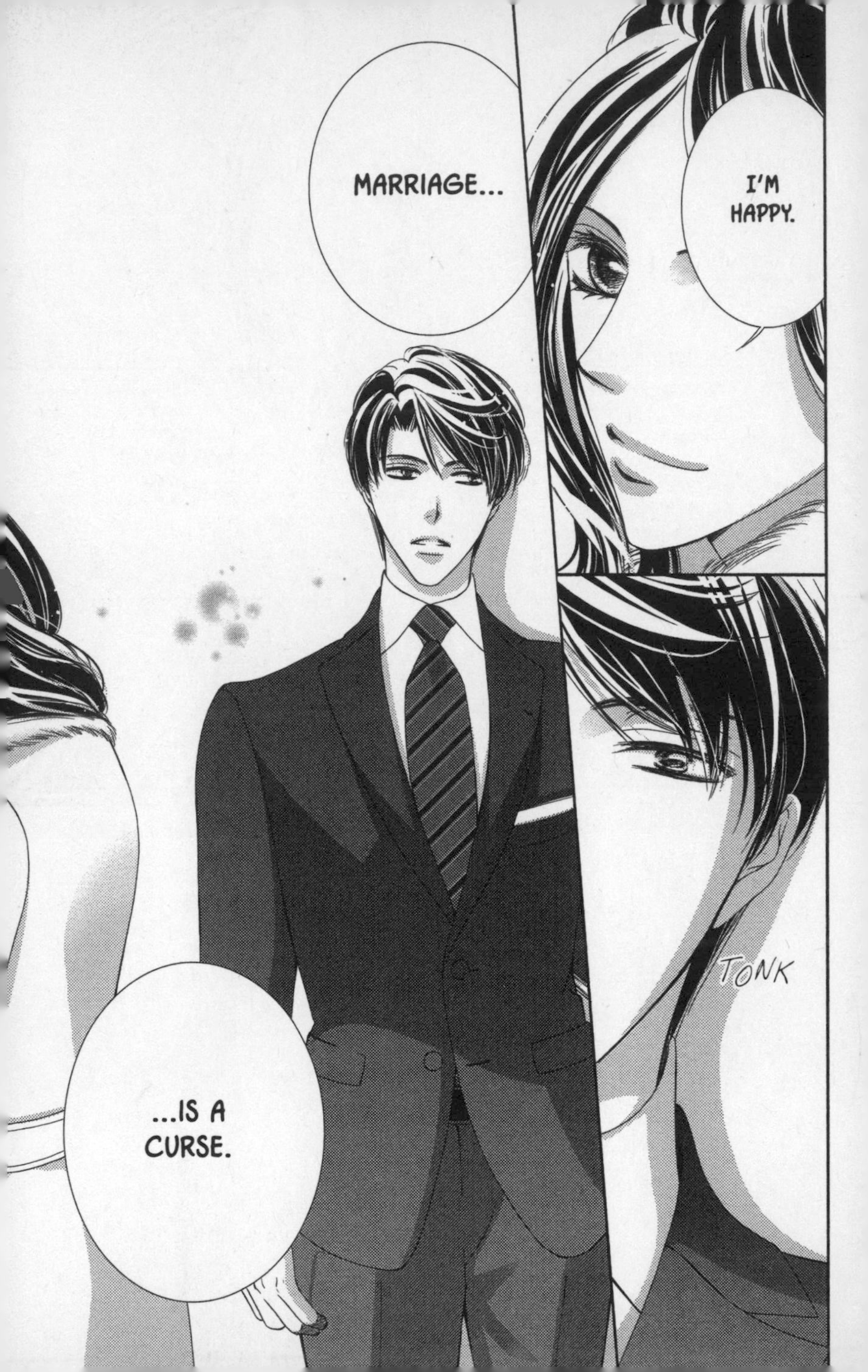
I'M HAPPY.
TONK
MARRIAGE...
...IS A CURSE.

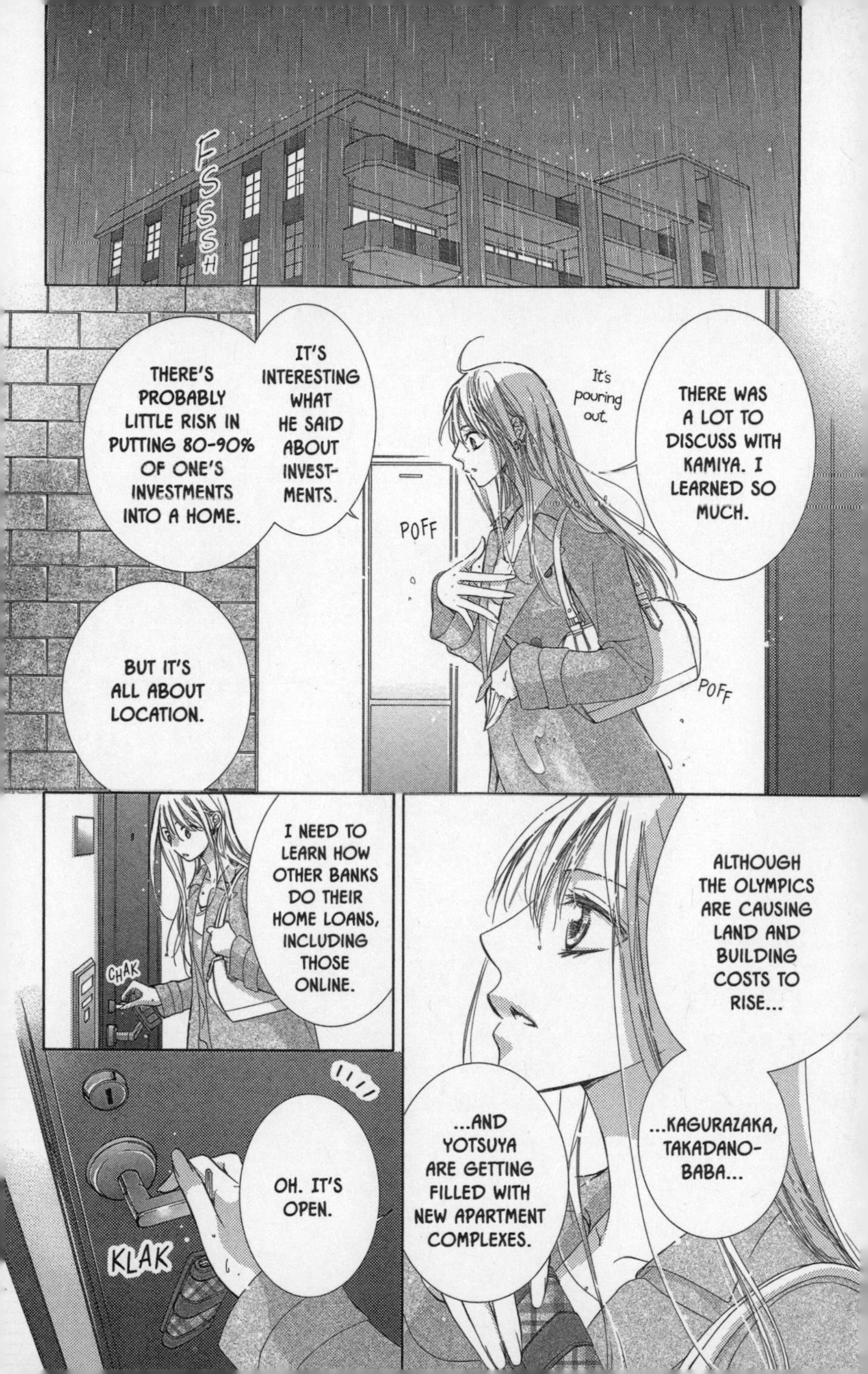
FSSSH
It's pouring out.
THERE WAS A LOT TO DISCUSS WITH KAMIYA. I LEARNED SO MUCH.
IT'S INTERESTING WHAT HE SAID ABOUT INVEST-MENTS.
THERE'S PROBABLY LITTLE RISK IN PUTTING 80-90% OF ONE'S INVESTMENTS INTO A HOME.
POFF
POFF
BUT IT'S ALL ABOUT LOCATION.
ALTHOUGH THE OLYMPICS ARE CAUSING LAND AND BUILDING COSTS TO RISE...
...KAGURAZAKA, TAKADANO-BABA...
...AND YOTSUYA ARE GETTING FILLED WITH NEW APARTMENT COMPLEXES.
I NEED TO LEARN HOW OTHER BANKS DO THEIR HOME LOANS, INCLUDING THOSE ONLINE.
CHAK
OH. IT'S OPEN.
KLAK

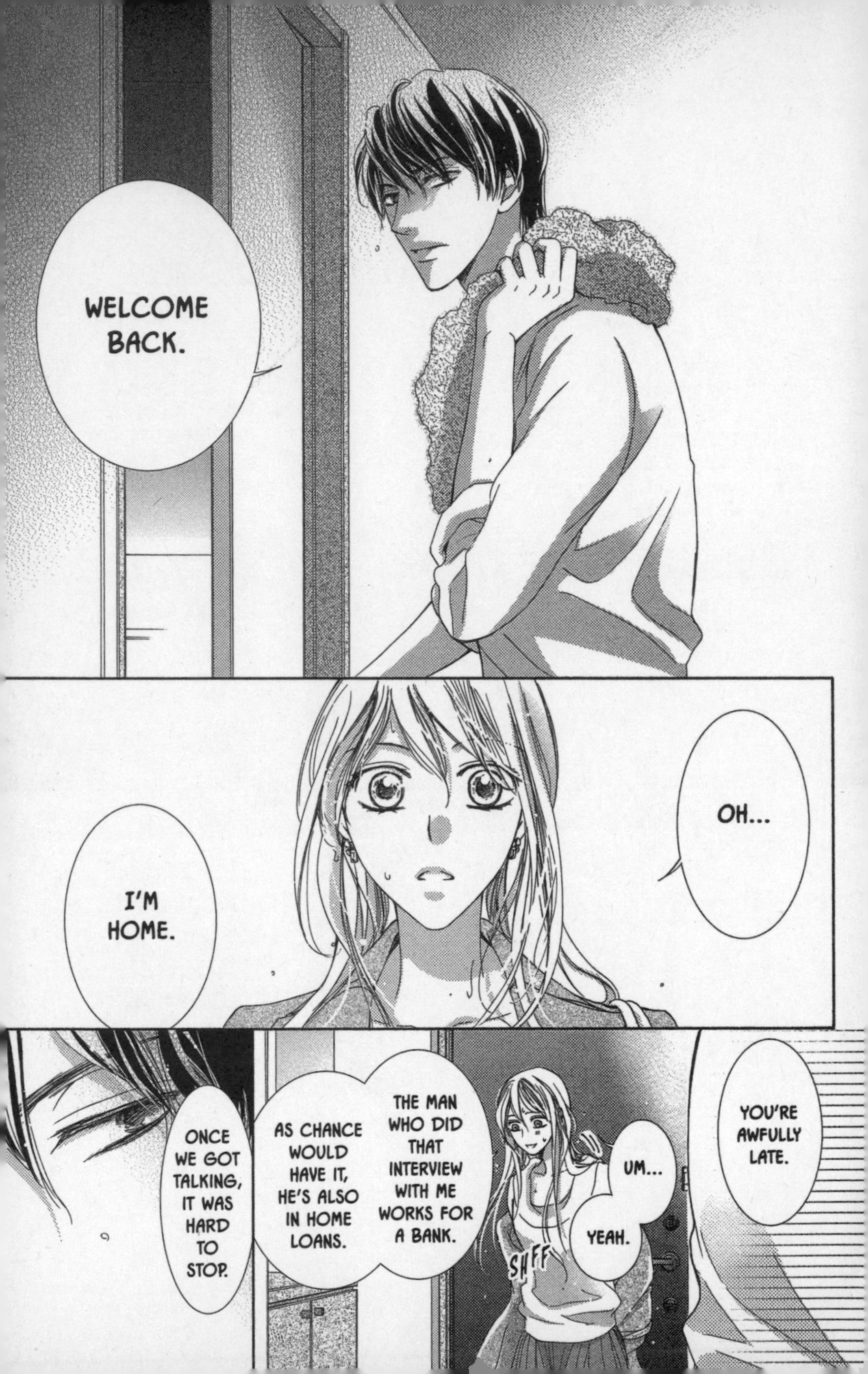
WELCOME BACK.
OH...
I'M HOME.
YOU'RE AWFULLY LATE.
UM...
YEAH.
SHFF
THE MAN WHO DID THAT INTERVIEW WITH ME WORKS FOR A BANK.
AS CHANCE WOULD HAVE IT, HE'S ALSO IN HOME LOANS.
ONCE WE GOT TALKING, IT WAS HARD TO STOP.

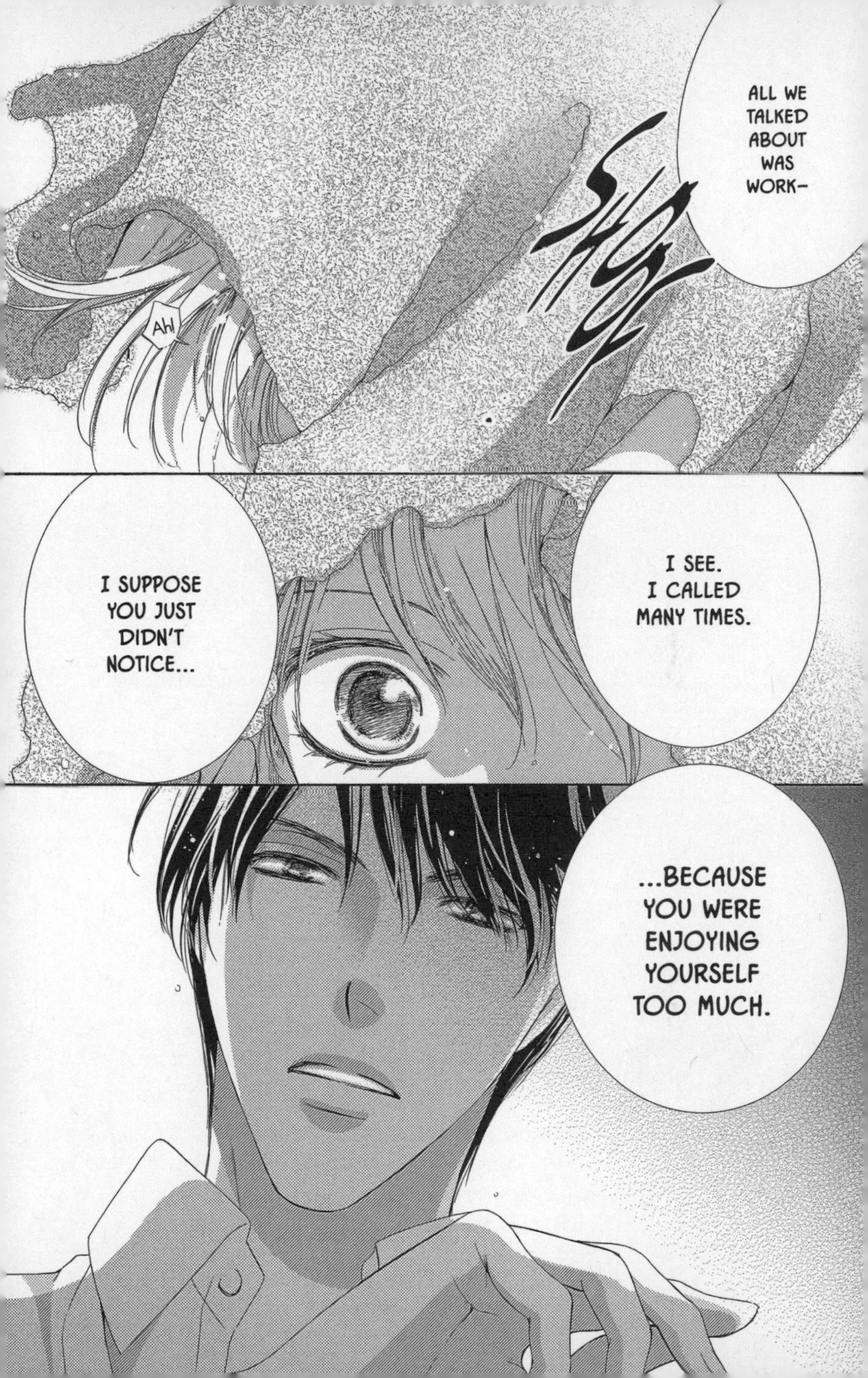
ALL WE TALKED ABOUT WAS WORK–
Ah!
I SEE. I CALLED MANY TIMES.
I SUPPOSE YOU JUST DIDN'T NOTICE...
...BECAUSE YOU WERE ENJOYING YOURSELF TOO MUCH.

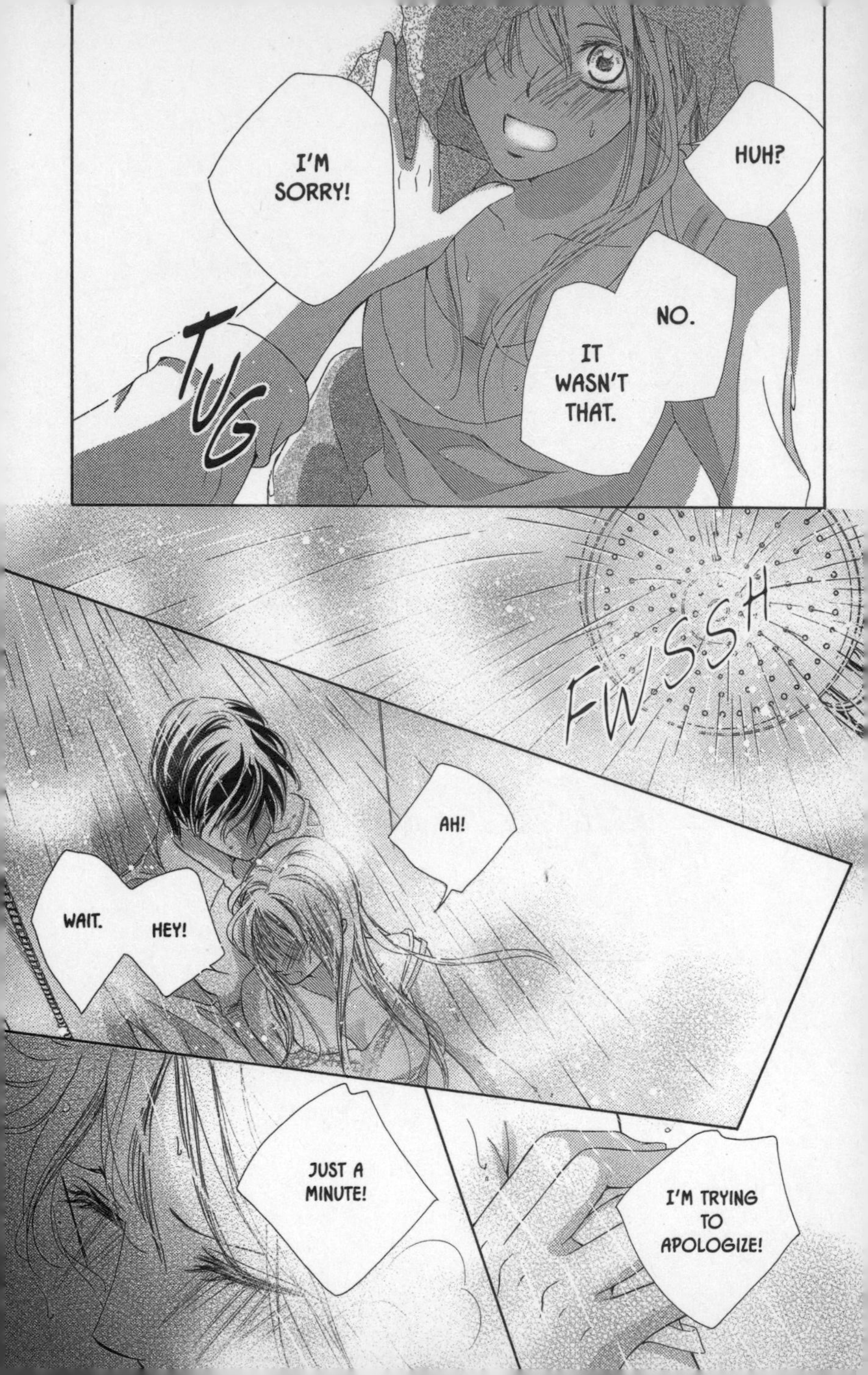
HUH?
I'M SORRY!
NO.
IT WASN'T THAT.
TUG
FWSSH
AH!
HEY!
WAIT.
I'M TRYING TO APOLOGIZE!
JUST A MINUTE!

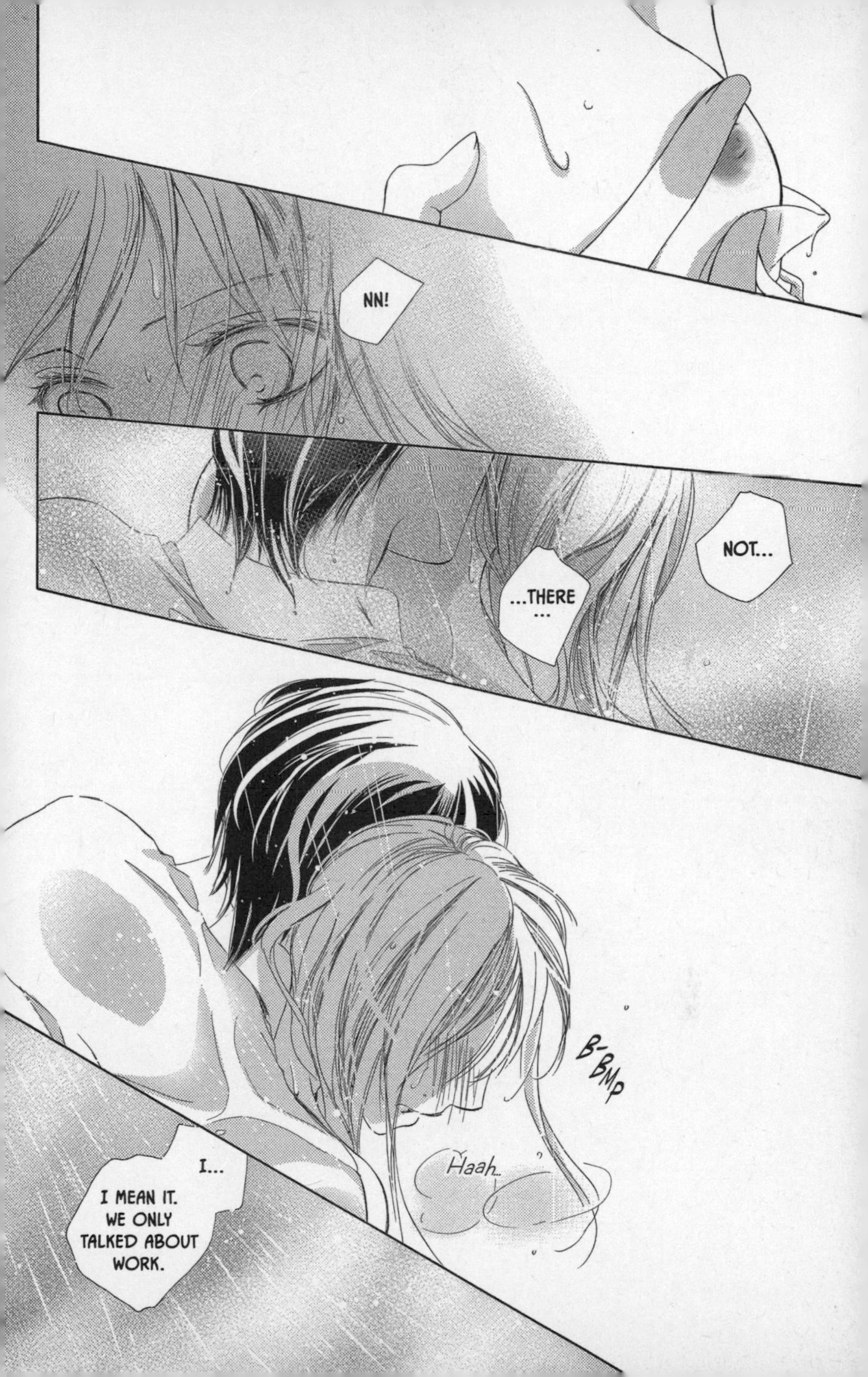
NN!
NOT...
...THERE ...
B-BMP
Haah..
I...
I MEAN IT. WE ONLY TALKED ABOUT WORK.

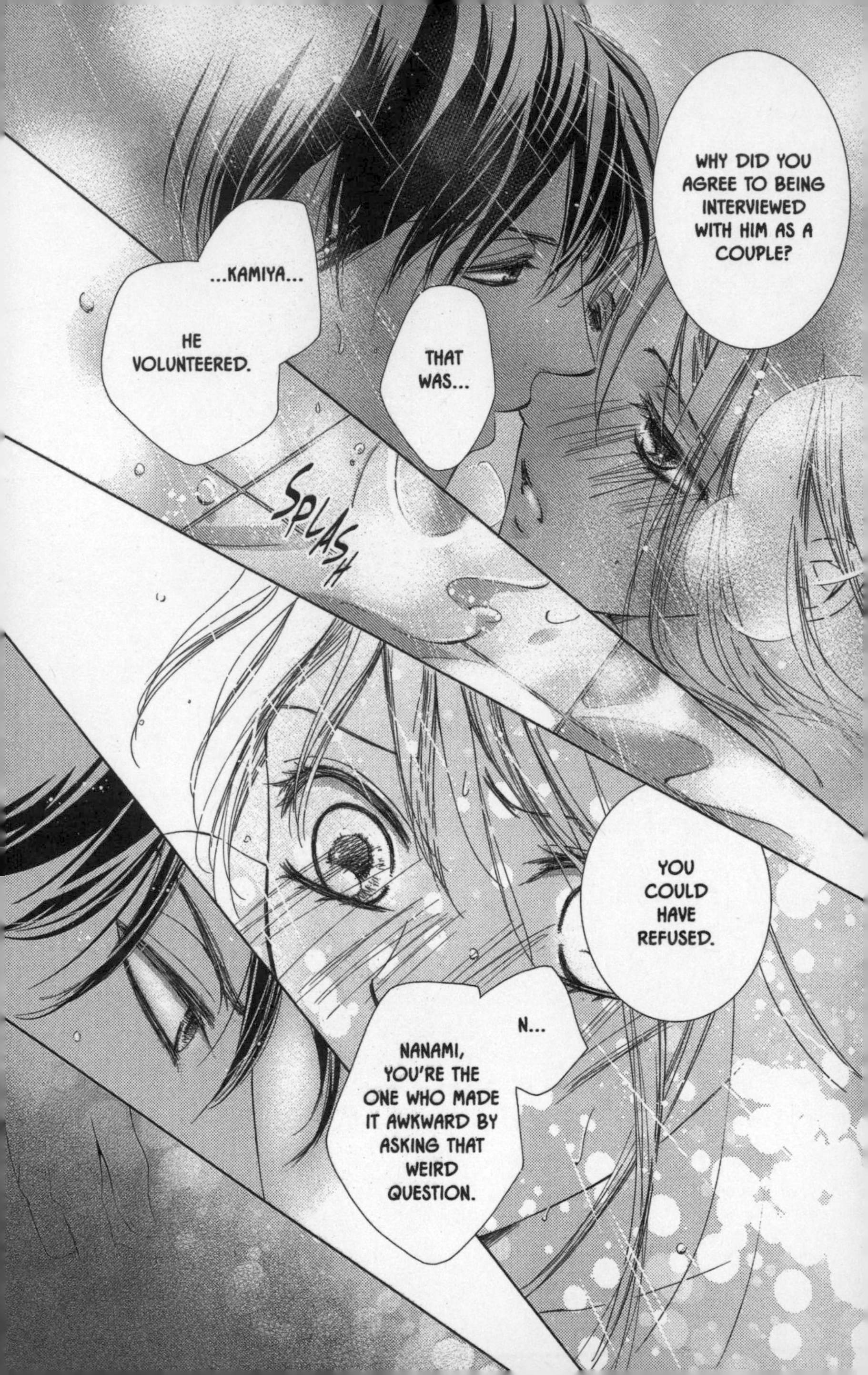
WHY DID YOU AGREE TO BEING INTERVIEWED WITH HIM AS A COUPLE?
THAT WAS...
...KAMIYA...
HE VOLUNTEERED.
SPLASH
YOU COULD HAVE REFUSED.
N...
NANAMI, YOU'RE THE ONE WHO MADE IT AWKWARD BY ASKING THAT WEIRD QUESTION.

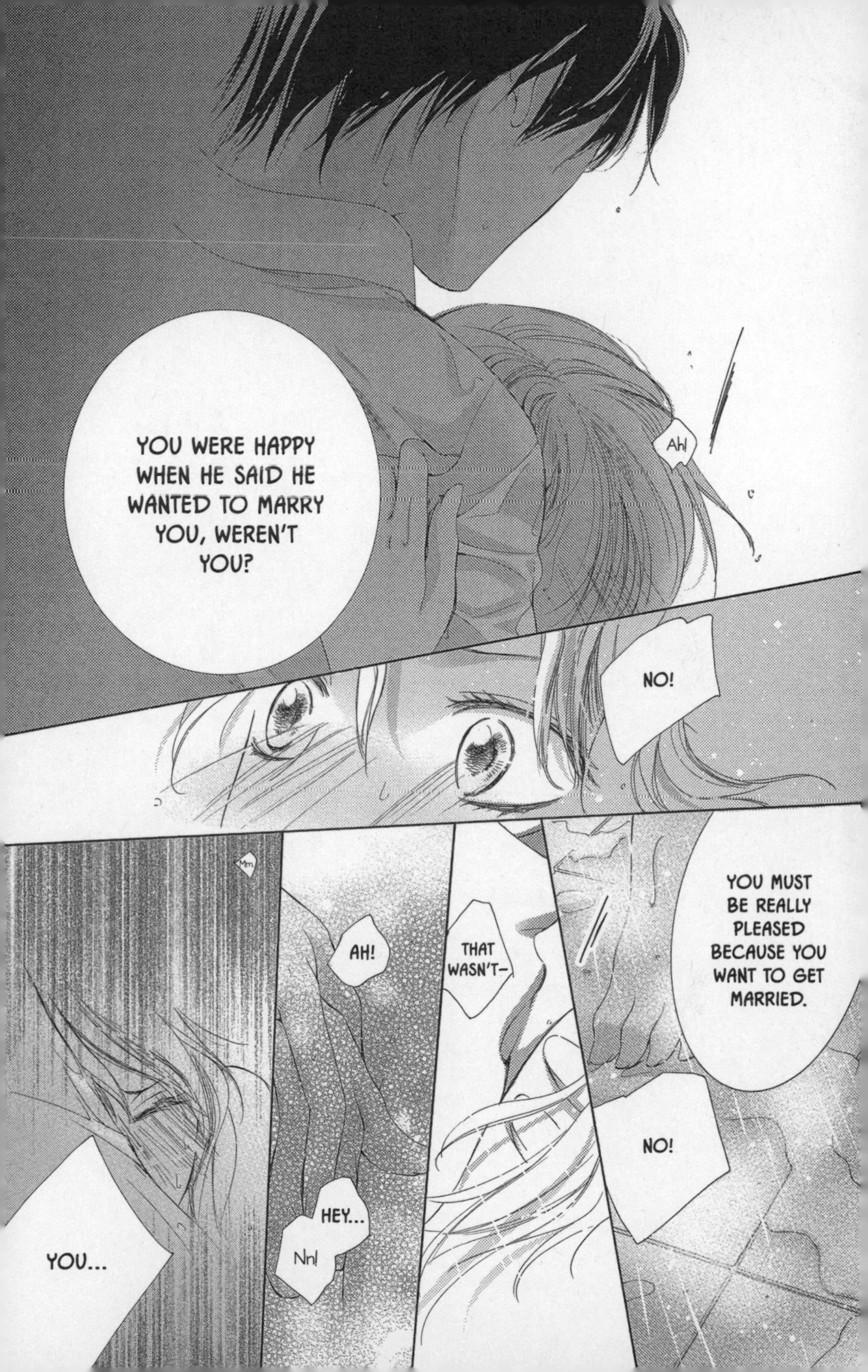
Ah!
YOU WERE HAPPY WHEN HE SAID HE WANTED TO MARRY YOU, WEREN'T YOU?
NO!
YOU MUST BE REALLY PLEASED BECAUSE YOU WANT TO GET MARRIED.
NO!
THAT WASN'T—
AH!
HEY...
Nn!
Mm.
YOU...

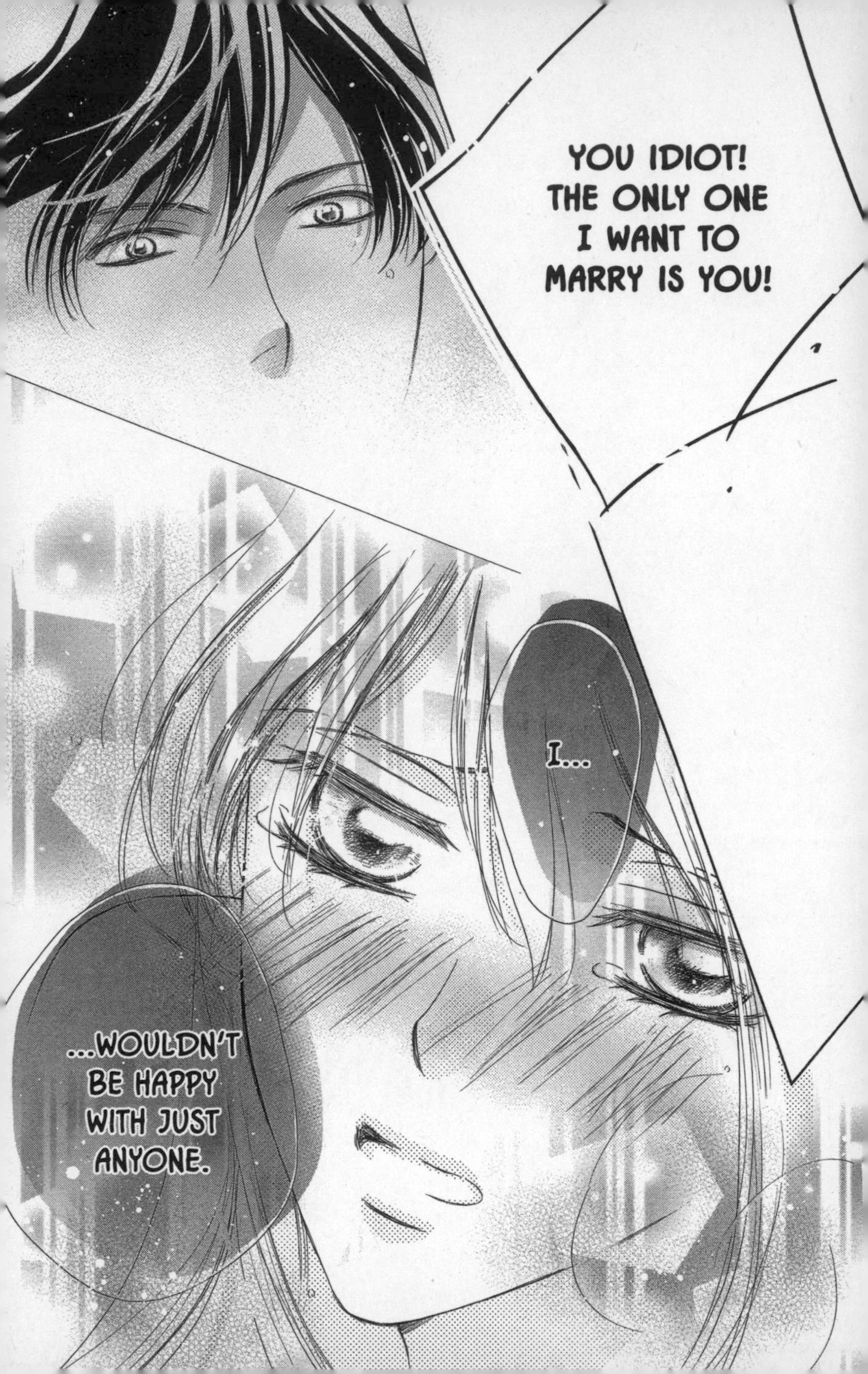
YOU IDIOT! THE ONLY ONE I WANT TO MARRY IS YOU!
I...
...WOULDN'T BE HAPPY WITH JUST ANYONE.

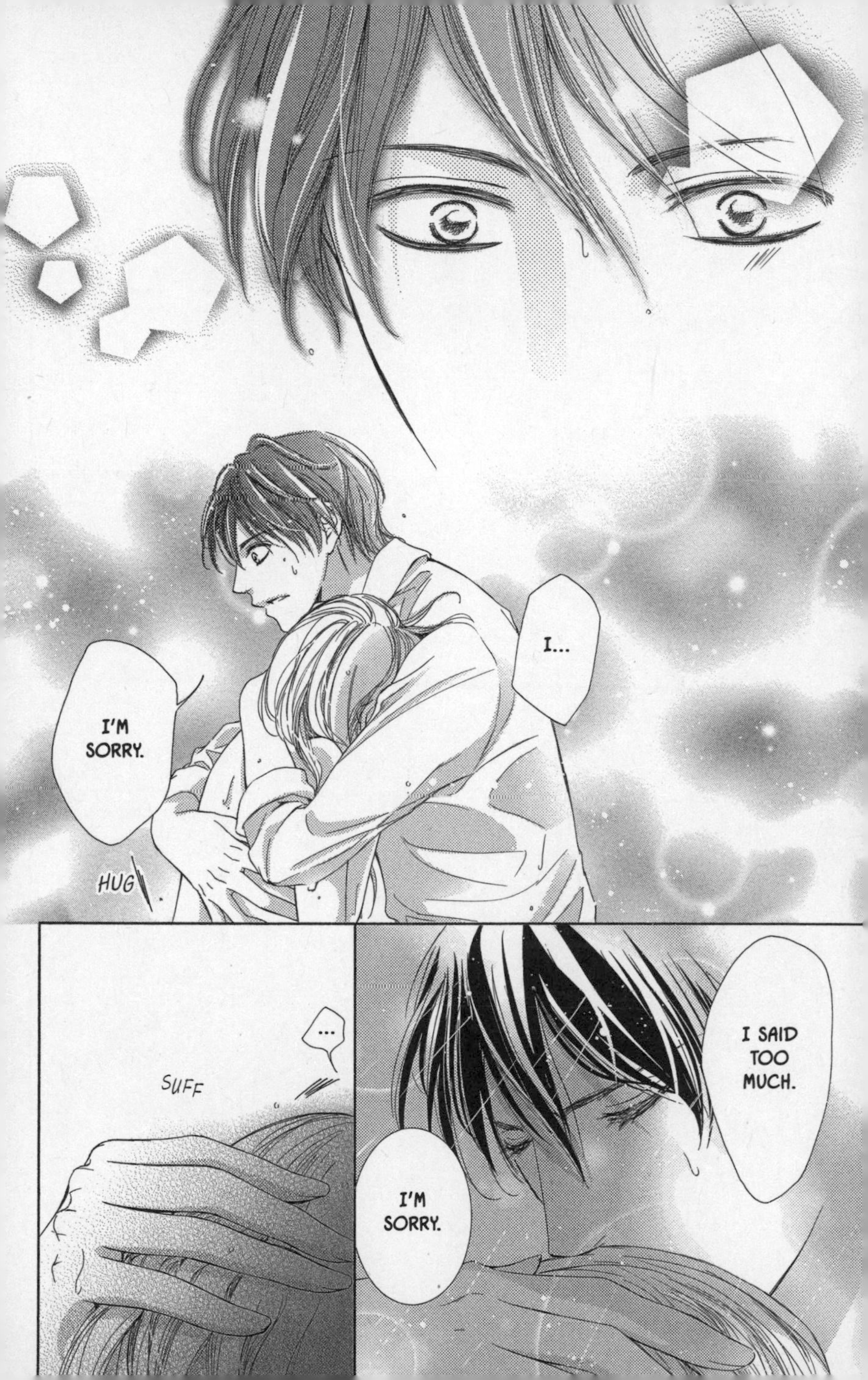
I...
I'M SORRY.
HUG
I SAID TOO MUCH.
I'M SORRY.
...
SUFF

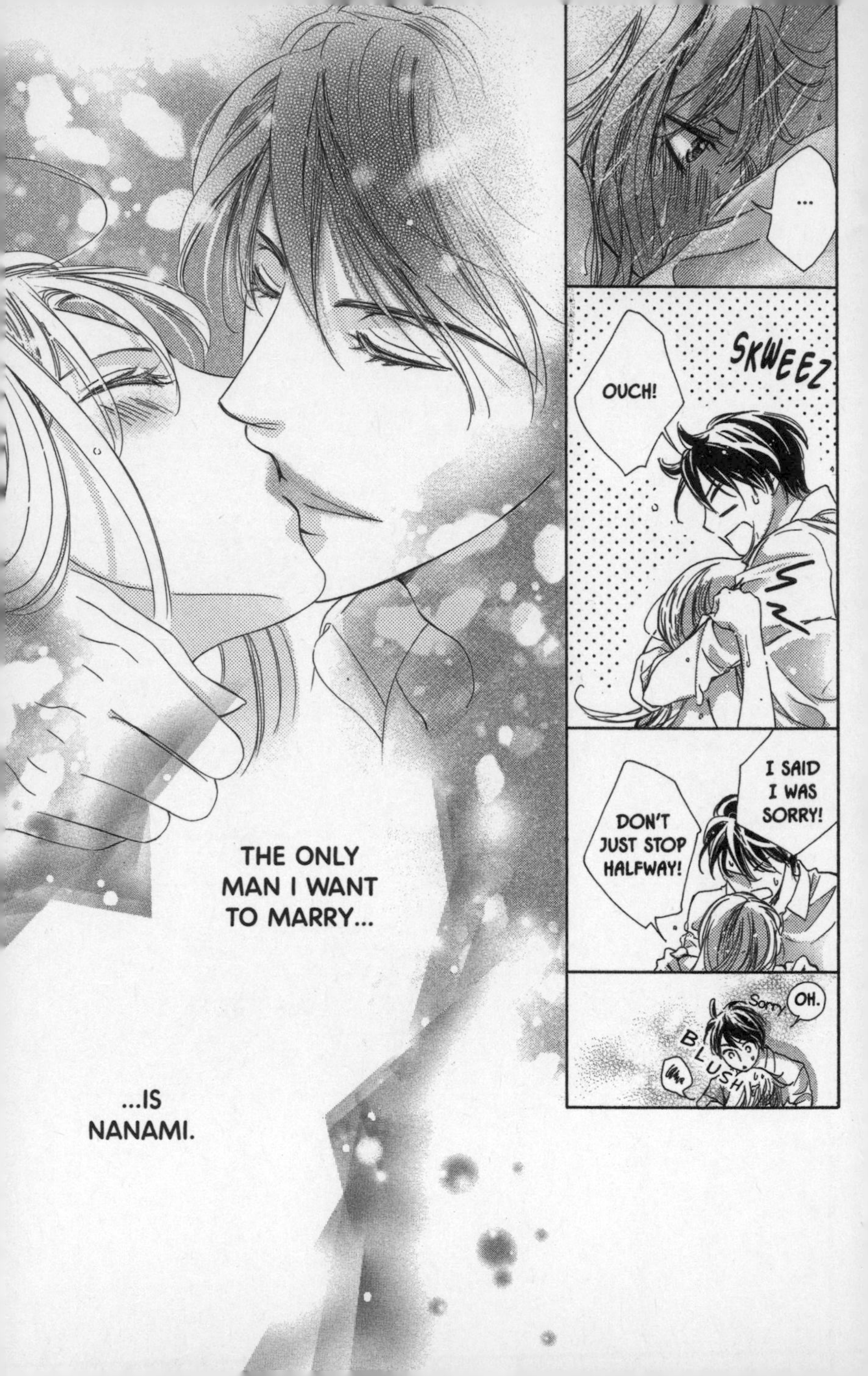
...
SKWEEZ
OUCH!
I SAID I WAS SORRY!
DON'T JUST STOP HALFWAY!
OH.
Sorry
BLUSH
THE ONLY MAN I WANT TO MARRY...
...IS NANAMI.

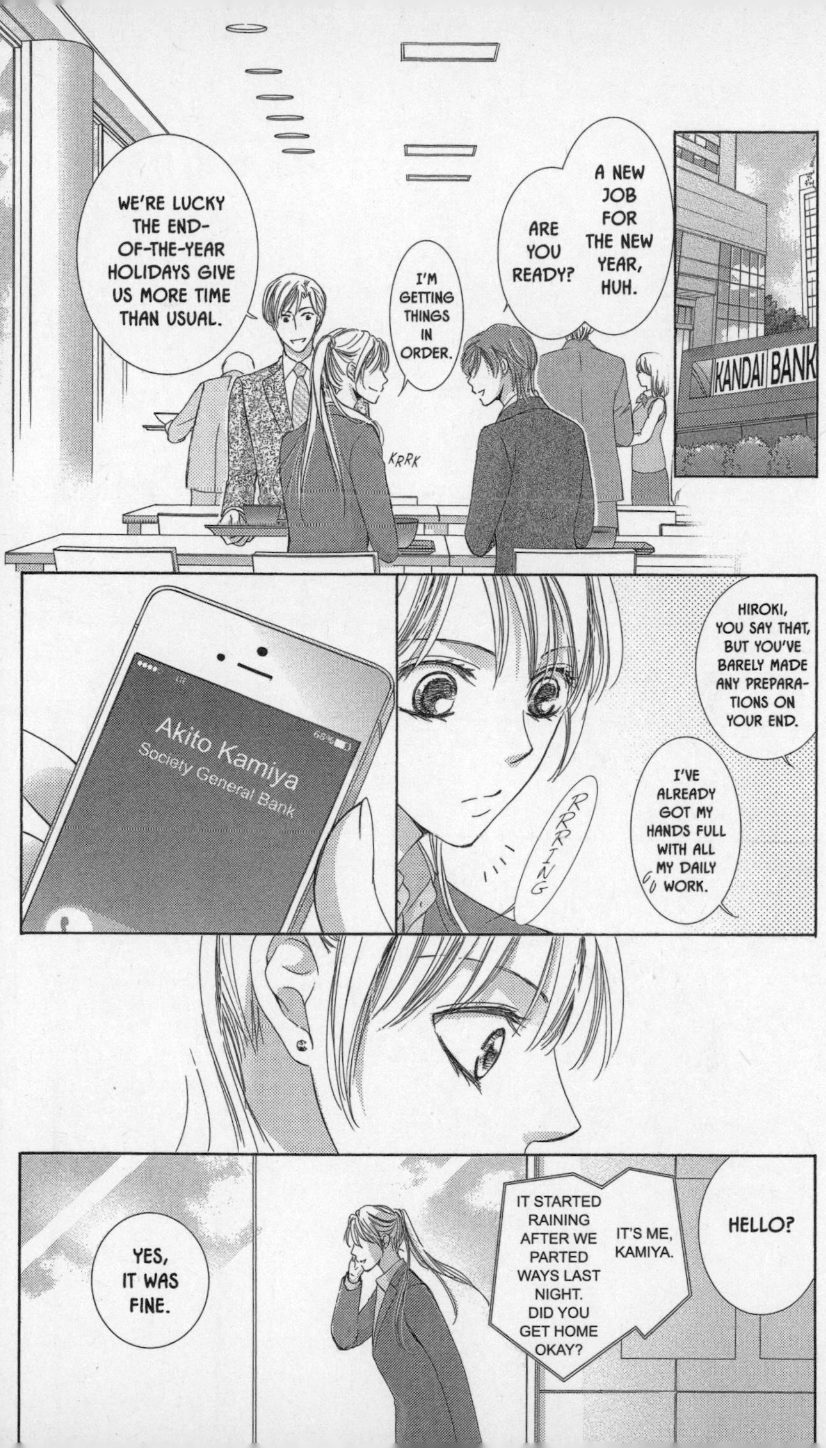
KANDAI BANK
A NEW JOB FOR THE NEW YEAR, HUH.
ARE YOU READY?
I'M GETTING THINGS IN ORDER.
WE'RE LUCKY THE END-OF-THE-YEAR HOLIDAYS GIVE US MORE TIME THAN USUAL.
KRRK
HIROKI, YOU SAY THAT, BUT YOU'VE BARELY MADE ANY PREPARATIONS ON YOUR END.
I'VE ALREADY GOT MY HANDS FULL WITH ALL MY DAILY WORK.
RRRING
Akito Kamiya
Society General Bank
68%
HELLO?
IT'S ME, KAMIYA.
IT STARTED RAINING AFTER WE PARTED WAYS LAST NIGHT. DID YOU GET HOME OKAY?
YES, IT WAS FINE.

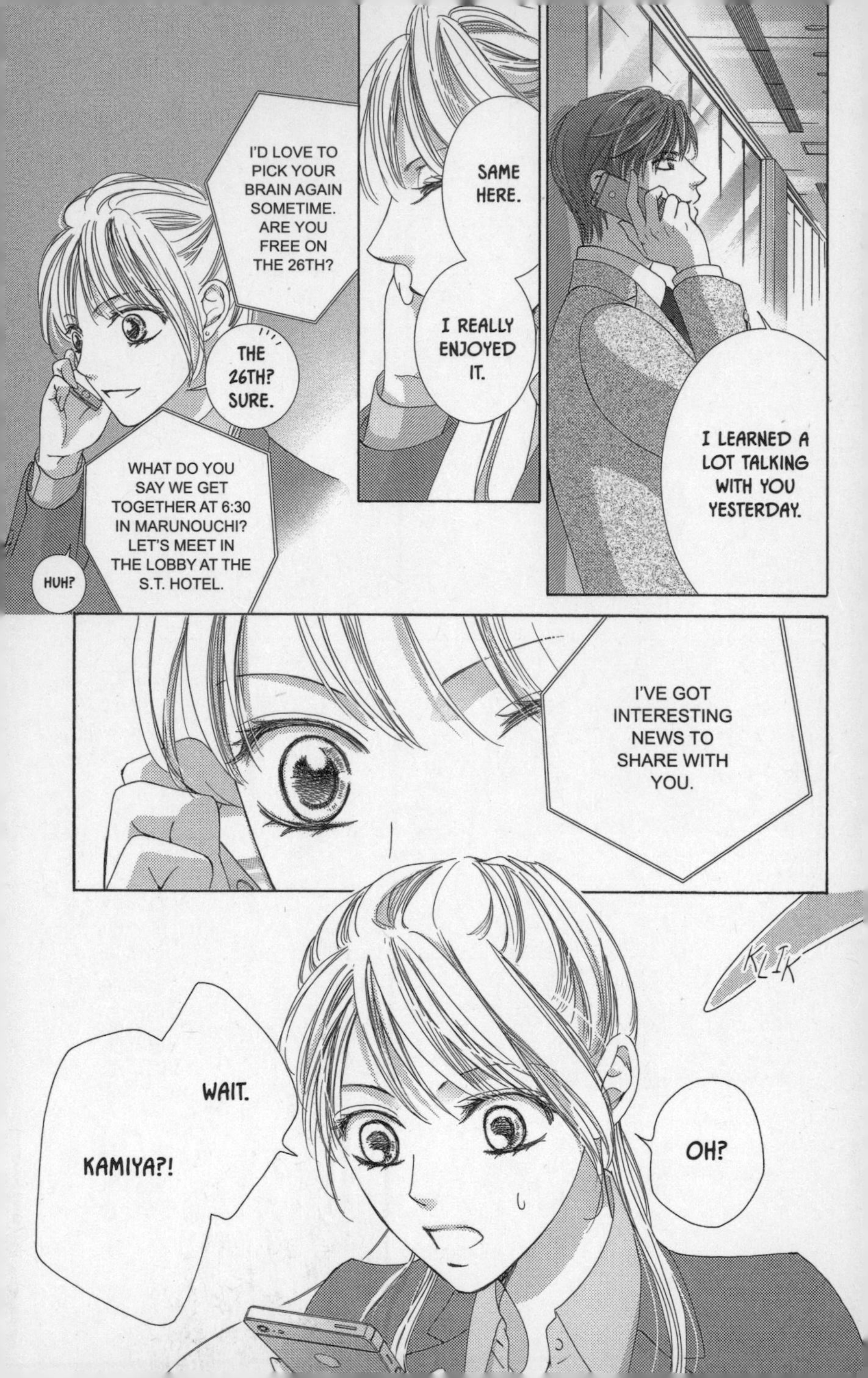
I LEARNED A LOT TALKING WITH YOU YESTERDAY.
SAME HERE.
I REALLY ENJOYED IT.
I'D LOVE TO PICK YOUR BRAIN AGAIN SOMETIME. ARE YOU FREE ON THE 26TH?
THE 26TH? SURE.
WHAT DO YOU SAY WE GET TOGETHER AT 6:30 IN MARUNOUCHI? LET'S MEET IN THE LOBBY AT THE S.T. HOTEL.
HUH?
I'VE GOT INTERESTING NEWS TO SHARE WITH YOU.
KLIK
OH?
WAIT.
KAMIYA?!

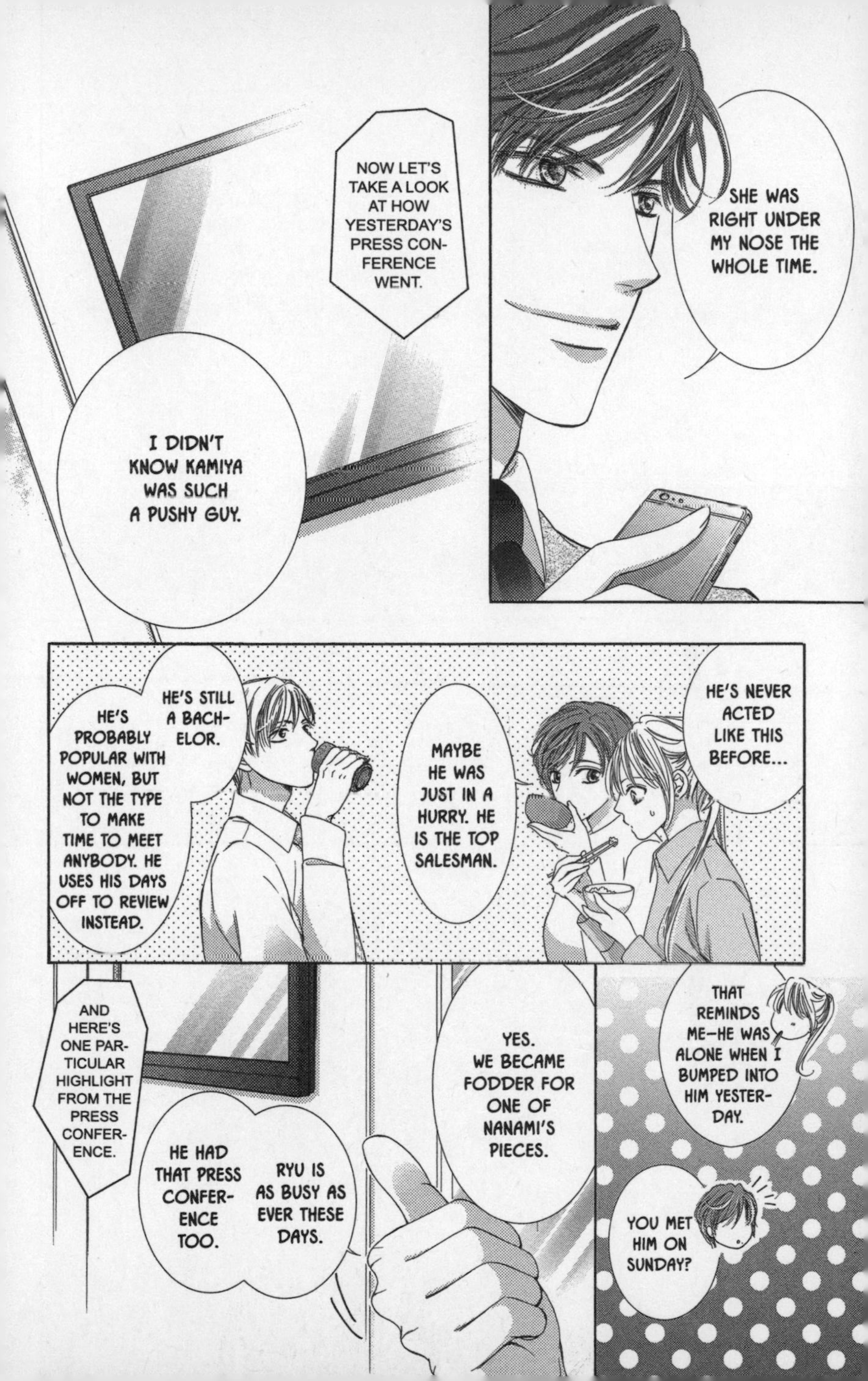
SHE WAS RIGHT UNDER MY NOSE THE WHOLE TIME.
NOW LET'S TAKE A LOOK AT HOW YESTERDAY'S PRESS CONFERENCE WENT.
I DIDN'T KNOW KAMIYA WAS SUCH A PUSHY GUY.
HE'S NEVER ACTED LIKE THIS BEFORE...
MAYBE HE WAS JUST IN A HURRY. HE IS THE TOP SALESMAN.
HE'S STILL A BACHELOR.
HE'S PROBABLY POPULAR WITH WOMEN, BUT NOT THE TYPE TO MAKE TIME TO MEET ANYBODY. HE USES HIS DAYS OFF TO REVIEW INSTEAD.
THAT REMINDS ME—HE WAS ALONE WHEN I BUMPED INTO HIM YESTERDAY.
YOU MET HIM ON SUNDAY?
YES. WE BECAME FODDER FOR ONE OF NANAMI'S PIECES.
RYU IS AS BUSY AS EVER THESE DAYS.
HE HAD THAT PRESS CONFERENCE TOO.
AND HERE'S ONE PARTICULAR HIGHLIGHT FROM THE PRESS CONFERENCE.

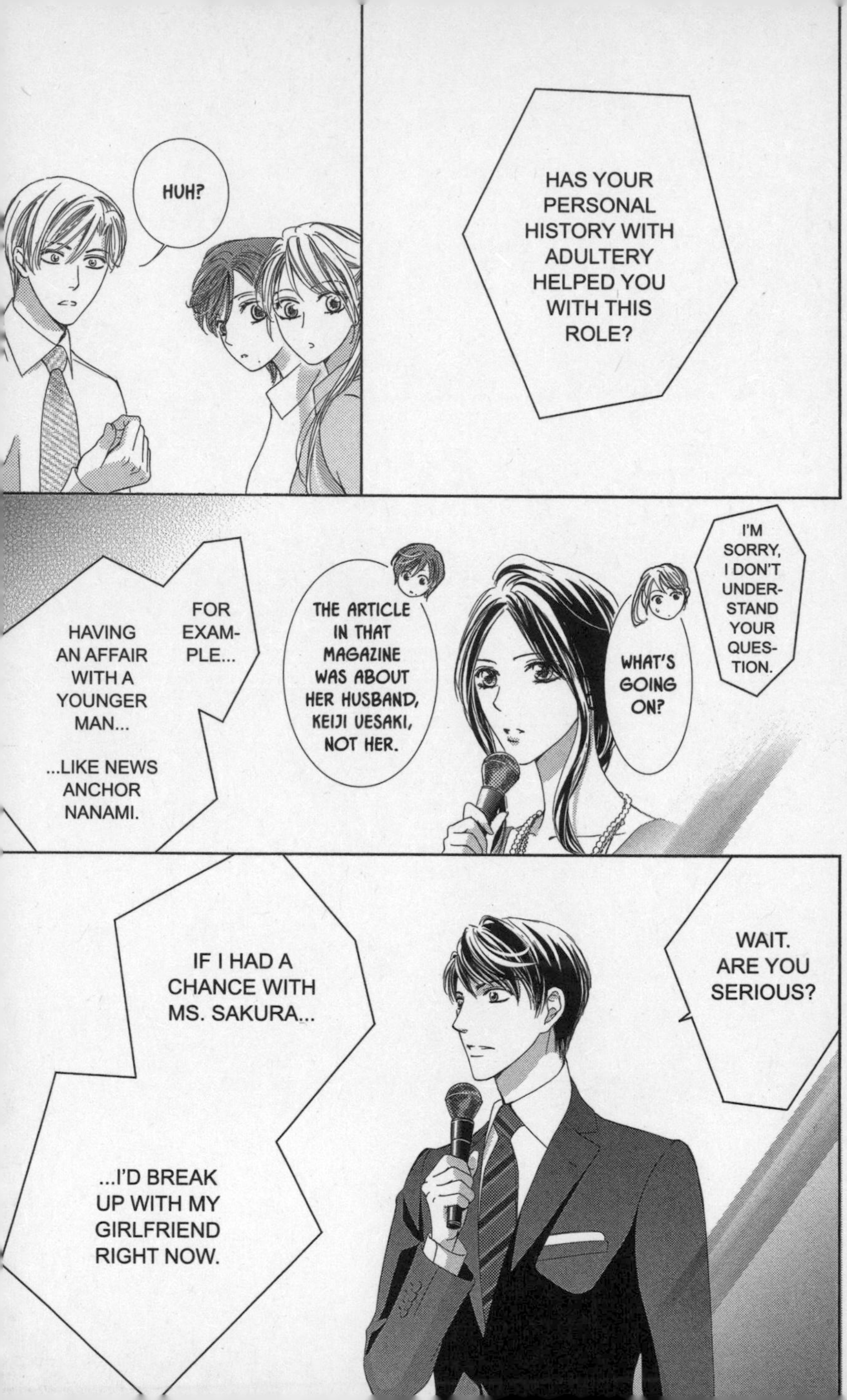

HAS YOUR PERSONAL HISTORY WITH ADULTERY HELPED YOU WITH THIS ROLE?
HUH?
I'M SORRY, I DON'T UNDER-STAND YOUR QUES-TION.
WHAT'S GOING ON?
THE ARTICLE IN THAT MAGAZINE WAS ABOUT HER HUSBAND, KEIJI UESAKI, NOT HER.
FOR EXAM-PLE...
HAVING AN AFFAIR WITH A YOUNGER MAN...
...LIKE NEWS ANCHOR NANAMI.
WAIT. ARE YOU SERIOUS?
IF I HAD A CHANCE WITH MS. SAKURA...
...I'D BREAK UP WITH MY GIRLFRIEND RIGHT NOW.

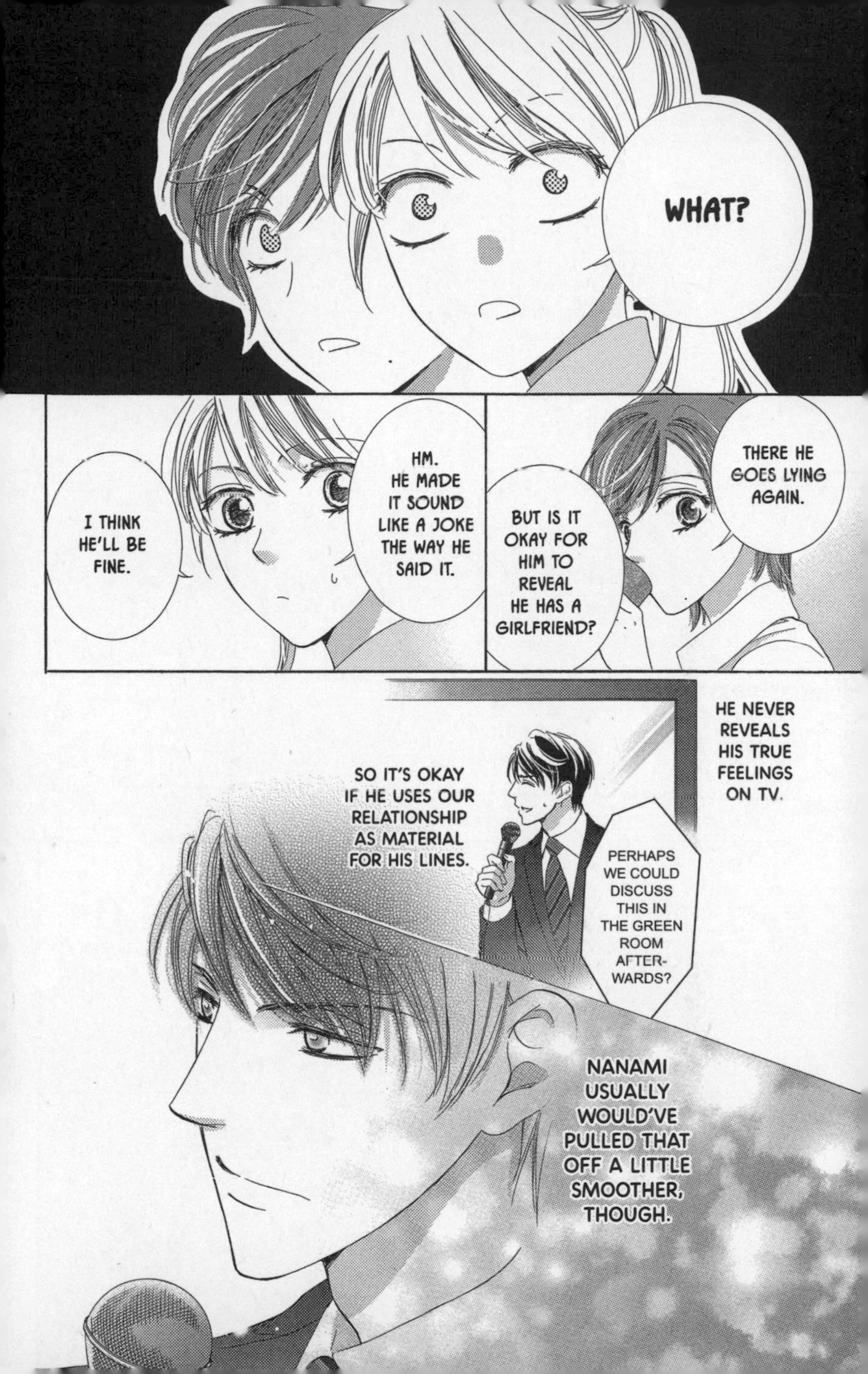
WHAT?
THERE HE GOES LYING AGAIN.
BUT IS IT OKAY FOR HIM TO REVEAL HE HAS A GIRLFRIEND?
HM. HE MADE IT SOUND LIKE A JOKE THE WAY HE SAID IT.
I THINK HE'LL BE FINE.
HE NEVER REVEALS HIS TRUE FEELINGS ON TV.
PERHAPS WE COULD DISCUSS THIS IN THE GREEN ROOM AFTER-WARDS?
SO IT'S OKAY IF HE USES OUR RELATIONSHIP AS MATERIAL FOR HIS LINES.
NANAMI USUALLY WOULD'VE PULLED THAT OFF A LITTLE SMOOTHER, THOUGH.

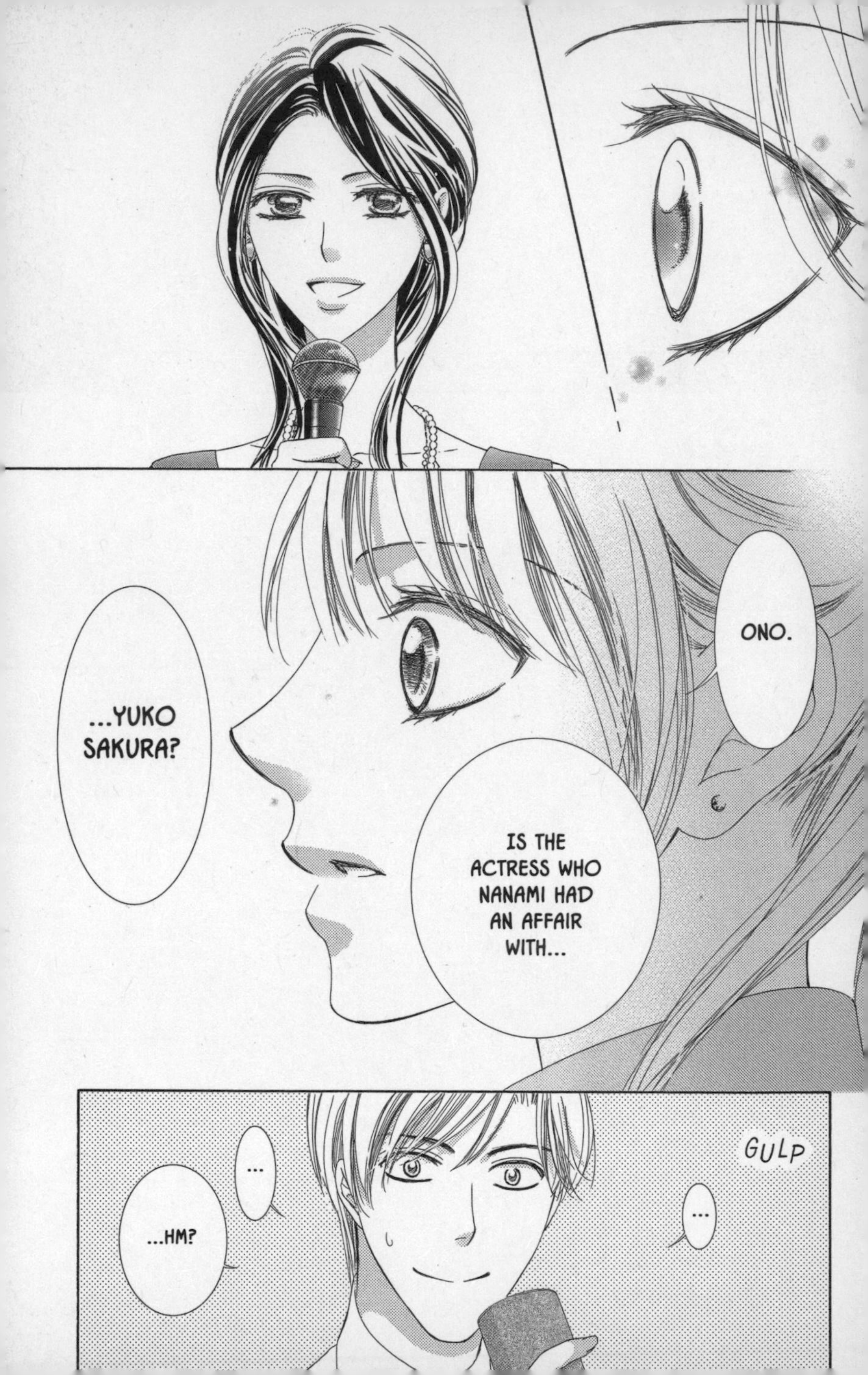
ONO.
IS THE ACTRESS WHO NANAMI HAD AN AFFAIR WITH...
...YUKO SAKURA?
GULP
...
...
...HM?

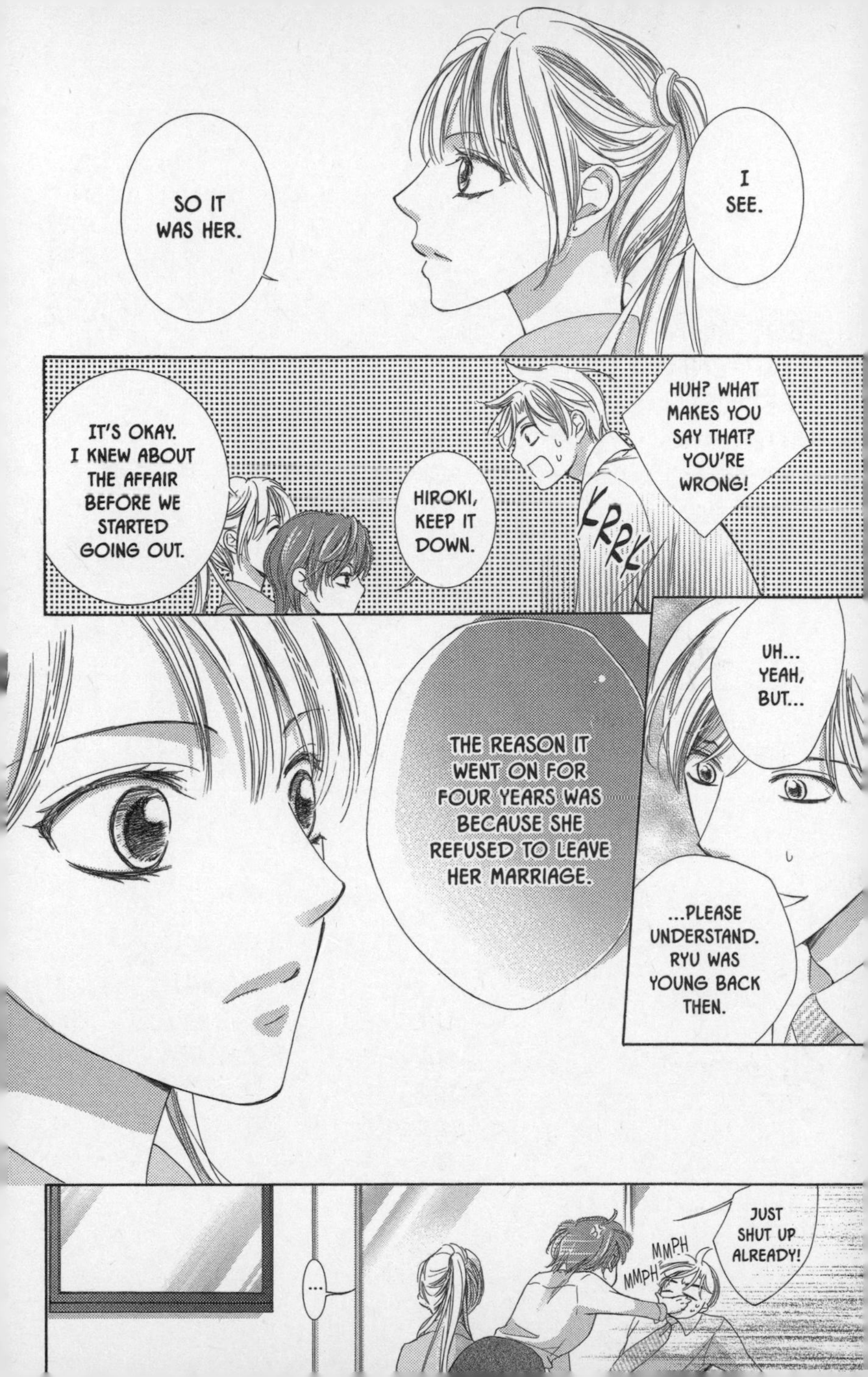
I SEE.
SO IT WAS HER.
HUH? WHAT MAKES YOU SAY THAT? YOU'RE WRONG!
KRRK
HIROKI, KEEP IT DOWN.
IT'S OKAY. I KNEW ABOUT THE AFFAIR BEFORE WE STARTED GOING OUT.
UH... YEAH, BUT...
...PLEASE UNDERSTAND. RYU WAS YOUNG BACK THEN.
THE REASON IT WENT ON FOR FOUR YEARS WAS BECAUSE SHE REFUSED TO LEAVE HER MARRIAGE.
JUST SHUT UP ALREADY!
MMPH
MMPH
...

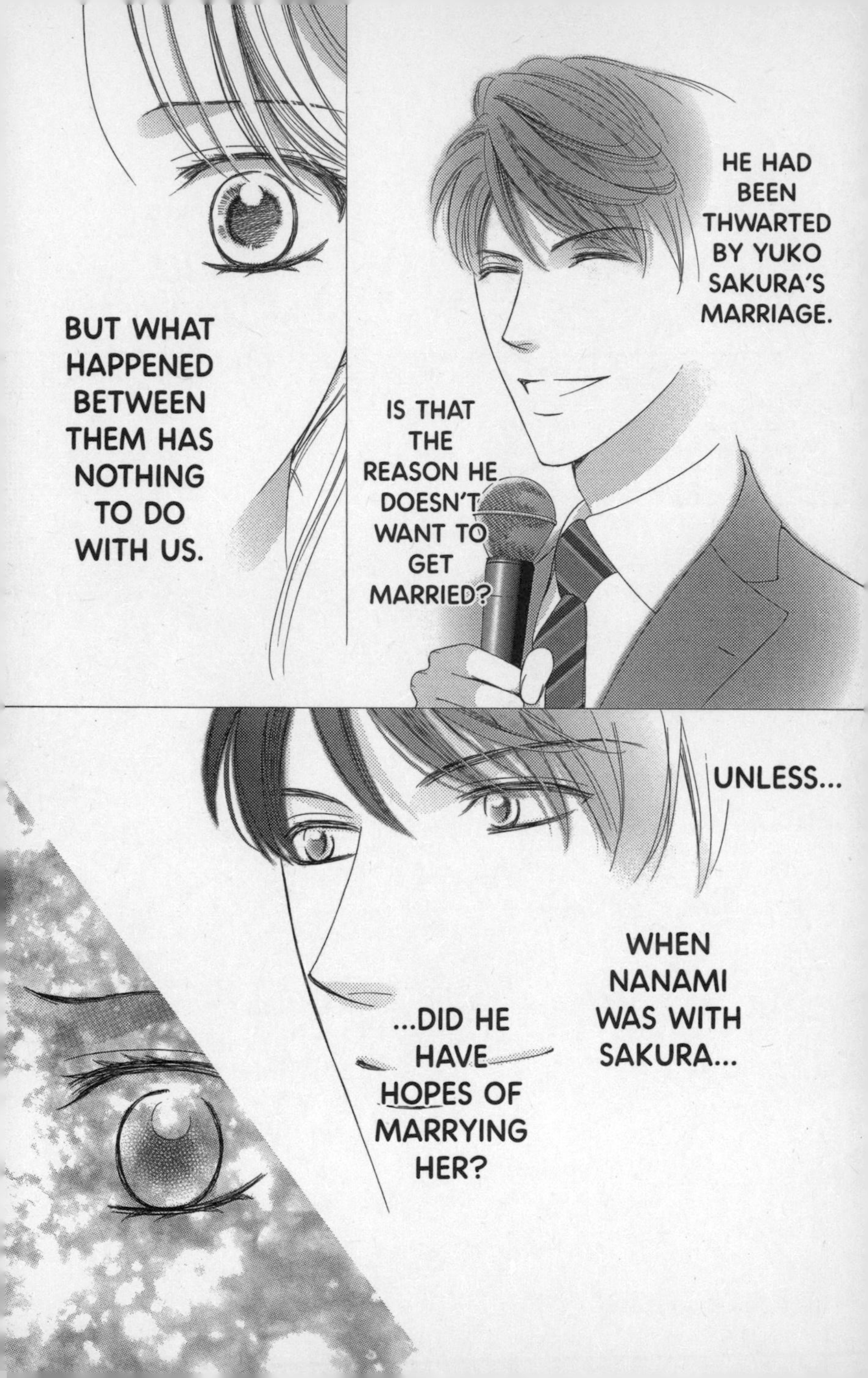
HE HAD BEEN THWARTED BY YUKO SAKURA'S MARRIAGE.
IS THAT THE REASON HE DOESN'T WANT TO GET MARRIED?
BUT WHAT HAPPENED BETWEEN THEM HAS NOTHING TO DO WITH US.
UNLESS...
WHEN NANAMI WAS WITH SAKURA...
...DID HE HAVE HOPES OF MARRYING HER?

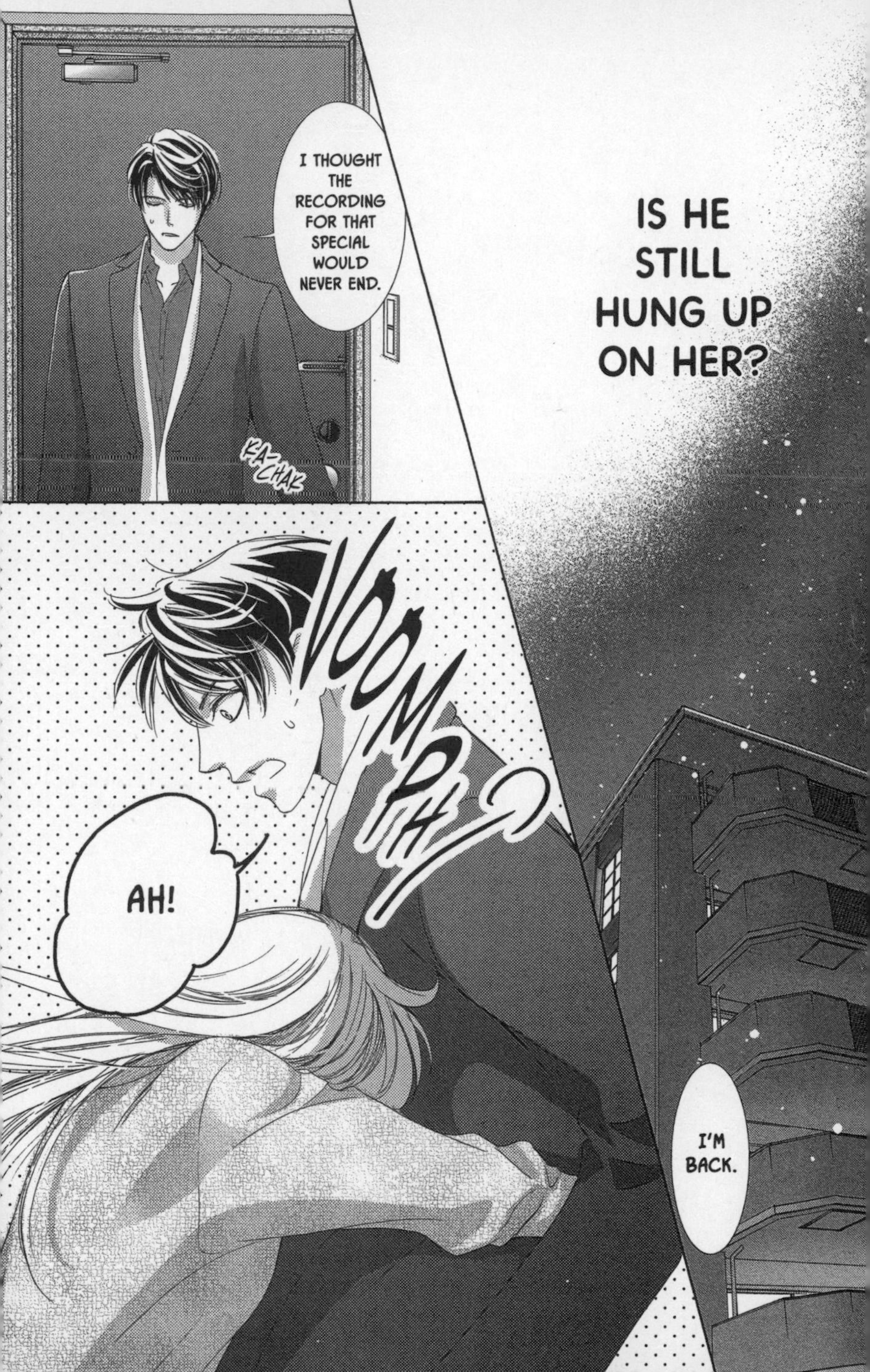
IS HE STILL HUNG UP ON HER?
I'M BACK.
I THOUGHT THE RECORDING FOR THAT SPECIAL WOULD NEVER END.
KA-CHAK
VOOMPH
AH!

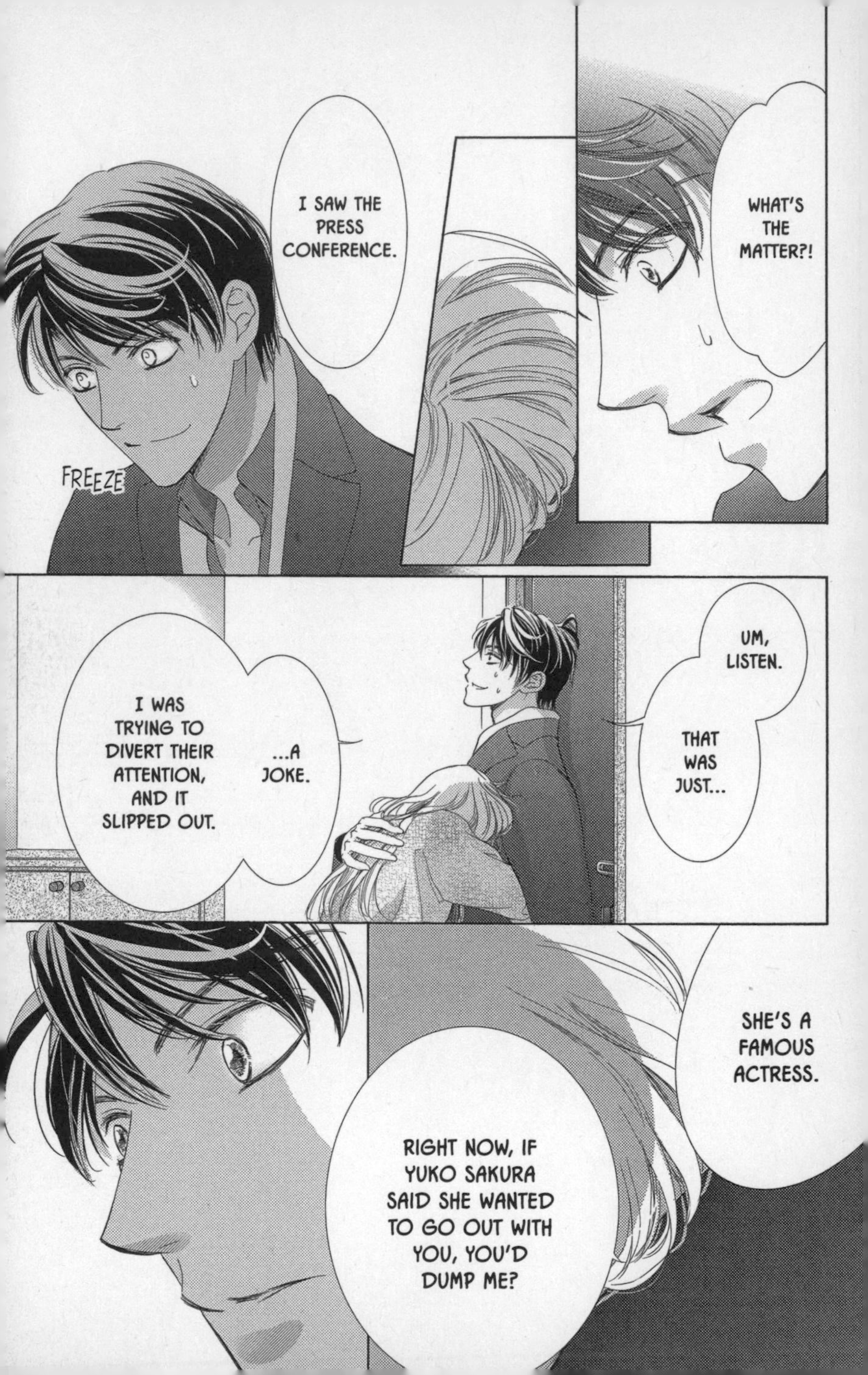
WHAT'S THE MATTER?!
I SAW THE PRESS CONFERENCE.
FREEZE
UM, LISTEN.
THAT WAS JUST...
...A JOKE.
I WAS TRYING TO DIVERT THEIR ATTENTION, AND IT SLIPPED OUT.
SHE'S A FAMOUS ACTRESS.
RIGHT NOW, IF YUKO SAKURA SAID SHE WANTED TO GO OUT WITH YOU, YOU'D DUMP ME?

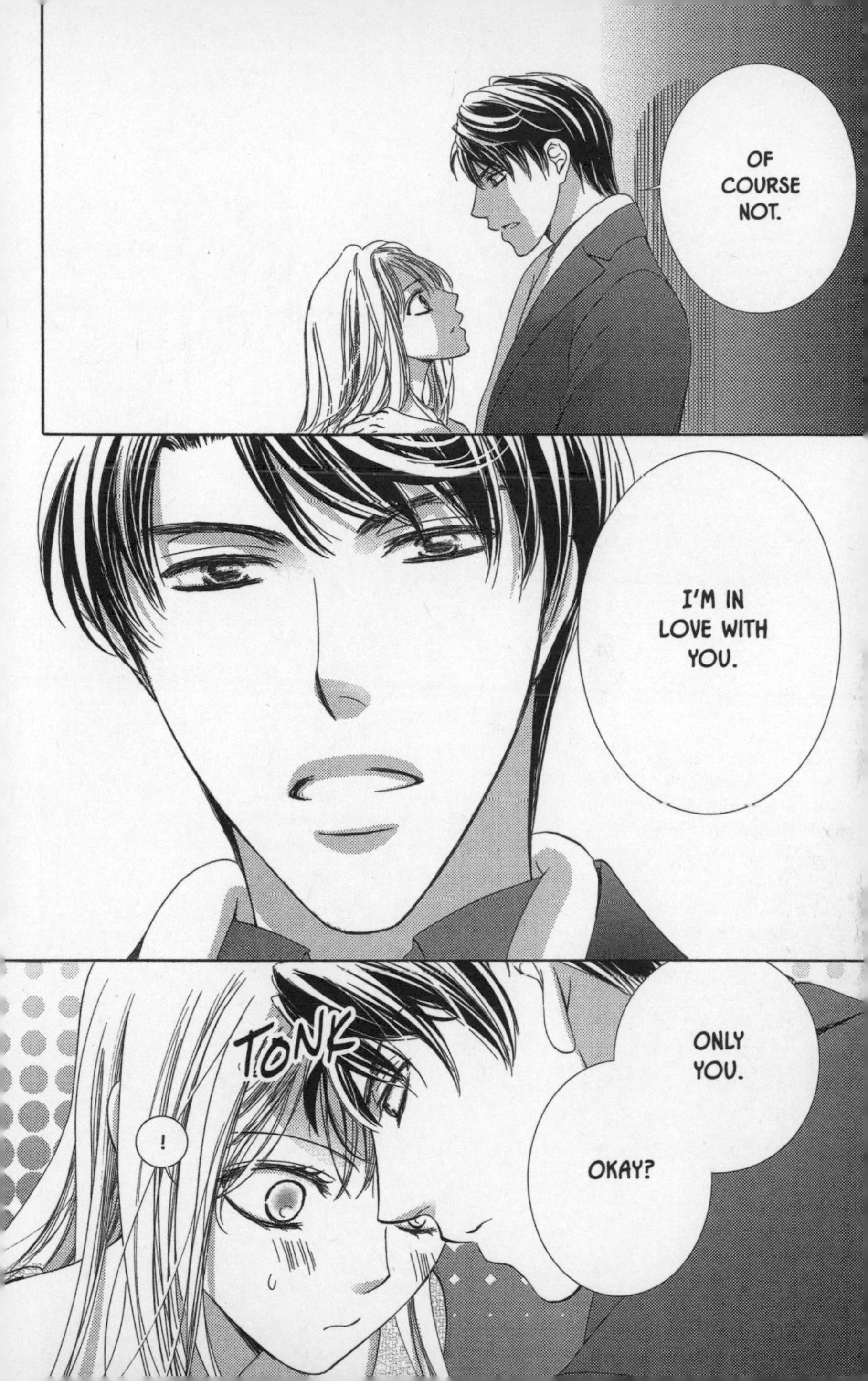
OF COURSE NOT.
I'M IN LOVE WITH YOU.
ONLY YOU.
TONK
!
OKAY?

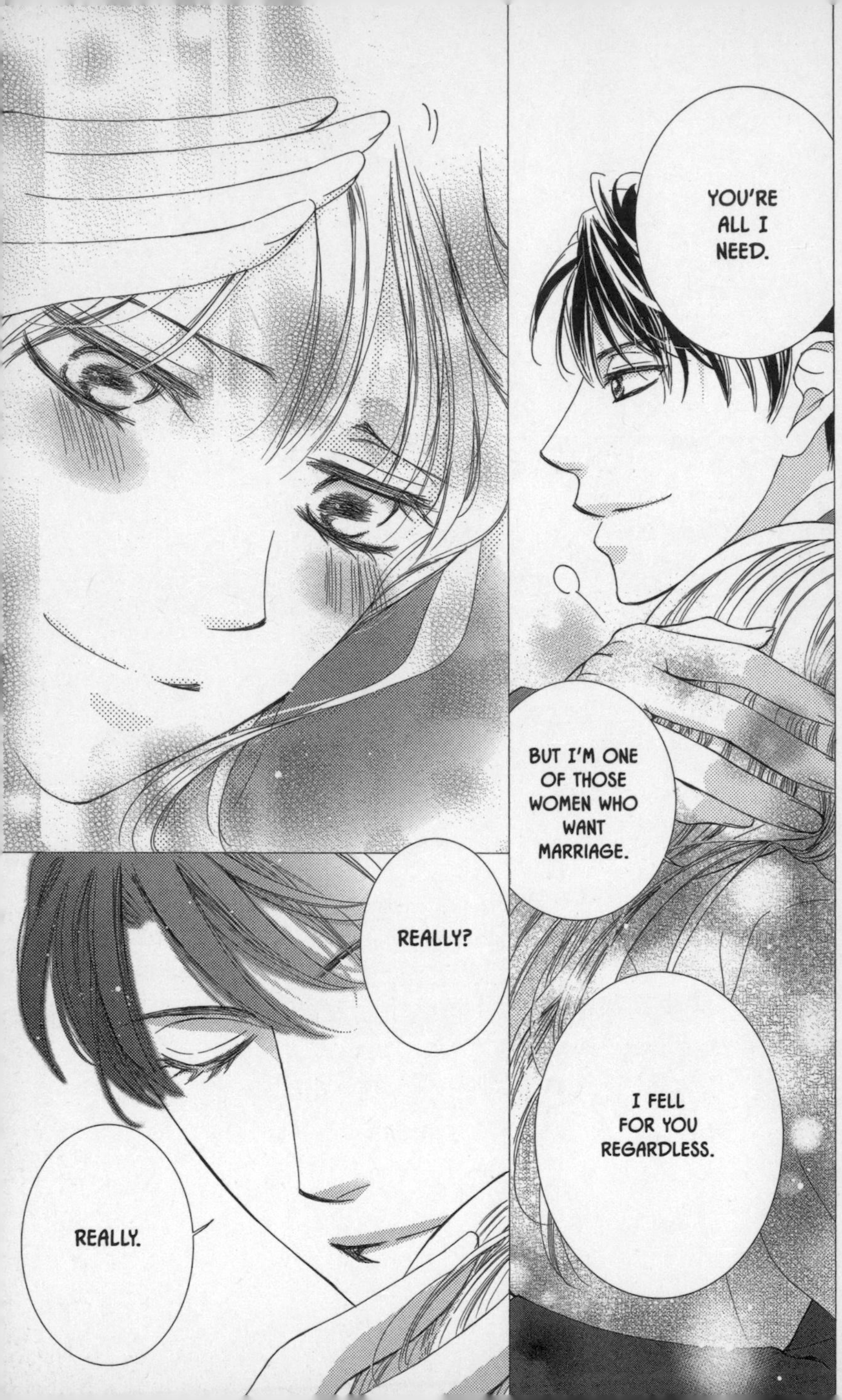
YOU'RE ALL I NEED.
BUT I'M ONE OF THOSE WOMEN WHO WANT MARRIAGE.
I FELL FOR YOU REGARDLESS.
REALLY?
REALLY.

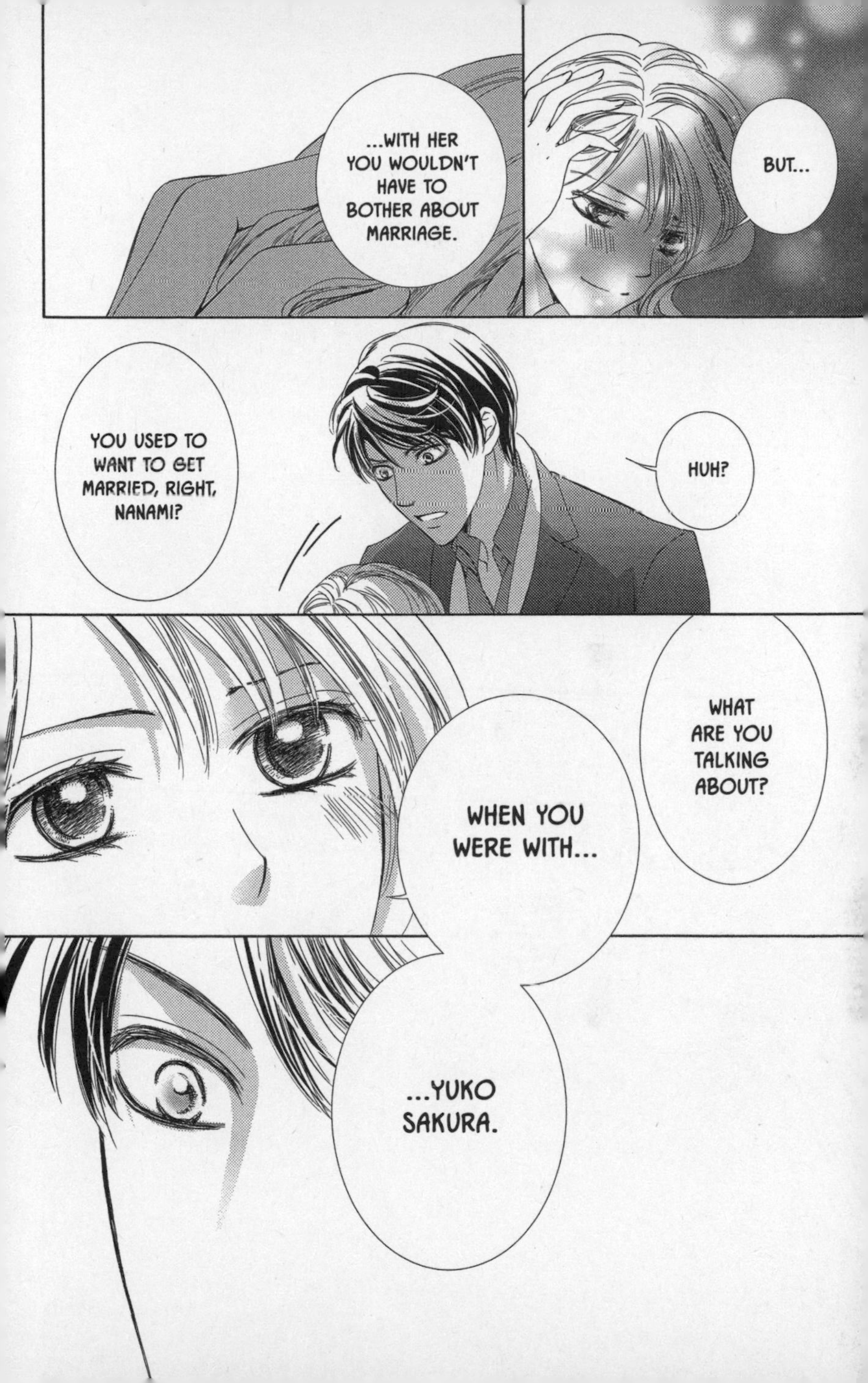
BUT...
...WITH HER YOU WOULDN'T HAVE TO BOTHER ABOUT MARRIAGE.
YOU USED TO WANT TO GET MARRIED, RIGHT, NANAMI?
HUH?
WHAT ARE YOU TALKING ABOUT?
WHEN YOU WERE WITH...
...YUKO SAKURA.

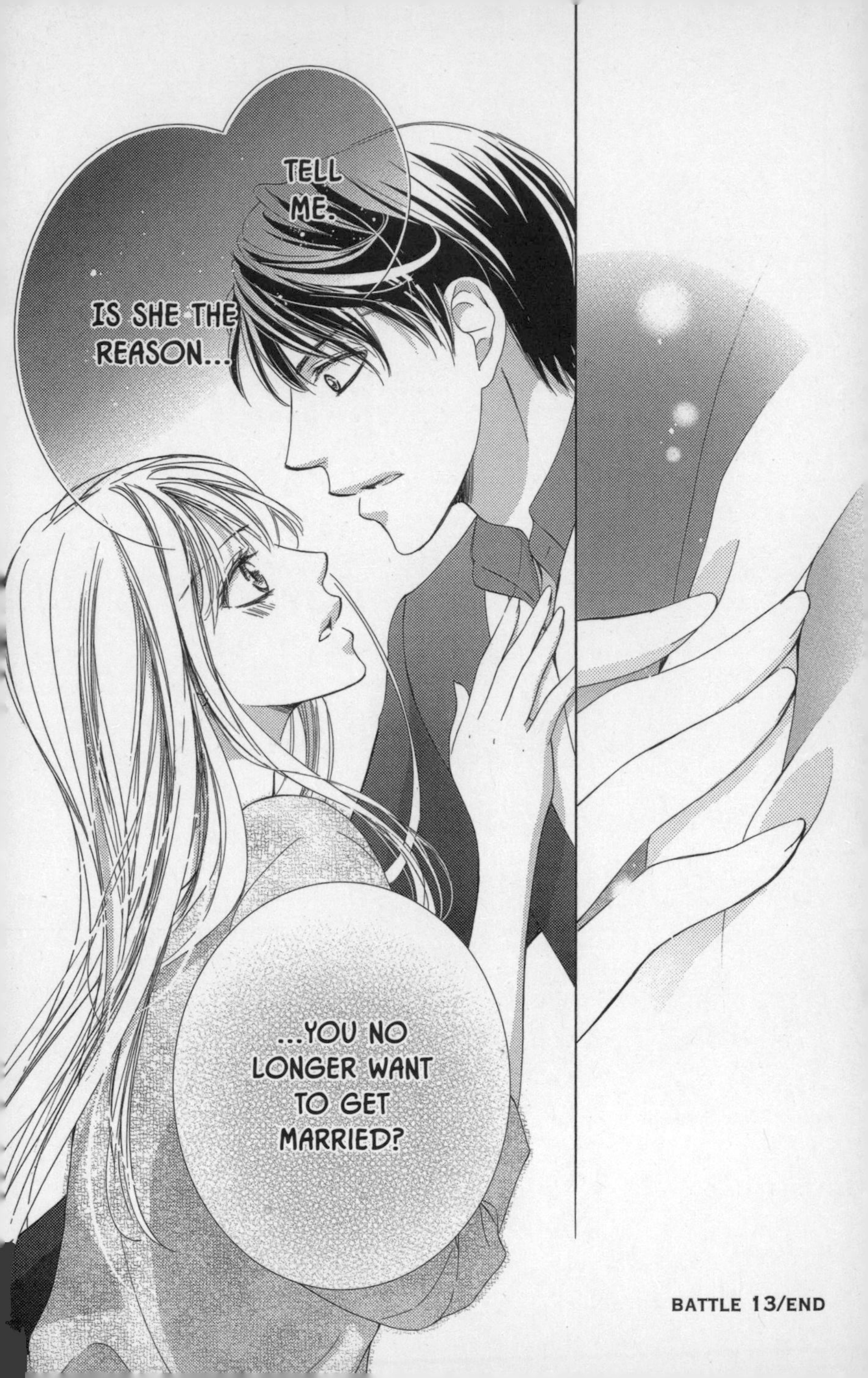
TELL ME.
IS SHE THE REASON...
...YOU NO LONGER WANT TO GET MARRIED?

BATTLE 13/END

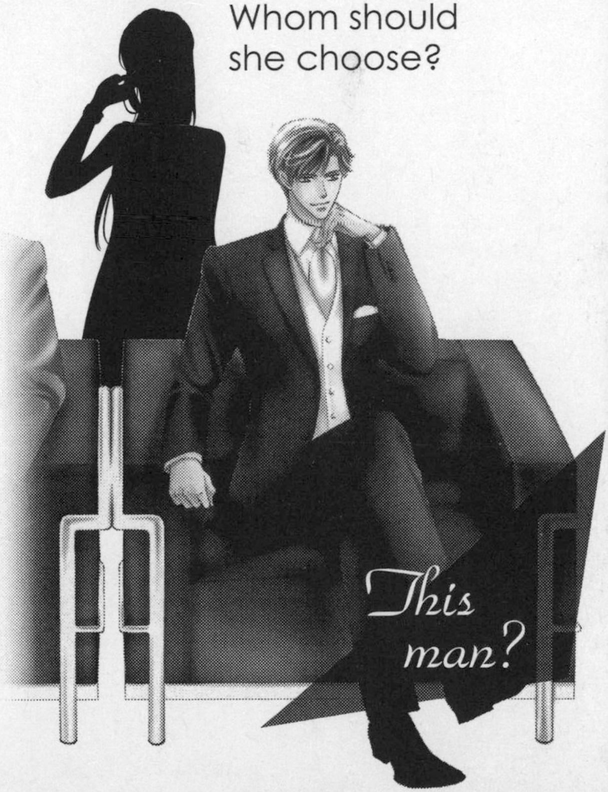
Whom should
she choose?
This
man?

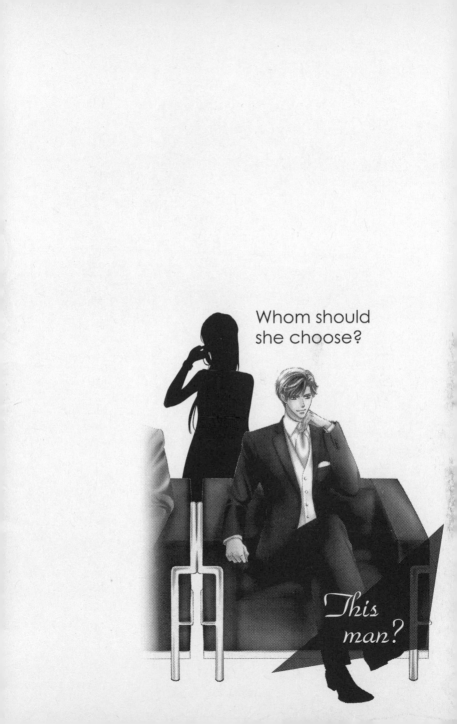

BATTLE 14:
We only love women we can make happy.

–Marcel Achard

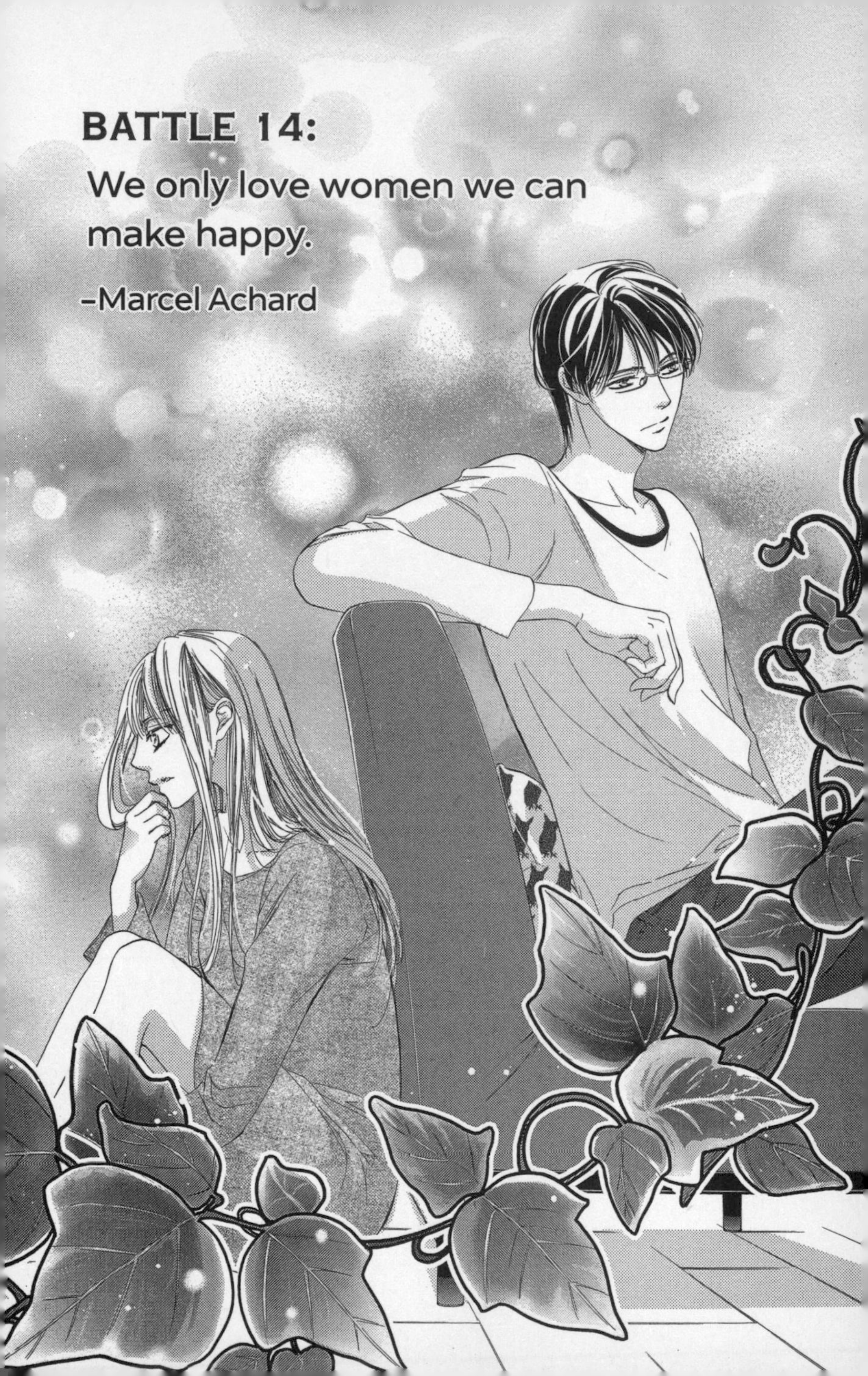

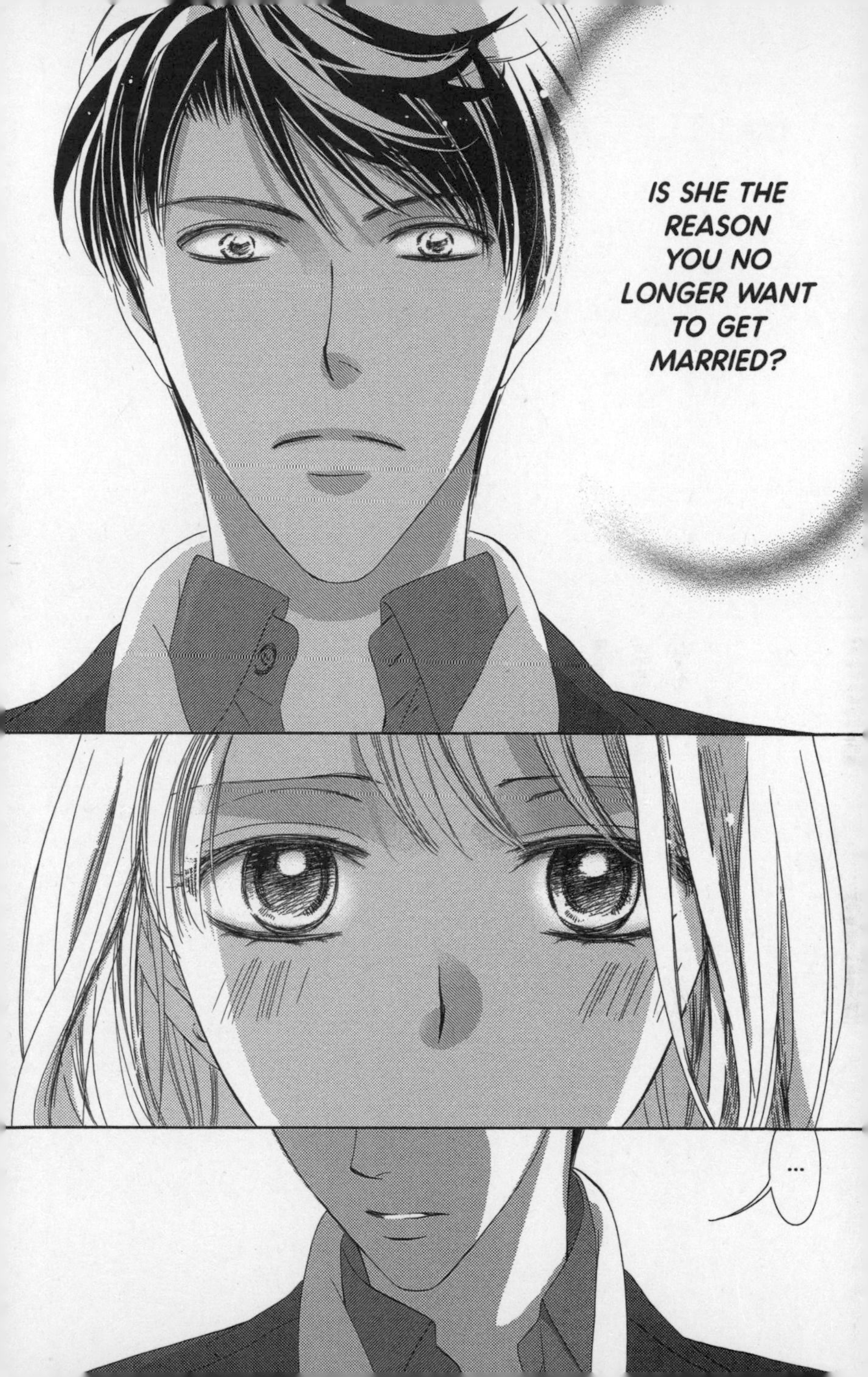
IS SHE THE REASON YOU NO LONGER WANT TO GET MARRIED?
...

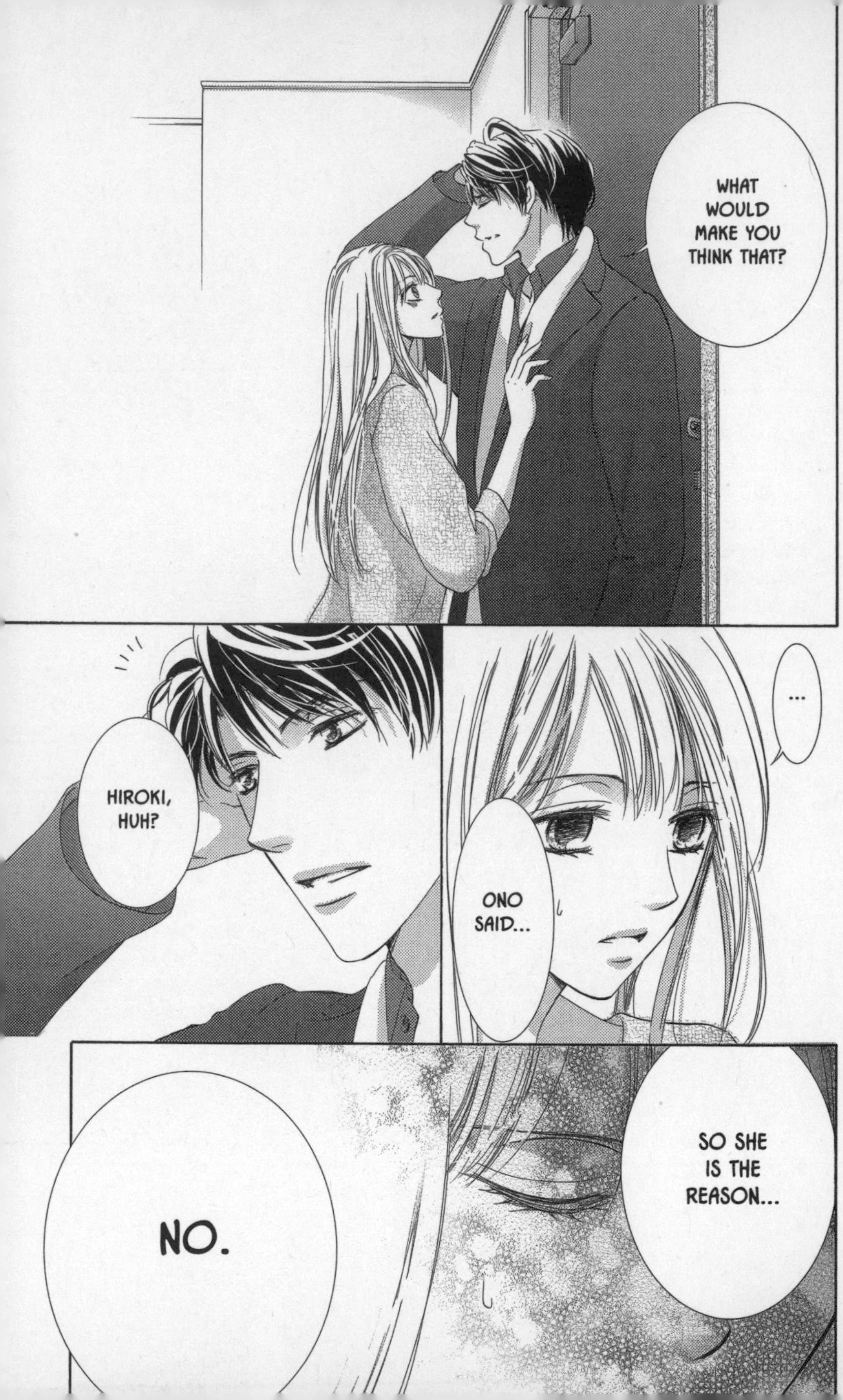
WHAT WOULD MAKE YOU THINK THAT?
...
ONO SAID...
HIROKI, HUH?
SO SHE IS THE REASON...
NO.

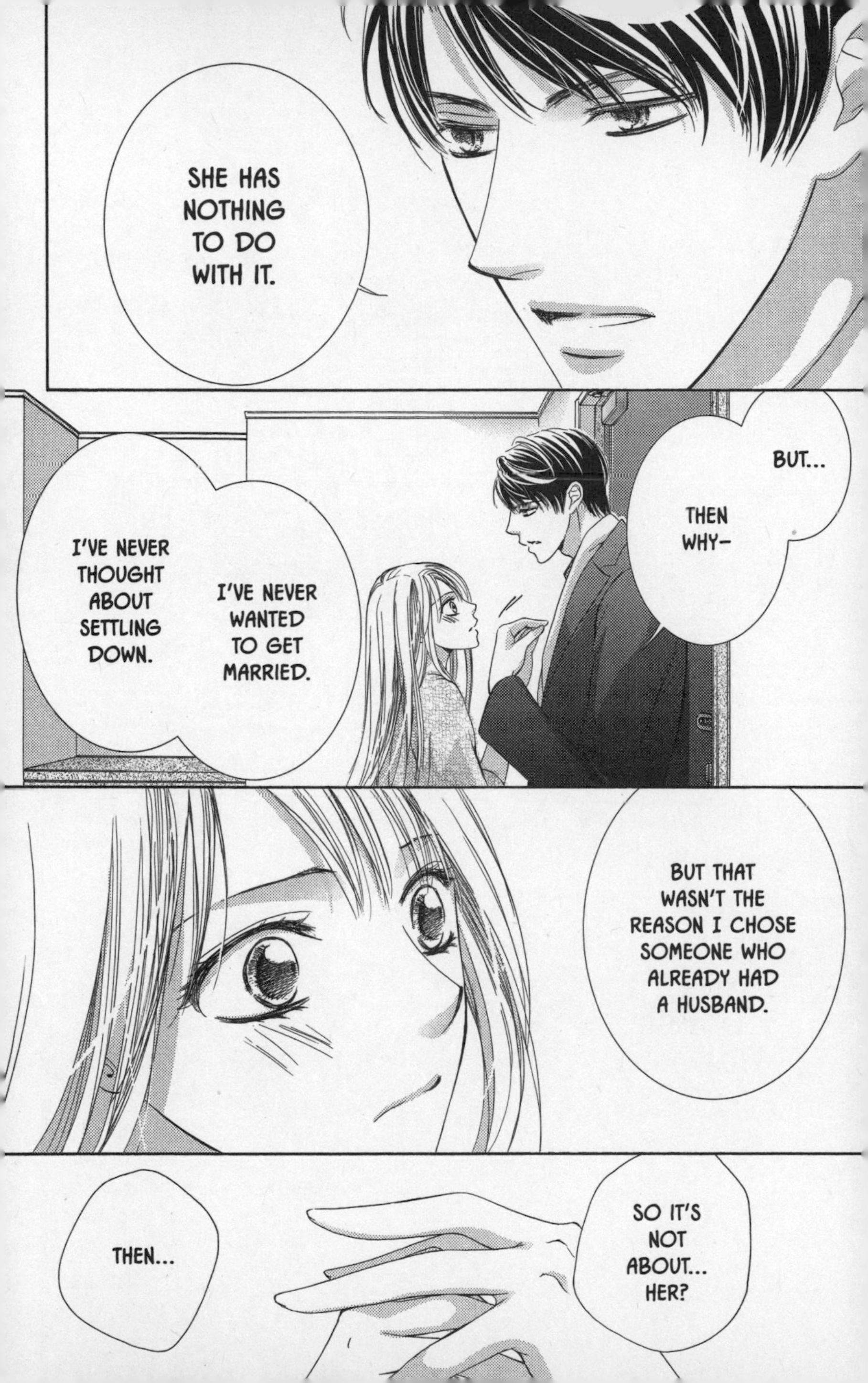
SHE HAS NOTHING TO DO WITH IT.
BUT...
THEN WHY–
I'VE NEVER WANTED TO GET MARRIED.
I'VE NEVER THOUGHT ABOUT SETTLING DOWN.
BUT THAT WASN'T THE REASON I CHOSE SOMEONE WHO ALREADY HAD A HUSBAND.
SO IT'S NOT ABOUT... HER?
THEN...

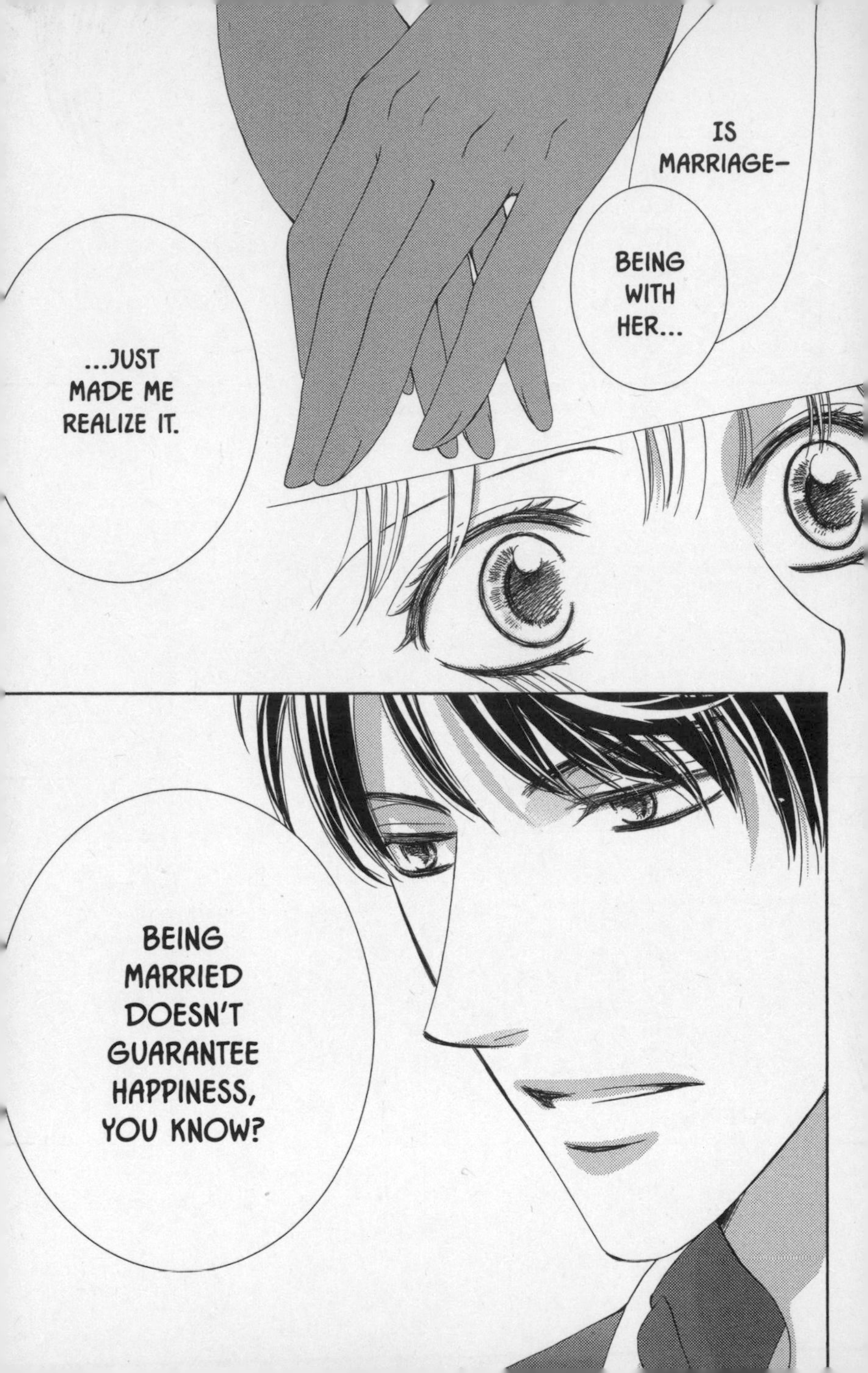
IS MARRIAGE—
BEING WITH HER...
...JUST MADE ME REALIZE IT.
BEING MARRIED DOESN'T GUARANTEE HAPPINESS, YOU KNOW?

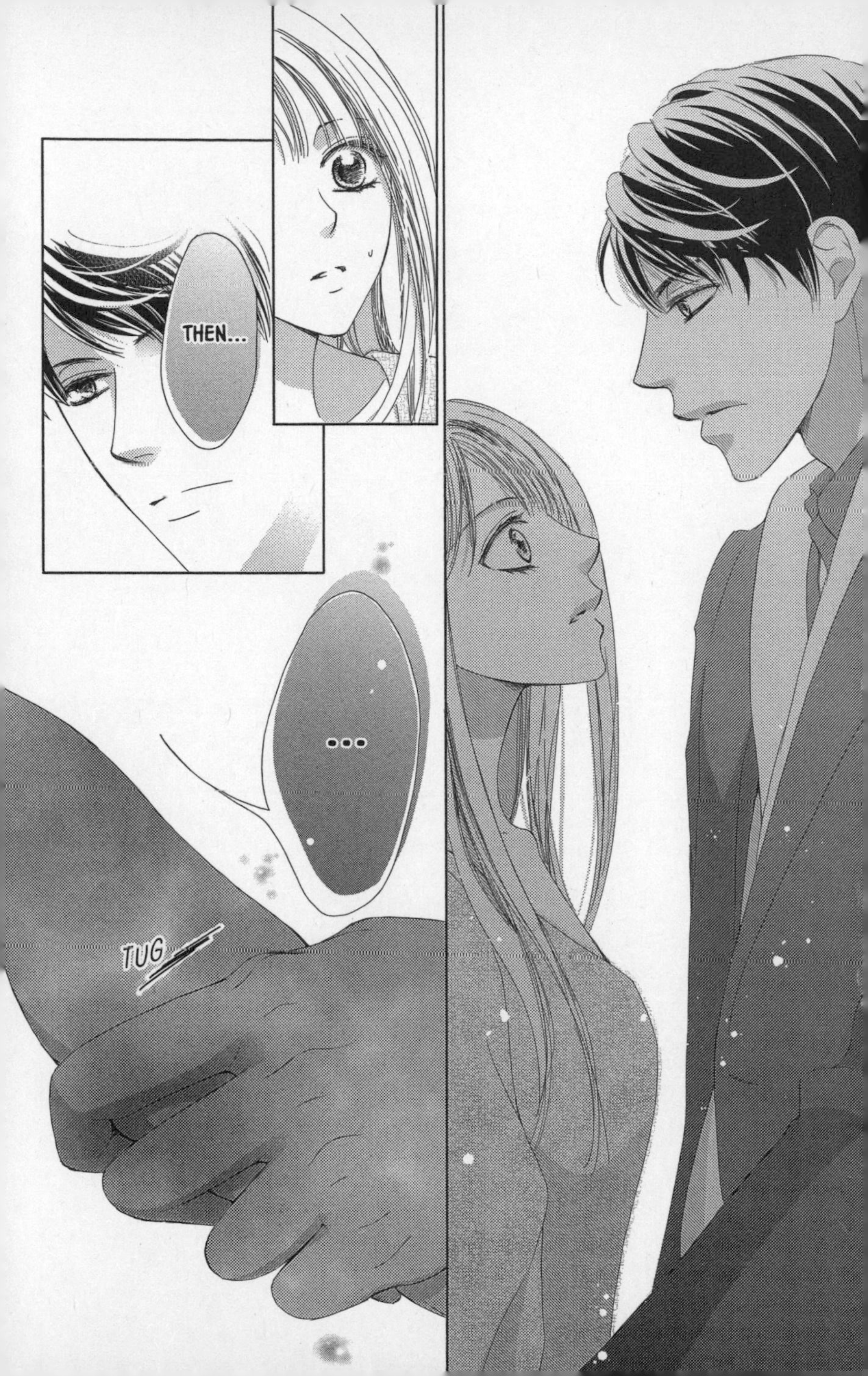
THEN...
...
TUG

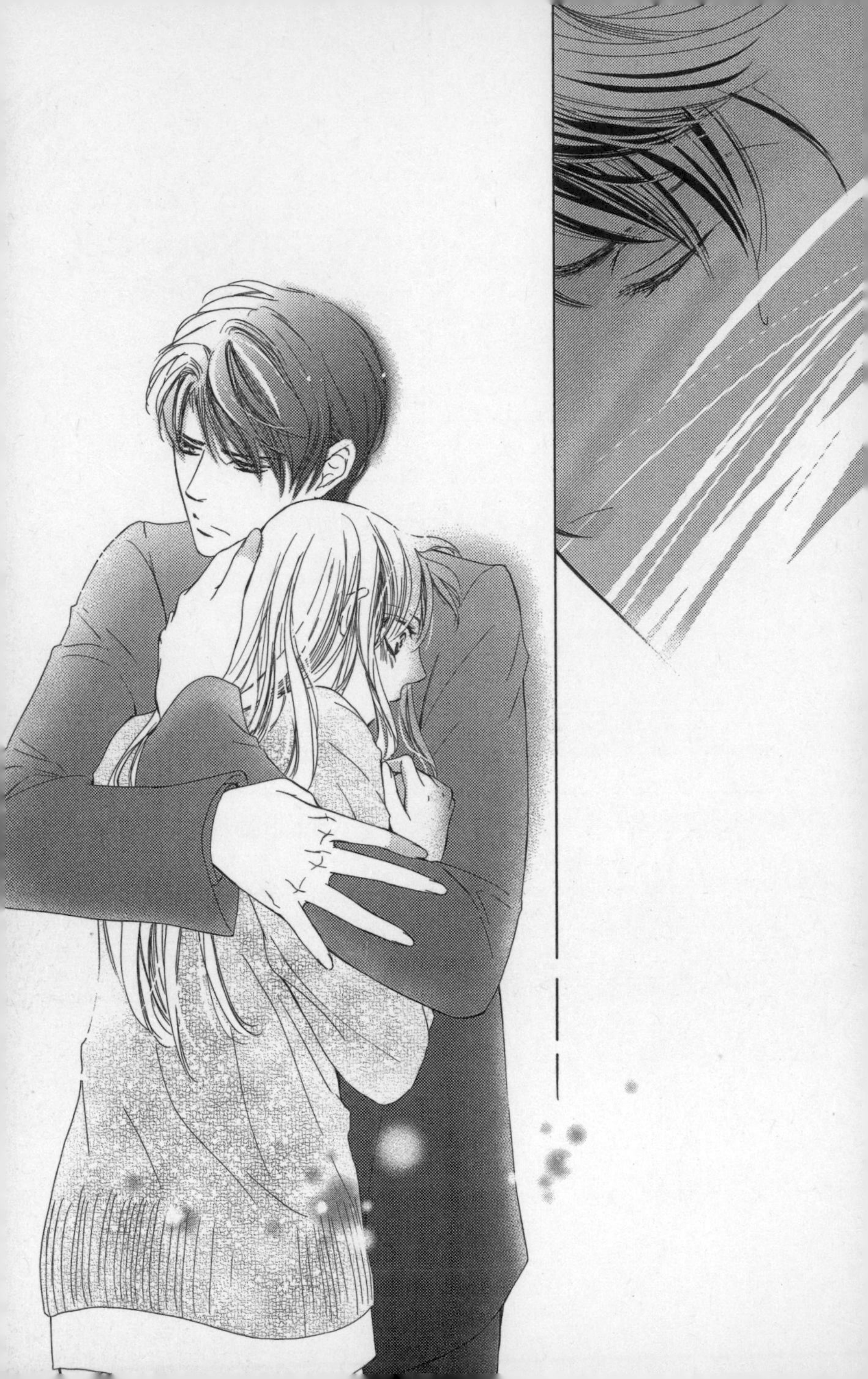

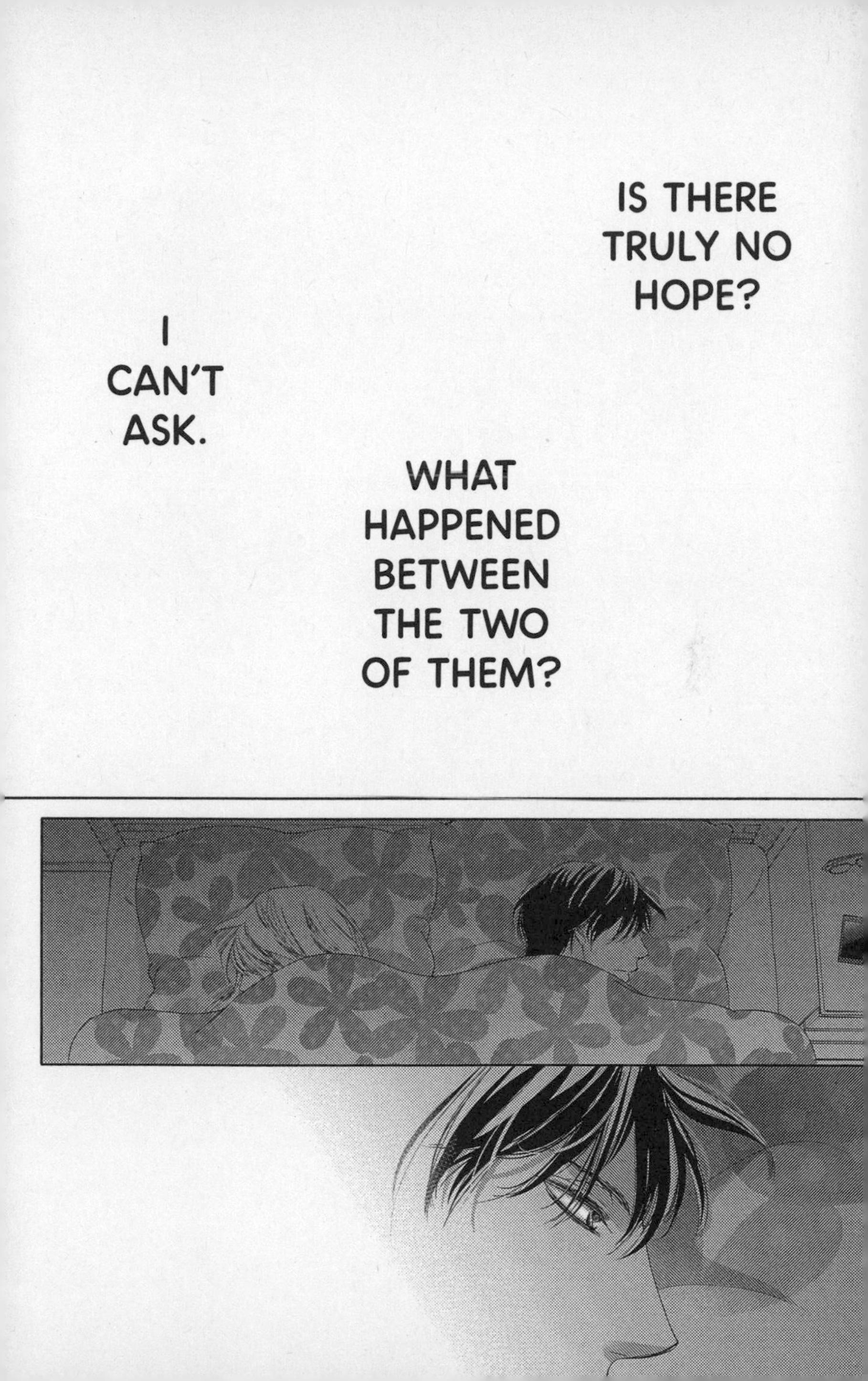
IS THERE TRULY NO HOPE?
WHAT HAPPENED BETWEEN THE TWO OF THEM?
I CAN'T ASK.

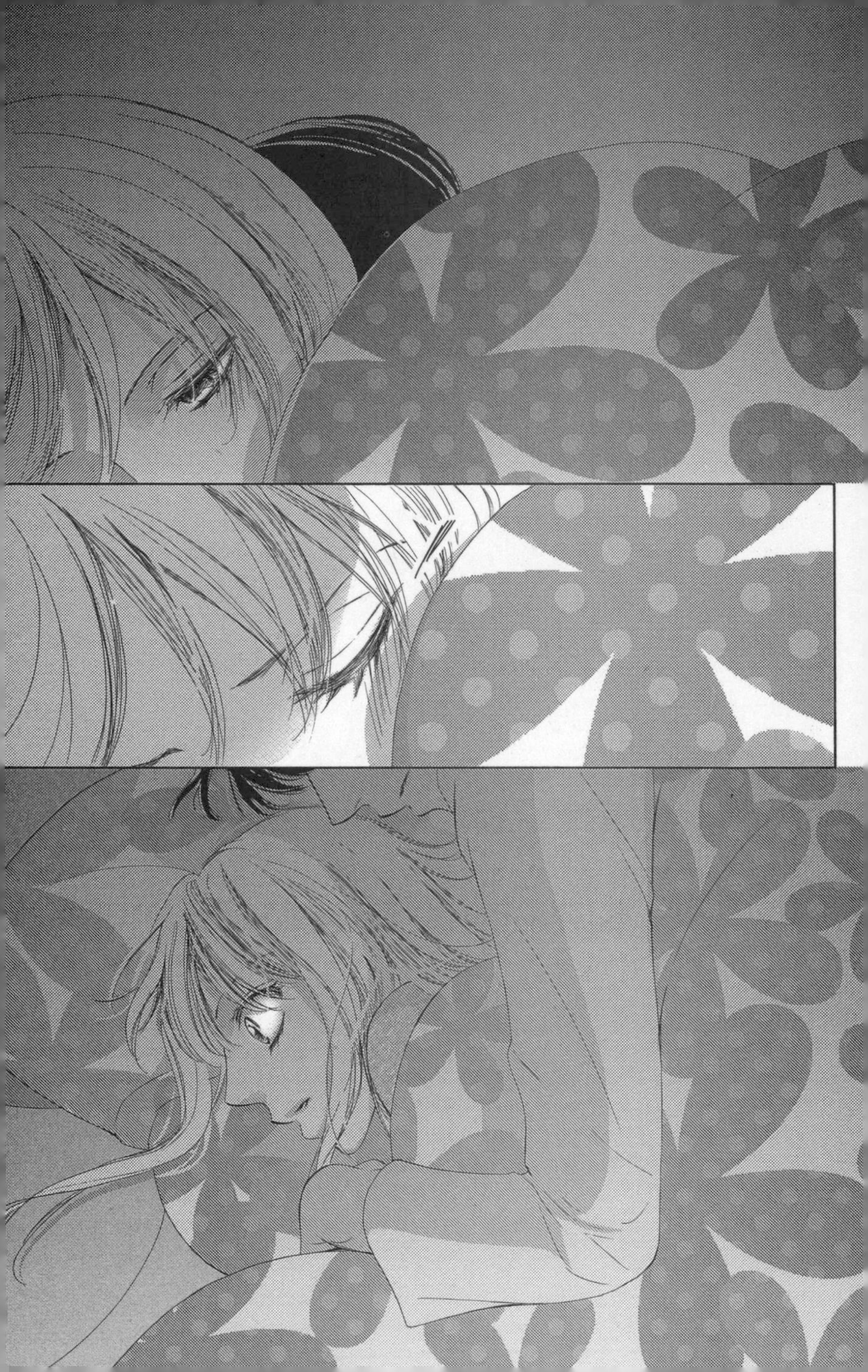

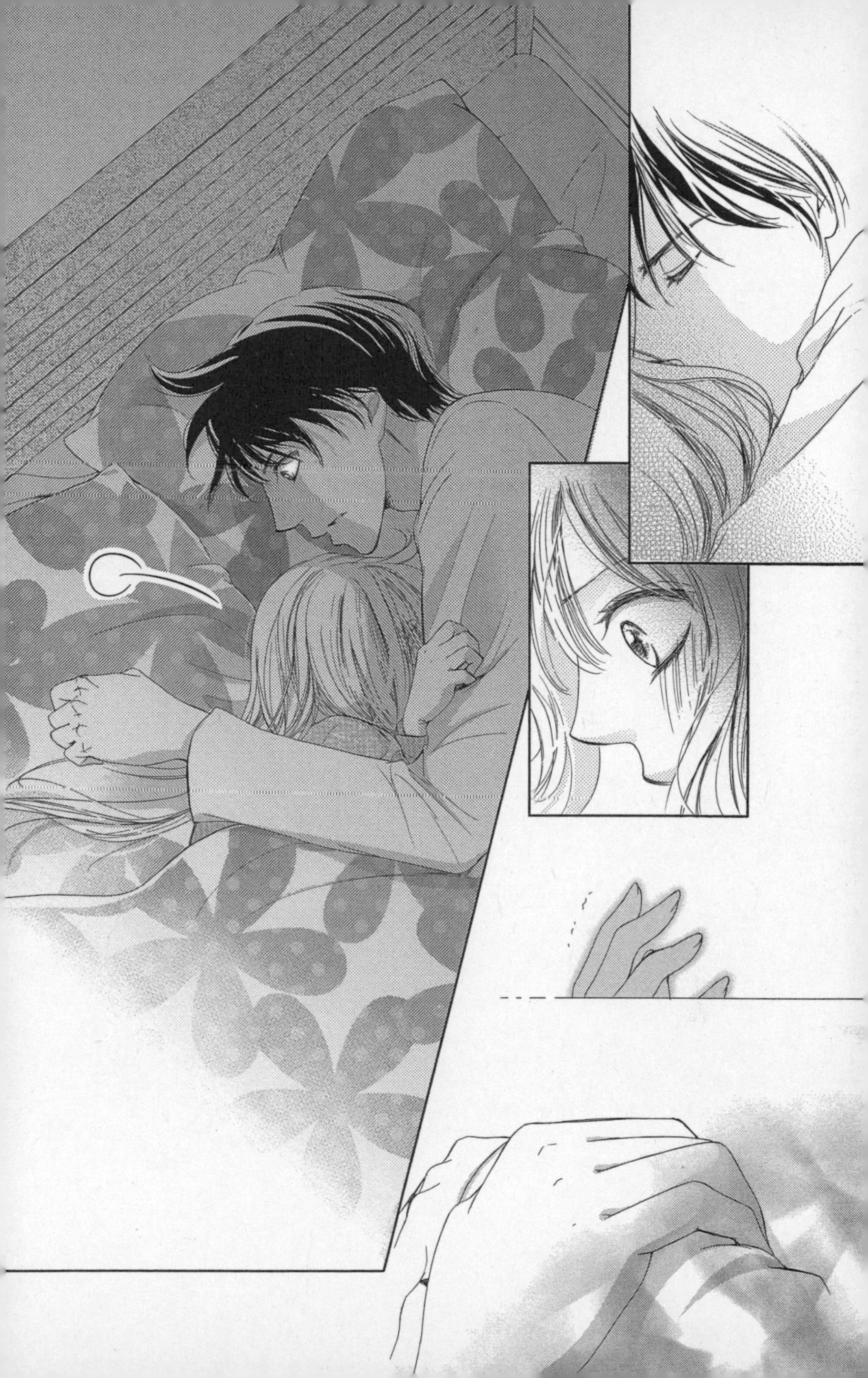

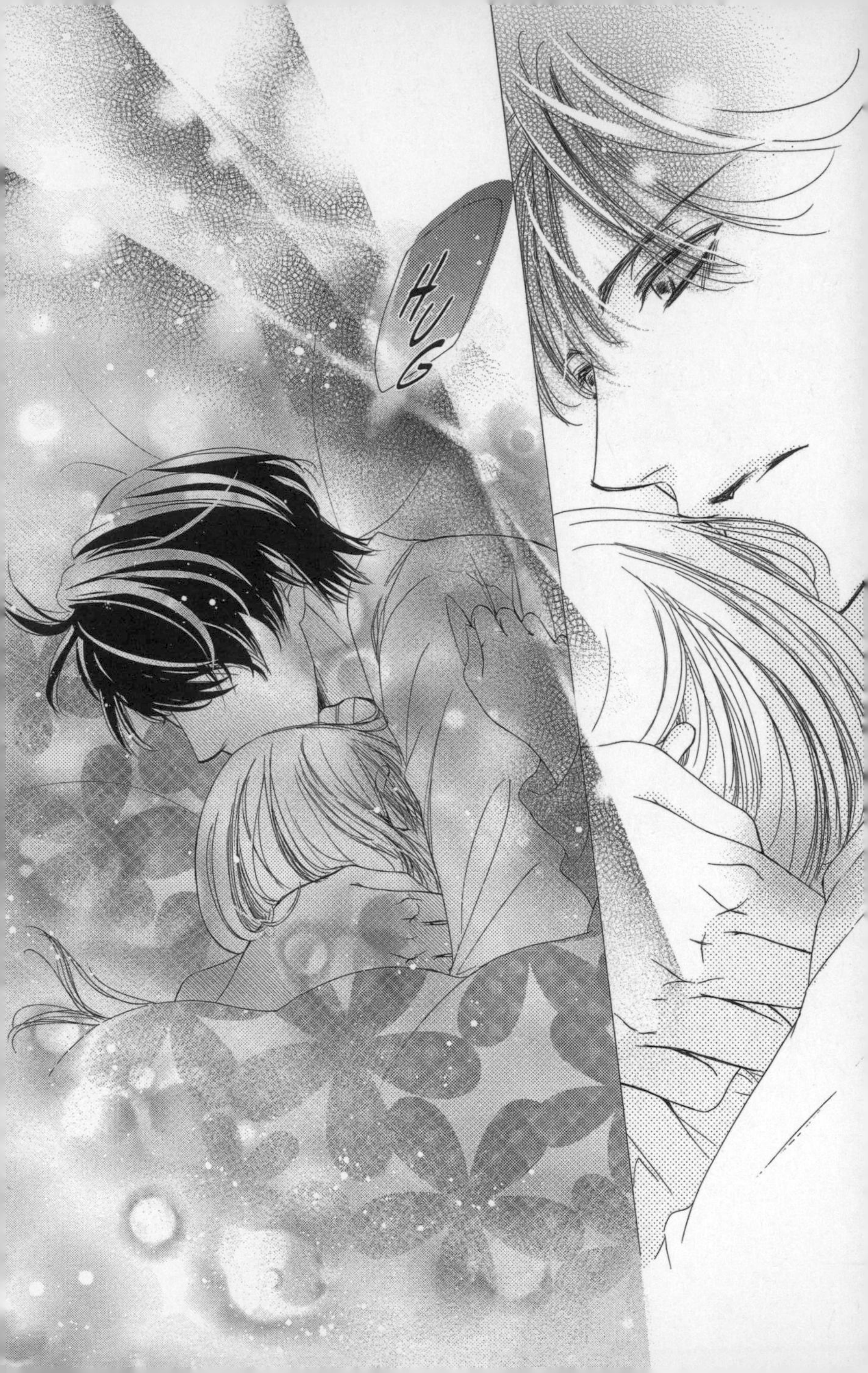
HUG

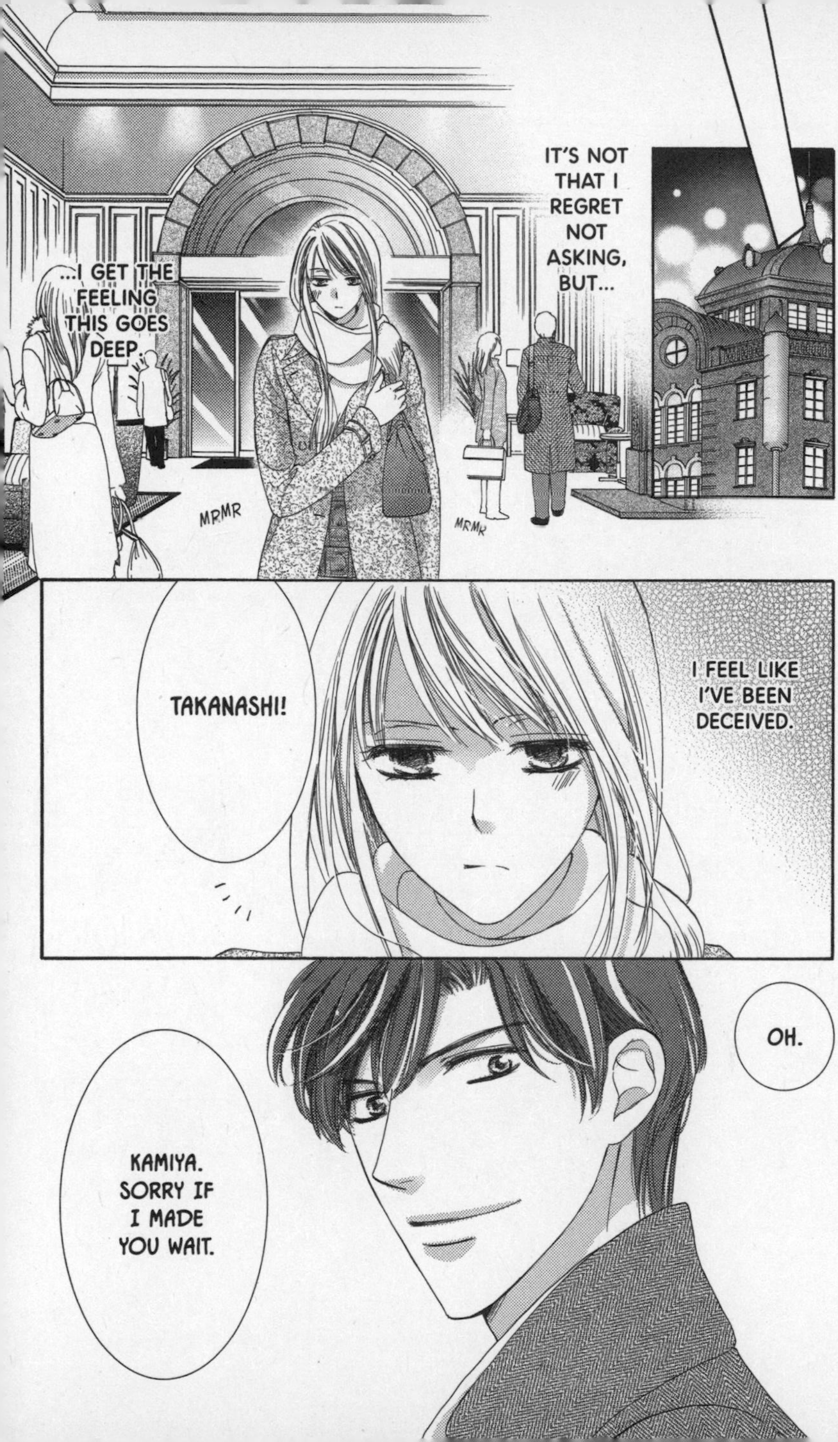
IT'S NOT THAT I REGRET NOT ASKING, BUT...
...I GET THE FEELING THIS GOES DEEP.
MRMR
MRMR
I FEEL LIKE I'VE BEEN DECEIVED.
TAKANASHI!
OH.
KAMIYA. SORRY IF I MADE YOU WAIT.

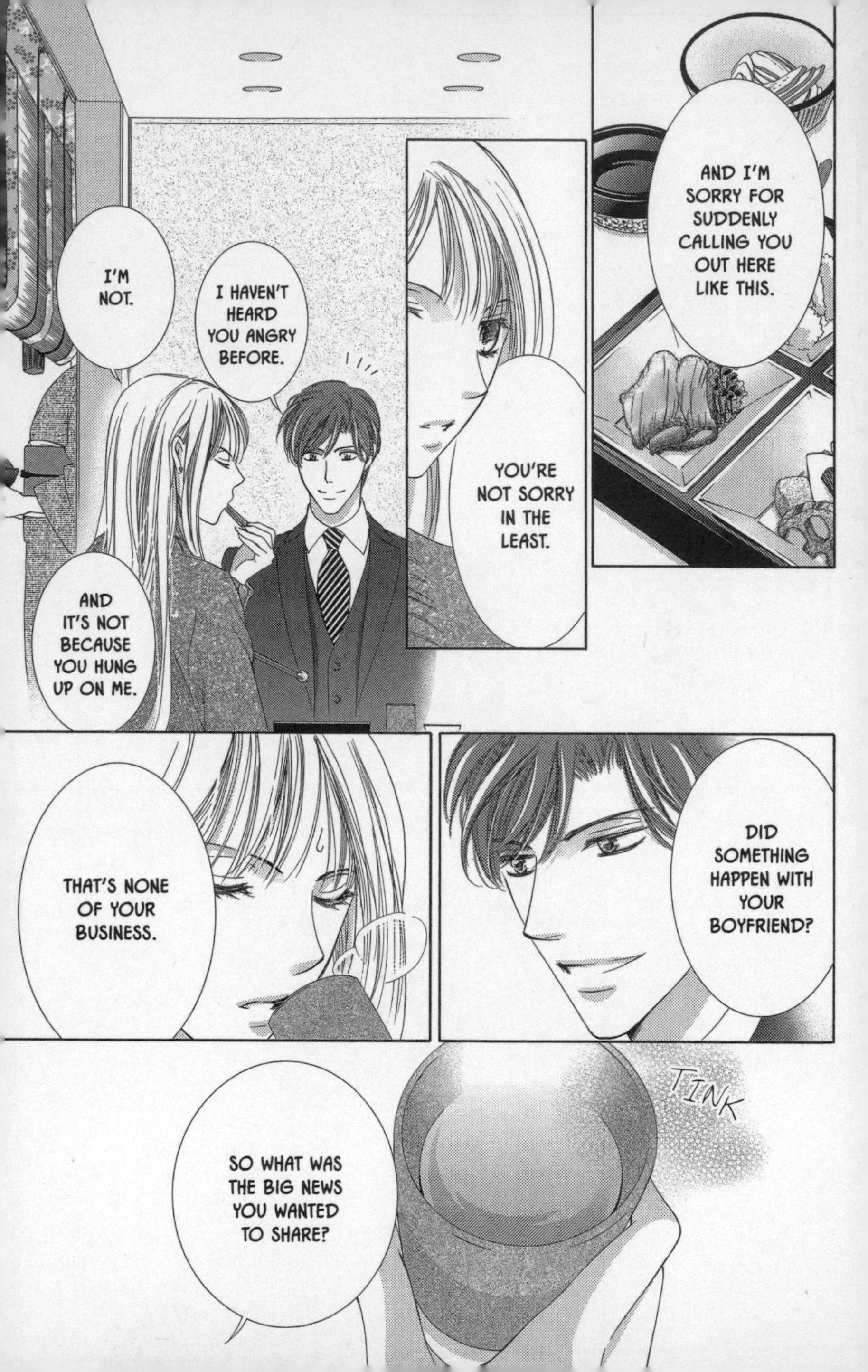
AND I'M SORRY FOR SUDDENLY CALLING YOU OUT HERE LIKE THIS.
YOU'RE NOT SORRY IN THE LEAST.
I HAVEN'T HEARD YOU ANGRY BEFORE.
I'M NOT.
AND IT'S NOT BECAUSE YOU HUNG UP ON ME.
DID SOMETHING HAPPEN WITH YOUR BOYFRIEND?
THAT'S NONE OF YOUR BUSINESS.
TINK
SO WHAT WAS THE BIG NEWS YOU WANTED TO SHARE?

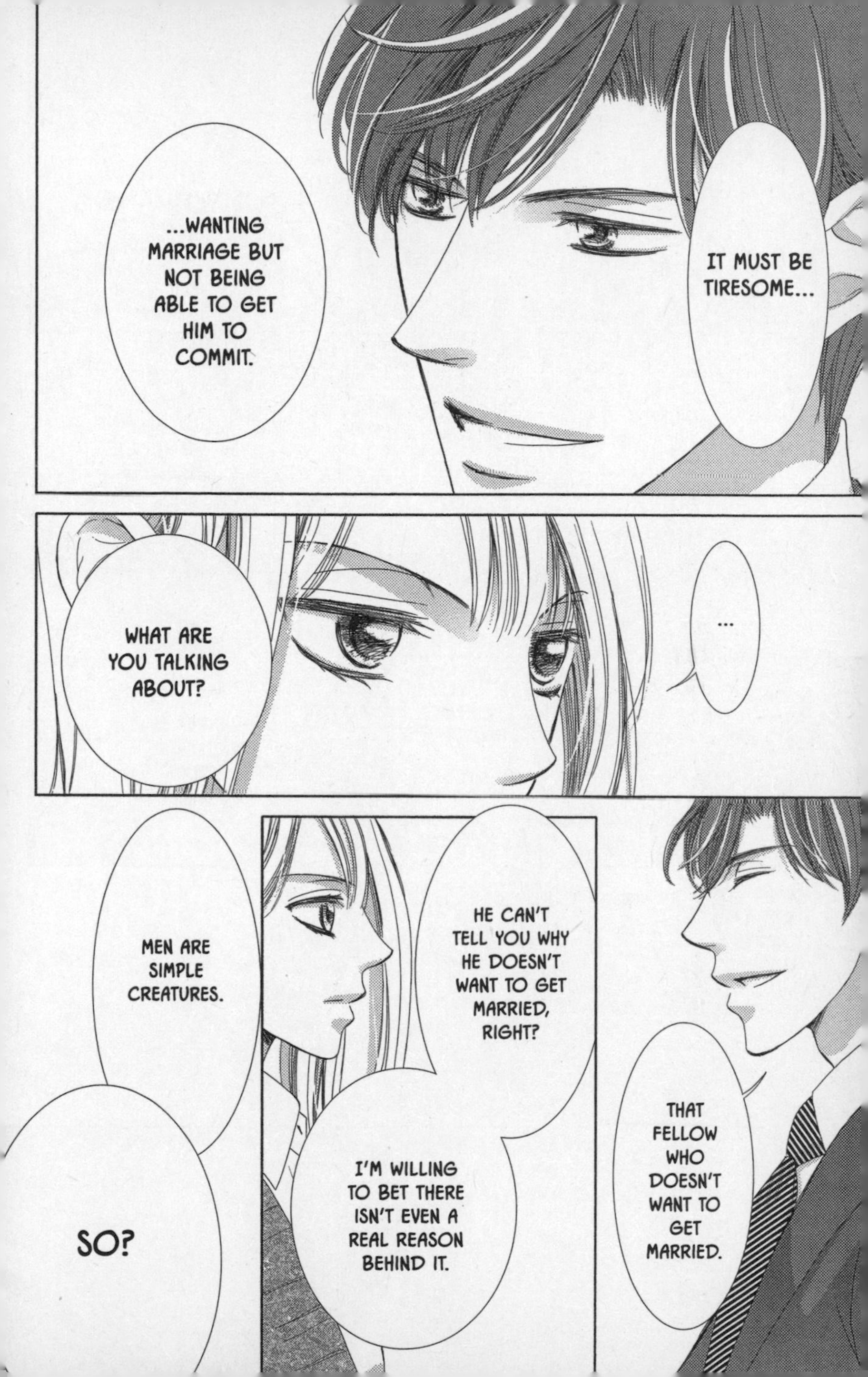
IT MUST BE TIRESOME...
...WANTING MARRIAGE BUT NOT BEING ABLE TO GET HIM TO COMMIT.
...
WHAT ARE YOU TALKING ABOUT?
THAT FELLOW WHO DOESN'T WANT TO GET MARRIED.
HE CAN'T TELL YOU WHY HE DOESN'T WANT TO GET MARRIED, RIGHT?
I'M WILLING TO BET THERE ISN'T EVEN A REAL REASON BEHIND IT.
MEN ARE SIMPLE CREATURES.
SO?

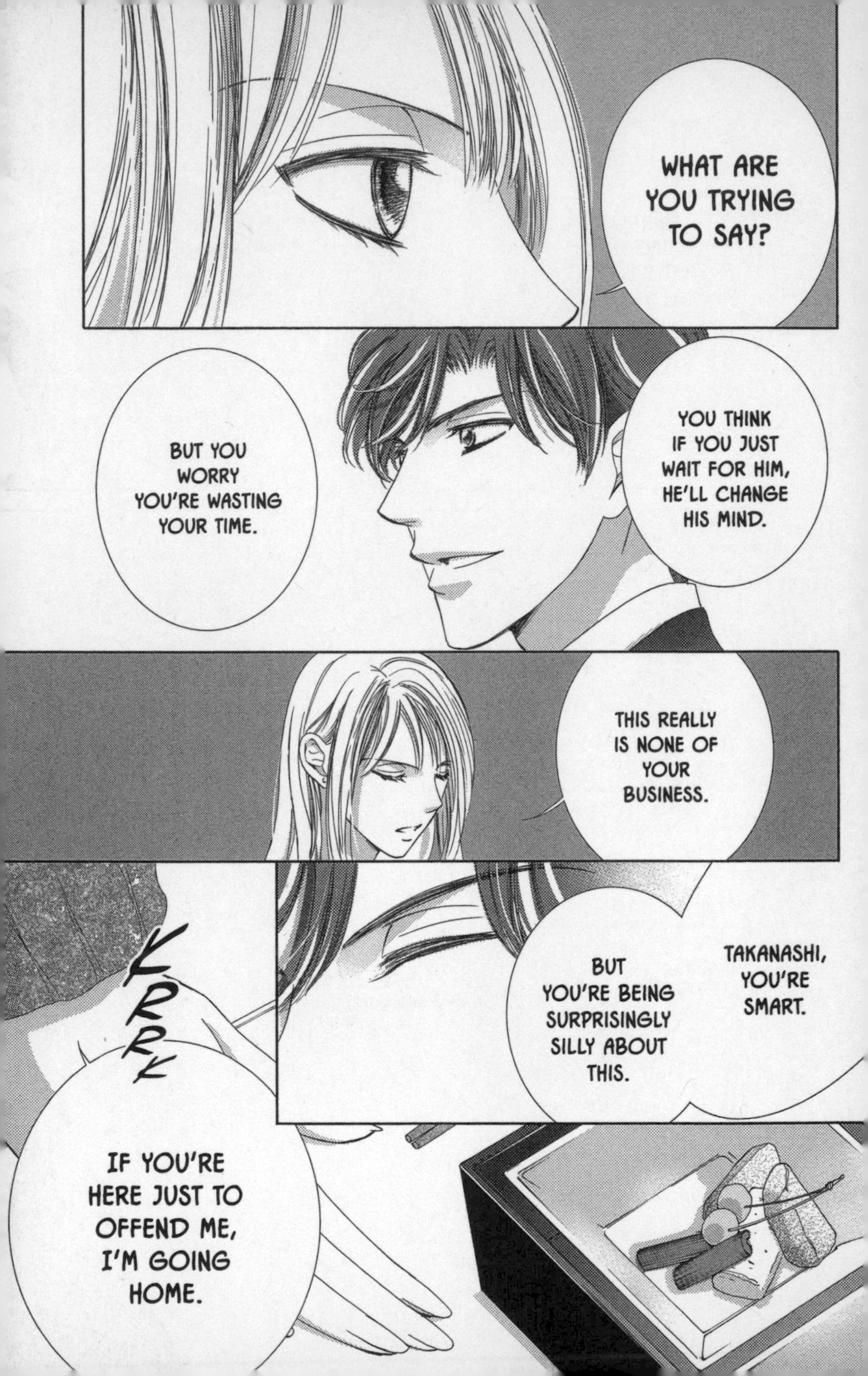
WHAT ARE YOU TRYING TO SAY?
YOU THINK IF YOU JUST WAIT FOR HIM, HE'LL CHANGE HIS MIND.
BUT YOU WORRY YOU'RE WASTING YOUR TIME.
THIS REALLY IS NONE OF YOUR BUSINESS.
TAKANASHI, YOU'RE SMART.
BUT YOU'RE BEING SURPRISINGLY SILLY ABOUT THIS.
KRRK
IF YOU'RE HERE JUST TO OFFEND ME, I'M GOING HOME.

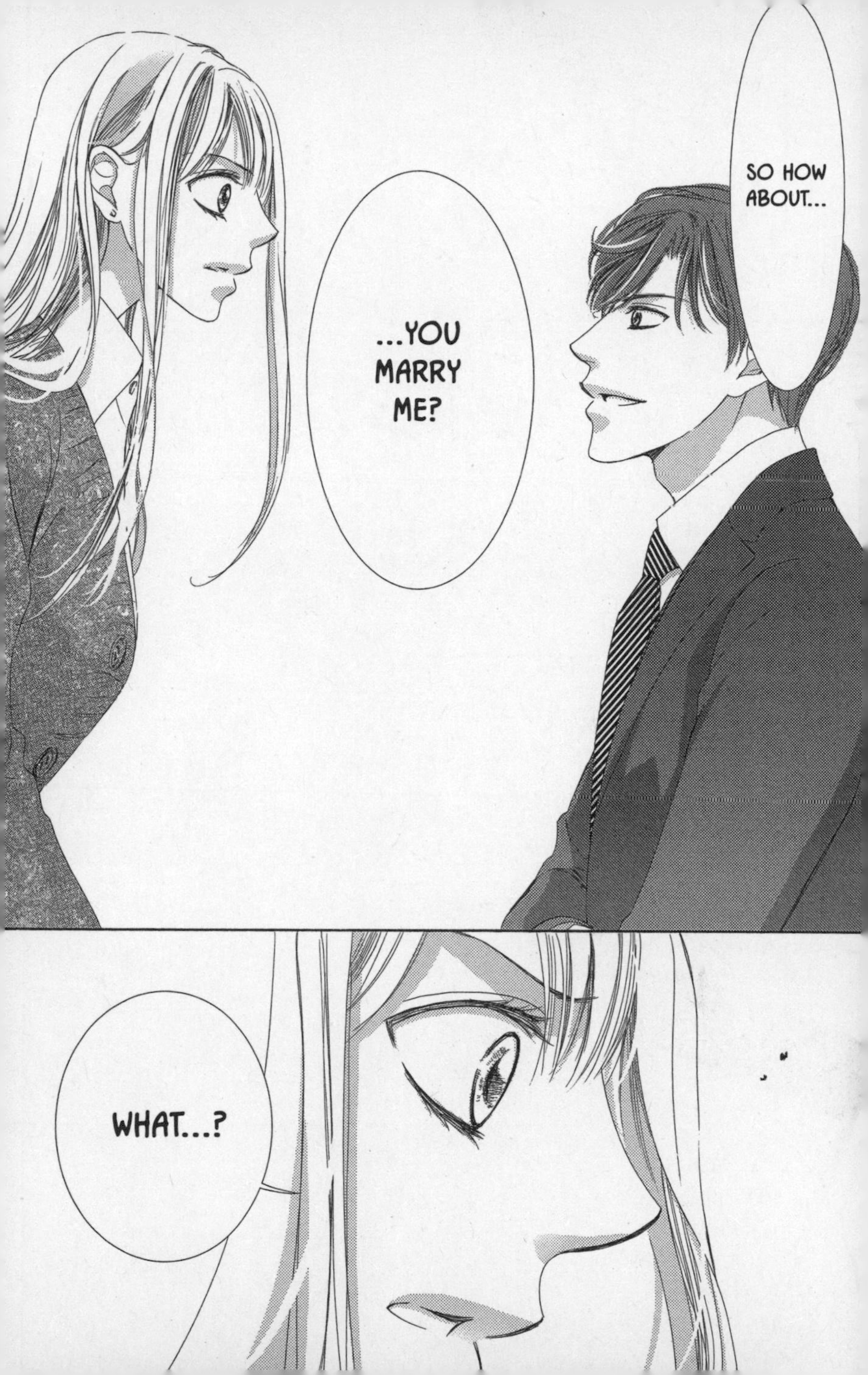
SO HOW ABOUT...
...YOU MARRY ME?
WHAT...?

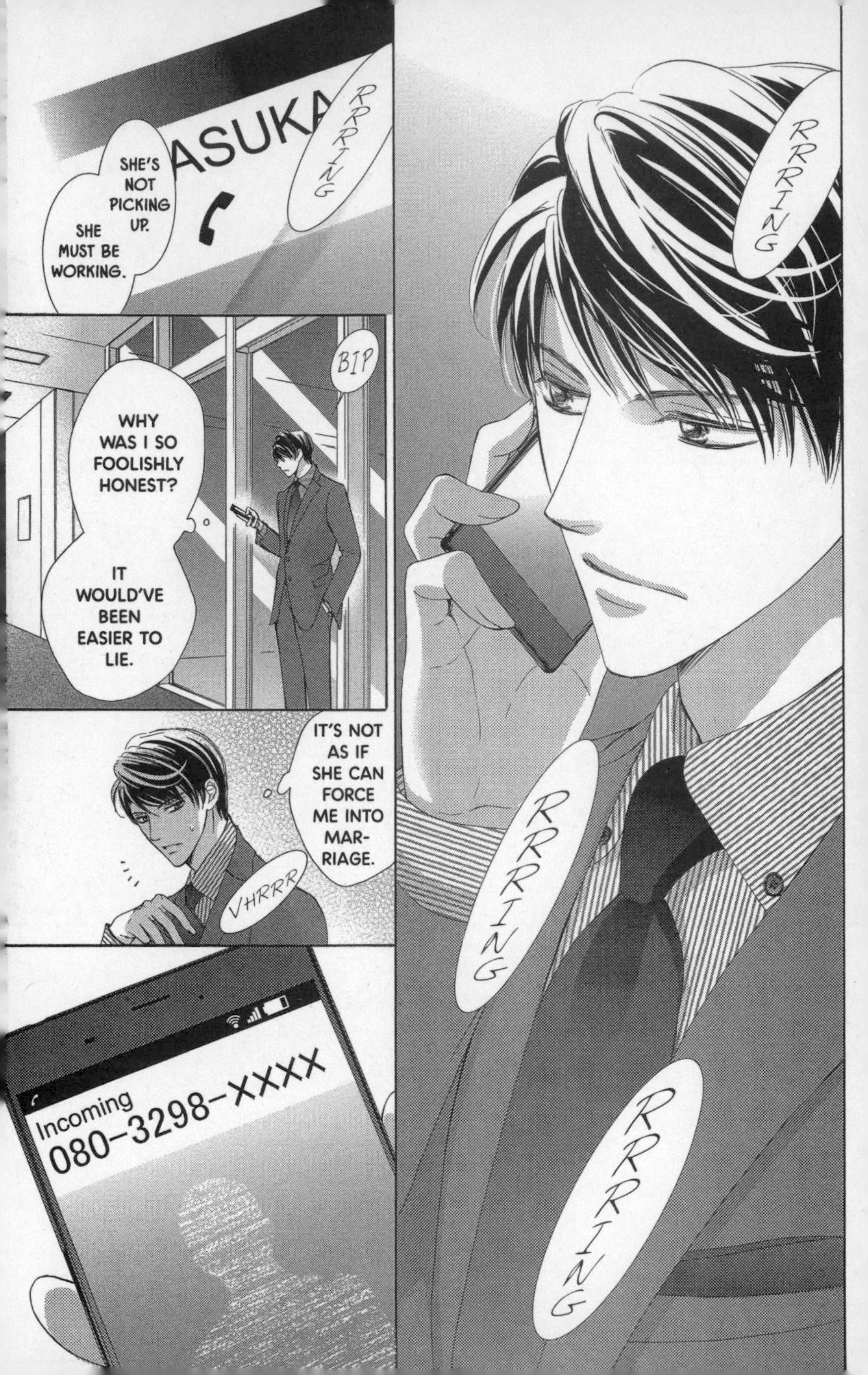
RRRING
ASUKA
RRRING
SHE'S NOT PICKING UP.
SHE MUST BE WORKING.
BIP
WHY WAS I SO FOOLISHLY HONEST?
IT WOULD'VE BEEN EASIER TO LIE.
IT'S NOT AS IF SHE CAN FORCE ME INTO MAR-RIAGE.
VHRRR
RRRING
RRRING
Incoming
080-3298-XXXX

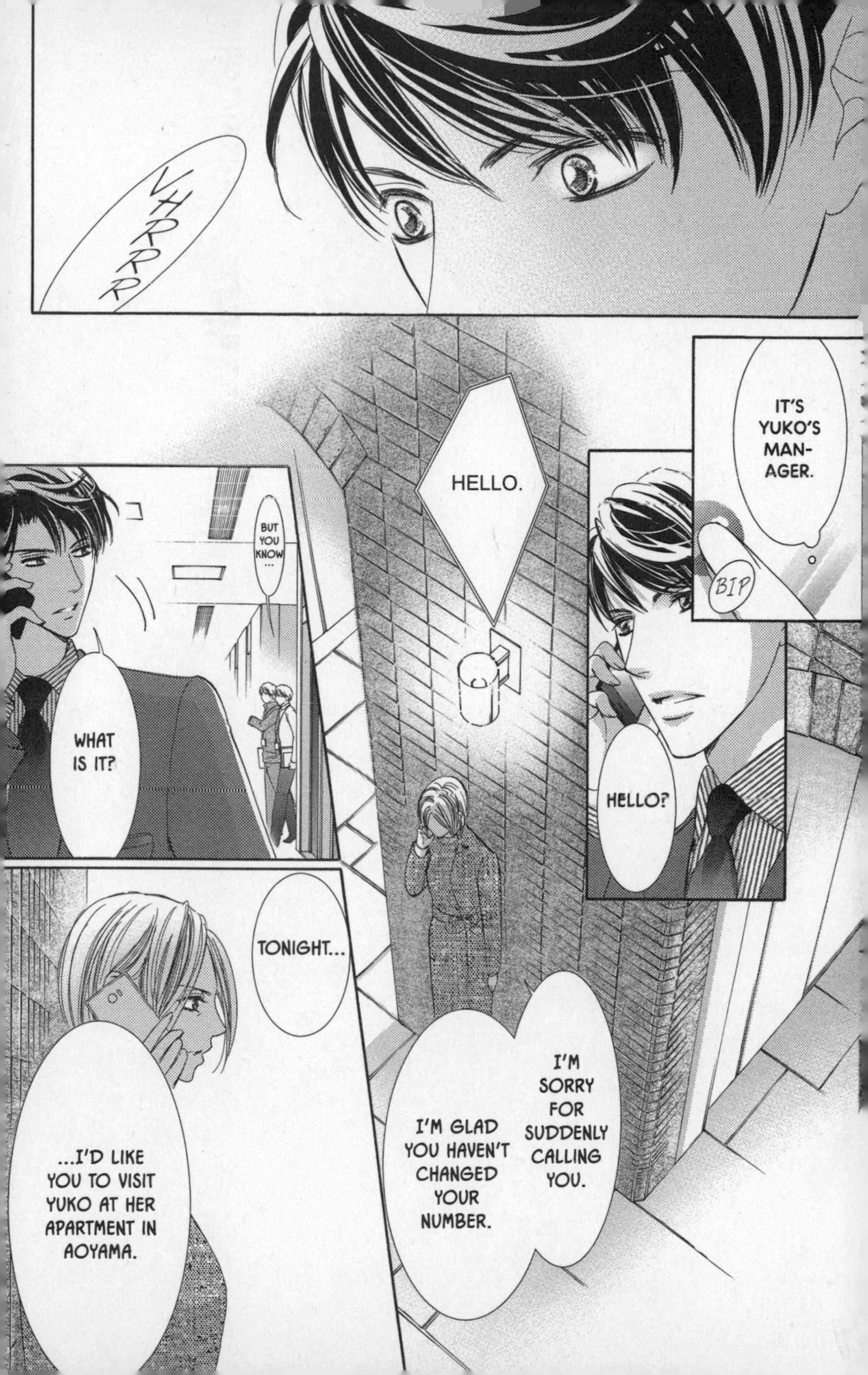
VHRRR
BIP
IT'S YUKO'S MAN-AGER.
HELLO?
HELLO.
WHAT IS IT?
BUT YOU KNOW...
I'M SORRY FOR SUDDENLY CALLING YOU.
I'M GLAD YOU HAVEN'T CHANGED YOUR NUMBER.
TONIGHT...
...I'D LIKE YOU TO VISIT YUKO AT HER APARTMENT IN AOYAMA.

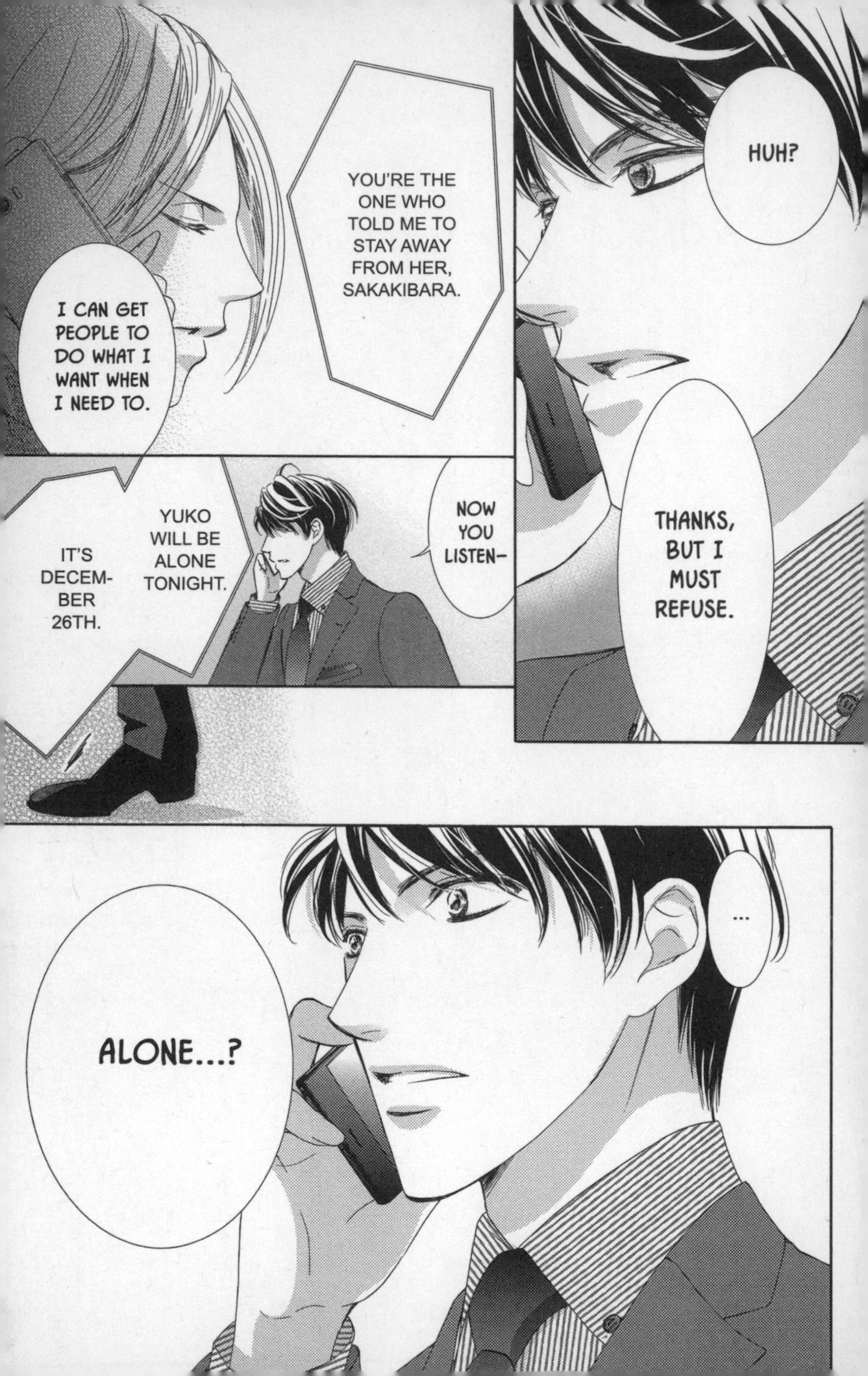
HUH?
THANKS, BUT I MUST REFUSE.
YOU'RE THE ONE WHO TOLD ME TO STAY AWAY FROM HER, SAKAKIBARA.
I CAN GET PEOPLE TO DO WHAT I WANT WHEN I NEED TO.
NOW YOU LISTEN—
YUKO WILL BE ALONE TONIGHT.
IT'S DECEMBER 26TH.
...
ALONE...?

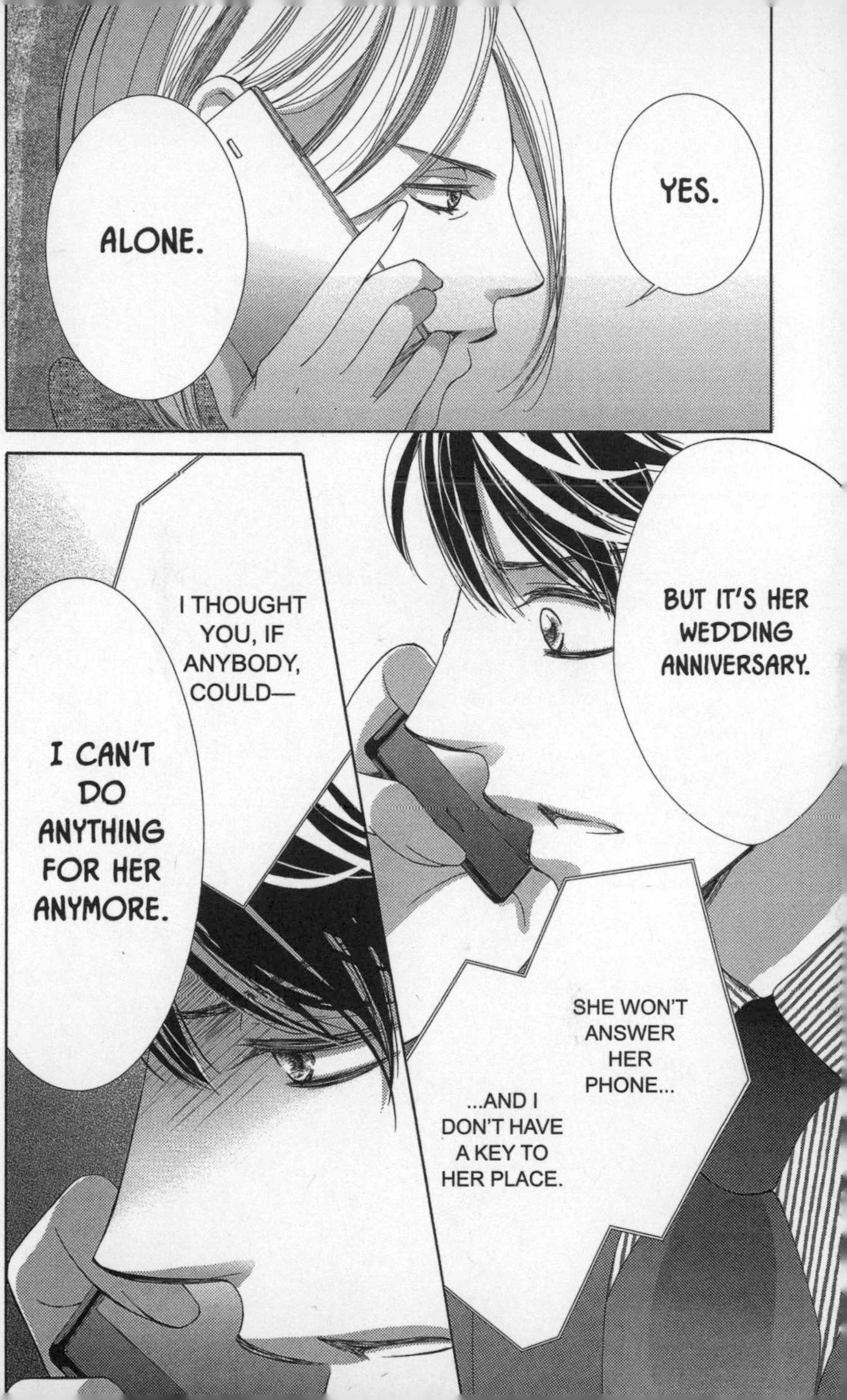
YES.
ALONE.
BUT IT'S HER WEDDING ANNIVERSARY.
SHE WON'T ANSWER HER PHONE...
...AND I DON'T HAVE A KEY TO HER PLACE.
I THOUGHT YOU, IF ANYBODY, COULD—
I CAN'T DO ANYTHING FOR HER ANYMORE.

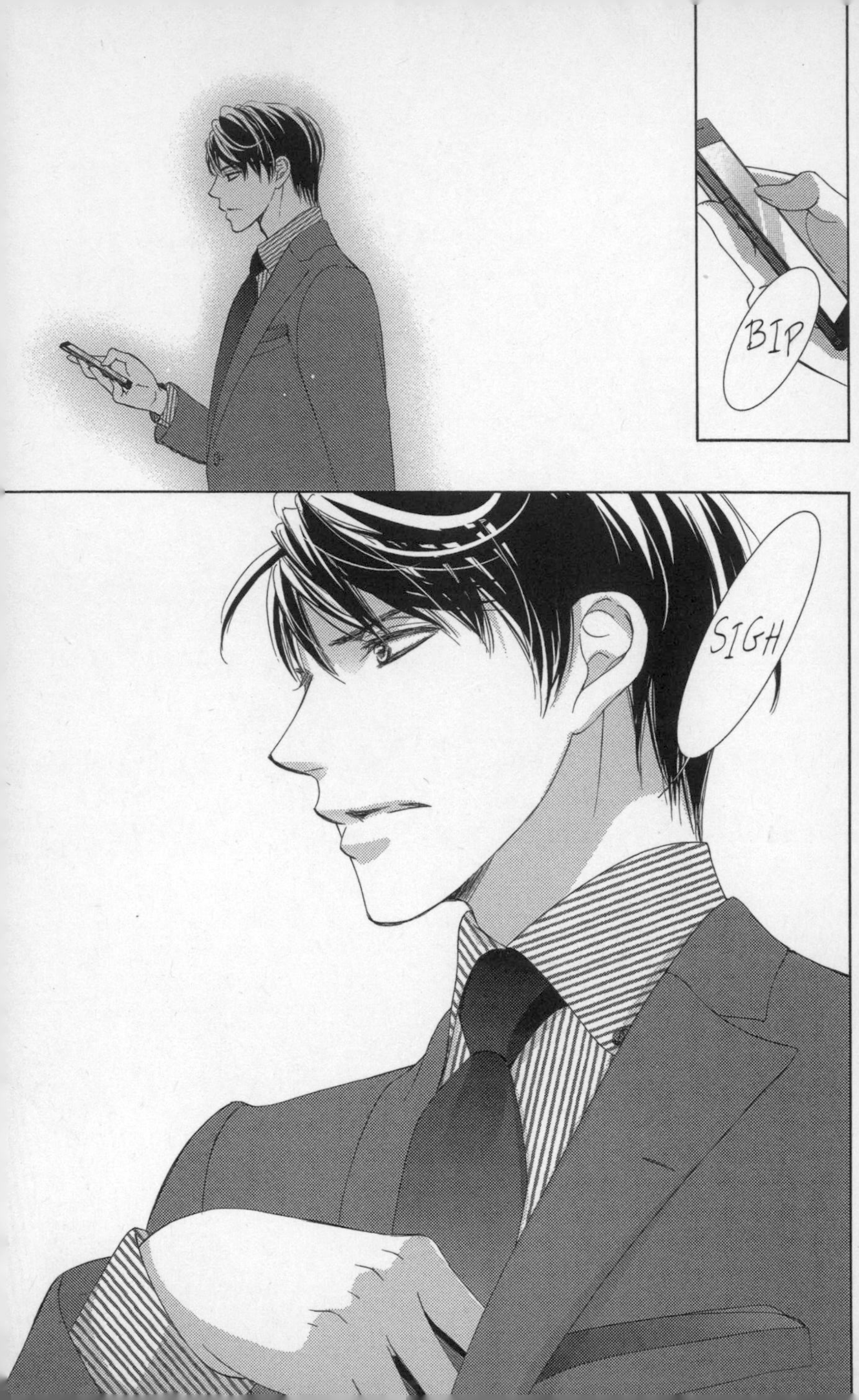
BIP
SIGH

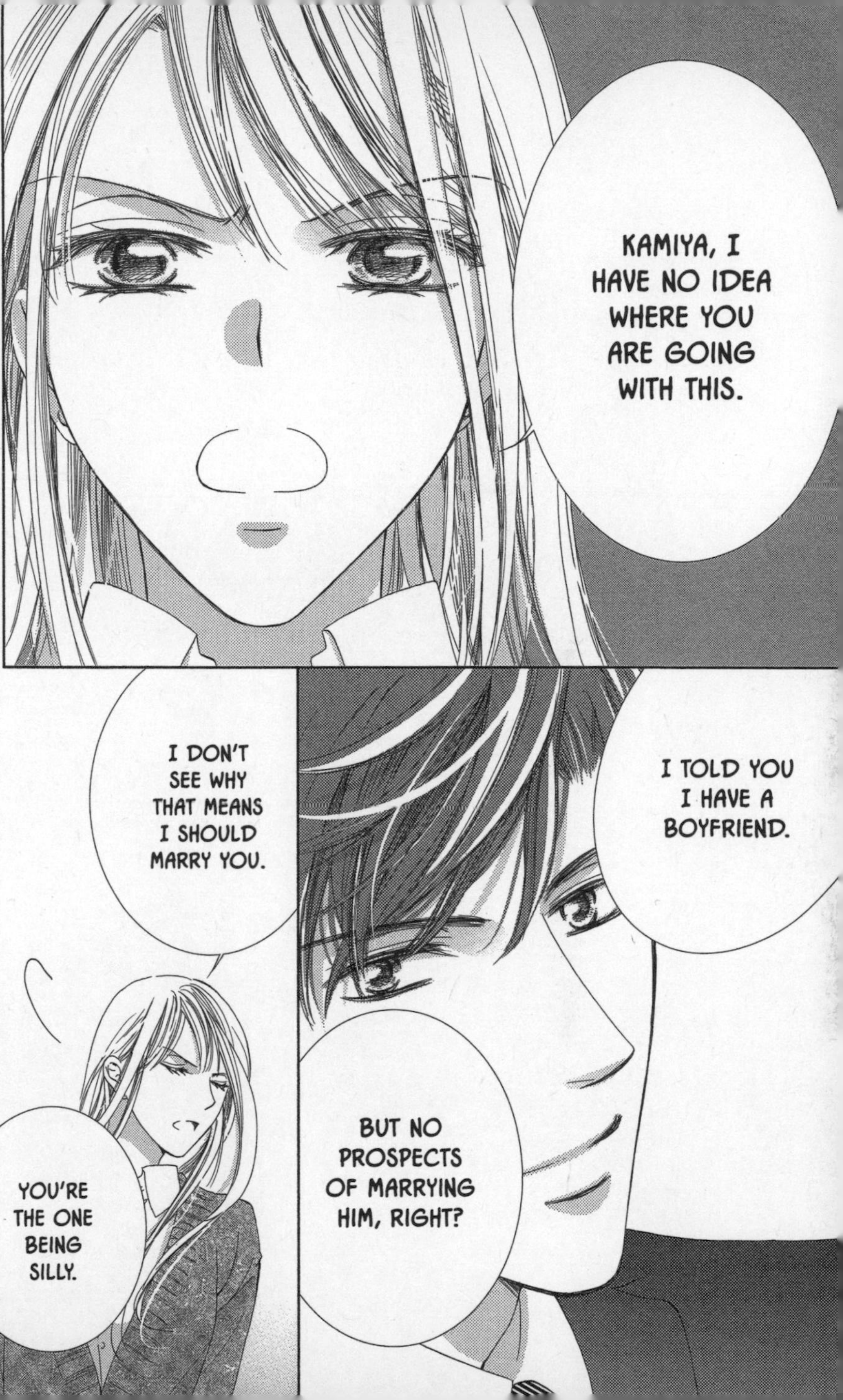
KAMIYA, I HAVE NO IDEA WHERE YOU ARE GOING WITH THIS.
I TOLD YOU I HAVE A BOYFRIEND.
BUT NO PROSPECTS OF MARRYING HIM, RIGHT?
I DON'T SEE WHY THAT MEANS I SHOULD MARRY YOU.
YOU'RE THE ONE BEING SILLY.

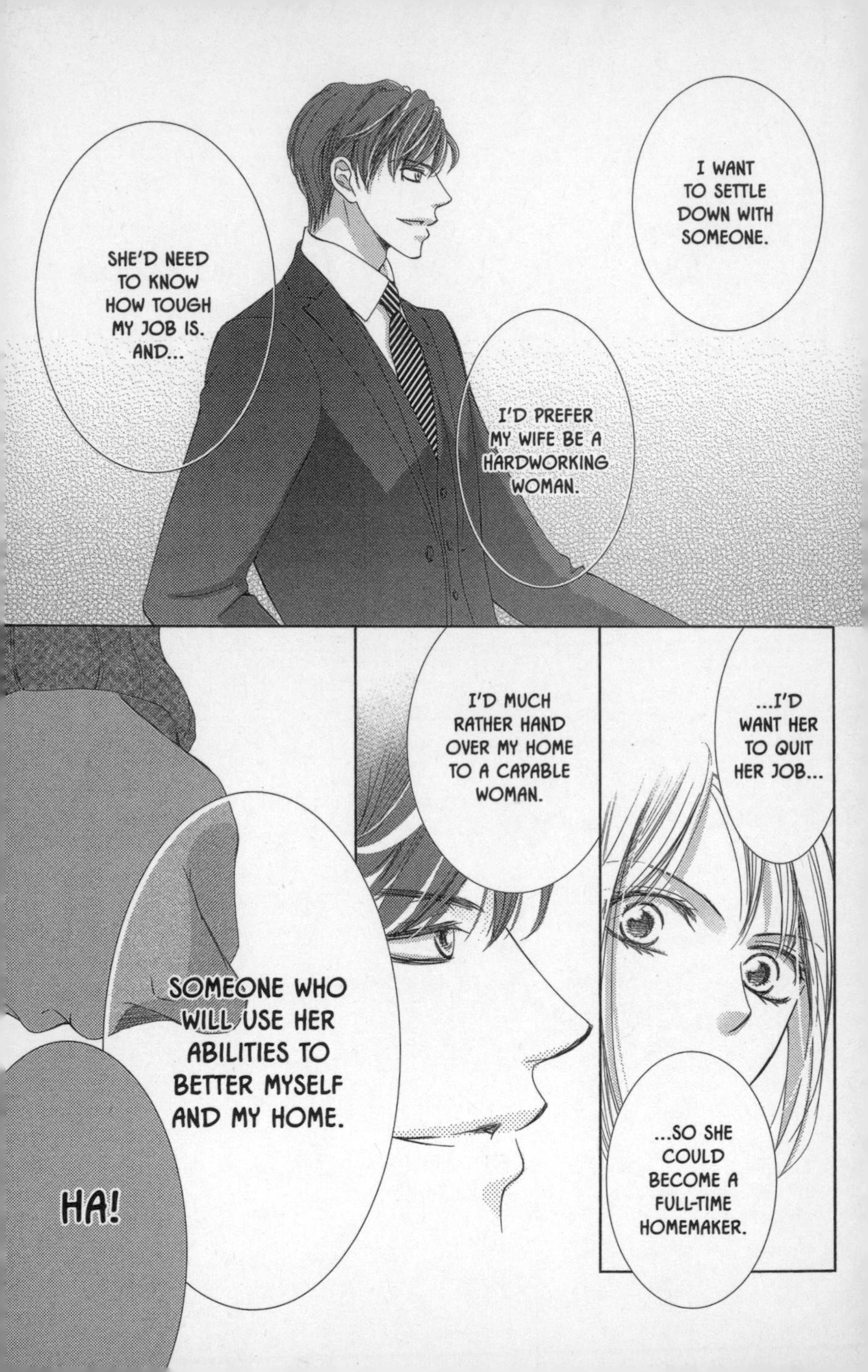
I WANT TO SETTLE DOWN WITH SOMEONE.
I'D PREFER MY WIFE BE A HARDWORKING WOMAN.
SHE'D NEED TO KNOW HOW TOUGH MY JOB IS. AND...
...I'D WANT HER TO QUIT HER JOB...
...SO SHE COULD BECOME A FULL-TIME HOMEMAKER.
I'D MUCH RATHER HAND OVER MY HOME TO A CAPABLE WOMAN.
SOMEONE WHO WILL USE HER ABILITIES TO BETTER MYSELF AND MY HOME.
HA!

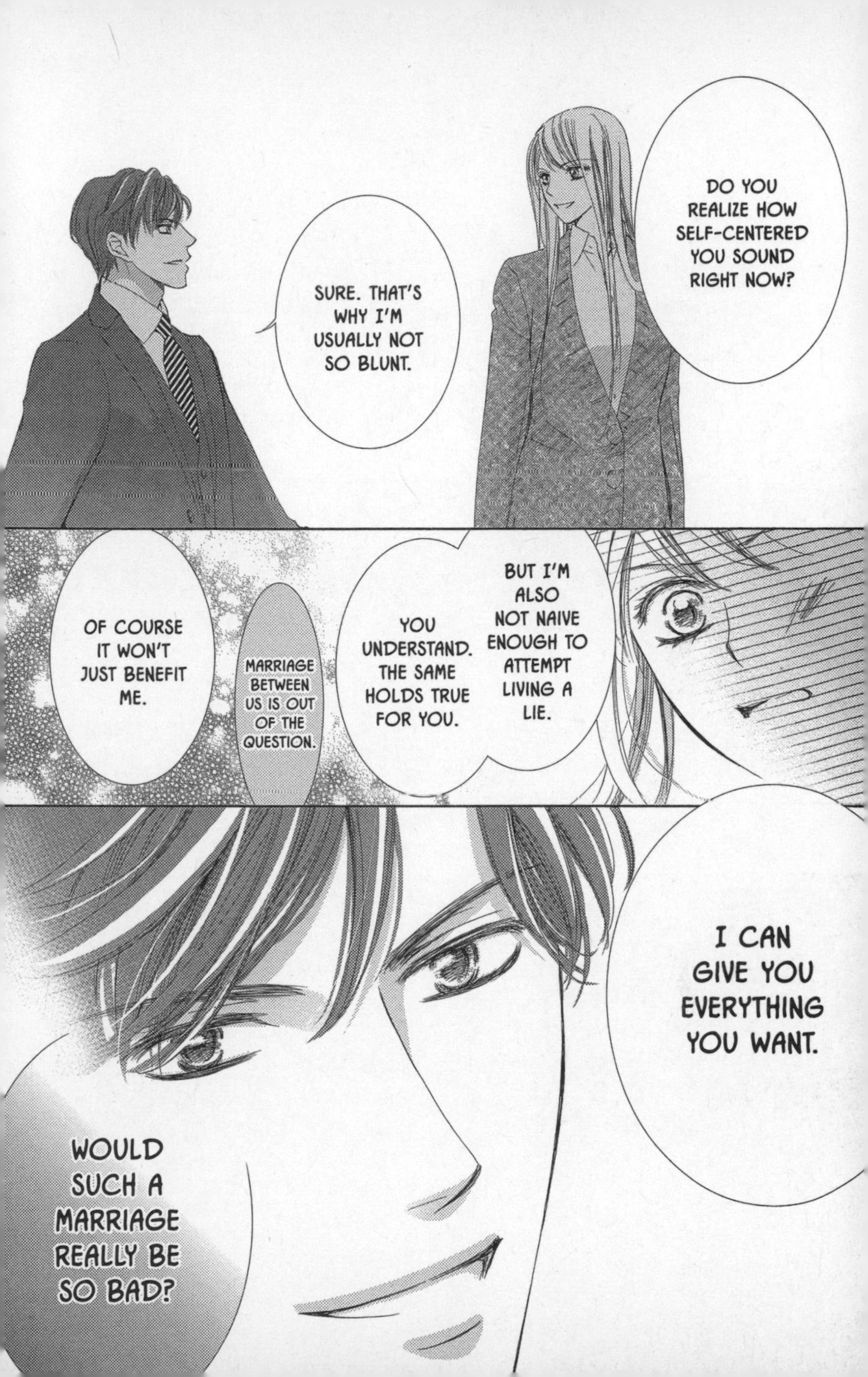
DO YOU REALIZE HOW SELF-CENTERED YOU SOUND RIGHT NOW?
SURE. THAT'S WHY I'M USUALLY NOT SO BLUNT.
BUT I'M ALSO NOT NAIVE ENOUGH TO ATTEMPT LIVING A LIE.
YOU UNDERSTAND. THE SAME HOLDS TRUE FOR YOU.
MARRIAGE BETWEEN US IS OUT OF THE QUESTION.
OF COURSE IT WON'T JUST BENEFIT ME.
I CAN GIVE YOU EVERYTHING YOU WANT.
WOULD SUCH A MARRIAGE REALLY BE SO BAD?

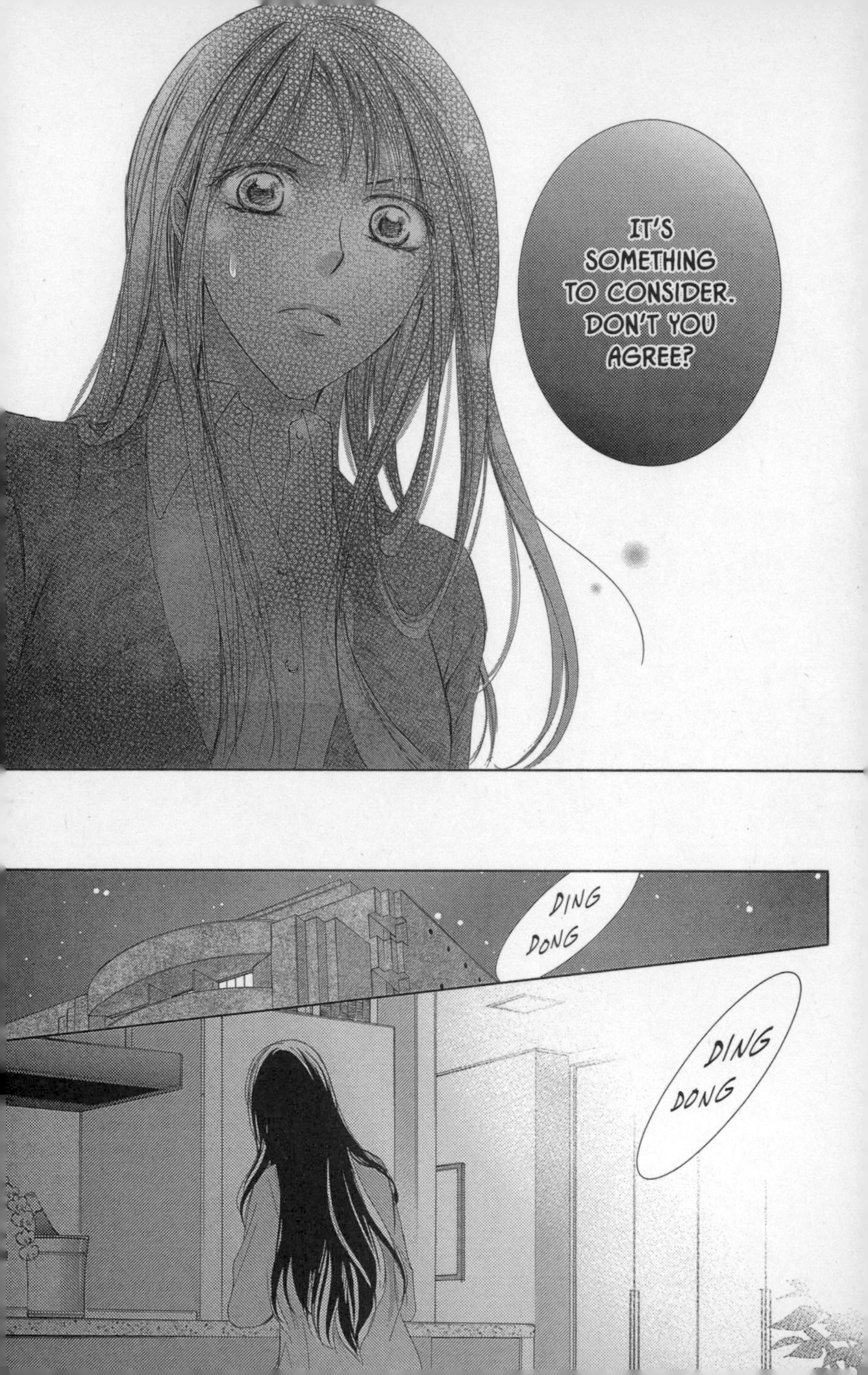
IT'S SOMETHING TO CONSIDER. DON'T YOU AGREE?
DING DONG
DING DONG

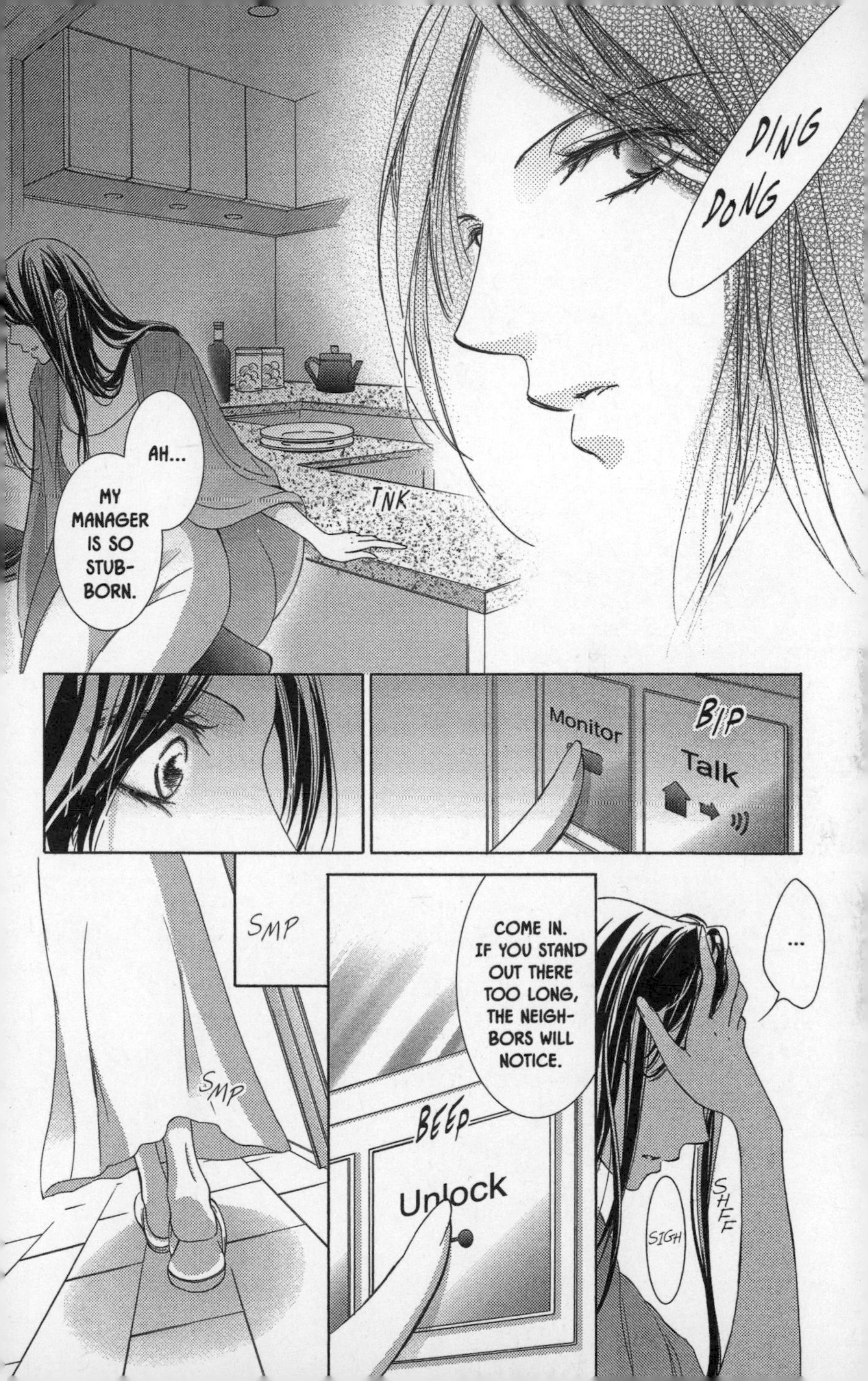
DING DONG
TNK
AH...
MY MANAGER IS SO STUB-BORN.
BIP
Monitor
Talk
...
COME IN. IF YOU STAND OUT THERE TOO LONG, THE NEIGH-BORS WILL NOTICE.
SHFF
SIGH
BEEP
Unlock
SMP
SMP

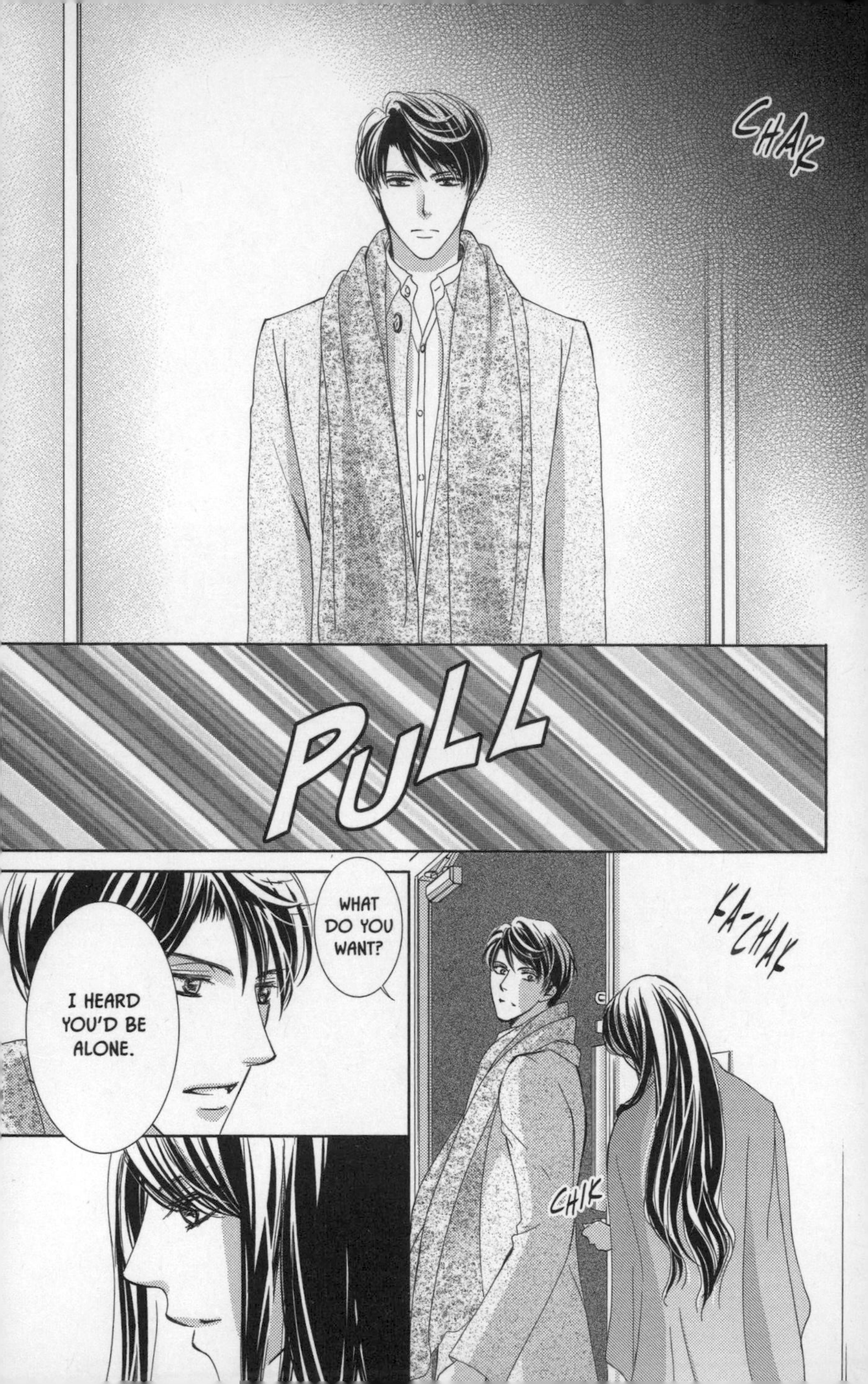
CHAK
PULL
KA-CHAK
CHIK
WHAT DO YOU WANT?
I HEARD YOU'D BE ALONE.

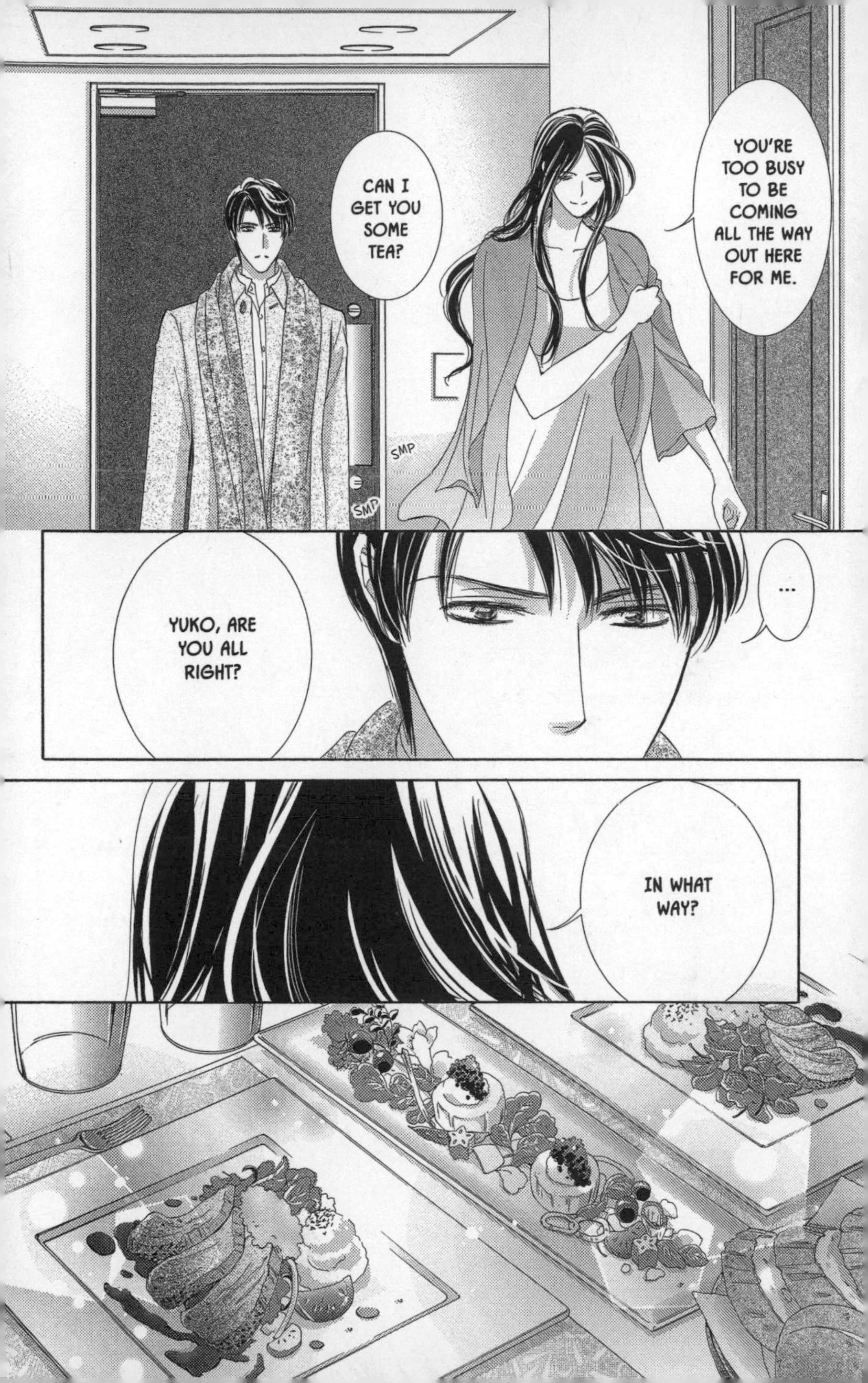
YOU'RE TOO BUSY TO BE COMING ALL THE WAY OUT HERE FOR ME.
CAN I GET YOU SOME TEA?
SMP
SMP
...
YUKO, ARE YOU ALL RIGHT?
IN WHAT WAY?

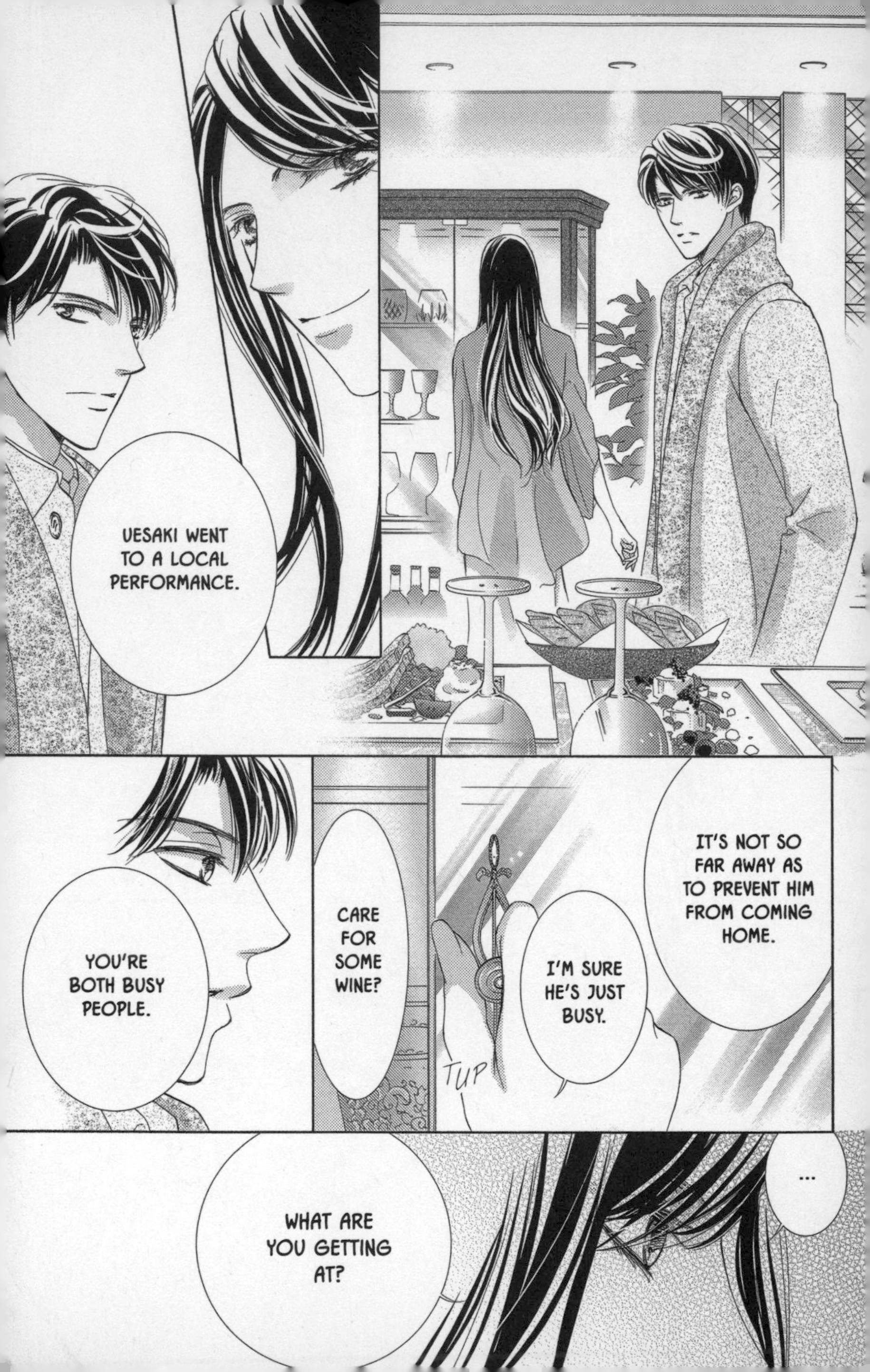
UESAKI WENT TO A LOCAL PERFORMANCE.
IT'S NOT SO FAR AWAY AS TO PREVENT HIM FROM COMING HOME.
I'M SURE HE'S JUST BUSY.
TUP
CARE FOR SOME WINE?
YOU'RE BOTH BUSY PEOPLE.
...
WHAT ARE YOU GETTING AT?

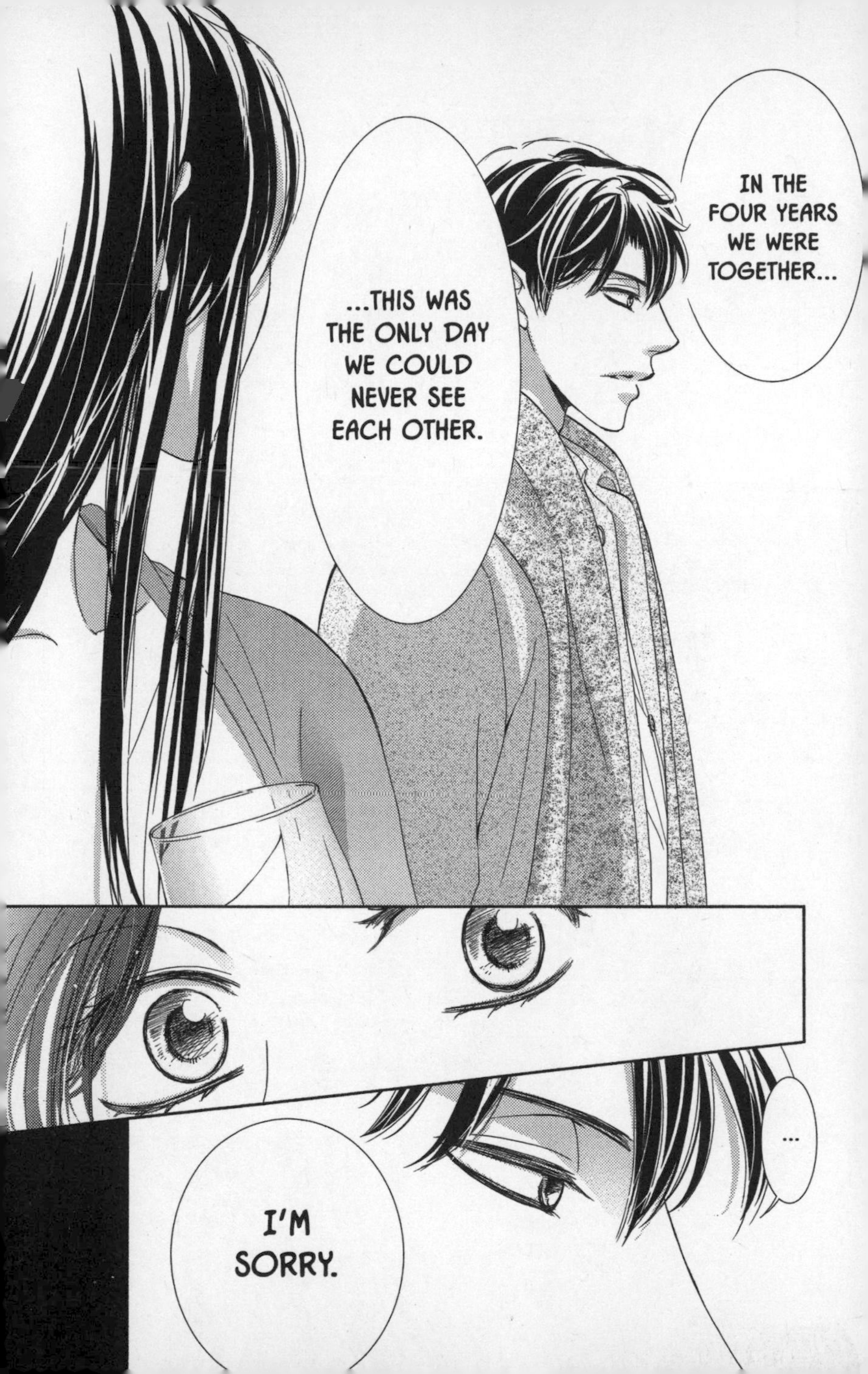
IN THE FOUR YEARS WE WERE TOGETHER...
...THIS WAS THE ONLY DAY WE COULD NEVER SEE EACH OTHER.
...
I'M SORRY.

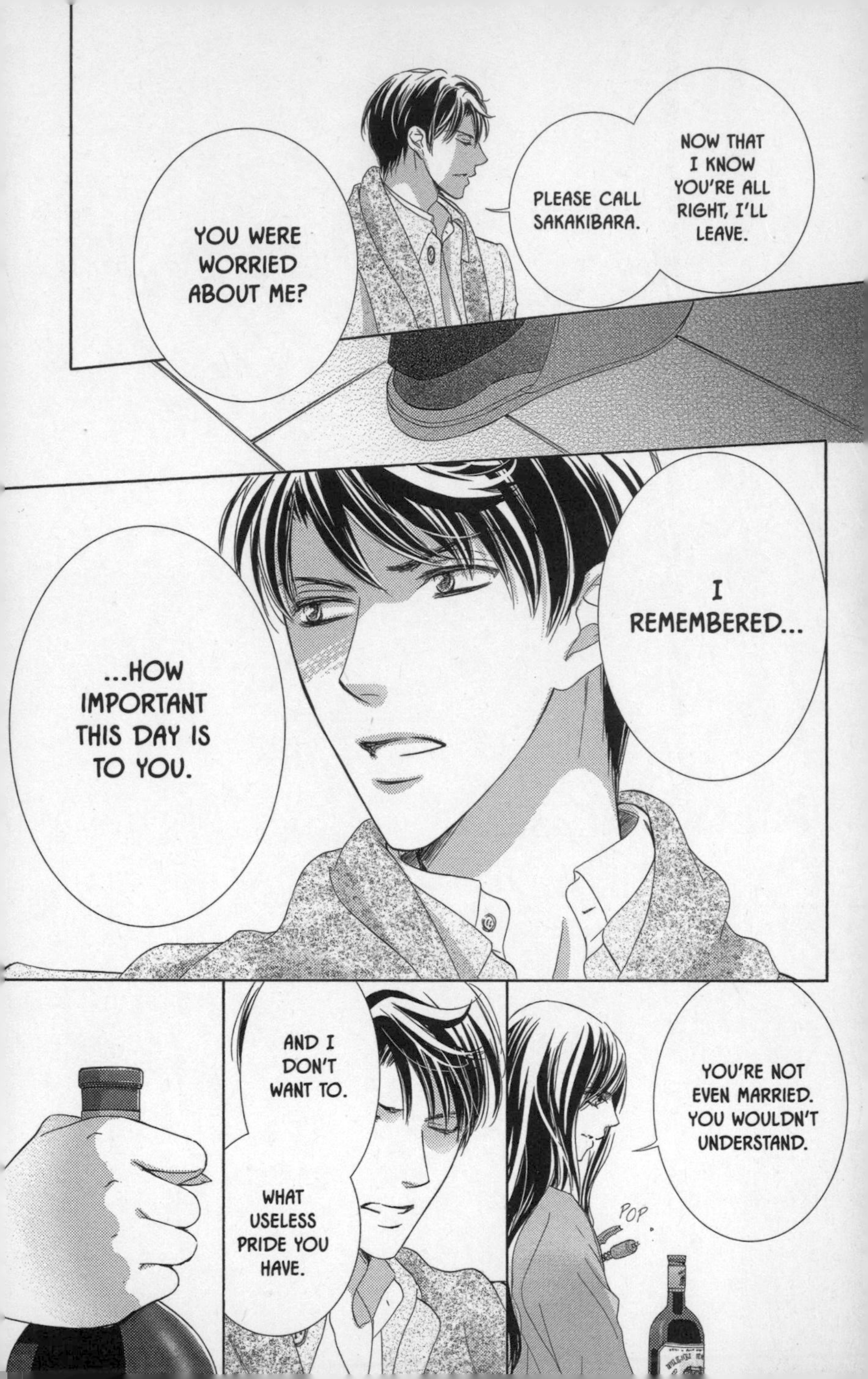
NOW THAT I KNOW YOU'RE ALL RIGHT, I'LL LEAVE.
PLEASE CALL SAKAKIBARA.
YOU WERE WORRIED ABOUT ME?
I REMEMBERED...
...HOW IMPORTANT THIS DAY IS TO YOU.
YOU'RE NOT EVEN MARRIED. YOU WOULDN'T UNDERSTAND.
POP
AND I DON'T WANT TO.
WHAT USELESS PRIDE YOU HAVE.

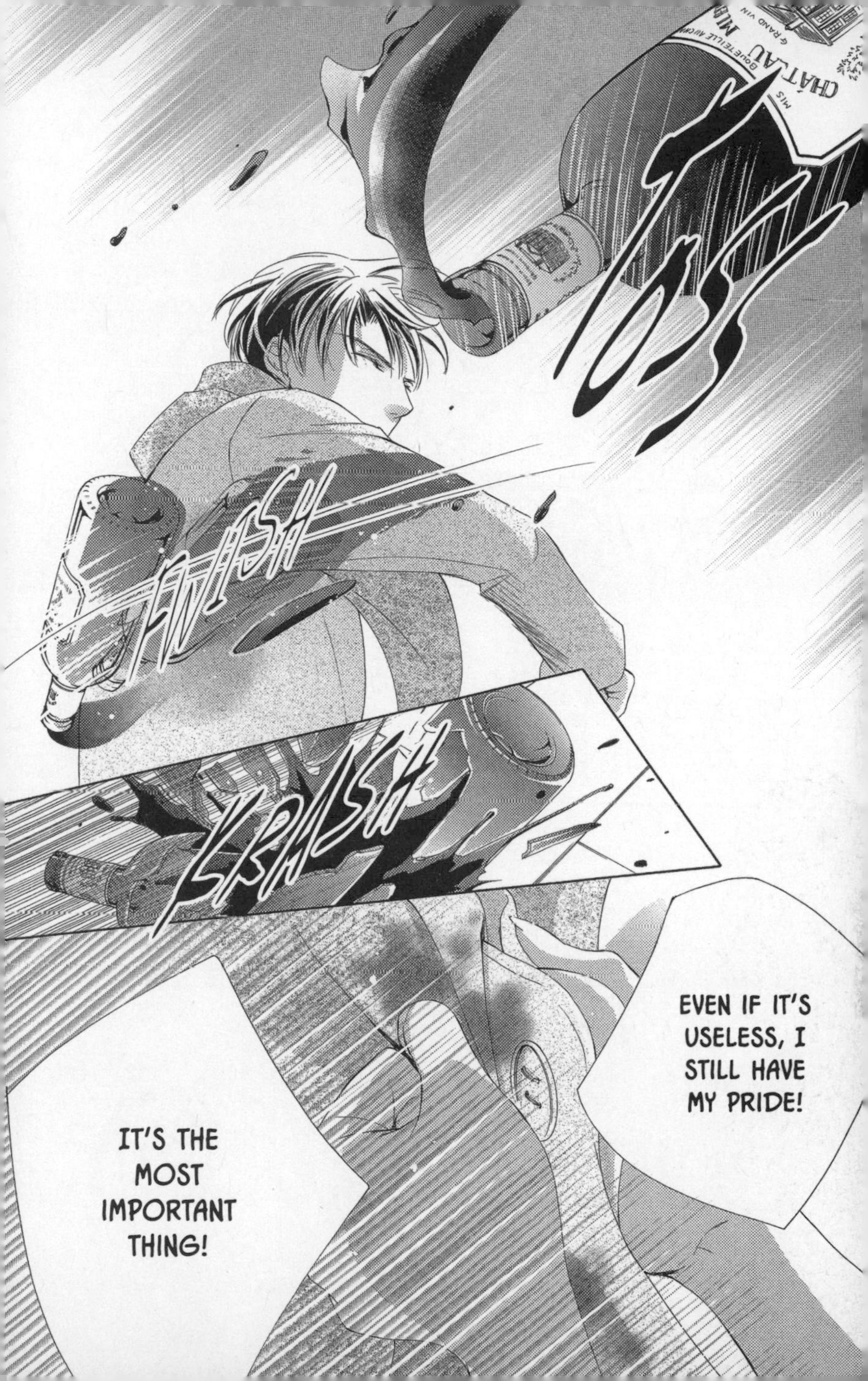
FWASH
KRASH
EVEN IF IT'S USELESS, I STILL HAVE MY PRIDE!
IT'S THE MOST IMPORTANT THING!

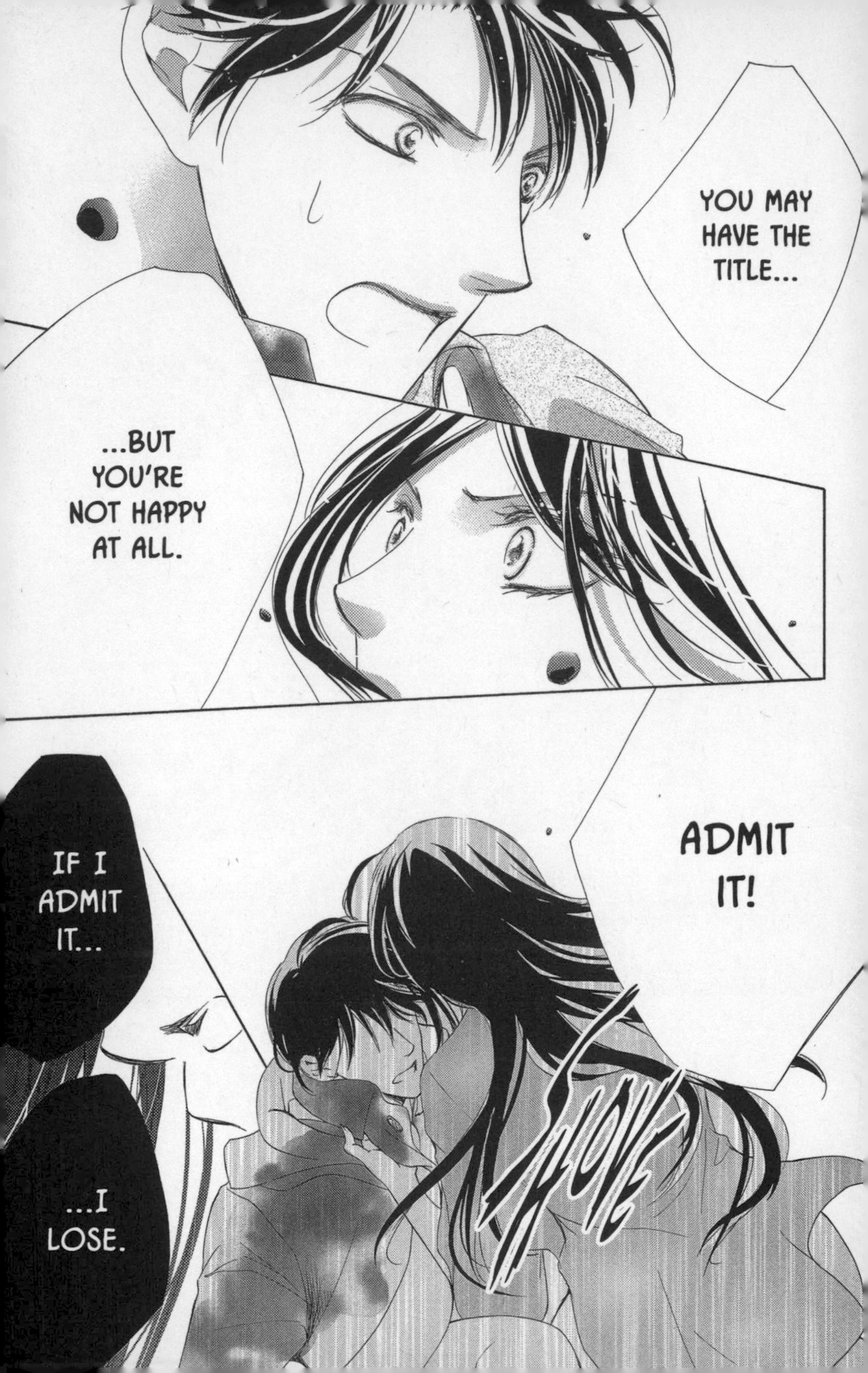
YOU MAY HAVE THE TITLE...
...BUT YOU'RE NOT HAPPY AT ALL.
ADMIT IT!
IF I ADMIT IT...
...I LOSE.

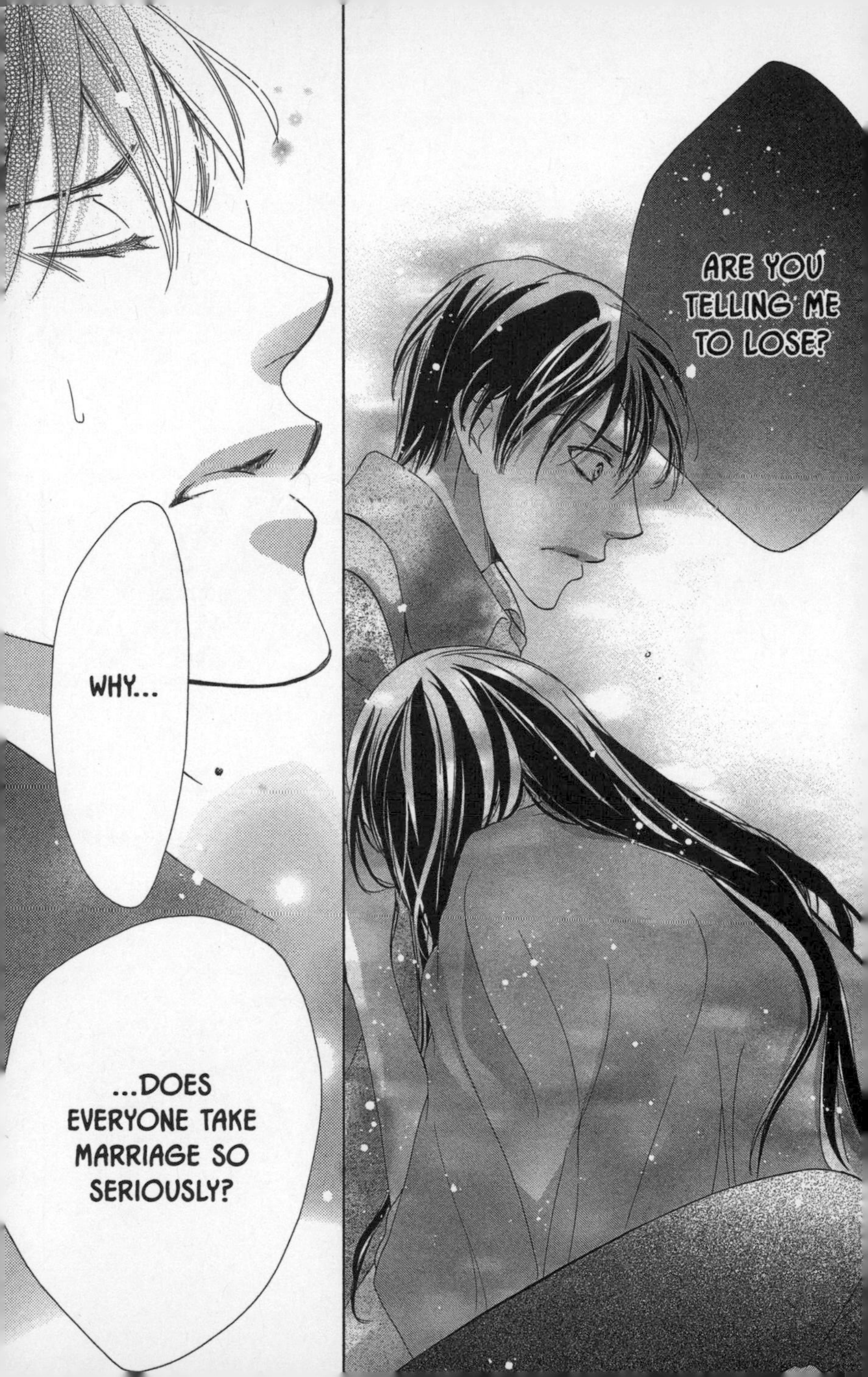
ARE YOU TELLING ME TO LOSE?
WHY...
...DOES EVERYONE TAKE MARRIAGE SO SERIOUSLY?

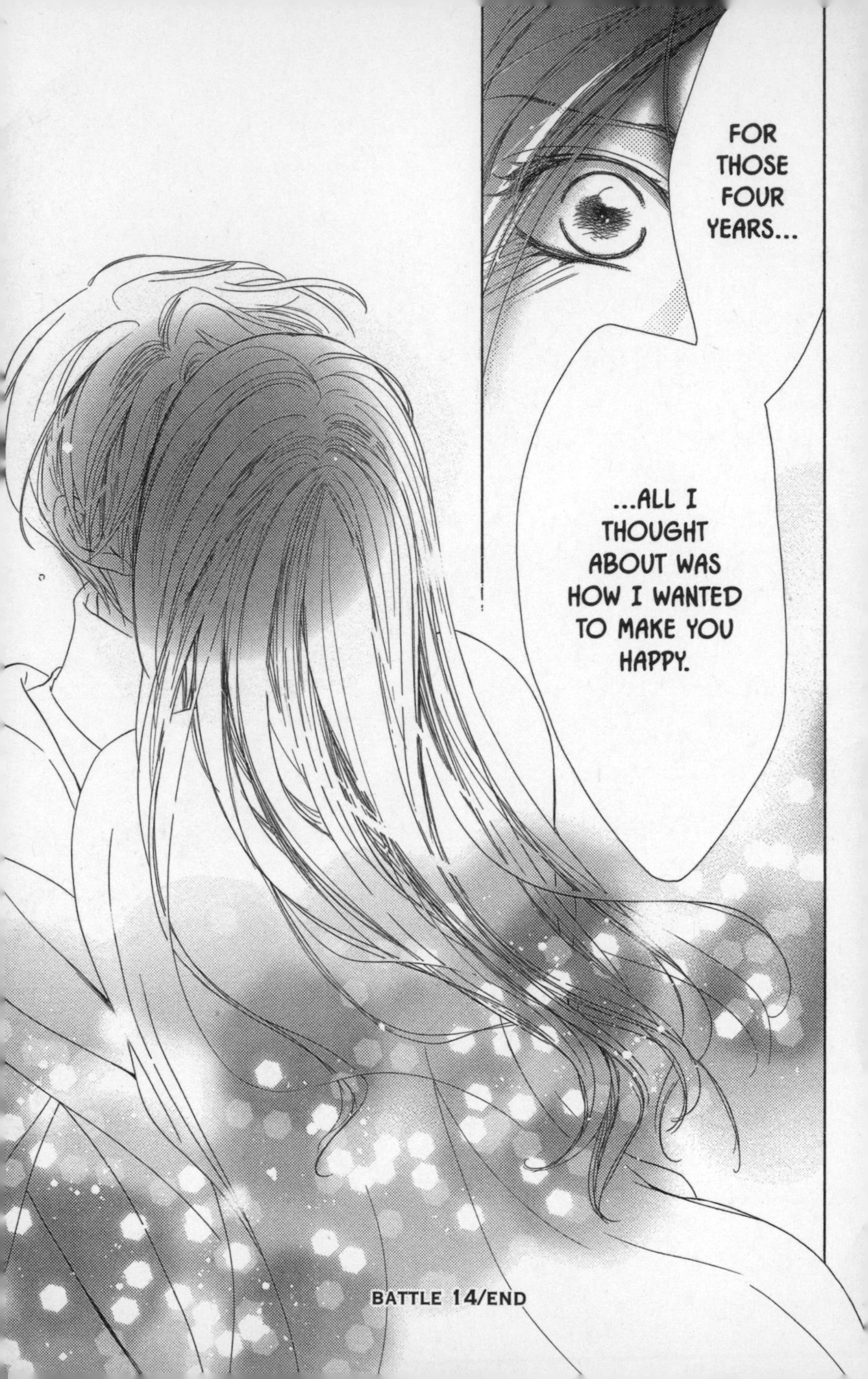
FOR THOSE FOUR YEARS...
...ALL I THOUGHT ABOUT WAS HOW I WANTED TO MAKE YOU HAPPY.
BATTLE 14/END

Or this man?

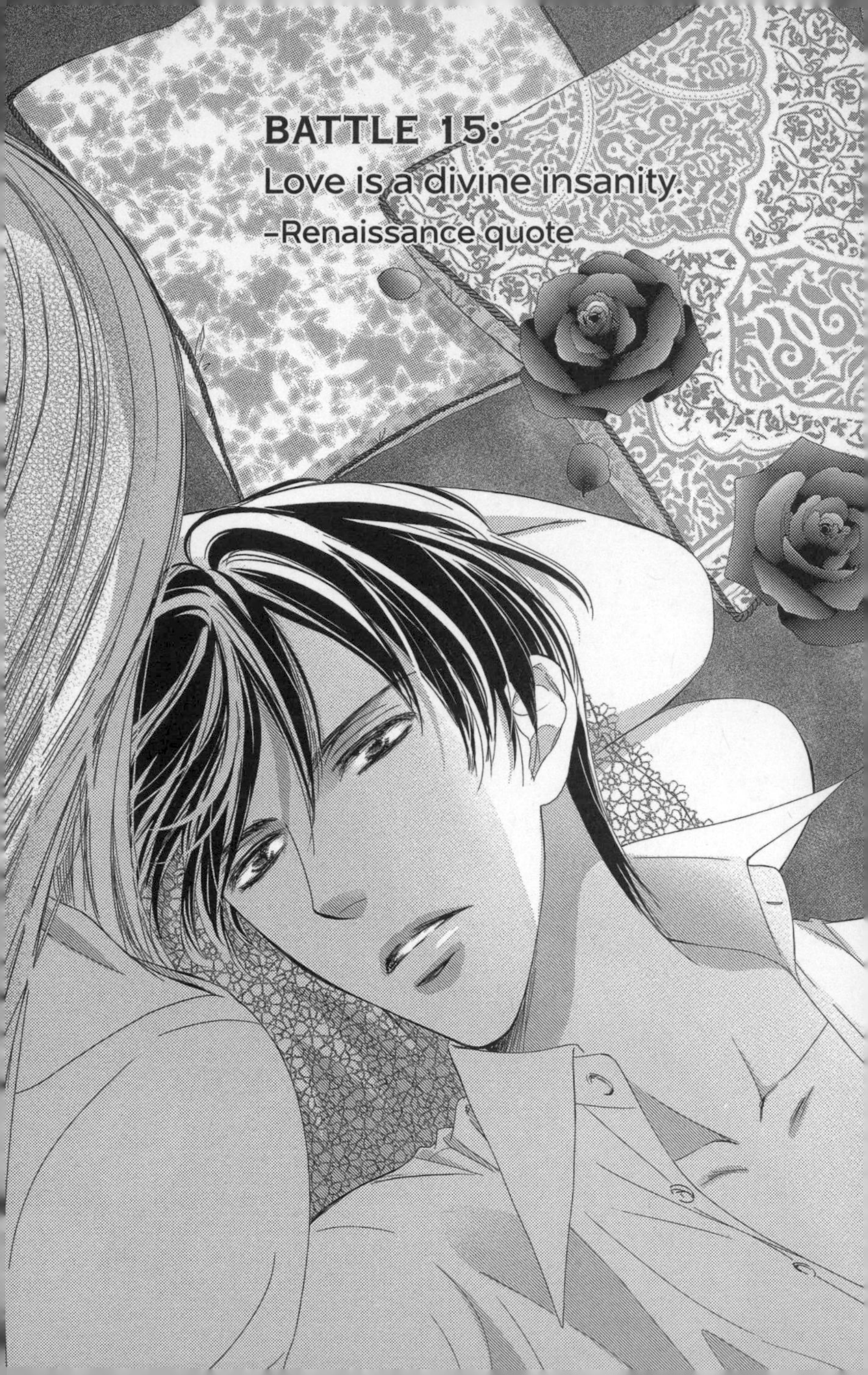
BATTLE 15:
Love is a divine insanity.
–Renaissance quote

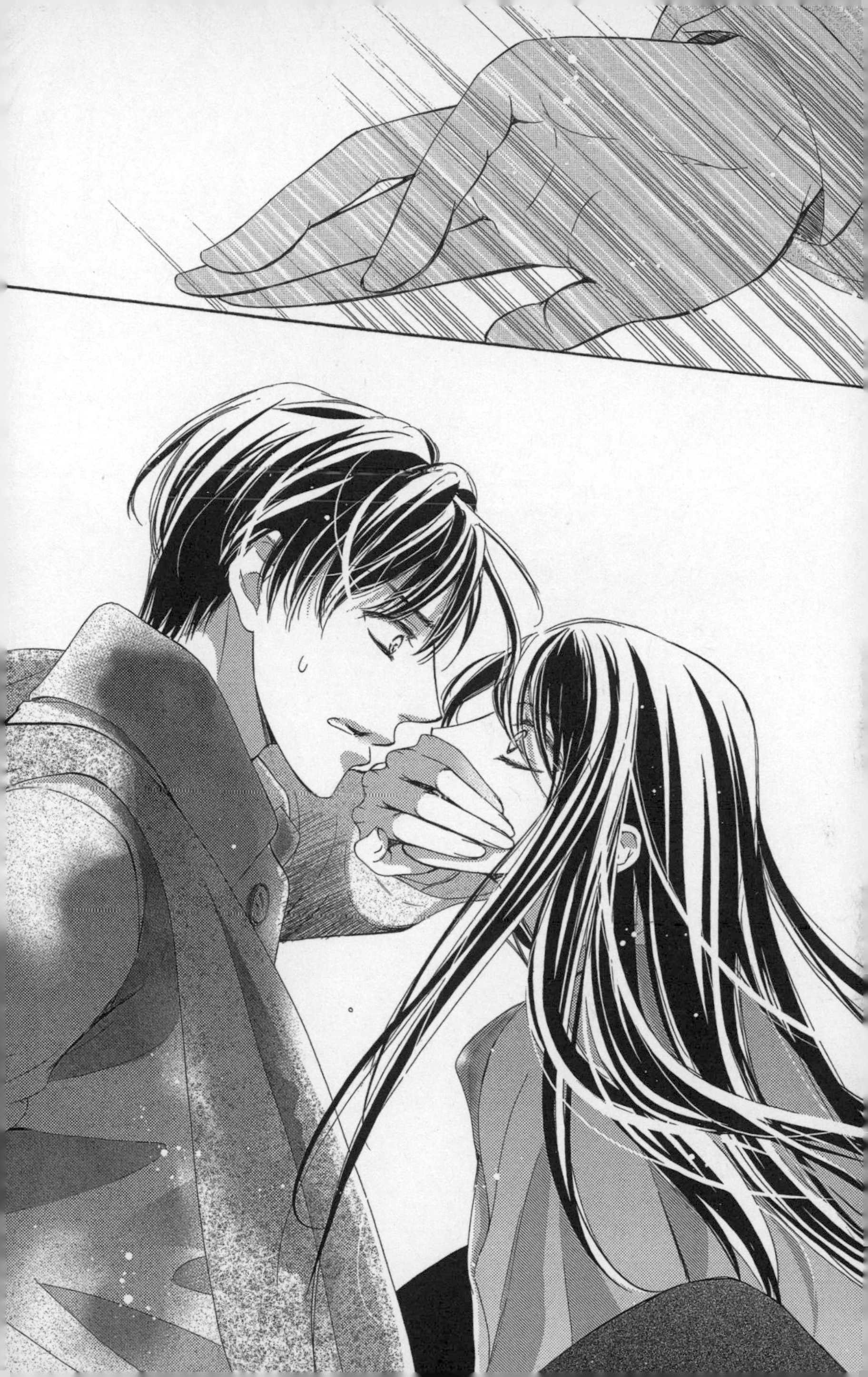

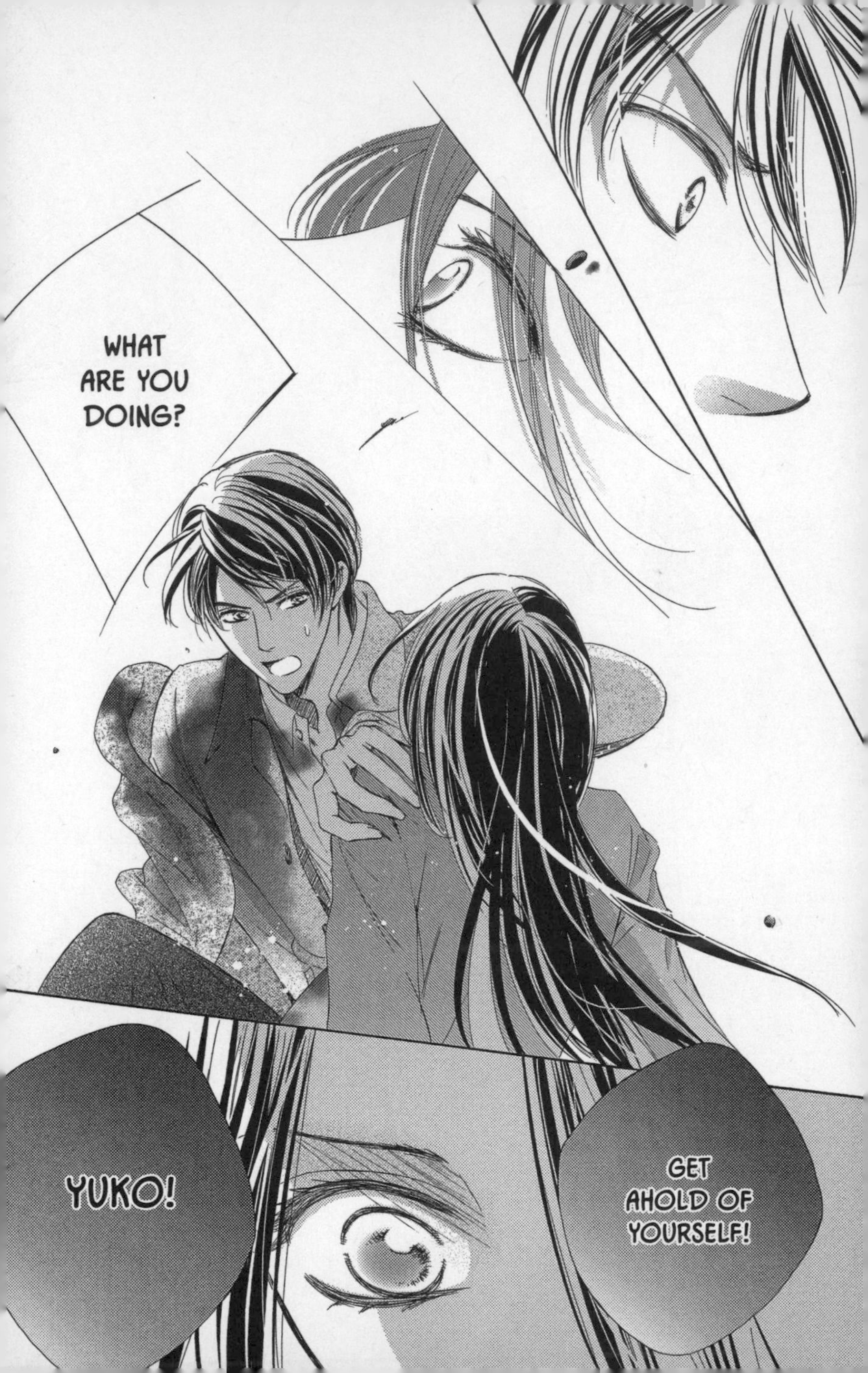
WHAT ARE YOU DOING?
GET AHOLD OF YOURSELF!
YUKO!

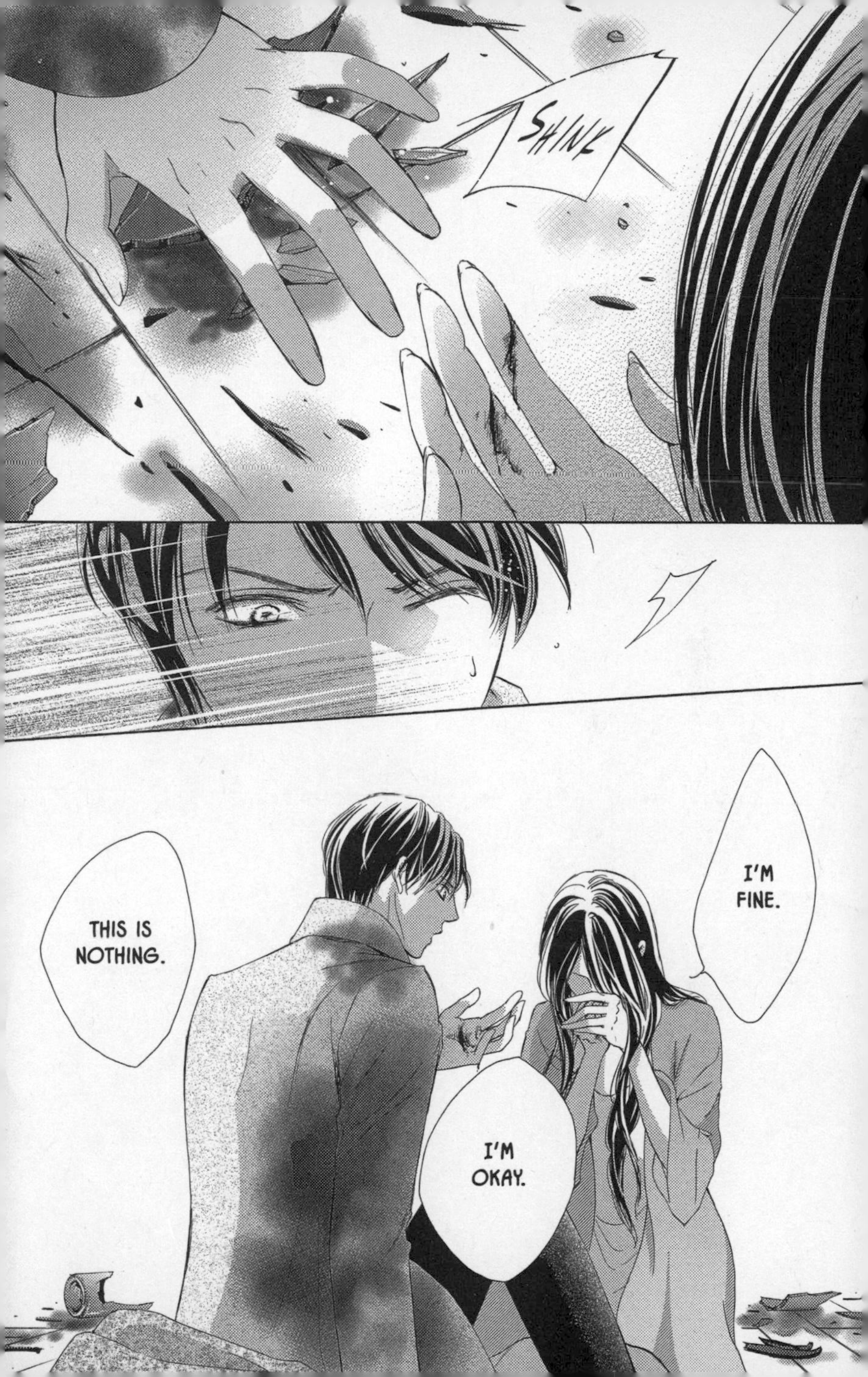
SHINK
I'M FINE.
I'M OKAY.
THIS IS NOTHING.

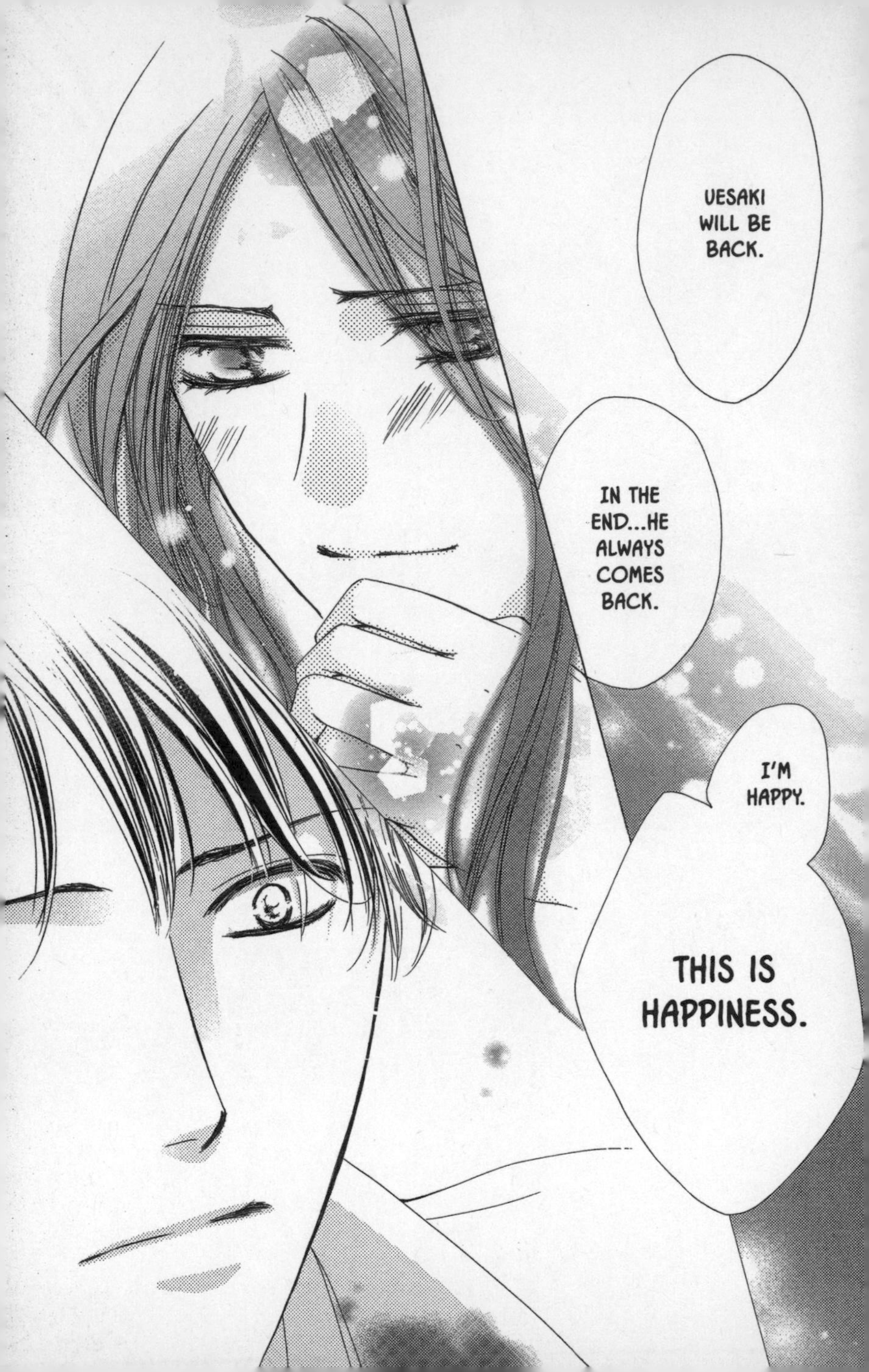
UESAKI WILL BE BACK.
IN THE END...HE ALWAYS COMES BACK.
I'M HAPPY.
THIS IS HAPPINESS.

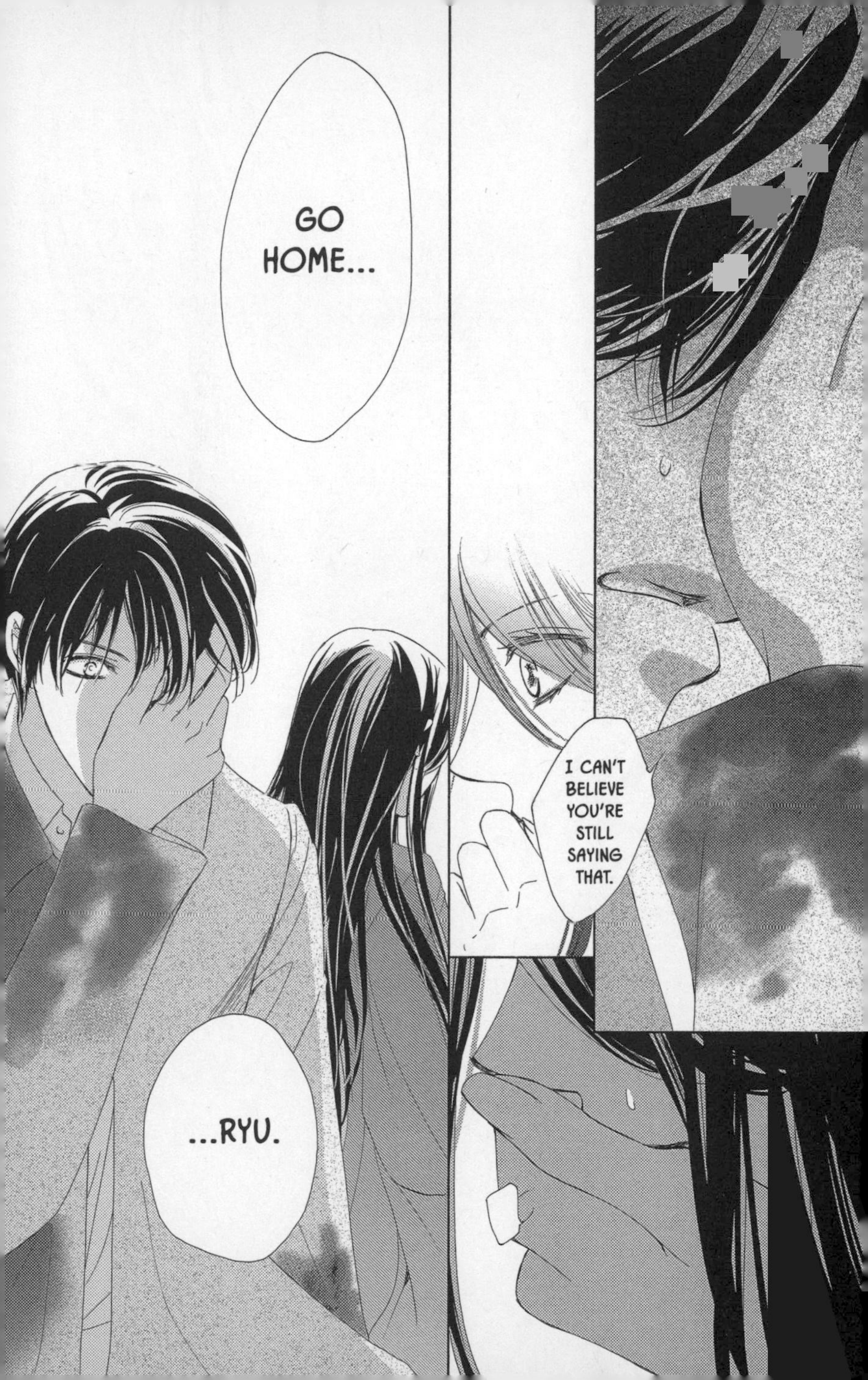
I CAN'T BELIEVE YOU'RE STILL SAYING THAT.
GO HOME...
...RYU.

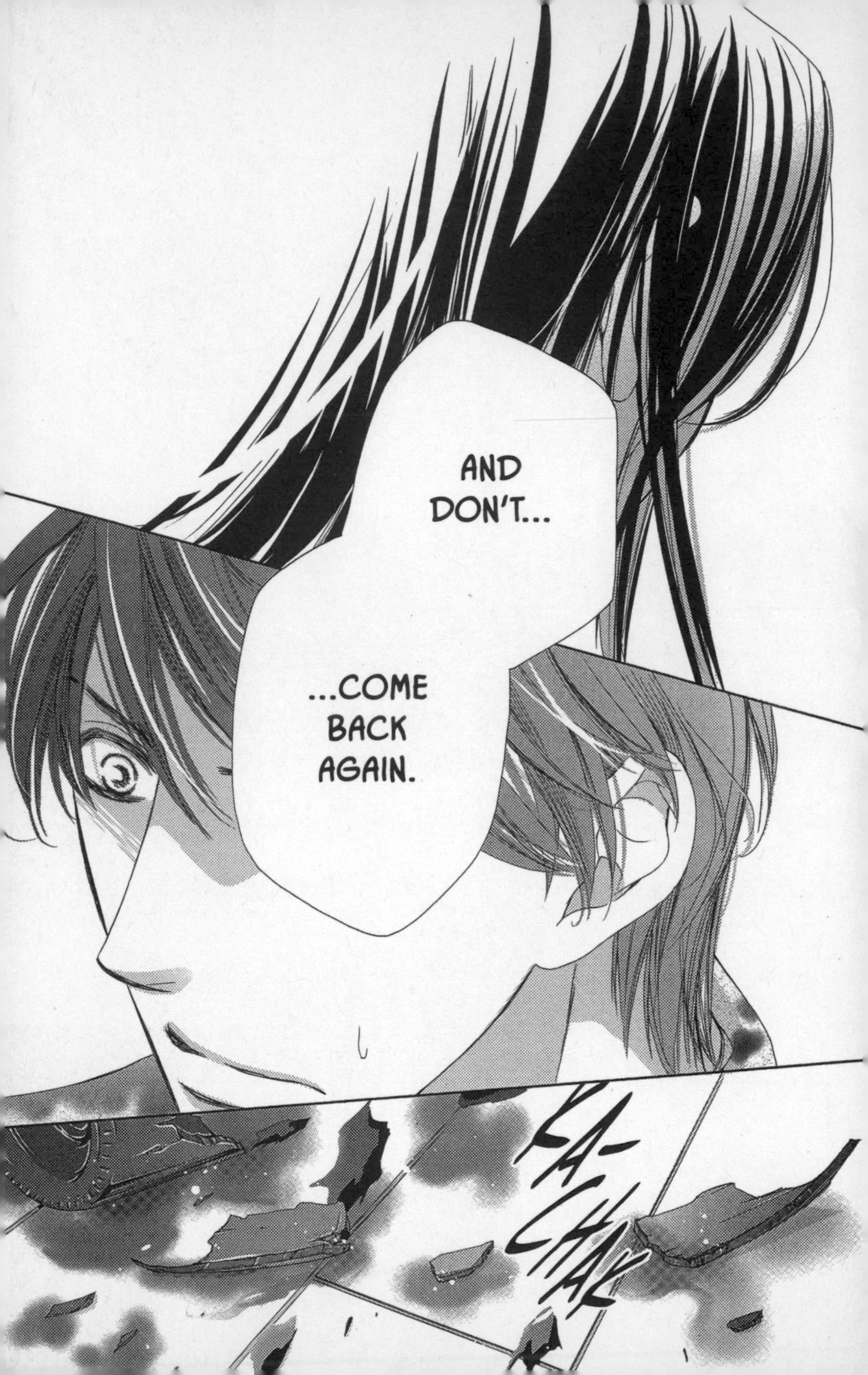
AND DON'T...
...COME BACK AGAIN.
KA-CHAK

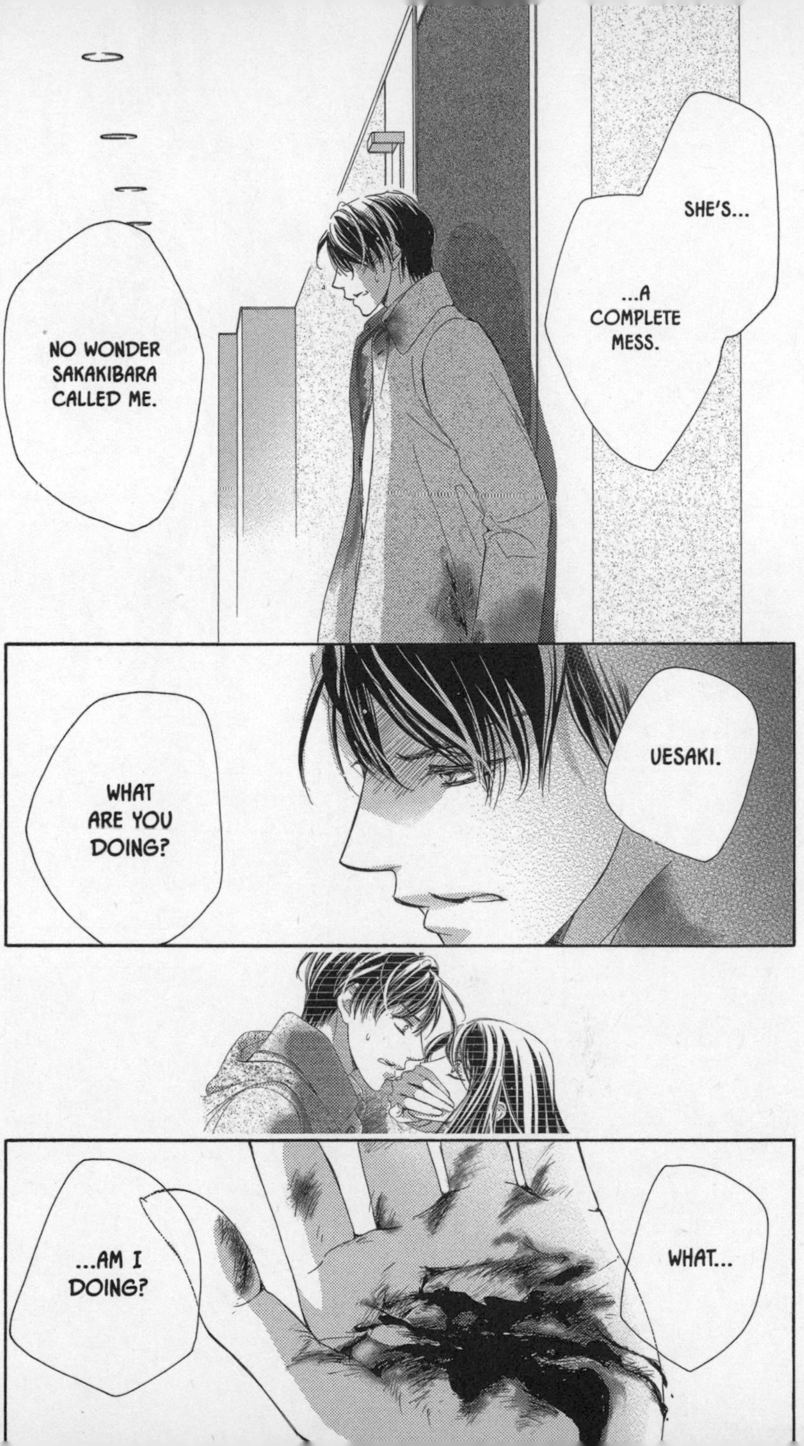
SHE'S...
...A COMPLETE MESS.
NO WONDER SAKAKIBARA CALLED ME.
UESAKI.
WHAT ARE YOU DOING?
WHAT...
...AM I DOING?

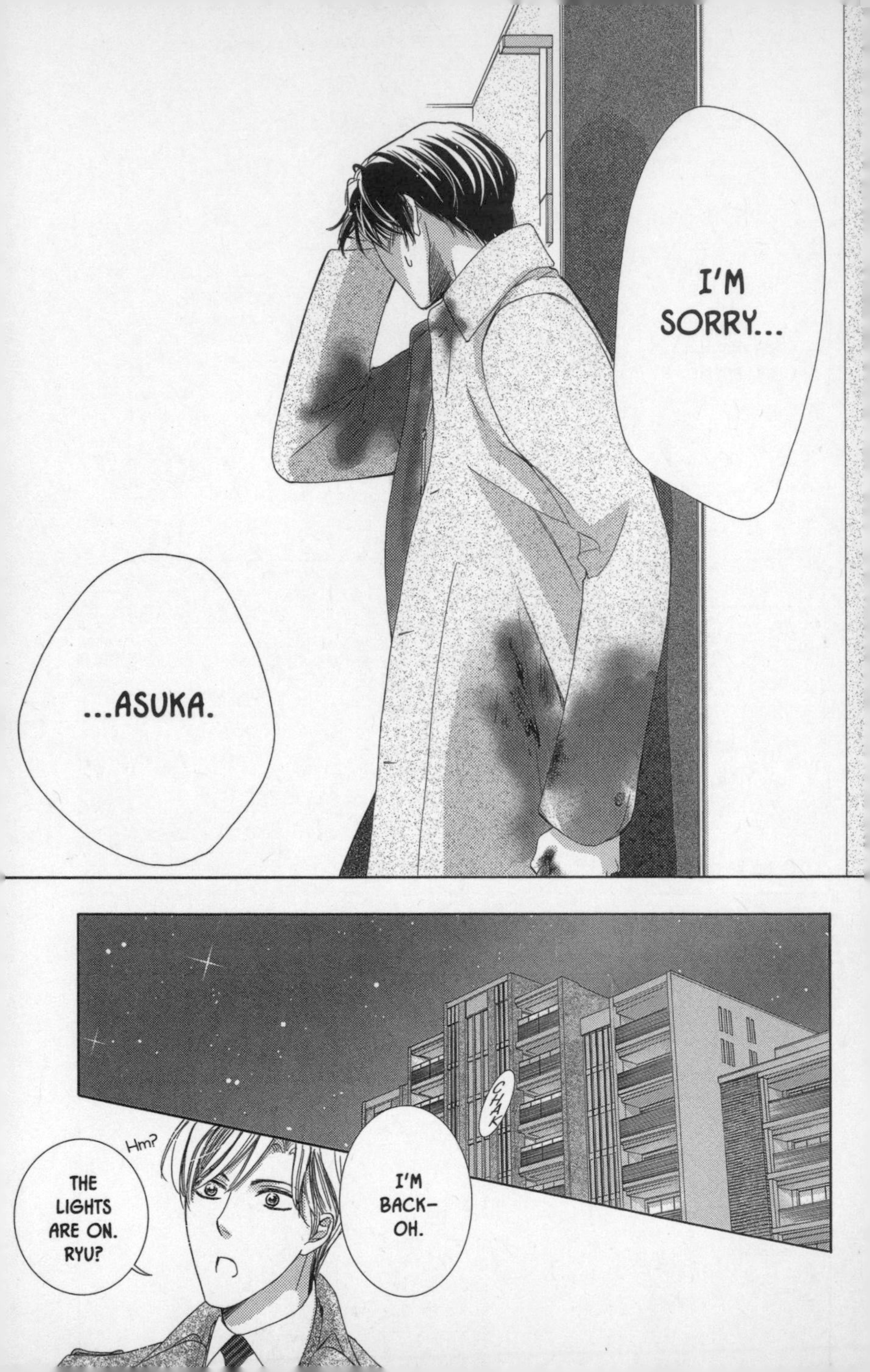
I'M SORRY...
...ASUKA.
CHAK
I'M BACK—OH.
Hm?
THE LIGHTS ARE ON. RYU?

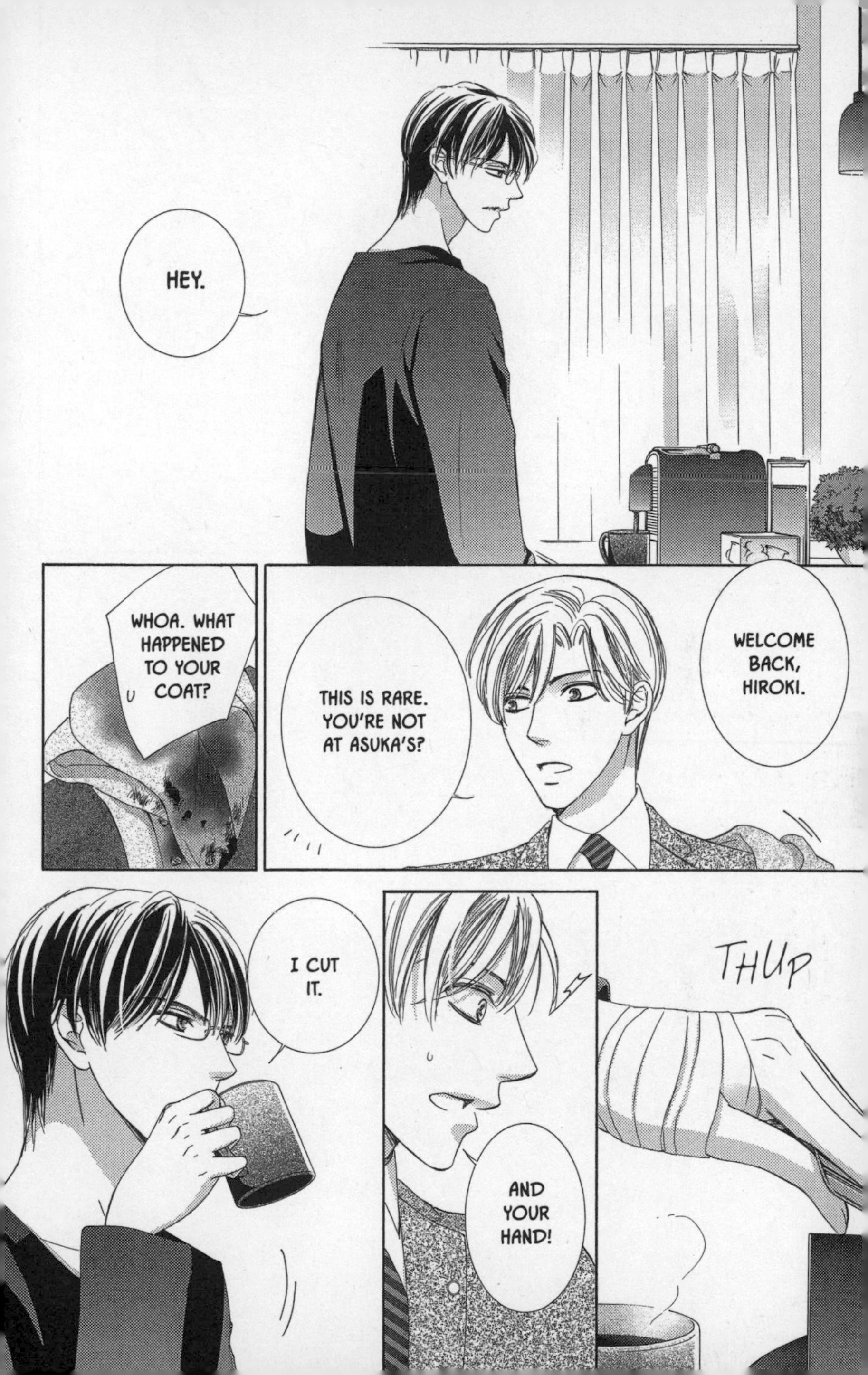
HEY.
WELCOME BACK, HIROKI.
THIS IS RARE. YOU'RE NOT AT ASUKA'S?
WHOA. WHAT HAPPENED TO YOUR COAT?
THUP
AND YOUR HAND!
I CUT IT.

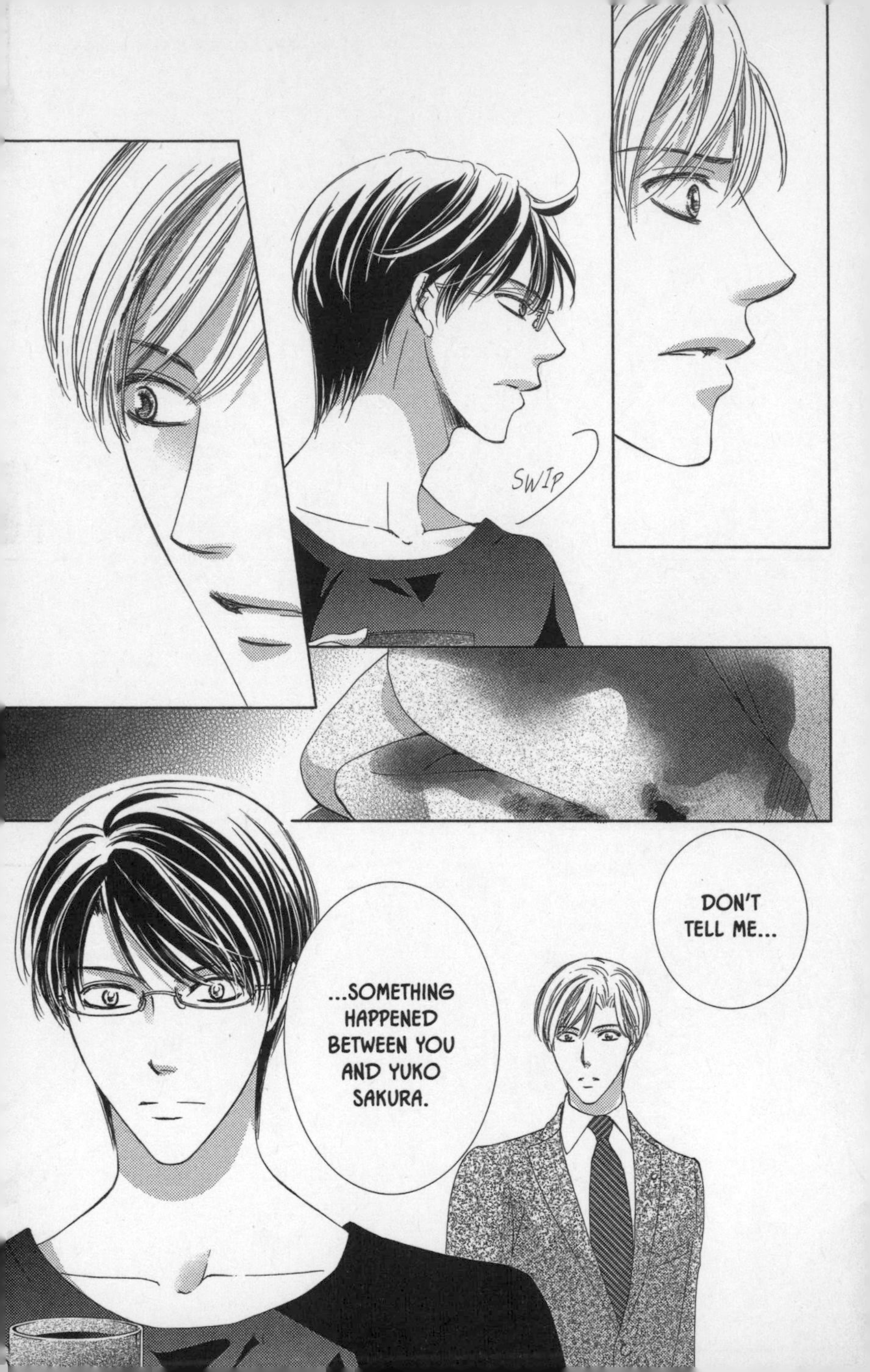
SWIP
DON'T TELL ME...
...SOMETHING HAPPENED BETWEEN YOU AND YUKO SAKURA.

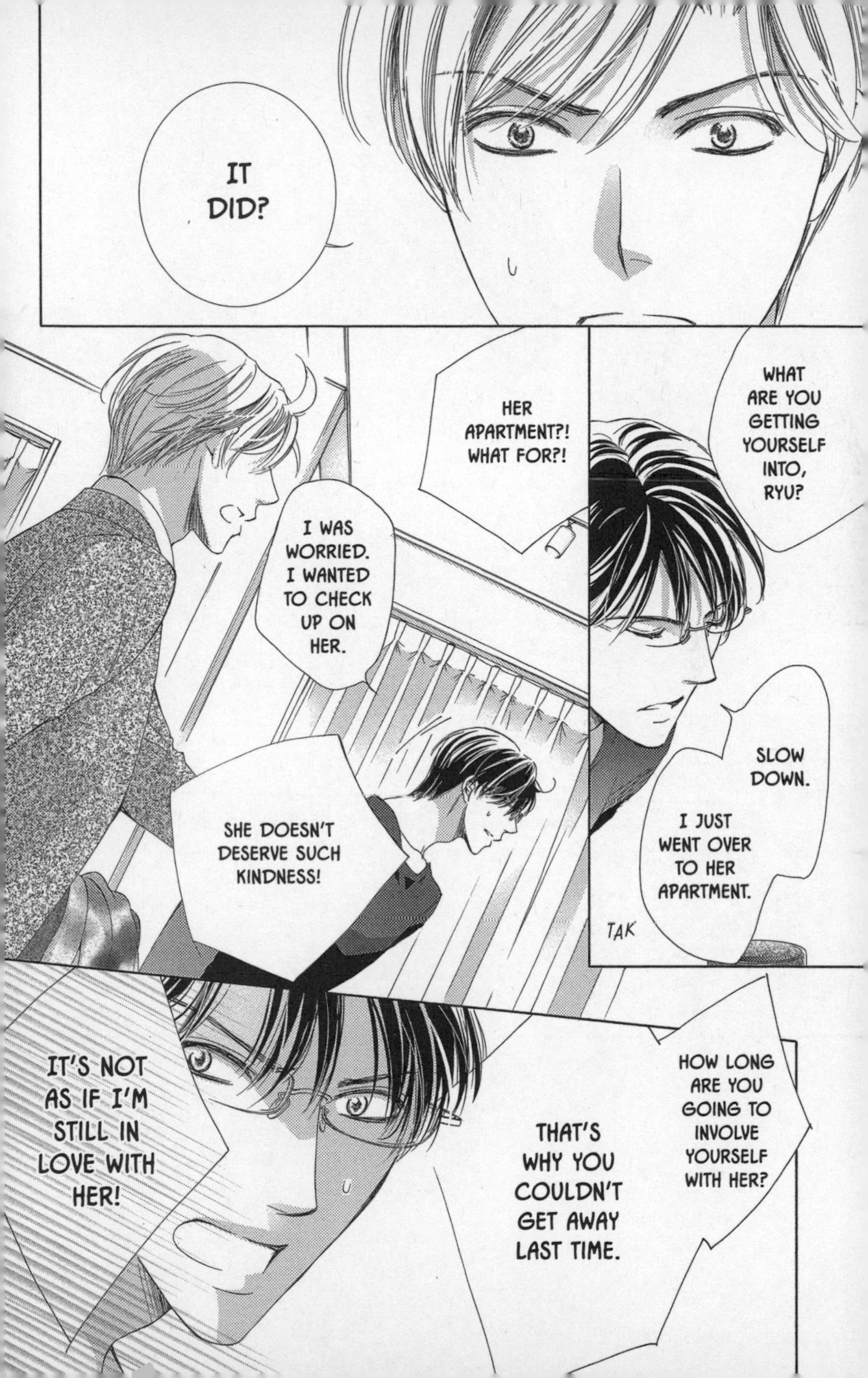
IT DID?
WHAT ARE YOU GETTING YOURSELF INTO, RYU?
SLOW DOWN.
I JUST WENT OVER TO HER APARTMENT.
TAK
HER APARTMENT?! WHAT FOR?!
I WAS WORRIED. I WANTED TO CHECK UP ON HER.
SHE DOESN'T DESERVE SUCH KINDNESS!
HOW LONG ARE YOU GOING TO INVOLVE YOURSELF WITH HER?
THAT'S WHY YOU COULDN'T GET AWAY LAST TIME.
IT'S NOT AS IF I'M STILL IN LOVE WITH HER!

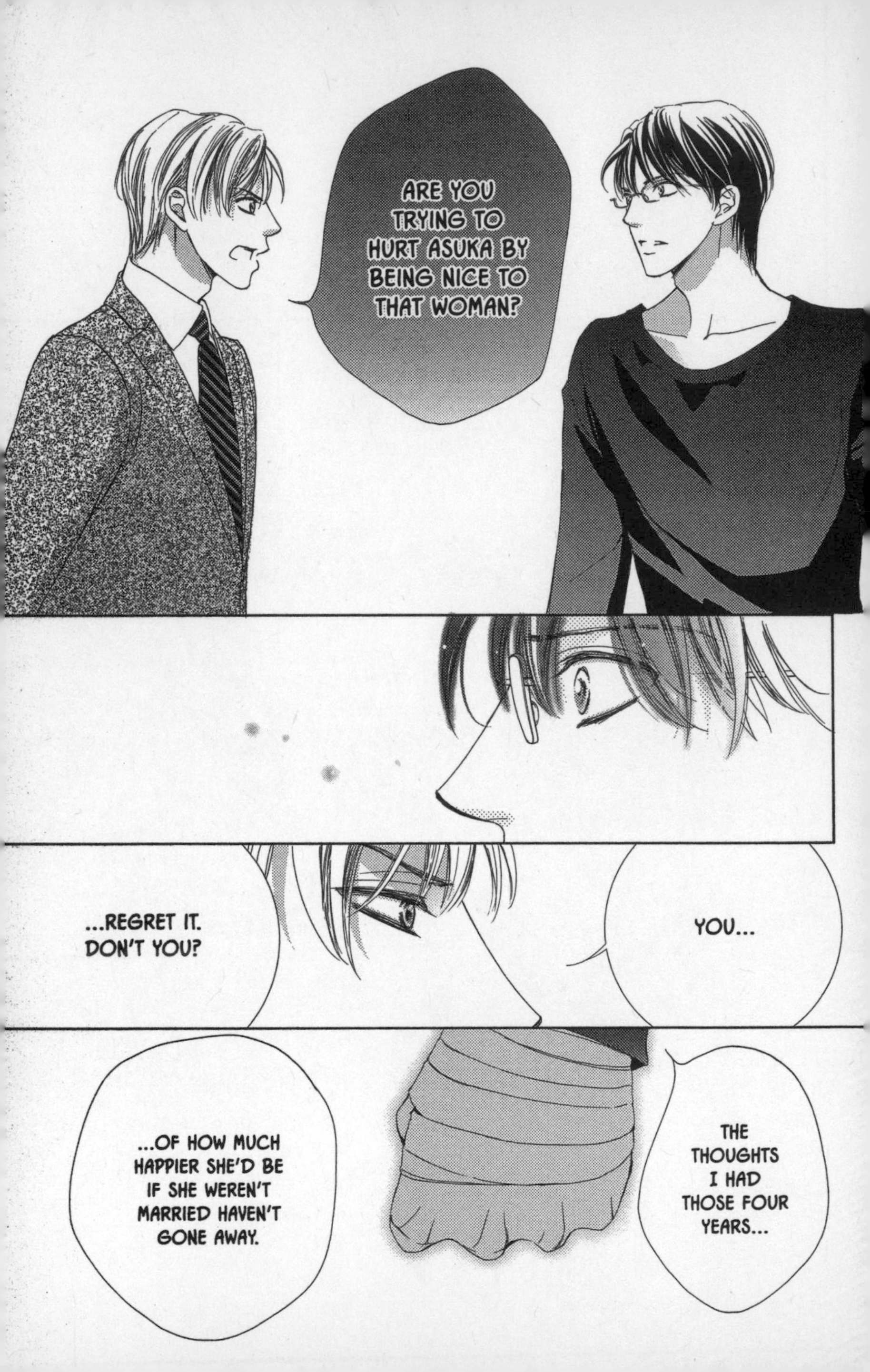
ARE YOU TRYING TO HURT ASUKA BY BEING NICE TO THAT WOMAN?
YOU...
...REGRET IT. DON'T YOU?
THE THOUGHTS I HAD THOSE FOUR YEARS...
...OF HOW MUCH HAPPIER SHE'D BE IF SHE WEREN'T MARRIED HAVEN'T GONE AWAY.

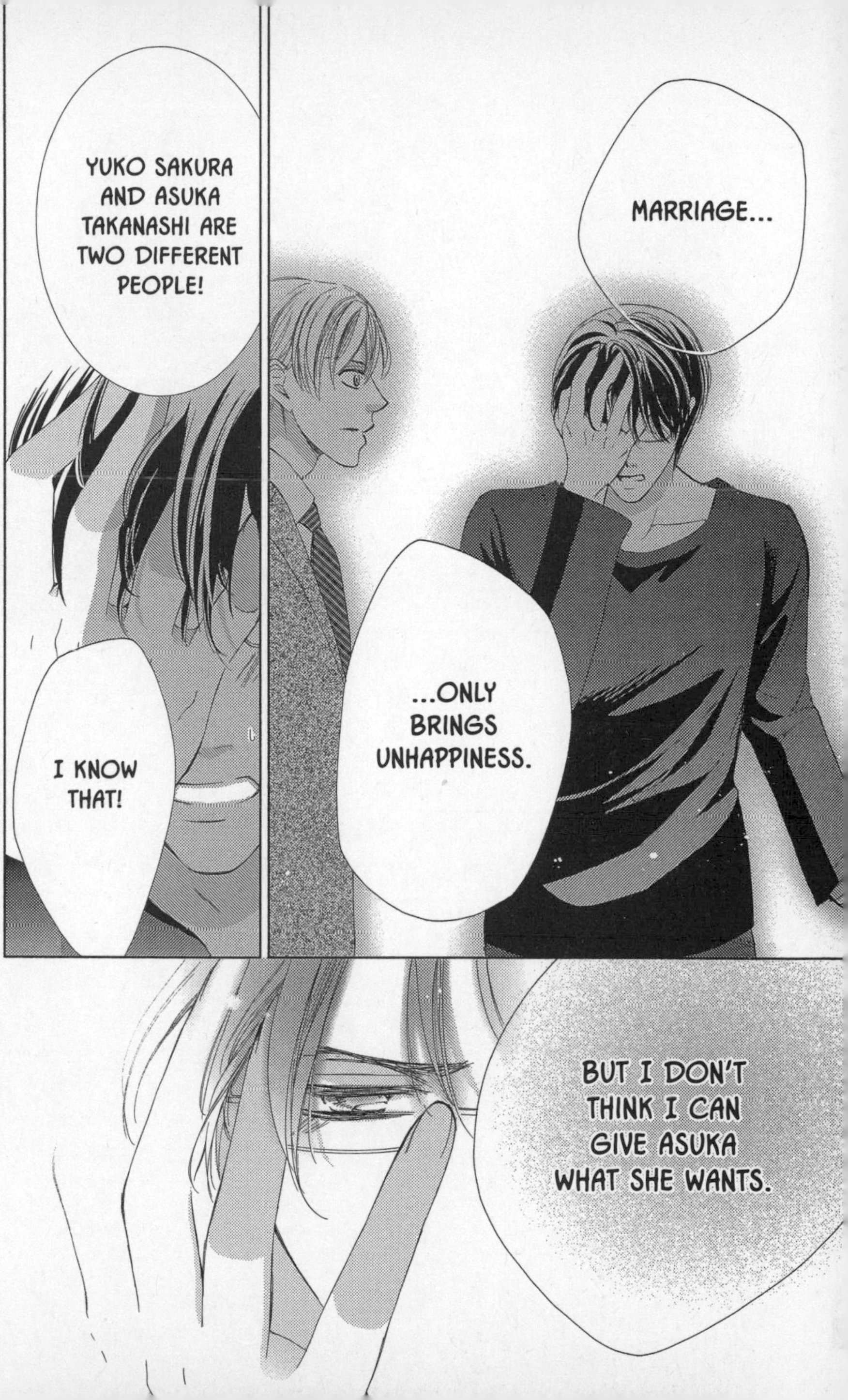
MARRIAGE...
...ONLY BRINGS UNHAPPINESS.
YUKO SAKURA AND ASUKA TAKANASHI ARE TWO DIFFERENT PEOPLE!
I KNOW THAT!
BUT I DON'T THINK I CAN GIVE ASUKA WHAT SHE WANTS.

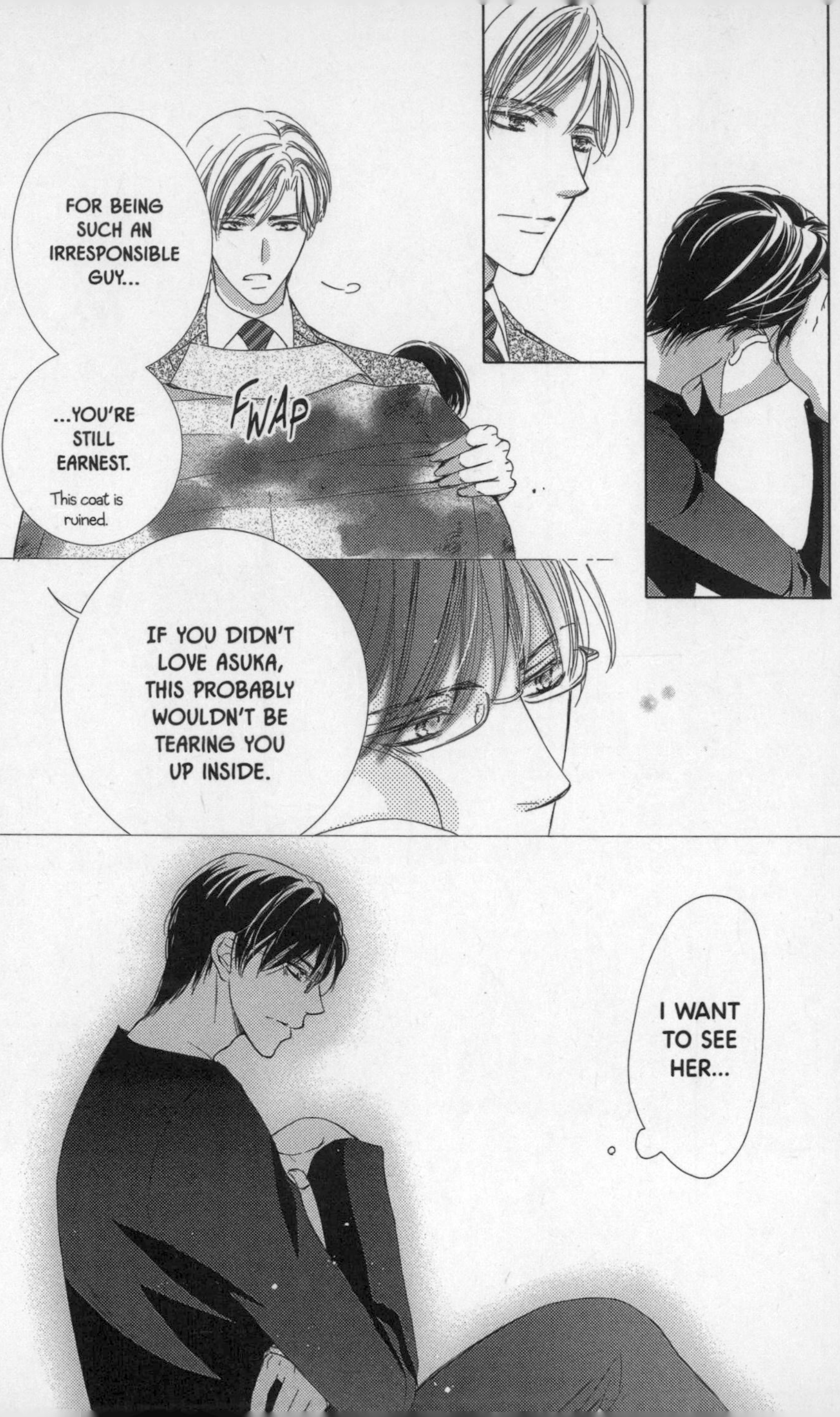
FOR BEING SUCH AN IRRESPONSIBLE GUY...
...YOU'RE STILL EARNEST.
This coat is ruined.
FWAP
IF YOU DIDN'T LOVE ASUKA, THIS PROBABLY WOULDN'T BE TEARING YOU UP INSIDE.
I WANT TO SEE HER...

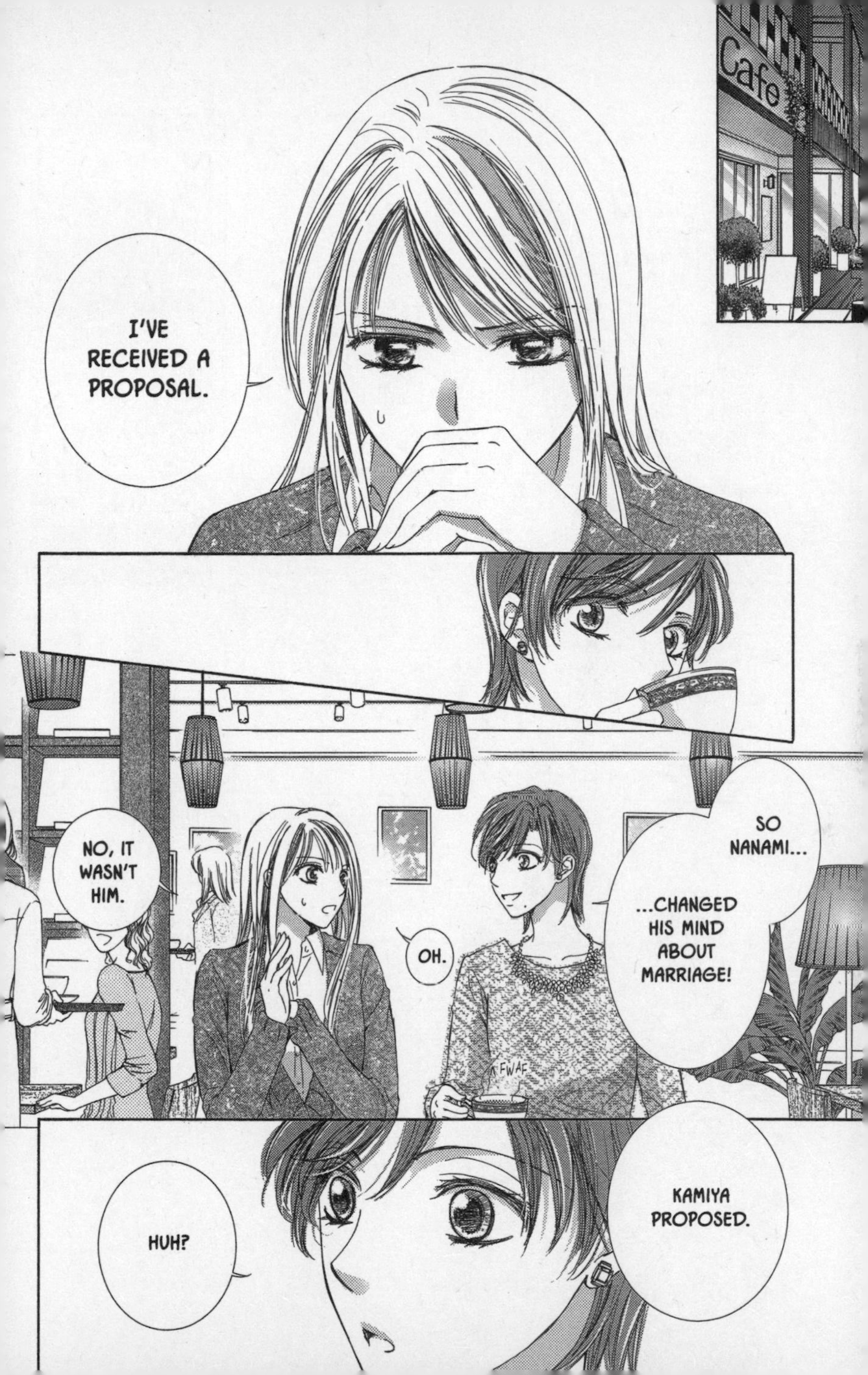
Cafe
I'VE RECEIVED A PROPOSAL.
SO NANAMI...
...CHANGED HIS MIND ABOUT MARRIAGE!
FWAF
OH.
NO, IT WASN'T HIM.
KAMIYA PROPOSED.
HUH?

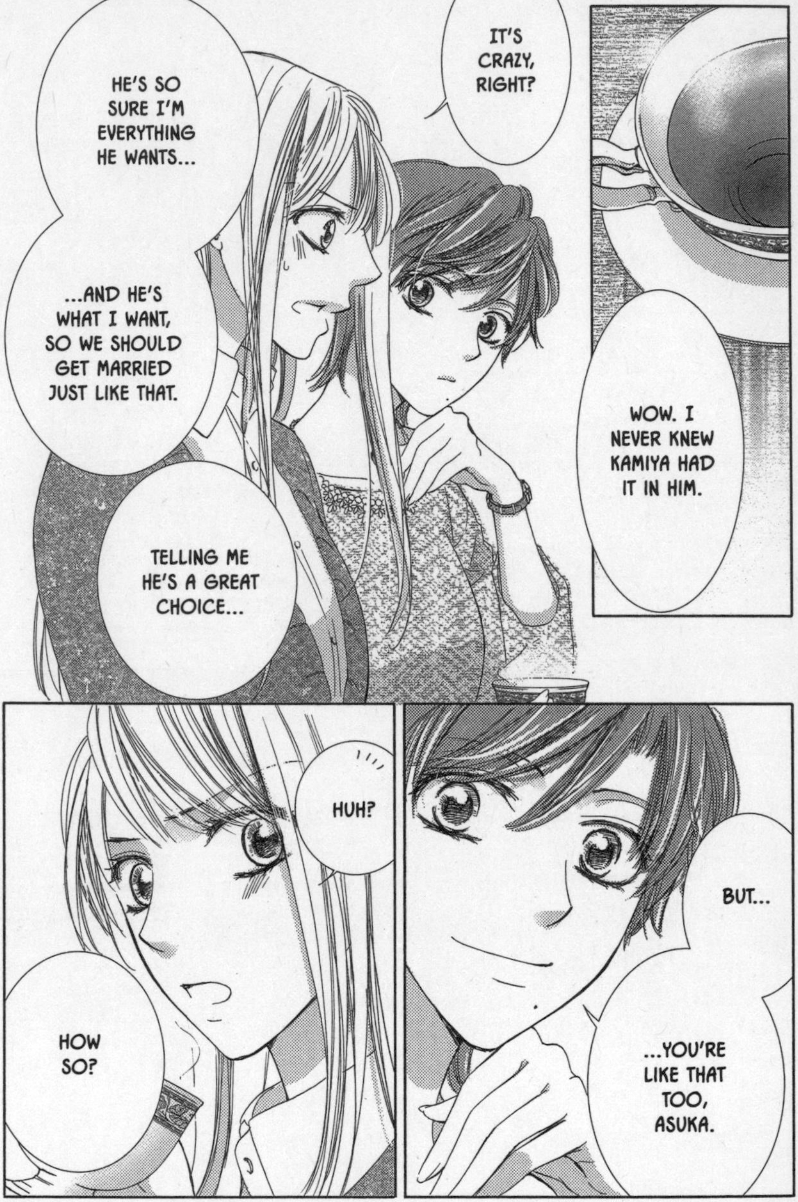
WOW. I NEVER KNEW KAMIYA HAD IT IN HIM.
IT'S CRAZY, RIGHT?
HE'S SO SURE I'M EVERYTHING HE WANTS...
...AND HE'S WHAT I WANT, SO WE SHOULD GET MARRIED JUST LIKE THAT.
TELLING ME HE'S A GREAT CHOICE...
BUT...
...YOU'RE LIKE THAT TOO, ASUKA.
HUH?
HOW SO?

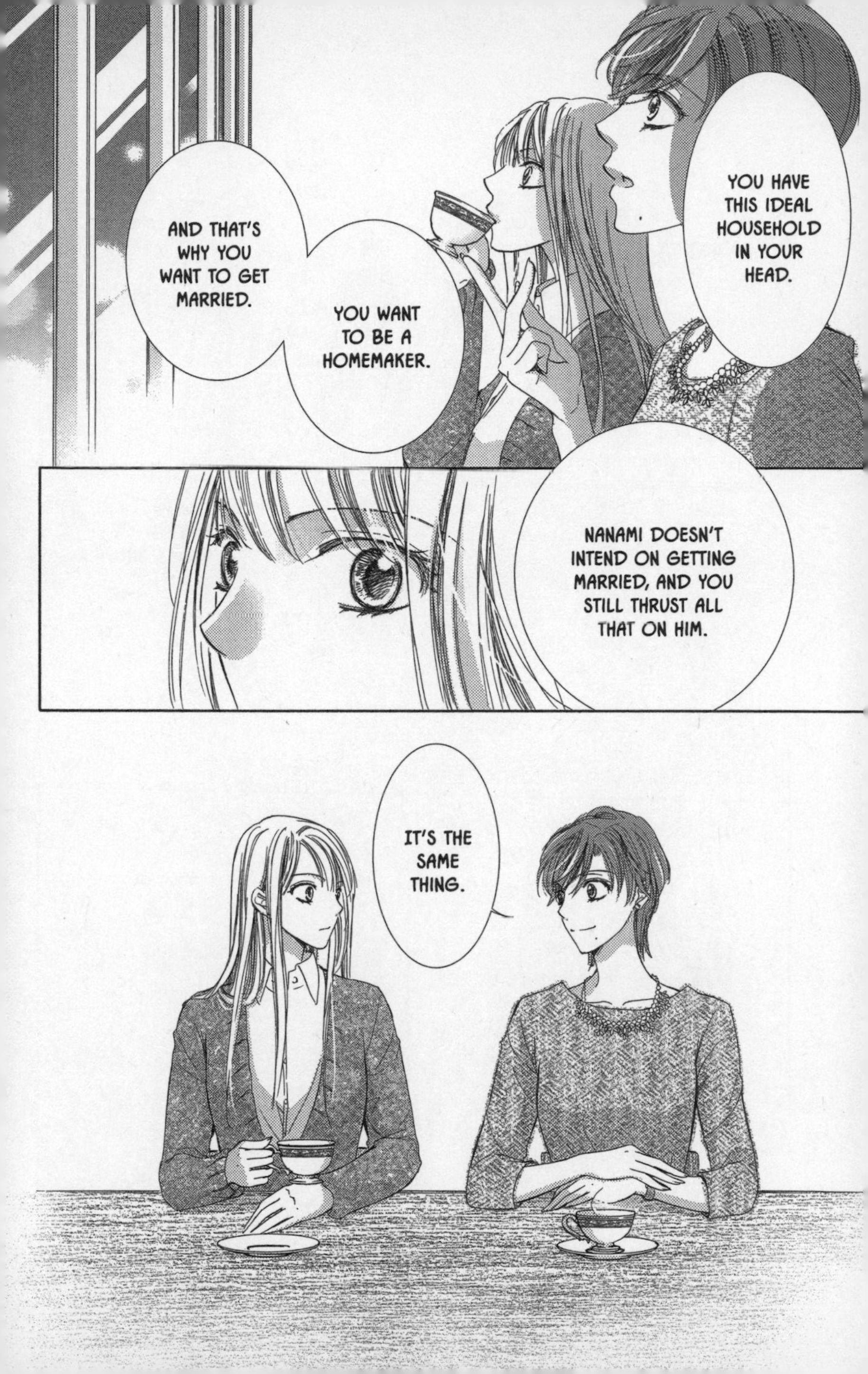
YOU HAVE THIS IDEAL HOUSEHOLD IN YOUR HEAD.
YOU WANT TO BE A HOMEMAKER.
AND THAT'S WHY YOU WANT TO GET MARRIED.
NANAMI DOESN'T INTEND ON GETTING MARRIED, AND YOU STILL THRUST ALL THAT ON HIM.
IT'S THE SAME THING.

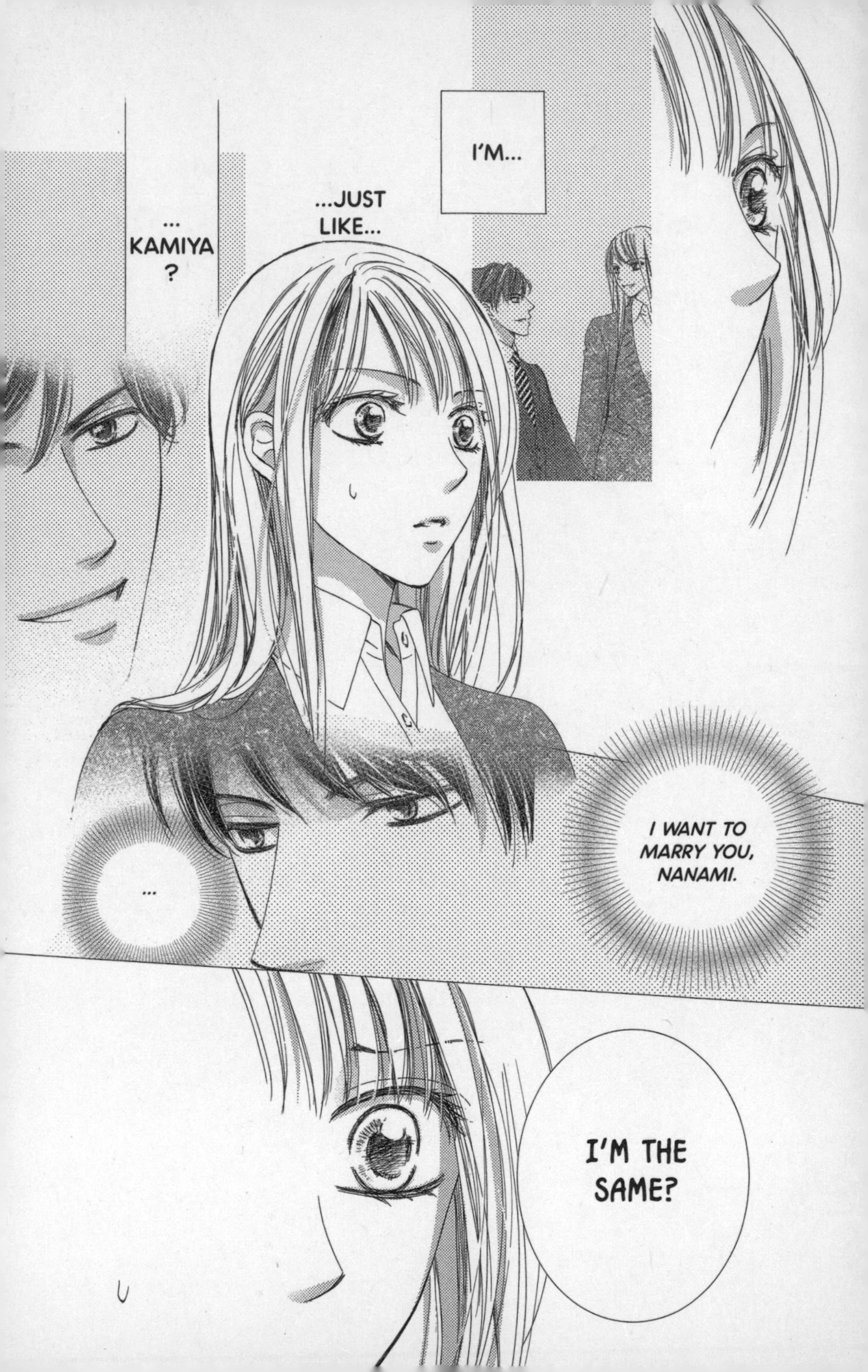
I'M...
...JUST LIKE...
...KAMIYA?
I WANT TO MARRY YOU, NANAMI.
...
I'M THE SAME?

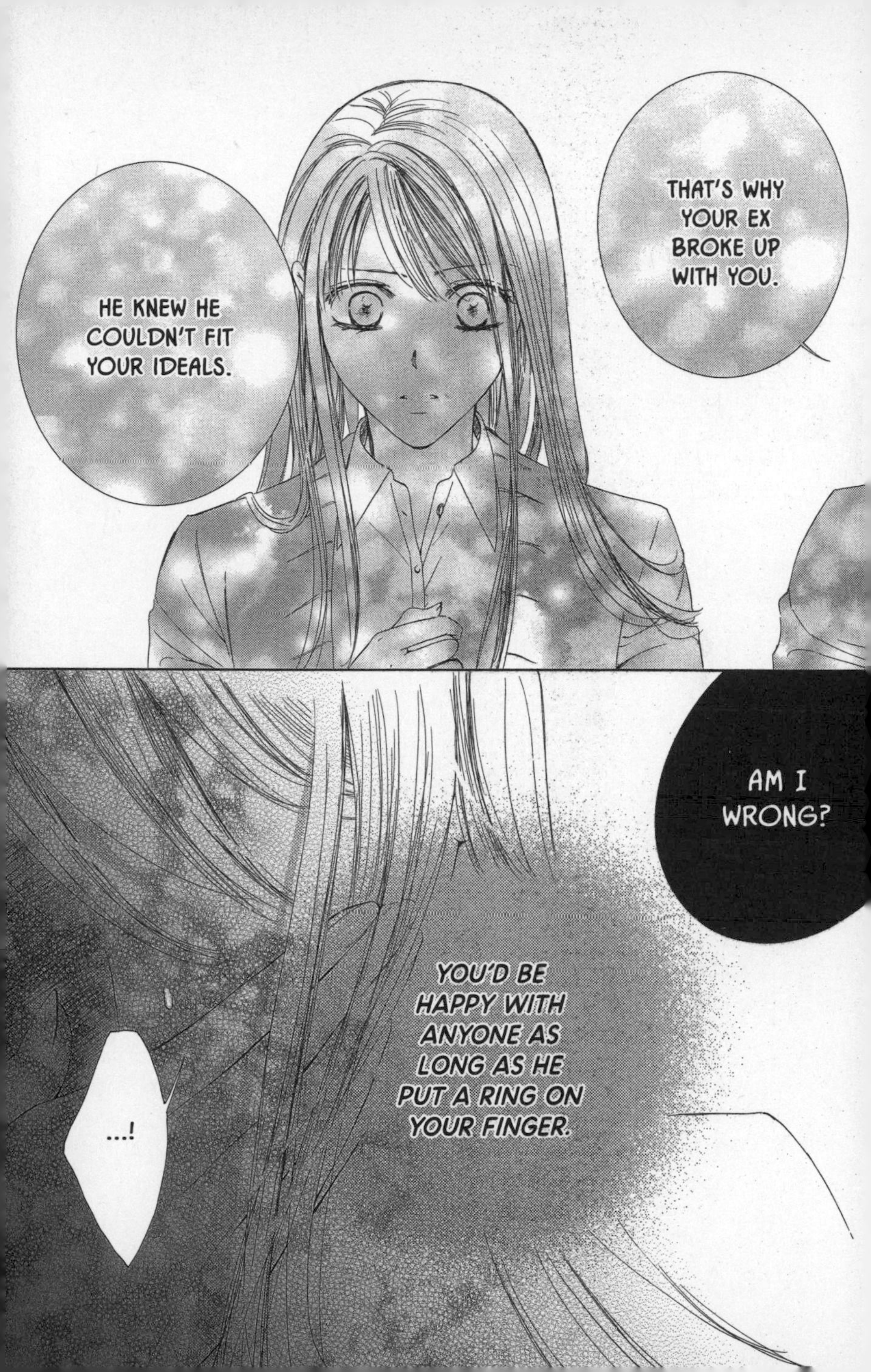
THAT'S WHY YOUR EX BROKE UP WITH YOU.
HE KNEW HE COULDN'T FIT YOUR IDEALS.
AM I WRONG?
YOU'D BE HAPPY WITH ANYONE AS LONG AS HE PUT A RING ON YOUR FINGER.
...!

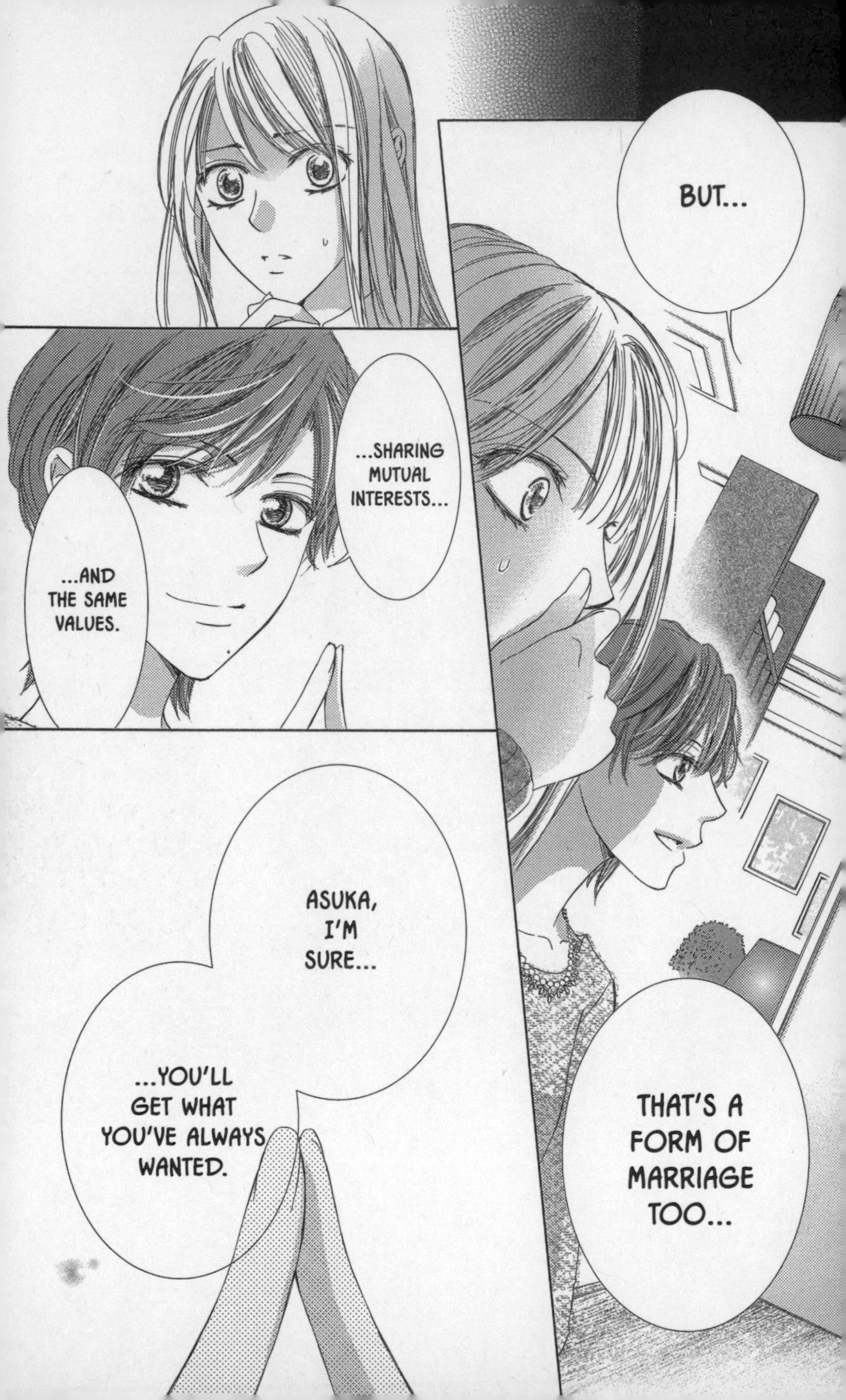
BUT...
THAT'S A FORM OF MARRIAGE TOO...
...SHARING MUTUAL INTERESTS...
...AND THE SAME VALUES.
ASUKA, I'M SURE...
...YOU'LL GET WHAT YOU'VE ALWAYS WANTED.

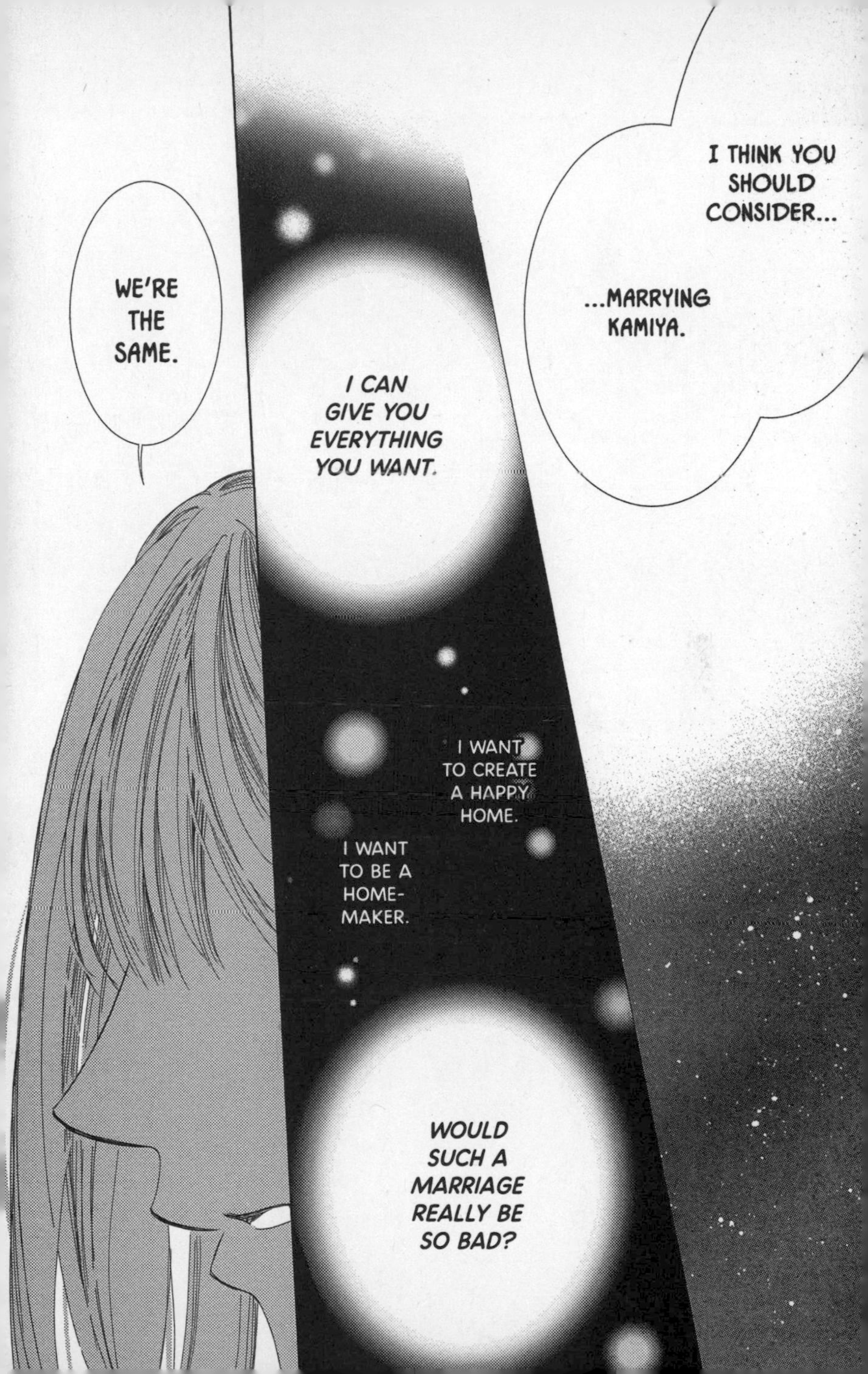

I THINK YOU SHOULD CONSIDER...
...MARRYING KAMIYA.
I CAN GIVE YOU EVERYTHING YOU WANT.
I WANT TO CREATE A HAPPY HOME.
I WANT TO BE A HOME-MAKER.
WOULD SUCH A MARRIAGE REALLY BE SO BAD?
WE'RE THE SAME.

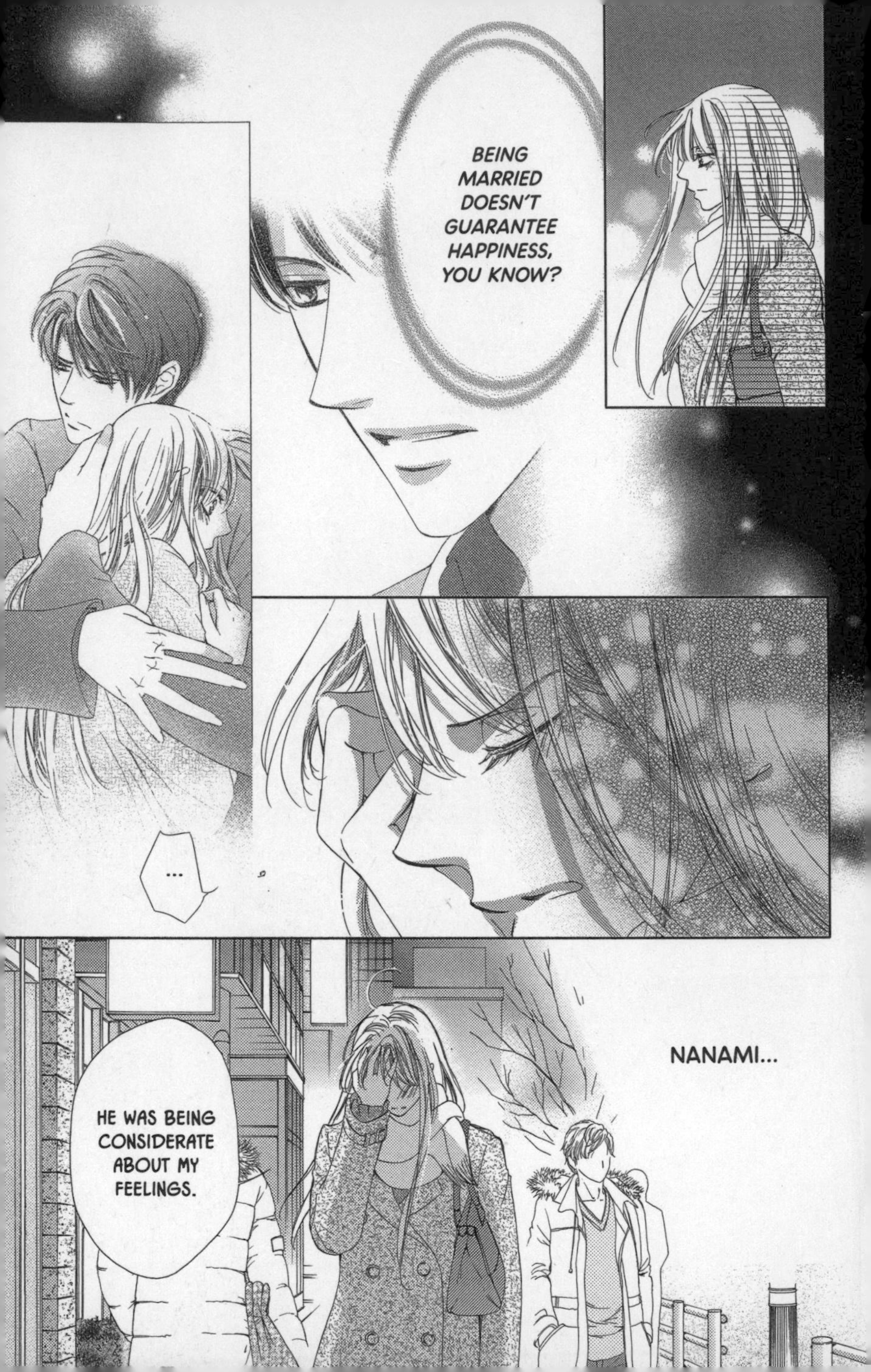
BEING MARRIED DOESN'T GUARANTEE HAPPINESS, YOU KNOW?
...
NANAMI...
HE WAS BEING CONSIDERATE ABOUT MY FEELINGS.

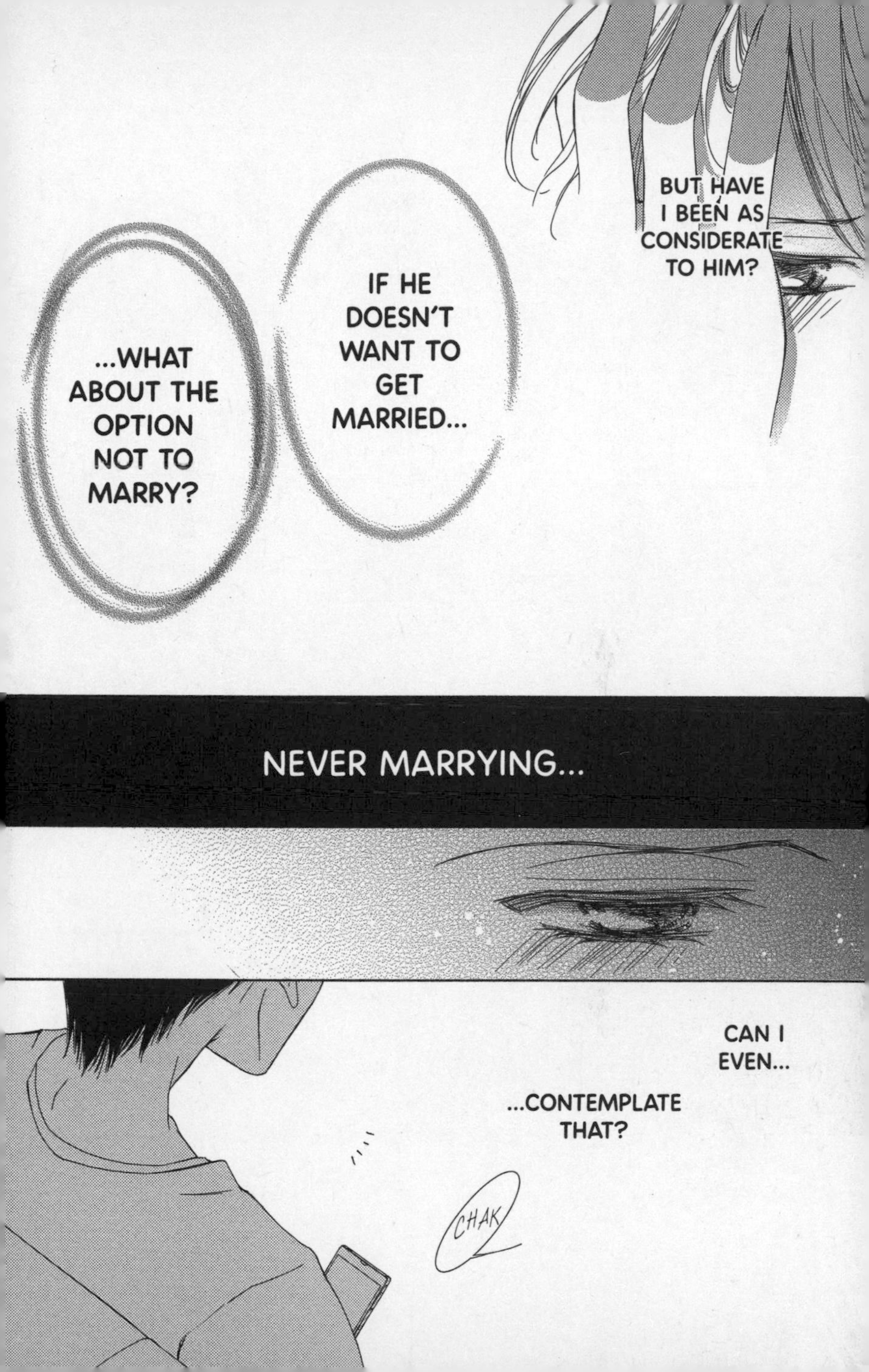
BUT HAVE I BEEN AS CONSIDERATE TO HIM?
IF HE DOESN'T WANT TO GET MARRIED...
...WHAT ABOUT THE OPTION NOT TO MARRY?
NEVER MARRYING...
CAN I EVEN...
...CONTEMPLATE THAT?
CHAK

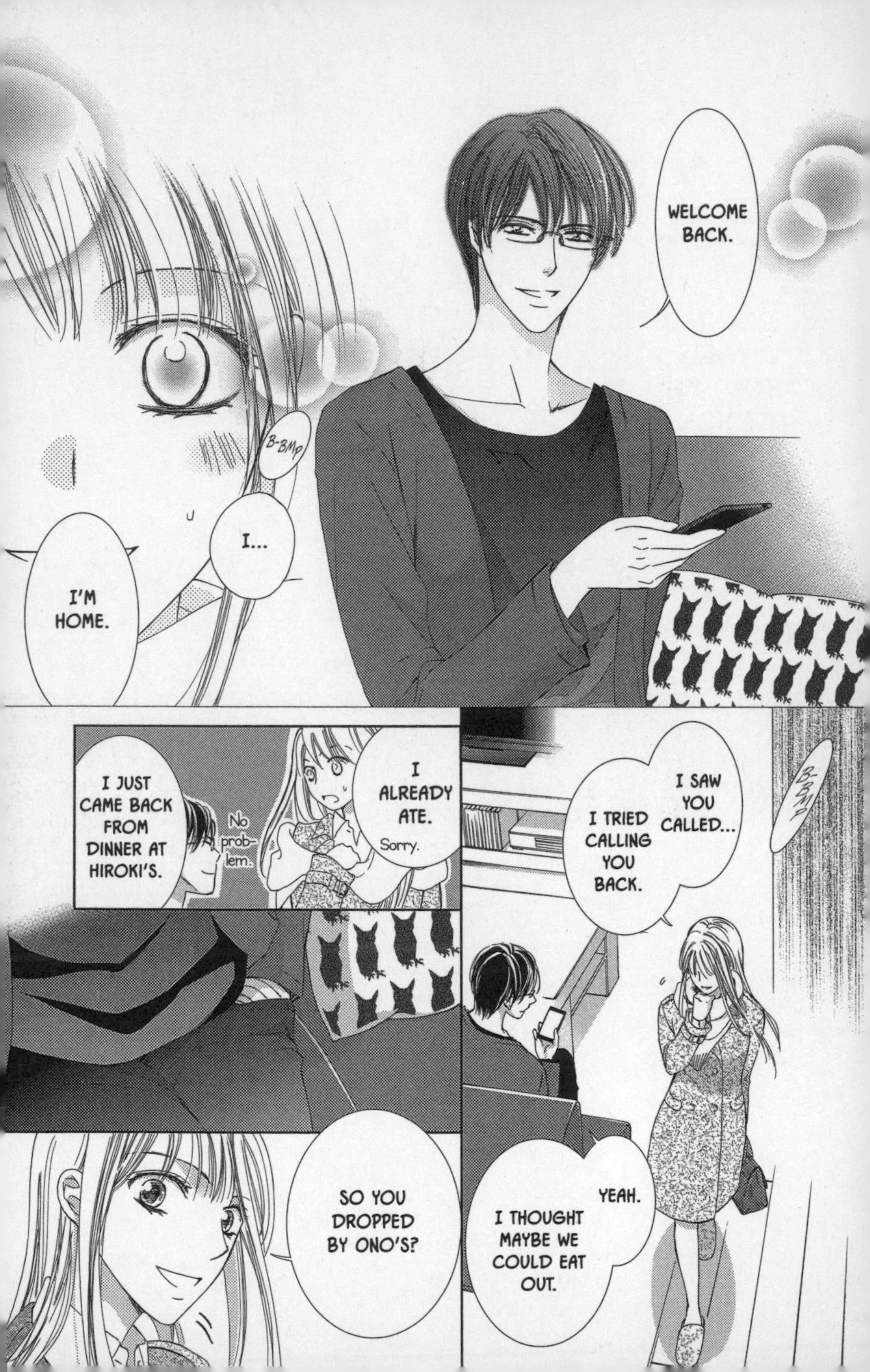
WELCOME BACK.
B-BMP
I...
I'M HOME.
B-BMP
I SAW YOU CALLED...
I TRIED CALLING YOU BACK.
YEAH.
I THOUGHT MAYBE WE COULD EAT OUT.
I ALREADY ATE.
Sorry.
No prob-lem.
I JUST CAME BACK FROM DINNER AT HIROKI'S.
SO YOU DROPPED BY ONO'S?

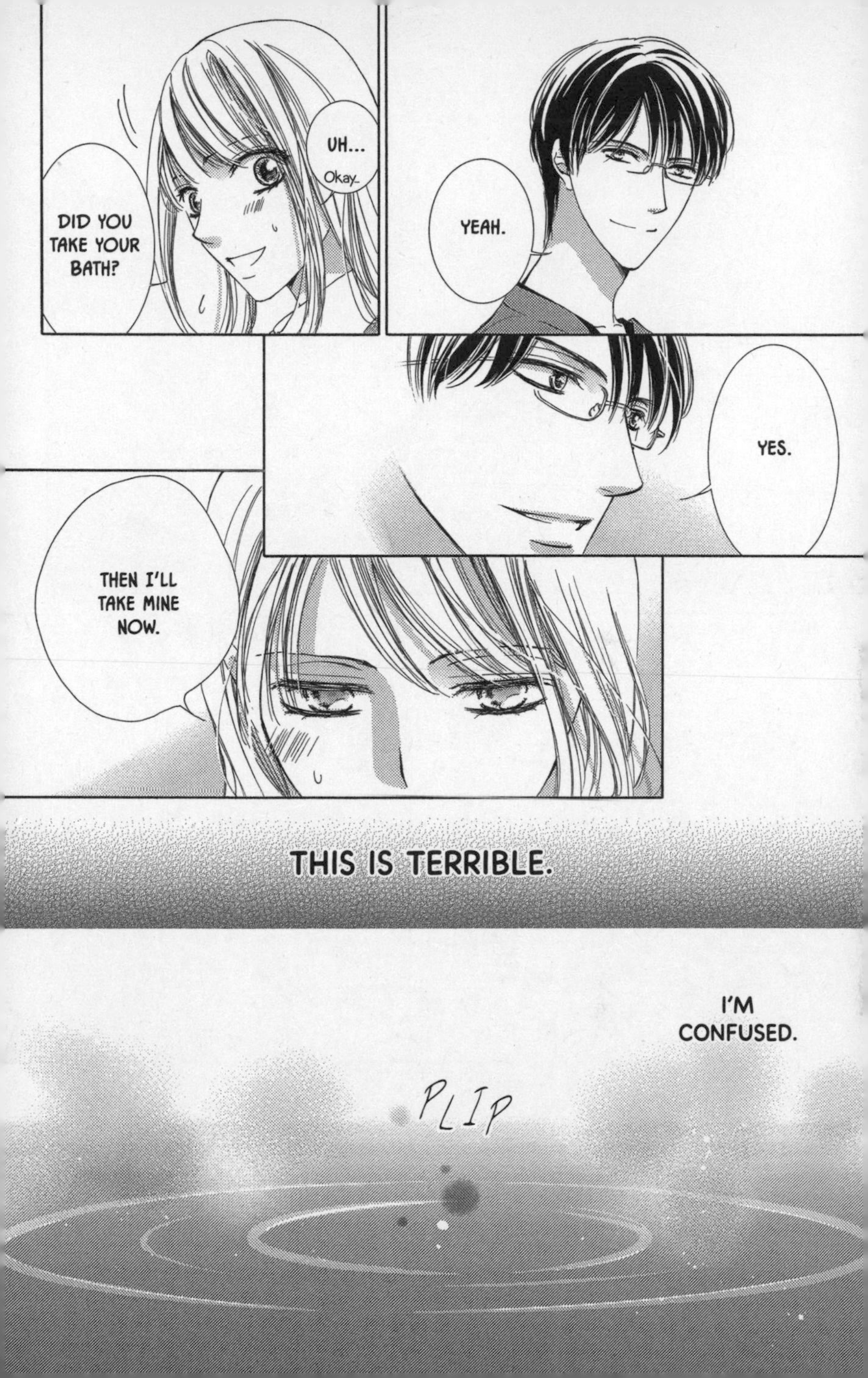
YEAH.
UH...
Okay..
DID YOU TAKE YOUR BATH?
YES.
THEN I'LL TAKE MINE NOW.
THIS IS TERRIBLE.
I'M CONFUSED.
PLIP

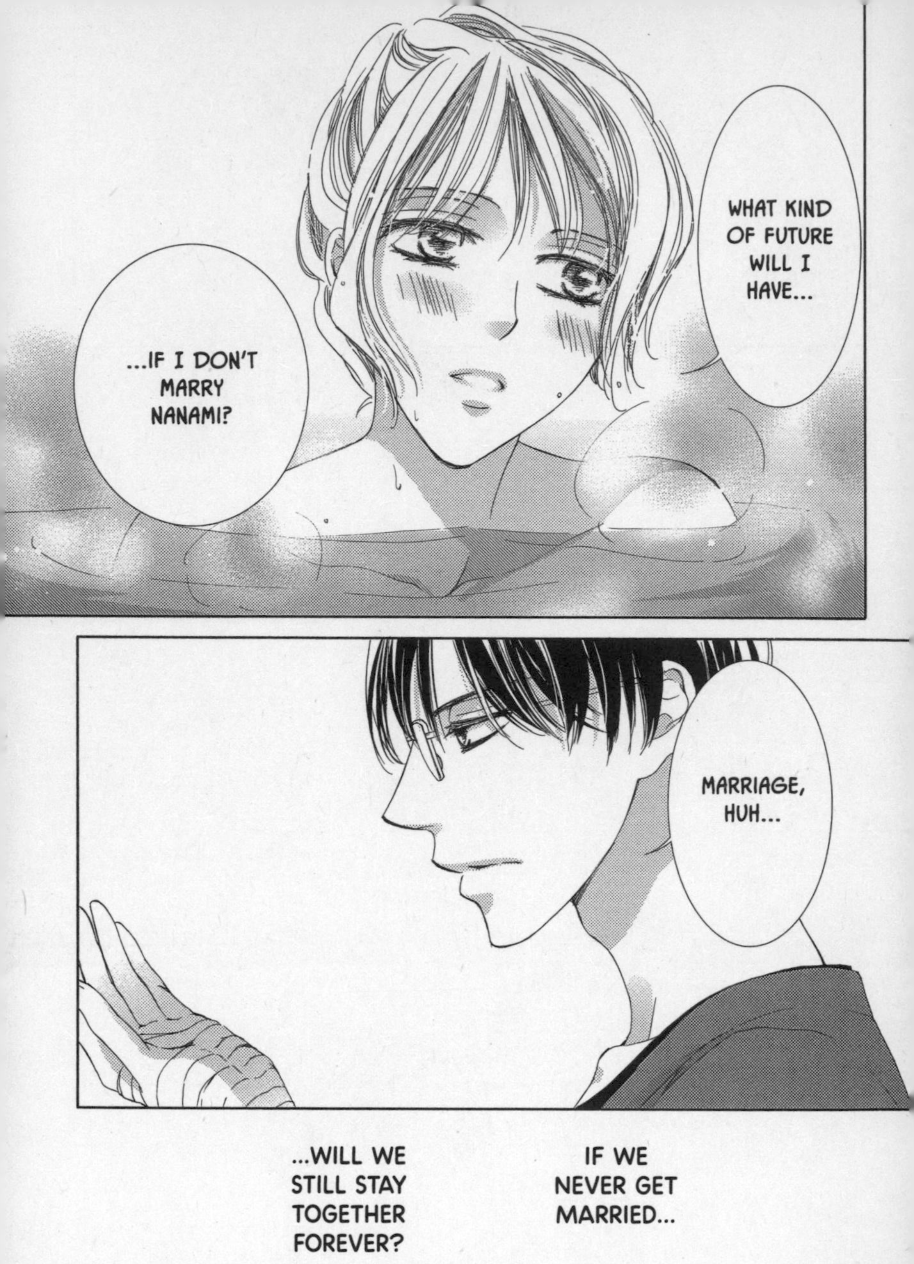
WHAT KIND OF FUTURE WILL I HAVE...
...IF I DON'T MARRY NANAMI?
MARRIAGE, HUH...
IF WE NEVER GET MARRIED...
...WILL WE STILL STAY TOGETHER FOREVER?

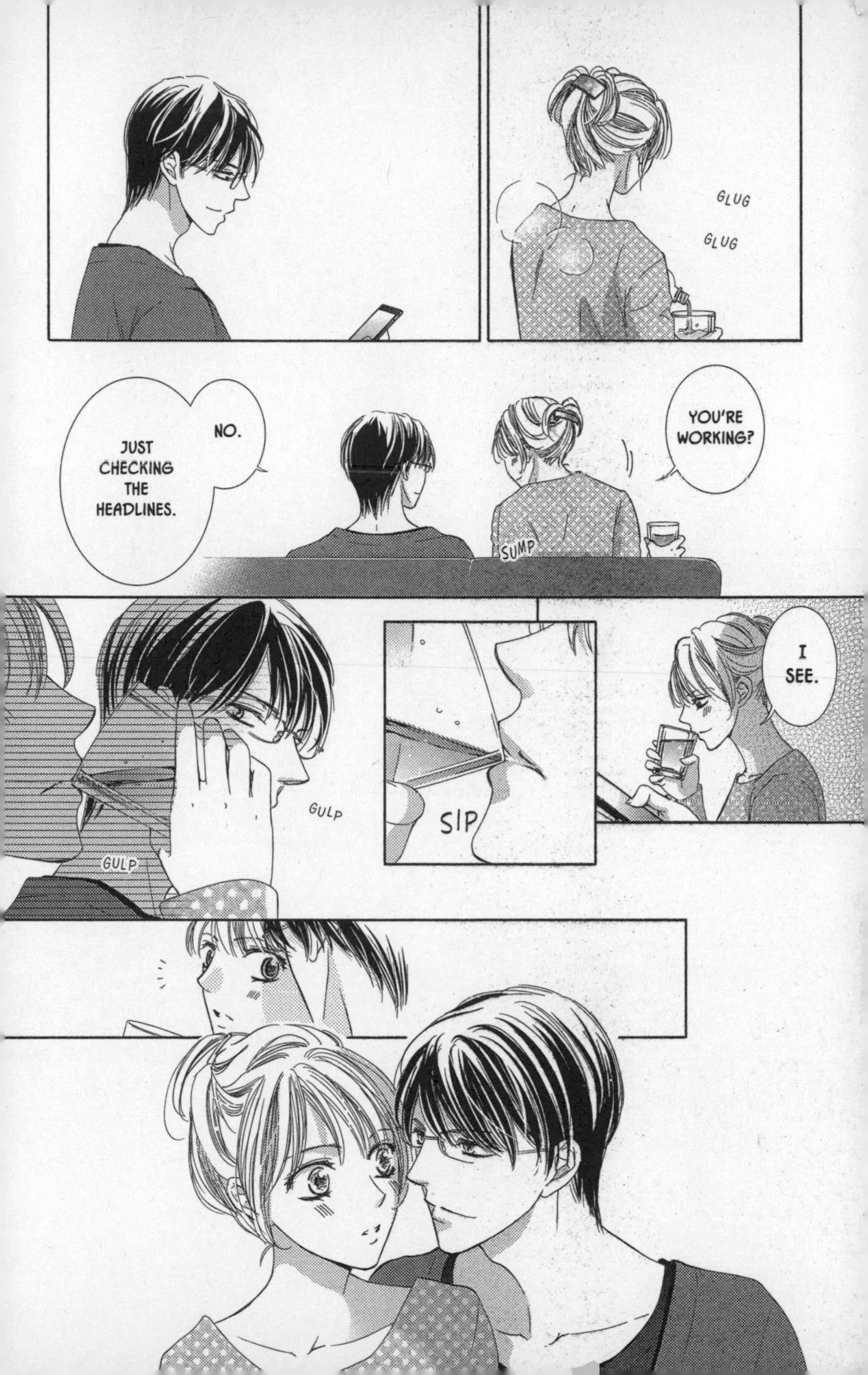
GLUG
GLUG
YOU'RE WORKING?
NO.
JUST CHECKING THE HEADLINES.
SUMP
I SEE.
SIP
GULP
GULP

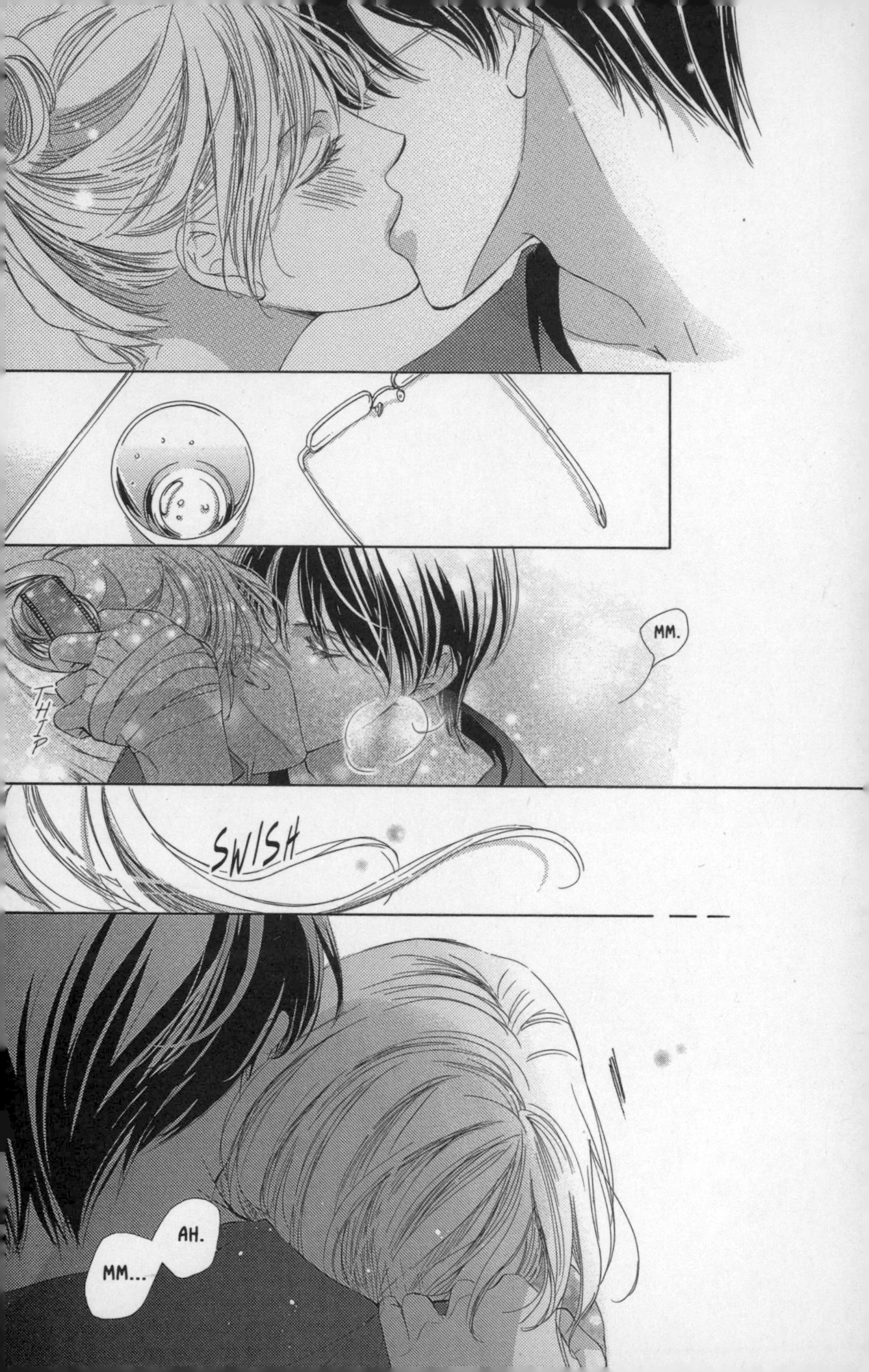
MM.
THIP
SWISH
AH.
MM...

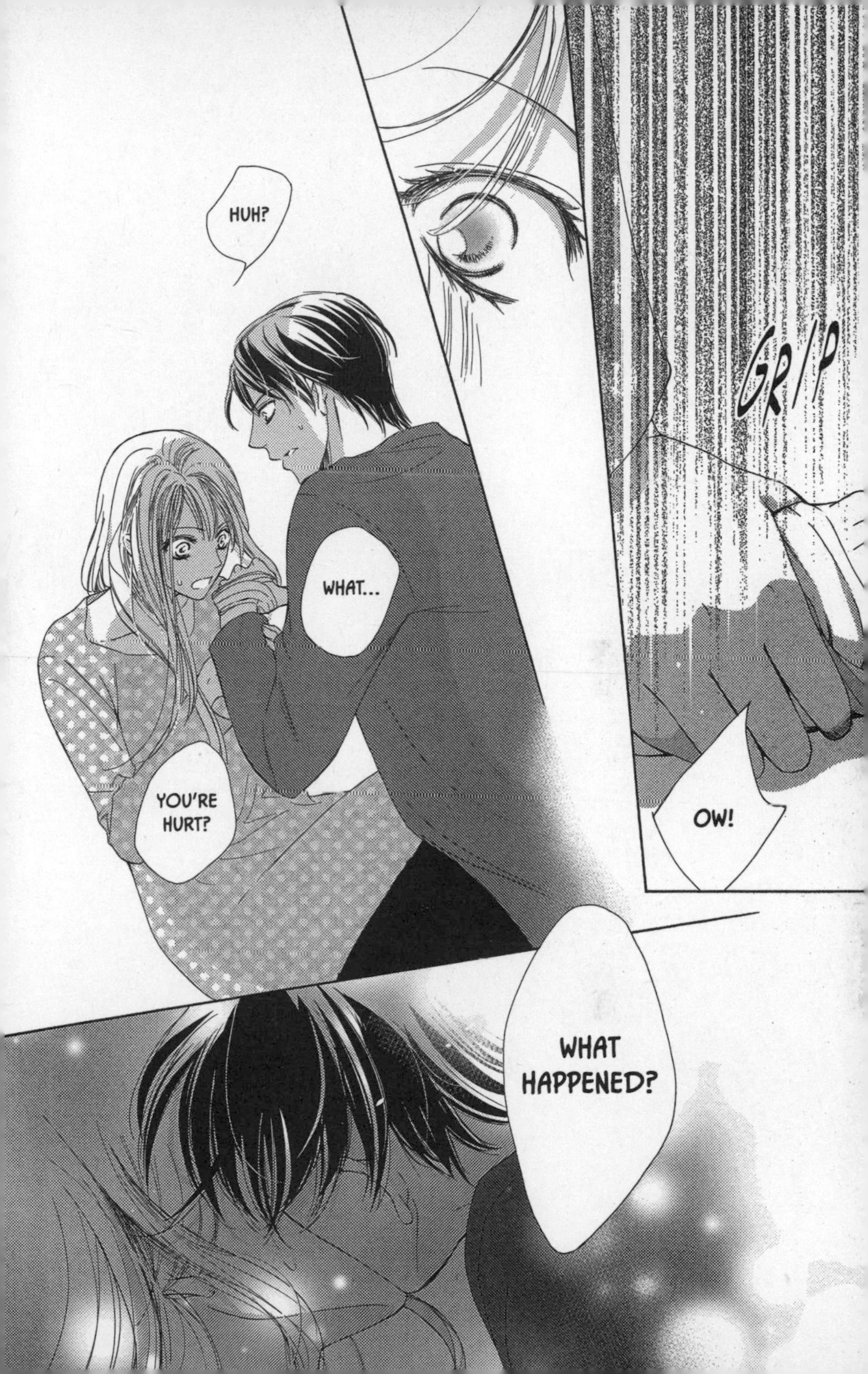
GRIP
OW!
HUH?
WHAT...
YOU'RE HURT?
WHAT HAPPENED?

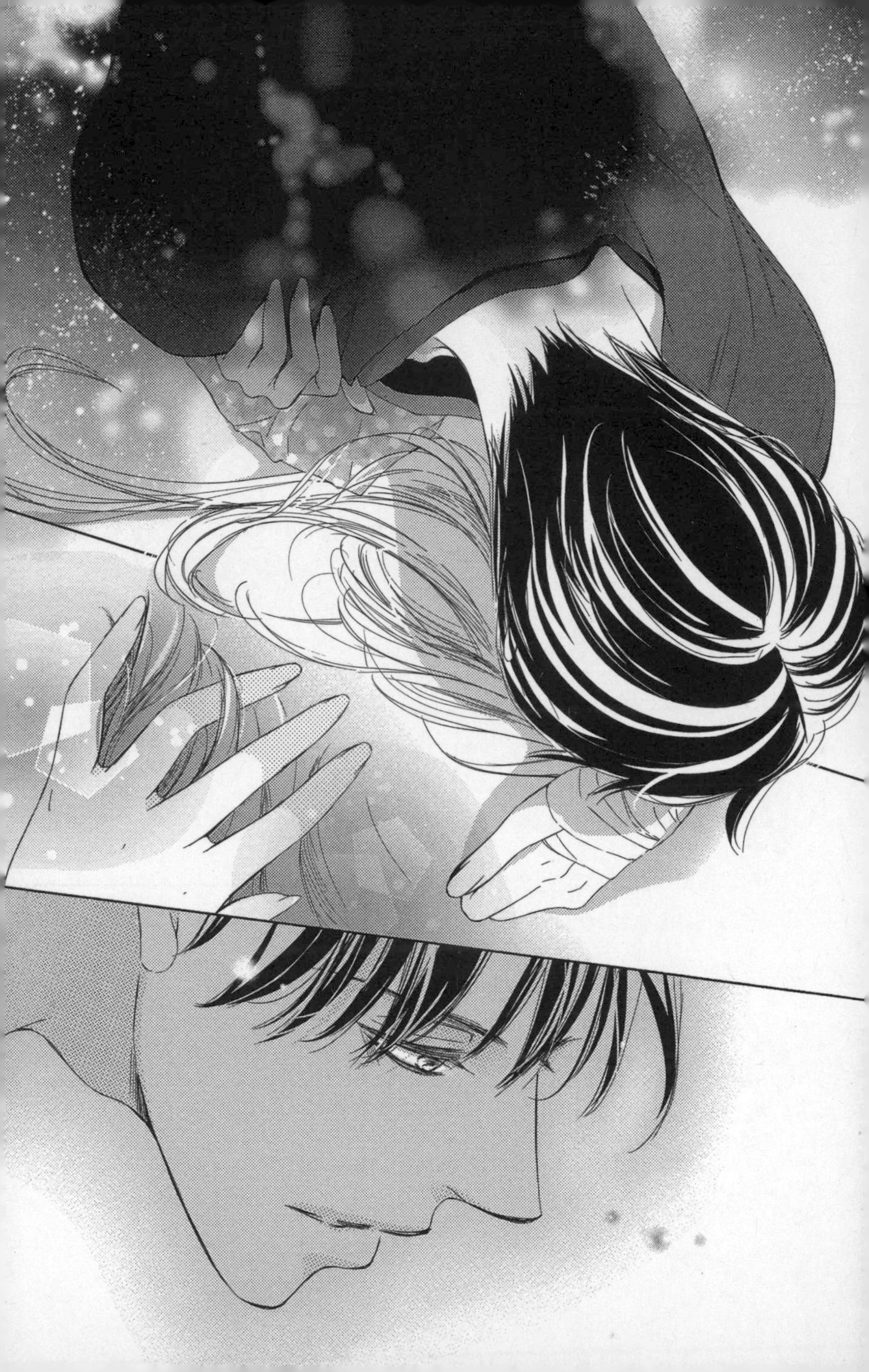

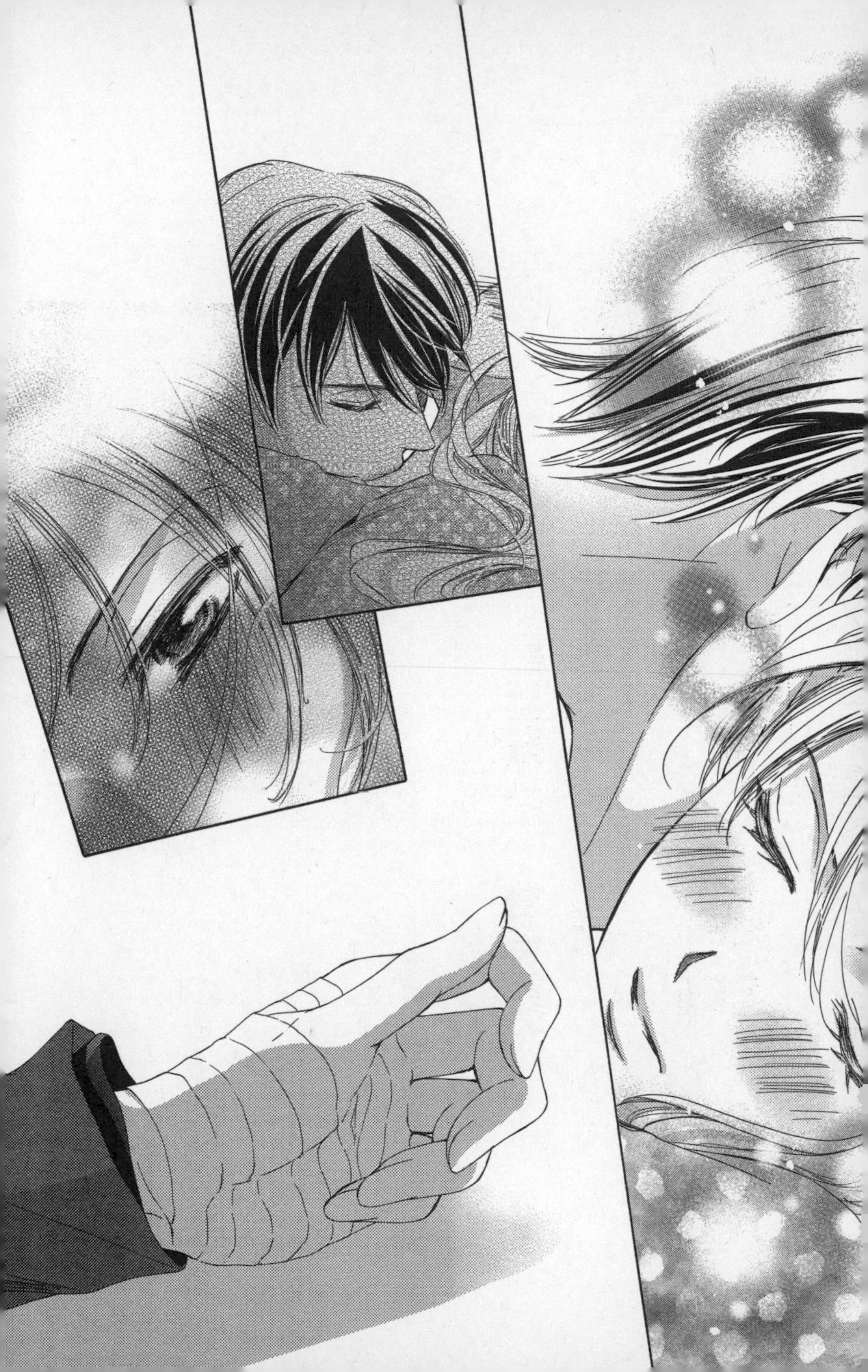

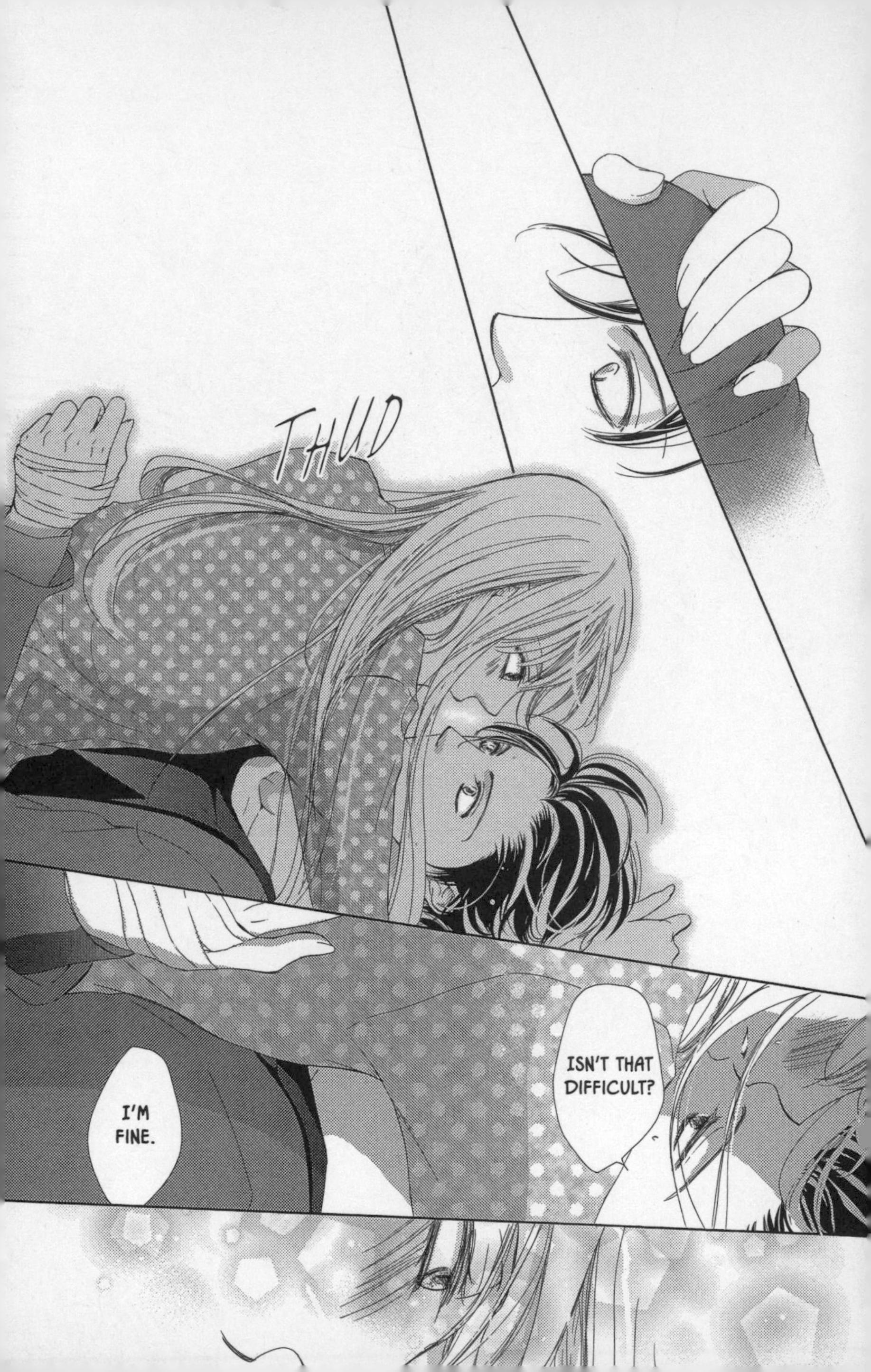
THUD
ISN'T THAT DIFFICULT?
I'M FINE.

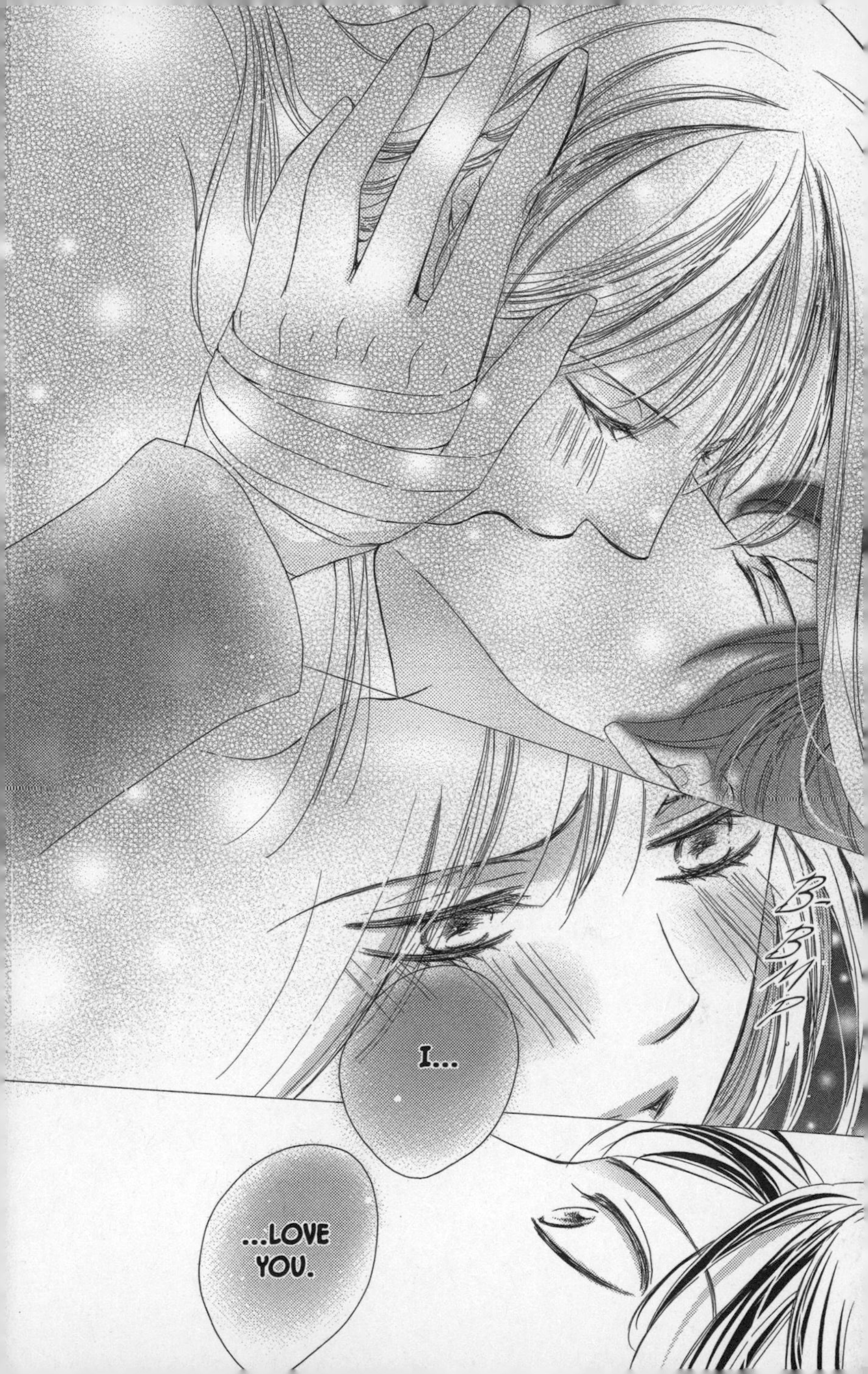
I...
...LOVE YOU.

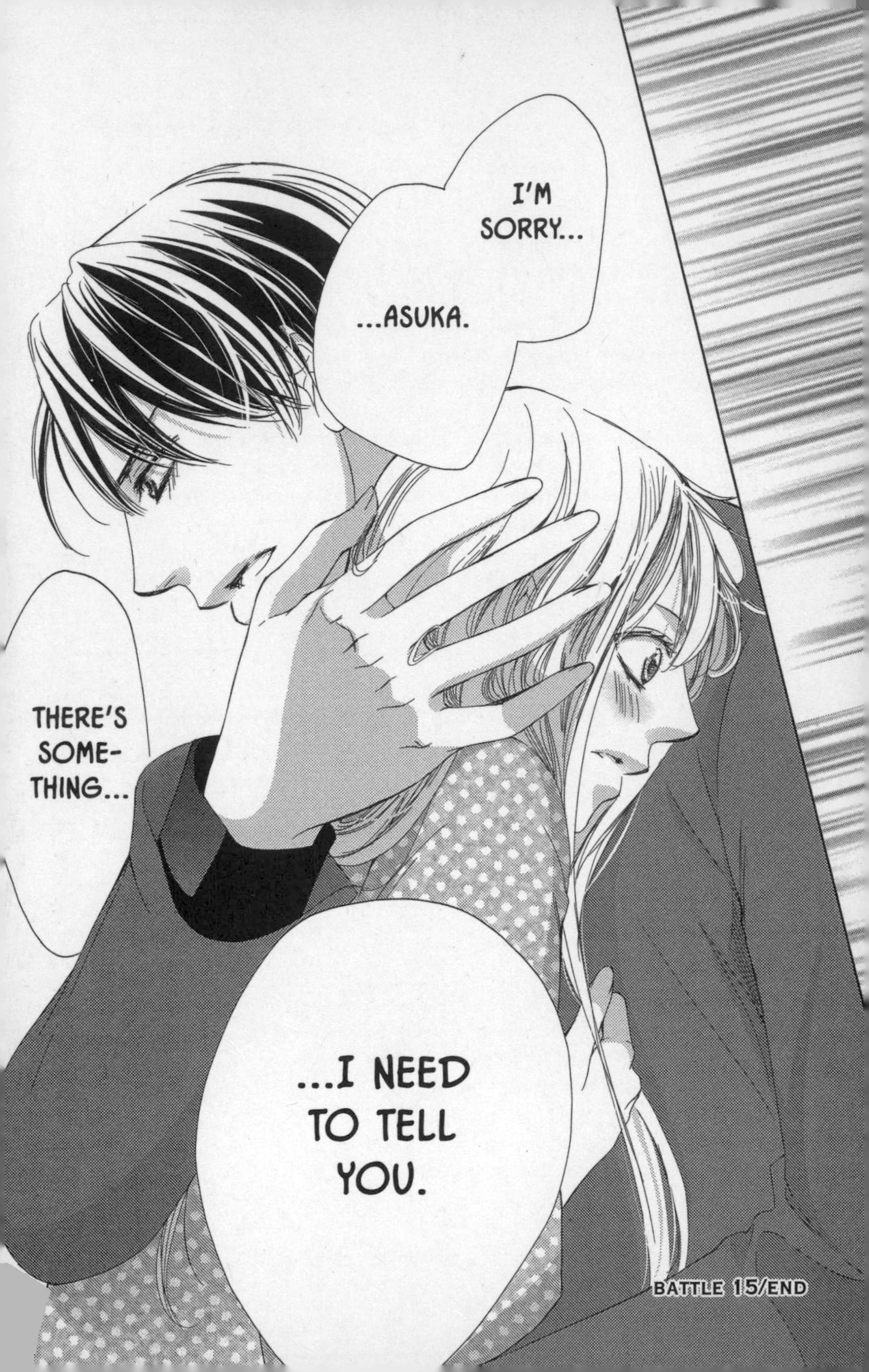
I'M SORRY...
...ASUKA.
THERE'S SOME-THING...
...I NEED TO TELL YOU.
BATTLE 15/END

GREETINGS

Hello. This is Izumi Miyazono.
Thank you very much for picking up volume 3 of *Everyone's Getting Married*! We'll see more of Asuka, Ryu, Rio, Hiroki, Yuko and Kamiya in volume 4.

To everyone who helped me out with the reference materials for this serialization despite their busy schedules: Thank you very much!

This volume contains a Nanaryu bonus story called "No Smoking for Nanaryu." I was happy to get to draw my favorite character Mikami.
...Truth be told, I wrote another little scribble in the margin of a page that never made it to the printer:

"Every year newscaster Mikami changes his hairdo. ✦✧"

After the pages had been submitted, my editor immediately called me up and said:

"This is the most irrelevant piece of information in the world..."
(↑Meaning: I'm not interested.)(*laugh*)
And attached a photo of that scribble.

So that's what I think about when I see this story. (*laugh*) Fun times.

I hope I get to see you in volume 4.
Thank you very much!

Thank you ♥ to Keiko S., Megumi M., Emi Y., Eri S., my family, my editor and everyone else involved.

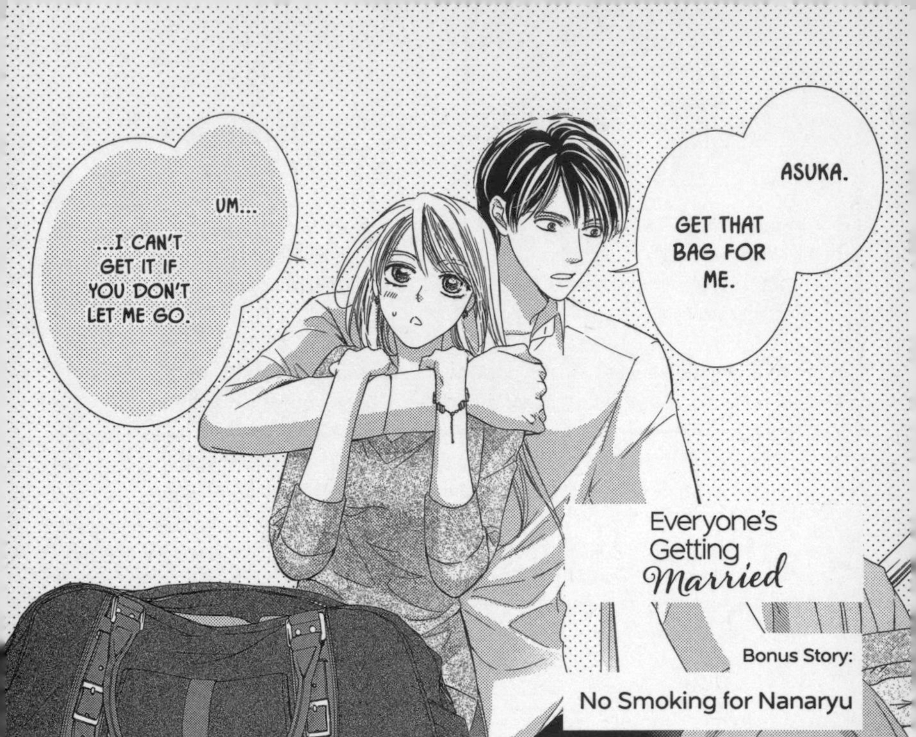
ASUKA.
GET THAT BAG FOR ME.
UM...
...I CAN'T GET IT IF YOU DON'T LET ME GO.
Everyone's Getting Married
Bonus Story:
No Smoking for Nanaryu

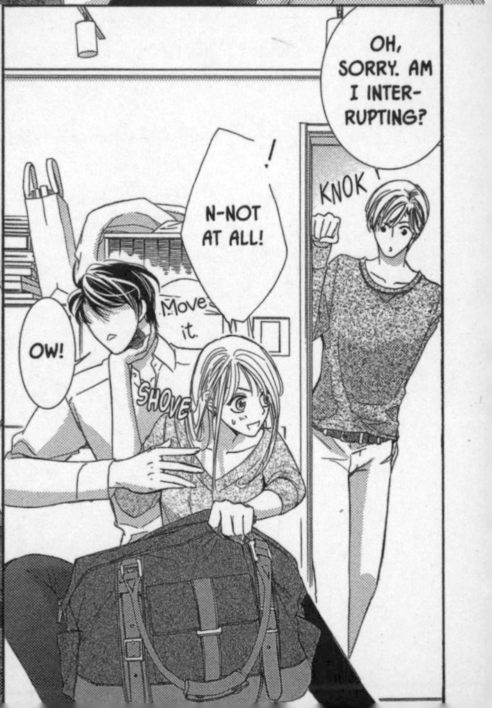
OH, SORRY. AM I INTER-RUPTING?
!
N-NOT AT ALL!
KNOK
Move it.
OW!
SHOVE

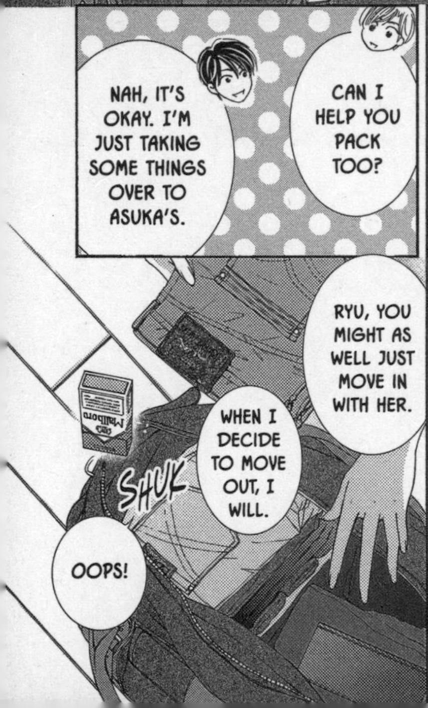
CAN I HELP YOU PACK TOO?
NAH, IT'S OKAY. I'M JUST TAKING SOME THINGS OVER TO ASUKA'S.
RYU, YOU MIGHT AS WELL JUST MOVE IN WITH HER.
WHEN I DECIDE TO MOVE OUT, I WILL.
SHUK
OOPS!

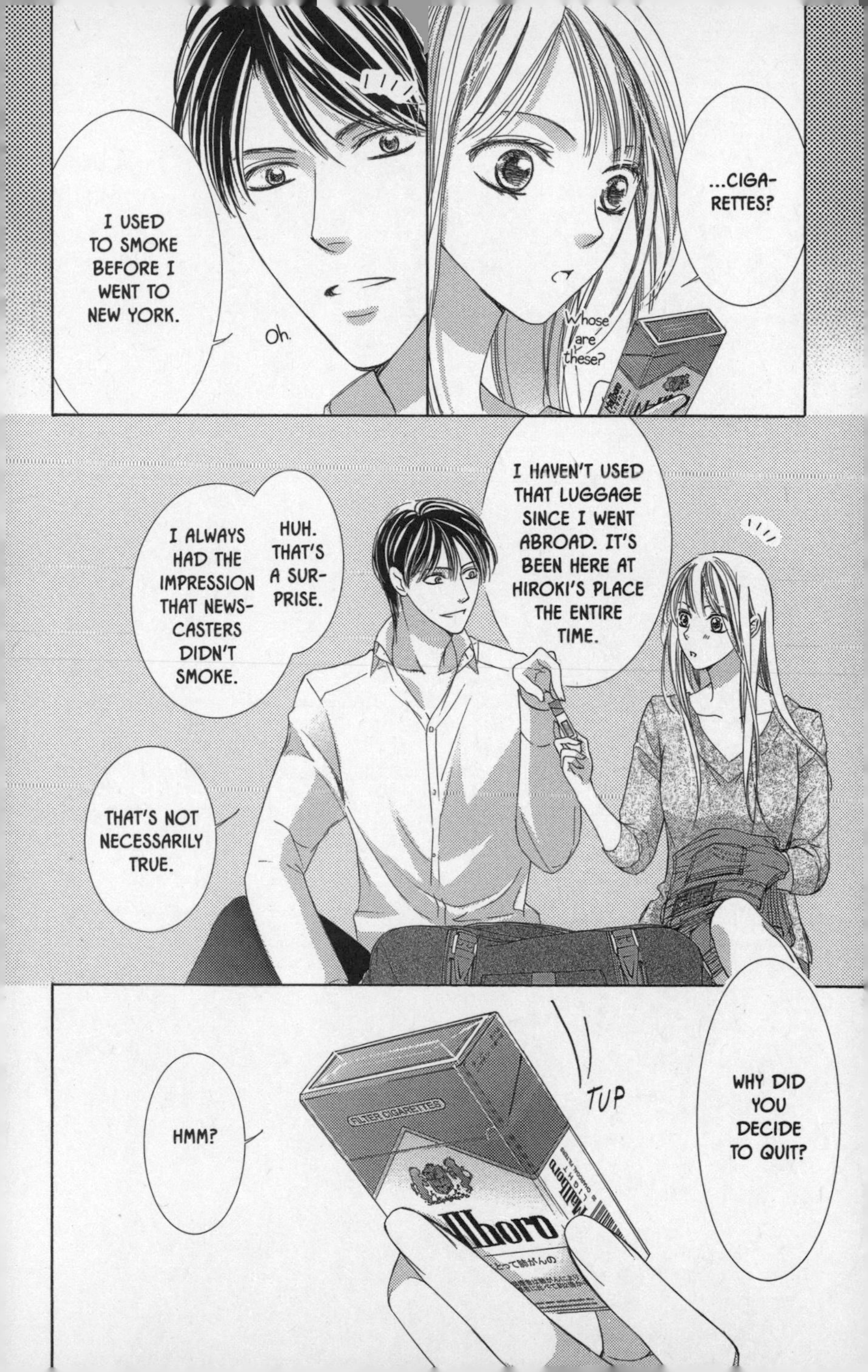
...CIGA-RETTES?
Whose are these?
Oh.
I USED TO SMOKE BEFORE I WENT TO NEW YORK.
I HAVEN'T USED THAT LUGGAGE SINCE I WENT ABROAD. IT'S BEEN HERE AT HIROKI'S PLACE THE ENTIRE TIME.
HUH. THAT'S A SUR-PRISE.
I ALWAYS HAD THE IMPRESSION THAT NEWS-CASTERS DIDN'T SMOKE.
THAT'S NOT NECESSARILY TRUE.
WHY DID YOU DECIDE TO QUIT?
TUP
HMM?
FILTER CIGARETTES

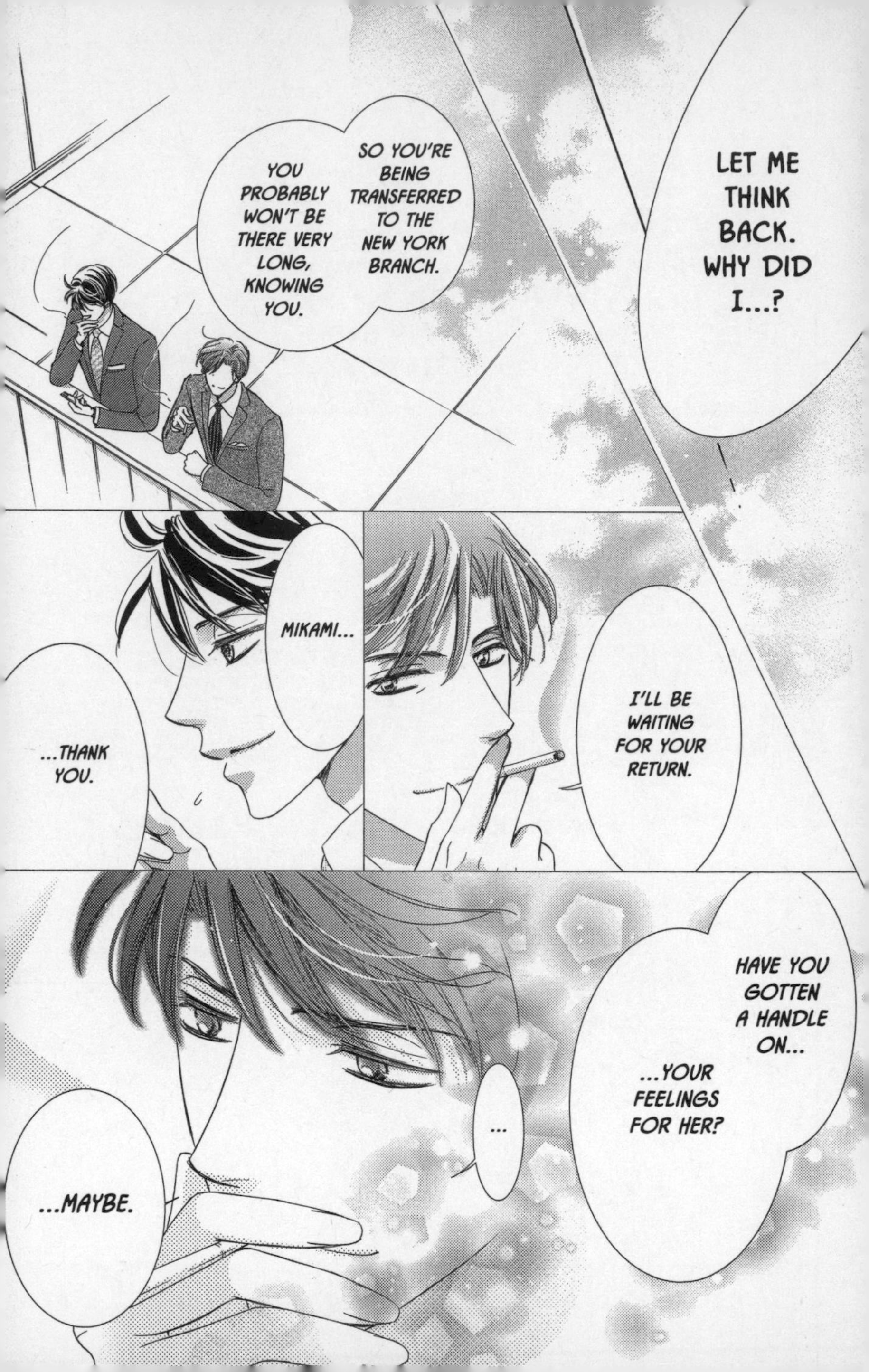
LET ME THINK BACK. WHY DID I...?
SO YOU'RE BEING TRANSFERRED TO THE NEW YORK BRANCH.
YOU PROBABLY WON'T BE THERE VERY LONG, KNOWING YOU.
I'LL BE WAITING FOR YOUR RETURN.
MIKAMI...
...THANK YOU.
HAVE YOU GOTTEN A HANDLE ON...
...YOUR FEELINGS FOR HER?
...
...MAYBE.

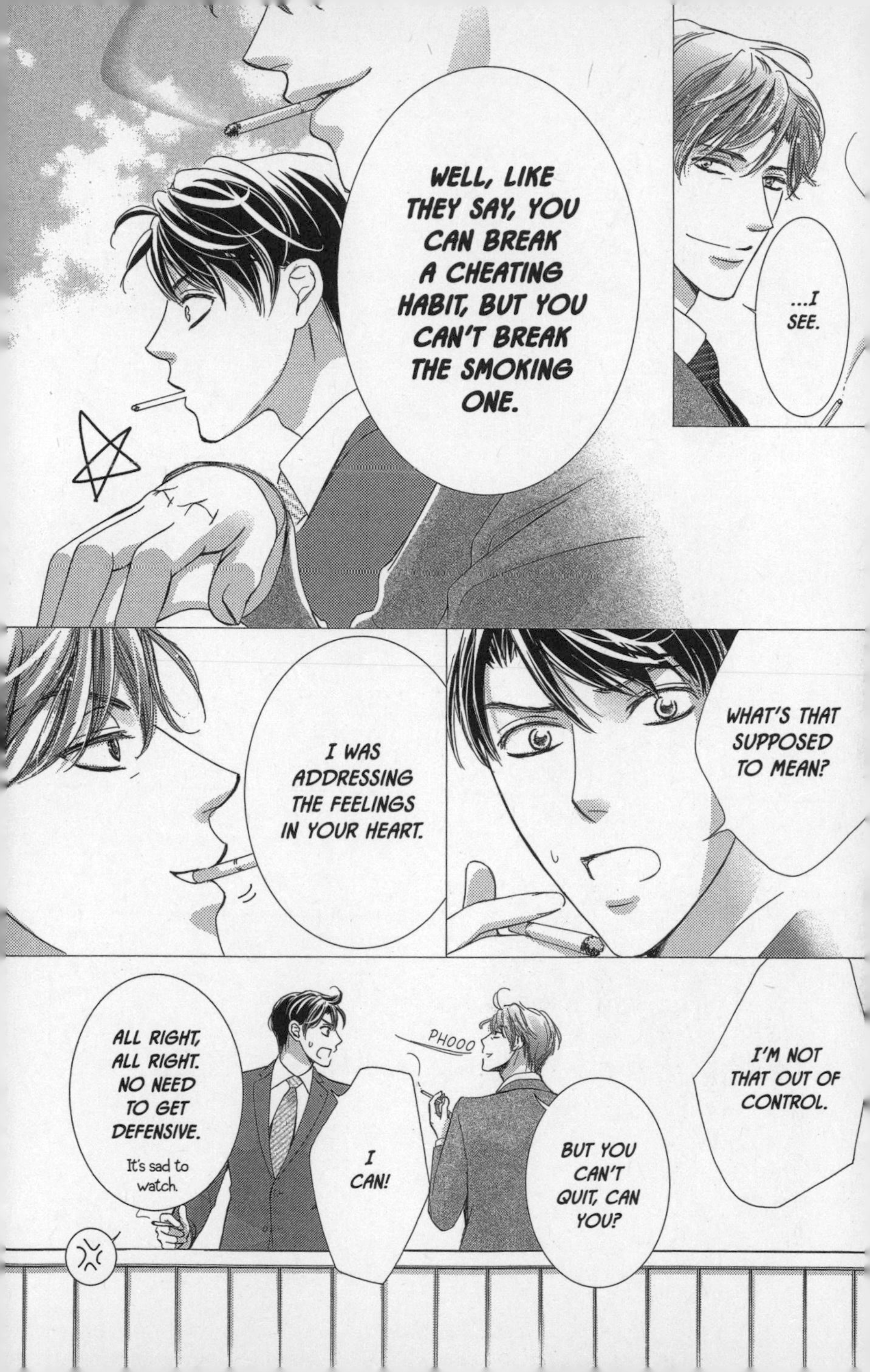
...I SEE.
WELL, LIKE THEY SAY, YOU CAN BREAK A CHEATING HABIT, BUT YOU CAN'T BREAK THE SMOKING ONE.
WHAT'S THAT SUPPOSED TO MEAN?
I WAS ADDRESSING THE FEELINGS IN YOUR HEART.
I'M NOT THAT OUT OF CONTROL.
PHOOO
BUT YOU CAN'T QUIT, CAN YOU?
I CAN!
ALL RIGHT, ALL RIGHT. NO NEED TO GET DEFENSIVE.
It's sad to watch.

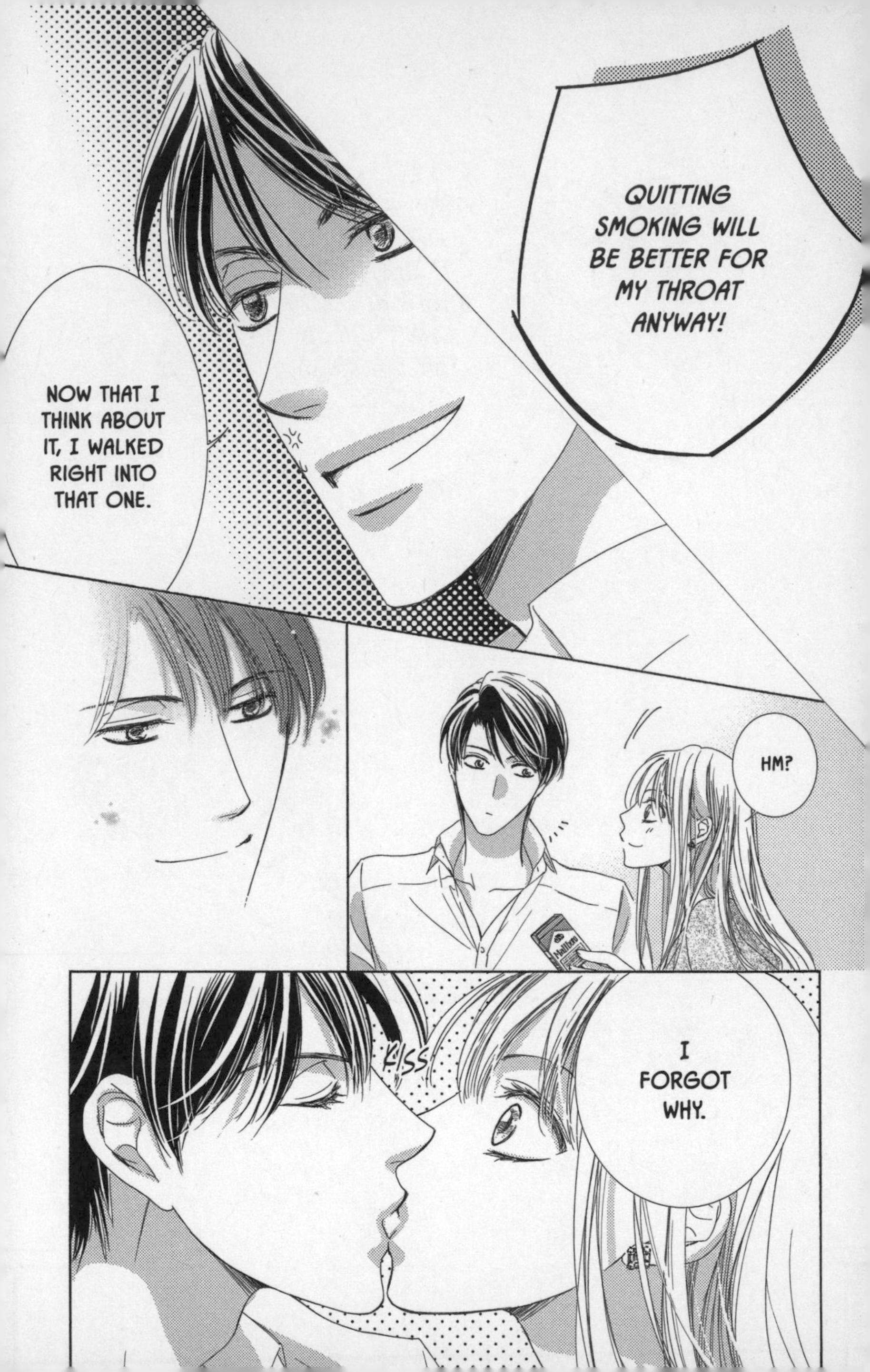
QUITTING SMOKING WILL BE BETTER FOR MY THROAT ANYWAY!
NOW THAT I THINK ABOUT IT, I WALKED RIGHT INTO THAT ONE.
HM?
I FORGOT WHY.
KISS

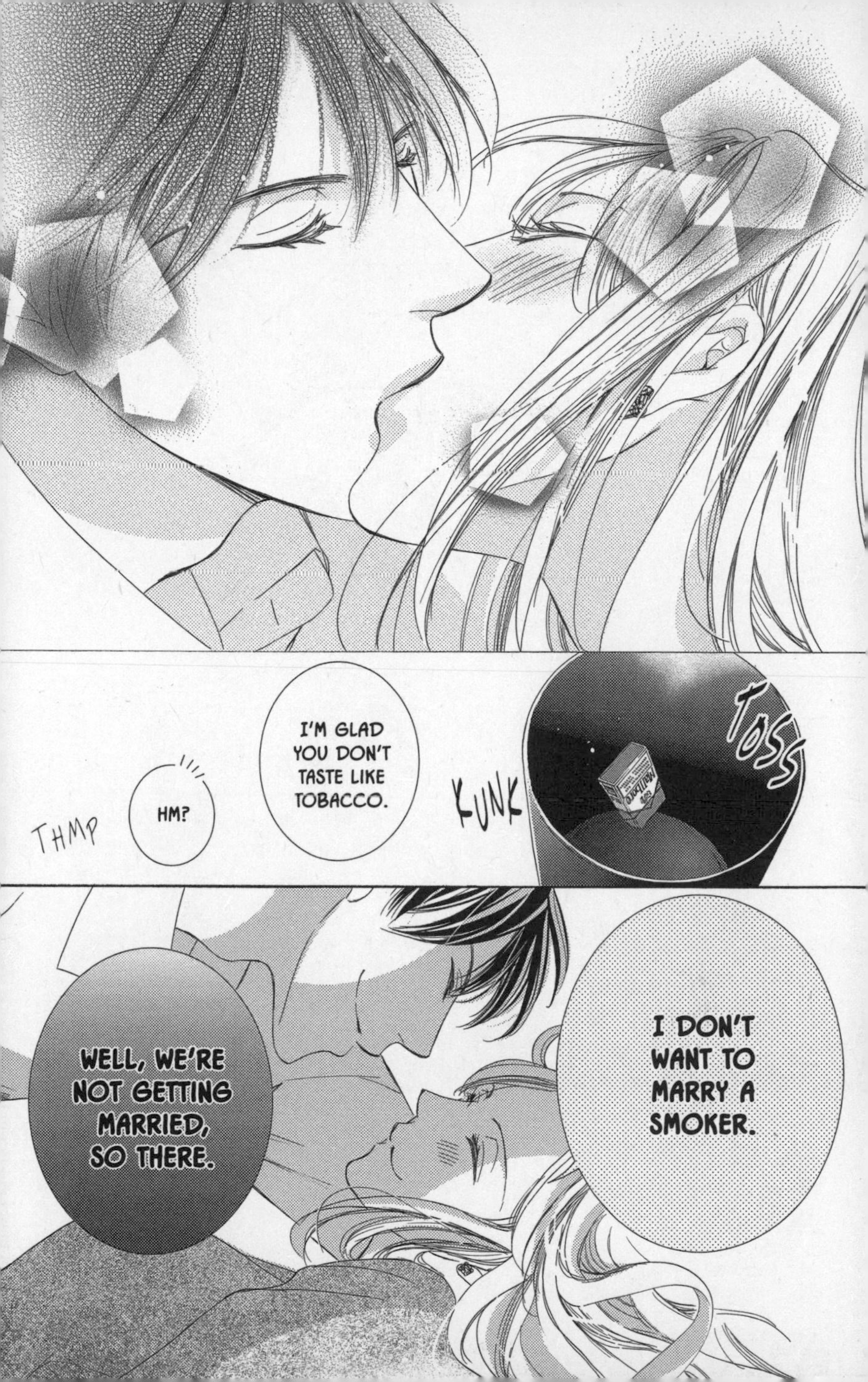
TOSS
KUNK
I'M GLAD YOU DON'T TASTE LIKE TOBACCO.
HM?
THMP
I DON'T WANT TO MARRY A SMOKER.
WELL, WE'RE NOT GETTING MARRIED, SO THERE.

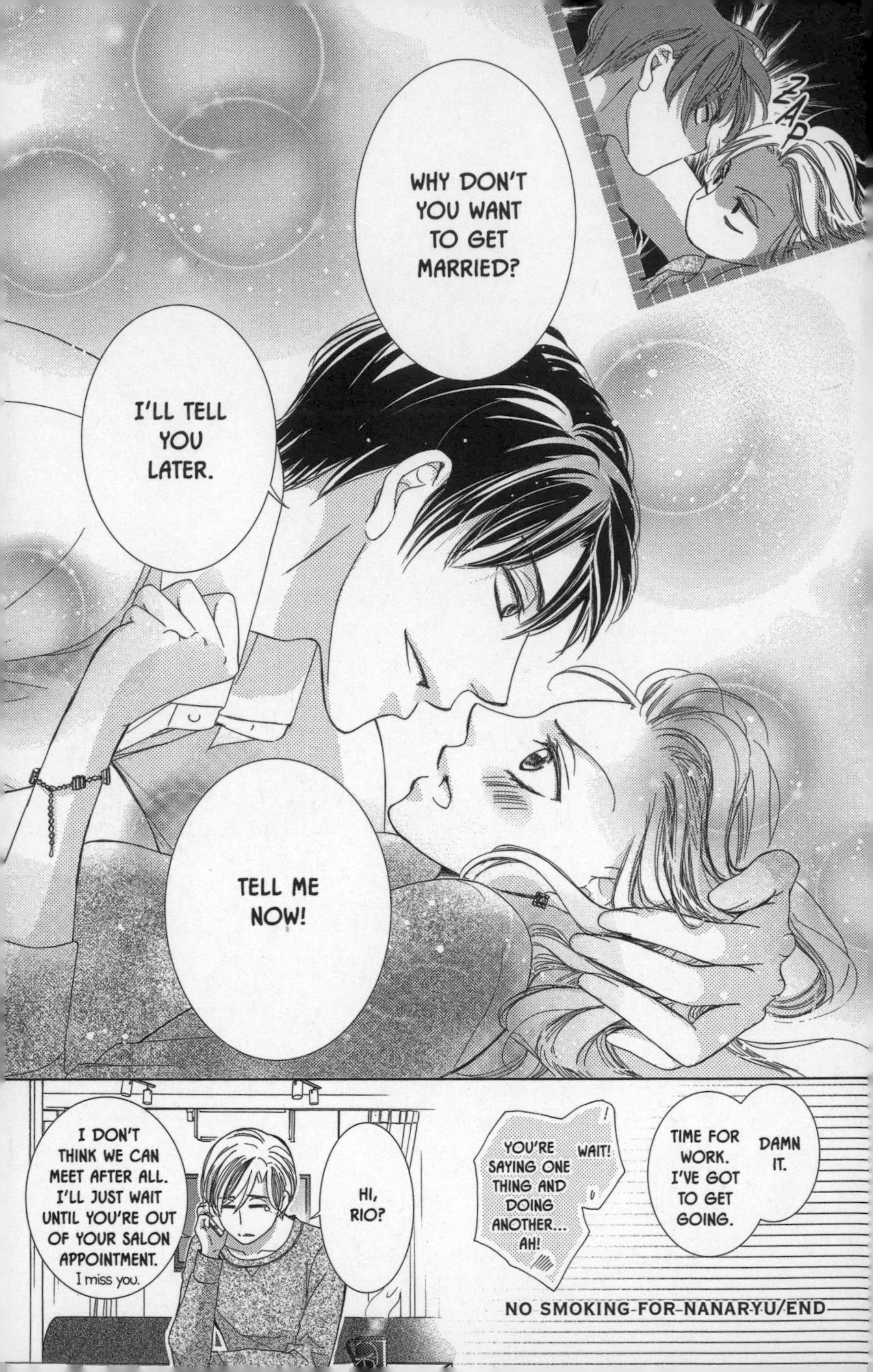
ZAP
WHY DON'T YOU WANT TO GET MARRIED?
I'LL TELL YOU LATER.
TELL ME NOW!
DAMN IT.
TIME FOR WORK. I'VE GOT TO GET GOING.
WAIT!
YOU'RE SAYING ONE THING AND DOING ANOTHER... AH!
HI, RIO?
I DON'T THINK WE CAN MEET AFTER ALL. I'LL JUST WAIT UNTIL YOU'RE OUT OF YOUR SALON APPOINTMENT.
I miss you.
NO SMOKING-FOR-NANARYU/END

...I made it.

Glad...

It's volume 3. The character above is one whose name has come up before, but he's finally making his first appearance.

I swear...he's so refreshing. I really like him.

IZUMI MIYAZONO

IZUMI MIYAZONO is from Niigata Prefecture in Japan. She debuted in 2005 with *Shunmin Shohousen* (*A Prescription for Sleep*). In 2014 she began serializing *Everyone's Getting Married* in *Petit Comic*.

Everyone's Getting Married ③

SHOJO BEAT EDITION

STORY AND ART BY **IZUMI MIYAZONO**

TOTSUZEN DESUGA, ASHITA KEKKON SHIMASU Vol. 3
by Izumi MIYAZONO
© 2014 Izumi MIYAZONO
All rights reserved.
Original Japanese edition published by SHOGAKUKAN.
English translation rights in the United States of America, Canada,
the United Kingdom and Ireland arranged with SHOGAKUKAN.

ORIGINAL COVER DESIGN Kaoru KUROKI, Saaya NISHINO + Bay Bridge Studio

TRANSLATION Katherine Schilling
TOUCH-UP ART & LETTERING Inori Fukuda Trant
DESIGN Shawn Carrico
EDITOR Nancy Thistlethwaite

The stories, characters and incidents mentioned
in this publication are entirely fictional.

Printed in the U.S.A.

Published by VIZ Media, LLC
P.O. Box 77010
San Francisco, CA 94107

10 9 8 7 6 5 4 3 2 1
First printing, December 2016

www.viz.com

www.shojobeat.com

STO

YOU MAY BE READING

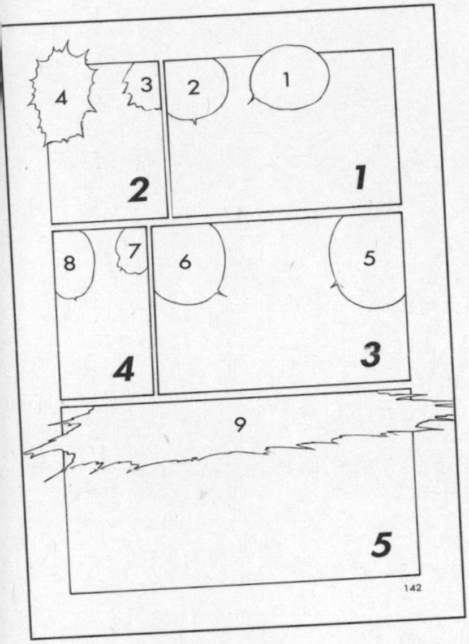
1
2
3
4
1
5
6
7
8
3
4
9
5
142

In

J

book reads

left—so action, sound effects and word balloons are completely reversed to preserve the orientation of the original artwork.

Check out the diagram shown here to get the hang of things, and then turn to the other side of the book to get started!

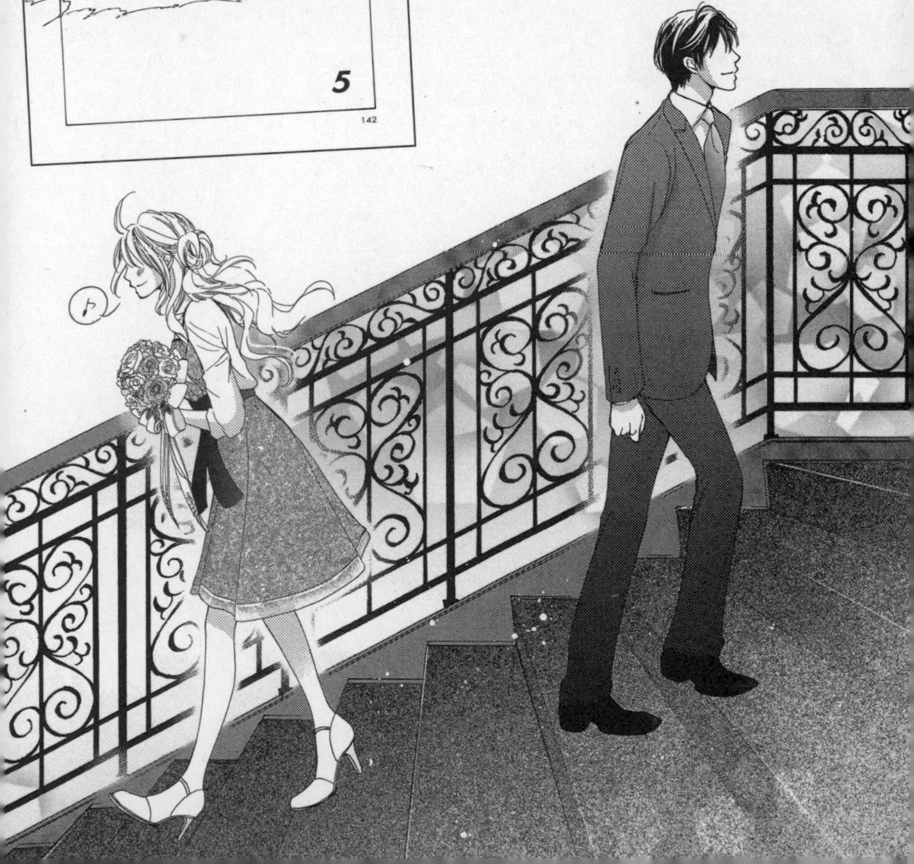